TOTAL MATH

AMERICAN
EDUCATION
PUBLISHING™
Columbus, Ohio

Send all inquiries to:
School Specialty Publishing
8720 Orion Place
Columbus, OH 43240-2111

ISBN 0-7696-3515-6

7 8 9 10 11 WAL 10 09 08 07 06

Table of Contents

Coin Crossword

Directions: Complete the puzzle. The answer to **A. Across** tells the month and day that the first U.S. coin was minted. The answer to **A. Down** gives the year.

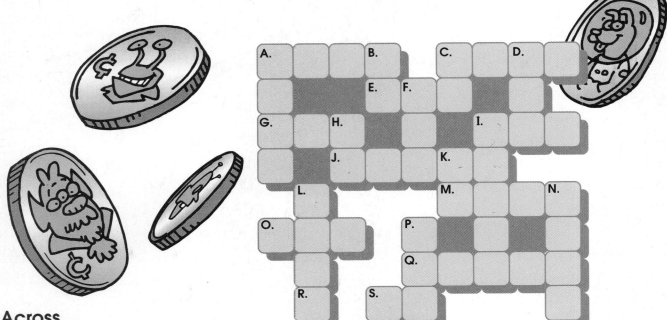

Across

A. One thousand, fifteen
C. Ten thousand less than 17,490
E. Same number in each place
G. 8, 9, and 2 scrambled
I. Reads the same forward and backward
J. Fifty-two thousand, ninety four
L. Six
M. One hundred less than 3,155
O. 2 hundreds, 1 ten, 8 ones
Q. Forty thousand, forty
S. Five more than twenty

Down

A. 5 hundred more than 1,294
B. One thousand less than 1,051
C. 7 tens and 1 one
D. One less than one thousand
F. One hundred more than zero
H. 10, 25, 40, 55, 70, ___
I. 3 ten thousands, 4 thousands
K. The tens digit is 3 times the ones digit
L. Same digit in the thousands and tens; same digit in the hundreds and ones
N. 5, 50, 500, ___
P. Consecutive digits

When was the first U.S. coin minted? _____

Roman Numerals

Example:

Roman Numeral	Value
I	1
V	5
X	10
L	50
C	100
D	500
M	1,000

Rules for Roman Numerals
◆ When a series of letters goes from a greater to a lesser value, add.
◆ When a series of letters goes from a lesser to a greater value, subtract.
◆ No letter repeats more than 3 times.

STAR GAMES
PART VI

VII = 5 + 1 + 1 = 7
CXV = 100 + 10 + 5 = 115
IV = 5 – 1 = 4
CD = 500 – 100 = 400
XIV = 10 + (5 – 1) = 10 + 4 = 14
MMCXL = 1,000 + 1,000 + 100 + (50 – 10) = 2,140

Directions: Match each Roman numeral in **Column A** with the correct number in **Column B.** Write the letter on the line.

Column A

1. _____ VII
2. _____ CXX
3. _____ IX
4. _____ MC
5. _____ DLIII
6. _____ CLXV
7. _____ MCMXI
8. _____ XXVI
9. _____ CIV
10. _____ DCXLII
11. _____ CCCXXXI
12. _____ XCVIII

Column B

a. 331
b. 165
c. 26
d. 120
e. 1,100
f. 98
g. 7
h. 104
i. 642
j. 9
k. 1,911
l. 553

Egyptian Numerals

The Egyptian numeral system is based on the number 10. The order of the symbols does not matter. The values of the numerals are added together.

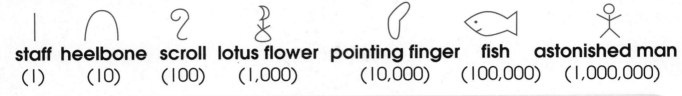

staff	heelbone	scroll	lotus flower	pointing finger	fish	astonished man
(1)	(10)	(100)	(1,000)	(10,000)	(100,000)	(1,000,000)

Example:

∩∩∣∣∣ = 23   fish ∩ scroll = 100,100

Directions: Match each Egyptian numeral in **Column A** with the correct number in **Column B.** Write the letter on the line.

Column A	Column B
1. ___	a. 25
2. ___	b. 10,300
3. ___	c. 200,010
4. ___	d. 3,000,000
5. ___	e. 41,213
6. ___	f. 103,010
7. ___	g. 1,000,212
8. ___	h. 4,101

Name _____

Place Value

The **place value** of a digit or numeral is shown by where it is in the number. In the number 1,234, 1 has the place value of thousands, 2 is hundreds, 3 is tens and 4 is ones.

Example: 1,250,000,000
   Read: One billion, two hundred fifty million
   Write: 1,250,000,000

Billions			Millions			Thousands			Ones		
h	t	o	h	t	o	h	t	o	h	t	o
		1,		2	5 0,		0	0 0,		0	0 0

Directions: Read the words. Then write the numbers.

twenty million, three hundred four thousand _____

five thousand, four hundred twenty-three _____

one hundred fifty billion, eight million,
one thousand, five hundred _____

sixty billion, seven hundred million,
one hundred thousand, three hundred twelve _____

four hundred million, fifteen thousand,
seven hundred one _____

six hundred ninety-nine million, four thousand,
nine hundred forty-two _____

Here's a game to play with a partner.

Write a ten-digit number using each digit, 0 to 9, only once. Do not show the number to your partner. Give clues like: "There is a five in the hundreds place." The clues can be given in any order. See if your partner can write the same number you have written.

Place Value

Directions: Draw a line to connect each number to its correct written form.

1. 791,000   Three hundred fifty thousand

2. 350,000   Seventeen million, five hundred thousand

3. 17,500,000   Seven hundred ninety-one thousand

4. 3,500,000   Seventy thousand, nine hundred ten

5. 70,910   Three million, five hundred thousand

6. 35,500,000   Seventeen billion, five hundred thousand

7. 17,000,500,000   Thirty-five million, five hundred thousand

Directions: Look carefully at this number: 2,071,463,548. Write the numeral for each of the following places:

8. _____ ten thousands

9. _____ millions

10. _____ hundreds

11. _____ billions

12. _____ hundred thousands

13. _____ ten millions

14. _____ one thousands

15. _____ hundred millions

Powers of 10

Example:

A power of 10 equals the number 10 multiplied by itself a given number of times.

100,000 = 10 x 10 x 10 x 10 x 10.

There are 5 zeros in 100,000, so 10 is multiplied by itself 5 times.

Directions: Write the missing number or numbers.

Example: 1,000 = 10 x 10 x 10

100,000 =   10 x 10 =

10,000 =   10 x 10 x 10 x 10 =

10 =   10 x 10 x 10 =

1,000,000 =   10 x 10 x 10 x 10 x 10 =

100 =   10 x 10 x 10 x 10 x 10 x 10 =

10,000,000 =

Name _____

Tens Trivia

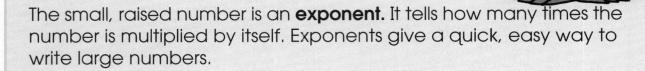

Example:

Use exponents to write large numbers.

$20,000 = 2 \times 10,000 = 2 \times 10 \times 10 \times 10 \times 10 = 2 \times 10^4$
$5,600 = 56 \times 100 = 56 \times 10 \times 10 = 56 \times 10^2$

The small, raised number is an **exponent.** It tells how many times the number is multiplied by itself. Exponents give a quick, easy way to write large numbers.

Directions: Rewrite each number using an exponent or rewrite the exponent in standard form.

1. There are about 3,000 hot dog vendors in New York City. _____

2. The Chinese alphabet has about 40,000 different characters. _____

3. A single beehive may have over 6×10^4 bees. _____

4. An ant can lift 50 times its own weight. _____

5. A caterpillar has about 2,000 muscles. _____

6. The average American will eat 35,000 cookies during his or her lifetime.

   _____

7. There are about 38,000 post offices in the United States. _____

8. A grasshopper can jump an obstacle 500 times its own height. _____

9. A gnat can flap its wings 1,000 times each second. _____

10. A quart-sized beach pail holds 8,000,000 grains of sand. _____

11. Las Vegas has over 15,000 miles of neon tubing. _____

12. Chicago has the largest public library with 2,000,000 books. _____

13. A mile-high stack of $1 bills would be worth 14×10^6. _____

14. Over 2 million pounds of meteor dust fall to the Earth every day. _____

15. The Empire State Building was built with over 10 million bricks. _____

16. The world consumes a billion gallons of petroleum each day. _____

Addition

Teachers of an Earth Science class planned to take 50 students on an overnight hiking and camping experience. After planning the menu, they went to the grocery store for supplies.

Breakfast	Lunch	Dinner	Snacks
bacon	hot dogs/buns	pasta	crackers
eggs	apples	sauce	marshmallows
bread	chips	garlic bread	chocolate bars
cereal	juice	salad	cocoa mix
juice	granola bars	cookies	
$34.50	$ 52.15	$ 47.25	$ 23.40

Directions: Answer the questions. Write the total amount spent on food for the trip.

What information do you need to answer the question? _____

_____

What is the total? _____

Directions: Add.

462	918	527	386	295
+ 574	+ 359	+ 582	+ 745	+ 764

397	524	906	750	891
+ 448	+ 725	+ 337	+ 643	+ 419

1,568	3,214	5,147	7,259	9,317
+ 2,341	+ 2,896	+ 4,285	+ 2,451	+ 3,583

Name _____

Addition

Directions: Add.

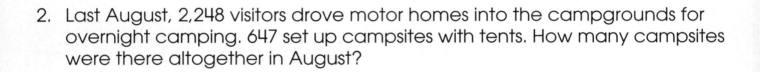

1. Tourists travel to national parks to see the many animals that live there. Park Rangers estimate 384 buffalo, 282 grizzly bears, and 426 deer are in the park. What is the total number of buffalo, bears, and deer estimated in the park?

    _____

2. Last August, 2,248 visitors drove motor homes into the campgrounds for overnight camping. 647 set up campsites with tents. How many campsites were there altogether in August?

    _____

3. During a 3-week camping trip, Tom and his family hiked 42 miles, took a 126-mile long canoeing trip, and drove their car 853 miles. How many miles did they travel in all?

    _____

4. Old Faithful is a geyser that spouts water high into the air. 10,000 gallons of water burst into the air regularly. Two other geysers spout 2,400 gallons of water during each eruption. What is the amount of water thrust into the air during one cycle?

    _____

5. Yellowstone National Park covers approximately 2,221,772 acres of land. Close by, the Grand Tetons cover approximately 310,350 acres. How many acres of land are there in these two parks?

    _____

6. Hiking trails cover 486 miles, motor routes around the north rim total 376 miles, and another 322 miles of road allow visitors to follow a loop around the southern part of the park. How many miles of trails and roadways are there?

    _____

Addition

Bob the butcher is popular with the dogs in town. He was making a delivery this morning when he noticed he was being followed by two dogs. Bob tried to climb a ladder to escape from the dogs.

Directions: Solve the following addition problems and shade in the answers on the ladder. If all the numbers are shaded when the problems have been solved, Bob made it up the ladder. Some answers may not be on the ladder.

1. 986,145 621,332 + 200,008	2. 1,873,402 925,666 + 4,689	3. 506,328 886,510 + 342,225
4. 43,015 2,811,604 + 987,053	5. 18,443 300,604 + 999,999	6. 8,075 14,608 + 33,914
7. 9,162 7,804 + 755,122	8. 88,714 213,653 + 5,441,298	9. 3,244,662 1,986,114 + 521,387
10. 4,581 22,983 + 5,618,775	11. 818,623 926 + 3,260,004	12. 80,436 9,159 + 3,028,761

Ladder numbers:

1,319,046
2,803,757
5,743,665
3,118,356
56,597
4,079,553
1,807,485
2,943,230
18,344,666
1,735,063
5,752,163
896,316
3,841,672
5,646,339

Does Bob make it? _____

Name _____

Go Fly a Kite!

Ben Franklin created this amazing square. It includes all numbers from **1** to **64**.

Directions: Follow these instructions to discover its special property.

1. Add the numbers in the 4 corners.
2. Choose any 4-by-4 section of the box and add the corners. Repeat.
3. Choose any 6-by-6 section and add the corners. Repeat.
4. Choose any 2-by-2 section add the numbers. Repeat.
5. Add the first or last 4 numbers in any row or column.

52	61	4	13	20	29	36	45
14	3	62	51	46	35	30	19
53	60	5	12	21	28	37	44
11	6	59	54	43	38	27	22
55	58	7	10	23	26	39	42
9	8	57	56	41	40	25	24
50	63	2	15	18	31	34	47
16	1	64	49	48	33	32	17

What is special about this amazing square? _____

Name _____

Mount Rushmore

Which four presidents are carved into Mount Rushmore?

Directions: To find out, solve these problems. Then, use the key.

472	853	507	644	999
− 251	− 731	− 502	− 230	− 633
S =	C =	O =	F =	I =

548	382	932	88	348
− 125	− 100	− 411	− 25	− 104
H =	N =	T =	A =	R =

111	794	716	820	835	800
− 101	− 392	− 315	− 520	− 722	− 600
J =	E =	V =	W =	L =	G =

___ ___ ___ ___ ___ ___ ___ ___ ___ ___
300   63 221 423 366 282 200 521   5   282

___ ___ ___ ___ ___ ___ ___ ___ ___
 10 402 414 414 402 244 221   5   282

___ ___ ___ ___ ___ ___ ___
113 366 282 122   5   113 282

___ ___ ___ ___ ___ ___ ___ ___ ___
244   5   5   221 402 401 402 113 521

Subtraction Squares

Directions: Subtract. If the first digit in the answer is odd, color the square gray or black. If the first digit is even, color the square red.

5,473 – 2,002	2,451 – 330	4,791 – 3,340	7,308 – 7,104	8,874 – 5,621	2,442 – 21
7,934 – 3,611	5,295 – 2,283	699 – 454	5,493 – 4,233	9,250 – 1,040	1,626 – 512
4,596 – 1,325	9,639 – 7,611	7,789 – 2,246	5,863 – 3,111	4,926 – 4,925	9,740 – 3,530
5,826 – 3,515	6,873 – 1,572	7,196 – 1,052	8,376 – 1,221	3,725 – 1,715	7,589 – 163
3,987 – 2,673	9,243 – 1,133	3,269 – 153	5,429 – 1,302	5,471 – 4,160	9,475 – 5,332
3,824 – 1,610	28,759 – 11,422	36,587 – 12,412	36,489 – 5,257	17,824 – 17,613	13,528 – 8,303

A mini-version of a game was made—use black and red game pieces to play it.

Subtraction

When working with larger numbers, it is important to keep the numbers lined up according to place value.

Directions: Subtract.

```
   398        543        491
 - 149      - 287      - 311


   786      1,825      4,172
 - 597      - 495      - 2,785


 8,391     63,852     24,107     52,900
- 5,492    - 34,765   -19,350    - 43,081
```

Eagle Peak is the highest mountain peak at Yellowstone National Park. It is 11,353 feet high. The next highest point at the park is Mount Washburn. It is 10,243 feet tall. How much higher is Eagle Peak?

_____

The highest mountain peak in North America is Mount McKinley, which stretches 20,320 feet toward the sky. Two other mountain ranges in North America have peaks at 10,302 feet and 8,194 feet. What is the greatest difference between the peaks?

_____

What's in a Name?

Example:

Follow the steps to do 4-digit addition with regrouping.

Add the ones. Regroup, if needed.	Add the tens. Regroup, if needed.	Add the hundreds. Regroup, if needed.	Add the thousands. Regroup, if needed.
I	I I	I I I	I I I
6,759	6,759	6,759	6,759
+ 5,854	+ 5,854	+ 5,854	+ 5,854
3	13	613	12,613

Directions: Add. Then, use this code to decode the sums. Write the letter for each numeral on the line.

Code: 0 = L, 1 = A, 2 = M, 3 = Y, 4 = T, 5 = O, 6 = I, 7 = R, 8 = S, 9 = N

593	1,921	101	3,846	4,945
+ 120	+ 223	+ 22	+ 1,622	+ 3,474
☐	☐	☐	☐	☐

1,043	1,782	1,251	3,357	3,526
1,000	50	1,266	321	1,261
+ 130	+ 2,744	+ 57	+ 4,493	+ 1,294
☐	☐	☐	☐	☐

3,180	9,923	22,854	14,356	17,911
+ 1,191	+ 9,718	+ 2,149	+ 12,487	+ 23,312
☐	☐	☐	☐	☐

What kinds of words have been spelled out?_____

Name _____

Subtraction Search

The Dead Sea is the lowest place on the earth.

Directions: To find how many feet below sea level it is, subtract. Then, find and circle each answer in the puzzle. Numbers can read forward, backward, up, down, or diagonally. Finally, read the four uncircled numbers from left to right to find the number of feet.

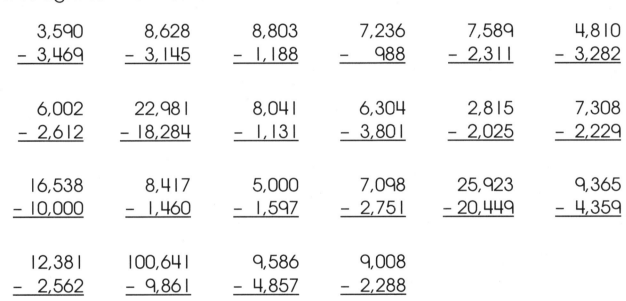

3,590 − 3,469	8,628 − 3,145	8,803 − 1,188	7,236 − 988	7,589 − 2,311	4,810 − 3,282
6,002 − 2,612	22,981 − 18,284	8,041 − 1,131	6,304 − 3,801	2,815 − 2,025	7,308 − 2,229
16,538 − 10,000	8,417 − 1,460	5,000 − 1,597	7,098 − 2,751	25,923 − 20,449	9,365 − 4,359
12,381 − 2,562	100,641 − 9,861	9,586 − 4,857	9,008 − 2,288		

How many feet below sea level is the Dead Sea? _____

4	7	2	9	1	5	2	8	1	9	2	6	5	3	8
1	6	8	5	0	0	6	3	2	0	5	4	7	4	6
7	1	3	0	5	4	8	3	1	7	0	3	1	9	2
9	5	2	7	8	0	1	9	6	8	3	4	5	5	4
0	4	6	9	7	3	4	0	3	0	6	7	2	0	8

Batting a Thousand

Directions: Add. If the sum is greater than 1,000, circle it.

```
  634        218        639        194
+ 253      + 235      + 647      + 133
```

```
  216        149        698        587
+ 345      + 459      + 388      + 524
```

```
  520        938        406        319
+ 416      + 491      + 439      + 508
```

```
  135        803        108        647
+ 185      + 262      + 801      + 886
```

How many sums were greater than 1,000? _____

Name _____

Checking Subtraction

You can check your subtraction by using addition.

Example:
$$34,436 \quad \text{Check:} \quad 22,172$$
$$- 12,264 \quad\quad\quad + 12,264$$
$$22,172 \quad\quad\quad\quad 34,436$$

Directions: Subtract. Then check your answers by adding.

15,326 − 11,532	Check:	28,615 − 25,329	Check:
96,521 − 47,378	Check:	46,496 − 35,877	Check:
77,911 − 63,783	Check:	156,901 −112,732	Check:
395,638 −187,569	Check:	67,002 − 53,195	Check:
16,075 −15,896	Check:	39,678 −19,769	Check:
84,654 − 49,997	Check:	12,335 −10,697	Check:

During the summer, 158,941 people visited Yellowstone National Park. During the fall, there were 52,397 visitors. How many more visitors went to the park during the summer than the fall?

_____

Making the Grade

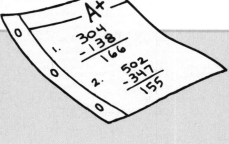

Example:

A subtraction problem can be checked with addition.

$$\begin{array}{r} 502 \\ -\ 347 \\ \hline 155 \end{array}$$

If the answer is correct, then 155 + 347 must equal 502.

Directions: Grade this test paper. Check each problem. Write a ✔ if it is correct and an **X** if it is incorrect. Then, use the key at the bottom to give yourself a grade.

Math Test

Grade = _____   Correct = _____

$\begin{array}{r}304\\-138\\\hline166\end{array}$	$\begin{array}{r}428\\-294\\\hline134\end{array}$	$\begin{array}{r}932\\-835\\\hline103\end{array}$	$\begin{array}{r}844\\-237\\\hline607\end{array}$	$\begin{array}{r}650\\-443\\\hline207\end{array}$
$\begin{array}{r}2,548\\-1,329\\\hline1,219\end{array}$	$\begin{array}{r}1,482\\-843\\\hline639\end{array}$	$\begin{array}{r}3,156\\-3,018\\\hline138\end{array}$	$\begin{array}{r}6,504\\-1,653\\\hline4,851\end{array}$	$\begin{array}{r}4,345\\-3,106\\\hline1,249\end{array}$
$\begin{array}{r}8,023\\-770\\\hline7,353\end{array}$	$\begin{array}{r}5,555\\-2,754\\\hline2,801\end{array}$	$\begin{array}{r}3,234\\-3,195\\\hline39\end{array}$	$\begin{array}{r}6,820\\-93\\\hline6,727\end{array}$	$\begin{array}{r}3,526\\-1,294\\\hline2,232\end{array}$
$\begin{array}{r}4,004\\-1,482\\\hline2,522\end{array}$	$\begin{array}{r}9,932\\-5,999\\\hline3,933\end{array}$	$\begin{array}{r}29,005\\-4,649\\\hline24,356\end{array}$	$\begin{array}{r}84,294\\-28,557\\\hline56,737\end{array}$	$\begin{array}{r}493,340\\-23,382\\\hline469,958\end{array}$

Number Correct:
18–20 = A   16–17 = B   14–15 = C   12–13 = D   11 or below = F

Name _____

Addition and Subtraction

Directions: Check the answers. Write **T** if the answer is true and **F** if it is false.

Example: 48,973   Check: 35,856
             − 35,856   **F**   +13,118
             13,118   48,974

```
  18,264    Check:              458,342    Check:
+ 17,893                       − 297,652
  36,157    ____                 160,680    _____
```

```
  39,854    Check:              631,928    Check:
+ 52,713                       − 457,615
  92,577    ____                 174,313    _____
```

```
  14,389    Check:              554,974    Check:
+ 93,587                       − 376,585
 107,976    ____                 178,389    _____
```

```
  87,321    Check:              109,568    Check:
− 62,348                       +  97,373
  24,973    ____                 206,941    _____
```

Directions: Read the story problem. Write the equation and check the answer.

A camper hikes 53,741 feet out into the wilderness. On his return trip he takes a shortcut, walking 36,752 feet back to his cabin. The shortcut saves him 16,998 feet of hiking. True or False?

Name _____

Addition and Subtraction

Directions: Add or subtract to find the answers.

Eastland School hosted a field day. Students could sign up for a variety of events. 175 students signed up for individual races. Twenty two-person teams competed in the mile relay and 36 kids took part in the high jump. How many students participated in the activities?

_____

Westmore School brought 42 students and 7 adults to the field day event. Northern School brought 84 students and 15 adults. There was a total of 300 students and 45 adults at the event. How many were from other schools?

_____

The Booster Club sponsored a concession stand during the day. Last year, they made $1,000 at the same event. This year they hoped to earn at least $1,250. They actually raised $1,842. How much more did they make than they had anticipated?

_____

Each school was awarded a trophy for participating in the field day activities. The Booster Club planned to purchase three plaques as awards, but they only wanted to spend $150. The first place trophy they selected was $68. The second place award was $59. How much would they be able to spend on the third place award to stay within their budgeted amount?

_____

The Booster Club decided to spend $1,000 to purchase several items for the school with the money they had earned. Study the list of items suggested and decide which combination of items they could purchase.

A. Swing set $425 _____

B. Sliding board $263 _____

C. Scoreboard $515 _____

D. Team uniforms $180 _____

Rounding

Rounding a number means to express it to the nearest ten, hundred, thousand, and so on. When rounding a number to the nearest ten, if the number has five or more ones, round up. Round down if the number has four or fewer ones.

Examples:

Round to the nearest ten:	84 → 80	86 → 90
Round to the nearest hundred:	187 → 200	120 → 100
Round to the nearest thousand:	981 → 1,000	5,480 → 5,000

Directions: Round these numbers to the nearest ten.

87 → _____   53 → _____   48 → _____   32 → _____   76 → _____

Directions: Round these numbers to the nearest hundred.

168 → _____   243 → _____   591 → _____   743 → _____   493 → _____

Directions: Round these numbers to the nearest thousand.

895 → _____   3,492 → _____   7,521 → _____   14,904 → _____   62,387 → _____

City Populations	
City	Population
Cleveland	492,801
Seattle	520,947
Omaha	345,033
Kansas City	443,878
Atlanta	396,052
Austin	514,013

Directions: Use the city population chart to answer the questions.

Which cities have a population of about 500,000?

_____

Which city has a population of about 350,000?

_____

How many cities have a population of about 400,000? _____

Which ones? _____

_____

Getting Around to Rounding

Example:

Round 36,528 to the nearest hundred.

36,<u>5</u>28
2 is less than 5.
Do not change the 5.
36,500

Round 36,528 to the nearest thousand.

3<u>6</u>,528
5 = 5.
Round the 6 to 7.
37,000

Round 36,528 to the nearest ten thousand.

<u>3</u>6,528
6 is greater than 5.
Round the 3 to 4.
40,000

Directions: Round each number to the nearest hundred, thousand, and ten thousand.

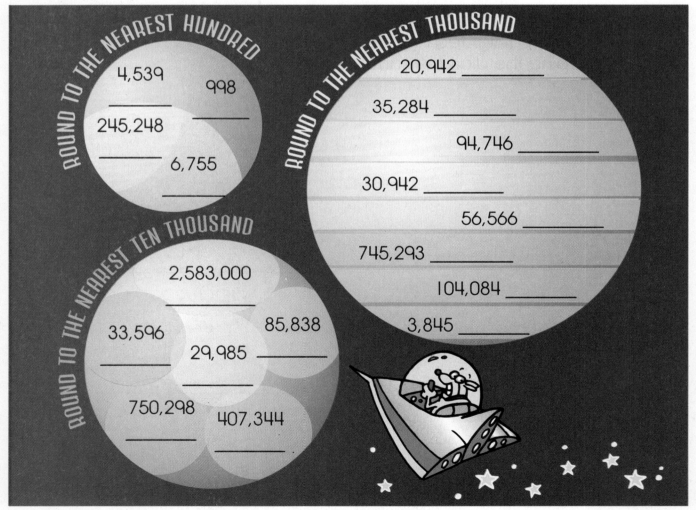

ROUND TO THE NEAREST HUNDRED

4,539 _____

998 _____

245,248 _____

6,755 _____

ROUND TO THE NEAREST THOUSAND

20,942 _____

35,284 _____

94,746 _____

30,942 _____

56,566 _____

745,293 _____

104,084 _____

3,845 _____

ROUND TO THE NEAREST TEN THOUSAND

2,583,000 _____

33,596 _____

85,838

29,985 _____

750,298 _____

407,344 _____

26

Rounding

Follow these steps to round numbers to a given place.

Example: Round 35,634 to the nearest thousand.

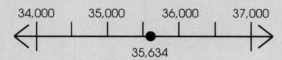

a. Locate and highlight the place to which the number is to be rounded.

▷ Highlight the digit in the thousands place: **3**5,634

b. Look at the digit to the right of the designated place. If the number is 5 or greater, round the highlighted number up. If the number is 4 or less, round the highlighted number down by keeping the digit the same.

▷ Six is greater than 5, so round the highlighted number up.

c. Rewrite the original number with the amended digit in the highlighted place and change all of the digits to the right to zeros.

▷ The rounded number is 36,000.

Example: Round 782 to the nearest 10.

▶ Highlight the digit in the tens place: 7**8**2

▶ Two is four or less, so round down by keeping the tens digit the same. 782

▶ The rounded number is 780.

Directions: Round each number to the given place.

nearest 10:	**1.** 855 _____	**2.** 333 _____
nearest 100:	**3.** 725 _____	**4.** 2,348 _____
nearest 1,000:	**5.** 4,317 _____	**6.** 8,650 _____
nearest 10,000:	**7.** 25,199 _____	**8.** 529,740 _____
nearest 100,000:	**9.** 496,225 _____	**10.** 97,008 _____

Number-line Rounding

Directions: Label the endpoints. Plot the given number. Circle the closer endpoint. The first three have been done for you.

1.

   Round 87 to the nearest ten.

2.

   Round 1,322 to the nearest hundred.

3.

   Round 1,475 to the nearest ten.

4.

   Round 8,274 to the nearest ten.

5.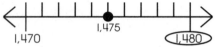

   Round 8,274 to the nearest hundred.

6.

   Round 1,452 to the nearest thousand.

7.

   Round 1,452 to the nearest ten.

8.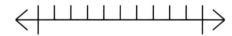

   Round 6,937 to the nearest thousand.

9.

   Round 8,485 to the nearest thousand.

10.

    Round 25,683 to the nearest ten thousand.

Rounding And Estimating

Rounding numbers and estimating answers is an easy way of finding the approximate answer without writing out the problem or using a calculator.

Directions: Circle the correct answer.

Round to the nearest **ten:**

$73 \longrightarrow$ 70
80

$48 \longrightarrow$ 40
50

$65 \longrightarrow$ 60
70

$85 \longrightarrow$ 80
90

$92 \longrightarrow$ 90
100

$37 \longrightarrow$ 30
40

Round to the nearest **hundred:**

$139 \rightarrow$ 100
200

$782 \rightarrow$ 700
800

$390 \rightarrow$ 300
400

$640 \rightarrow$ 600
700

$525 \rightarrow$ 500
600

$457 \rightarrow$ 400
500

Round to the nearest **thousand:**

$1,375 \longrightarrow$ 1,000
2,000

$21,800 \longrightarrow$ 21,000
22,000

$36,240 \longrightarrow$ 36,000
37,000

Sam wanted to buy a new computer. He knew he had only about $1,200 to spend. Which of the following ones could he afford to buy?

 $1,165

 $1,279

 $1,249

If Sam spent $39 on software for his new computer, $265 for a printer, and $38 for a cordless mouse, about how much money did he need?

_____

Estimating

To **estimate** means to give an approximate rather than an exact answer. Rounding each number first makes it easy to estimate an answer.

Example:

$$\begin{array}{r} 93 \\ + 48 \\ \hline \end{array} \longrightarrow \begin{array}{r} 90 \\ + 50 \\ \hline 140 \end{array} \qquad \begin{array}{r} 321 \\ + 597 \\ \hline \end{array} \longrightarrow \begin{array}{r} 300 \\ + 600 \\ \hline 900 \end{array} \qquad \begin{array}{r} 1,859 \\ - 997 \\ \hline \end{array} \longrightarrow \begin{array}{r} 2,000 \\ - 1,000 \\ \hline 1,000 \end{array}$$

Directions: Estimate the sums and differences by rounding the numbers first.

$\begin{array}{r} 68 \\ + 34 \\ \hline \end{array} \longrightarrow$	$\begin{array}{r} 12 \\ + 98 \\ \hline \end{array} \longrightarrow$	$\begin{array}{r} 89 \\ + 23 \\ \hline \end{array} \longrightarrow$
$\begin{array}{r} 638 \\ - 395 \\ \hline \end{array} \longrightarrow$	$\begin{array}{r} 281 \\ - 69 \\ \hline \end{array} \longrightarrow$	$\begin{array}{r} 271 \\ - 126 \\ \hline \end{array} \longrightarrow$
$\begin{array}{r} 1,532 \\ - 998 \\ \hline \end{array} \longrightarrow$	$\begin{array}{r} 8,312 \\ - 4,789 \\ \hline \end{array} \longrightarrow$	$\begin{array}{r} 6,341 \\ + 9,286 \\ \hline \end{array} \longrightarrow$

Bonnie has $50 to purchase tennis shoes, a tennis racquet, and tennis balls. Does she have enough money?

_____

What Do You Think?

Directions: Estimate the answer to each question. Use a timer, watch, or clock that measures seconds to time the activity. Then, record the actual answer. How close was the estimate?

Question	Estimate	Actual Number
1. How many jumping jacks can you do in 15 seconds?		
2. How many seconds does it take to say the alphabet backwards?		
3. How many light bulbs are there in your home?		
4. How many seconds does it take to tie both shoes?		
5. How many times does the letter **p** appear on this page?		
6. How many spoonfuls of water does it take to fill a small drinking glass?		
7. How high can you count out loud in 15 seconds?		
8. How many steps does it take to walk around the edge of the largest room in your home?		
9. How many numbers between 1 and 99 have the numeral 2 in them?		
10. How many seconds does it take to sing "Happy Birthday to You"?		

Name _____

The Missing Link

Directions: Round each number to the nearest thousand, ten thousand, hundred thousand, and million.

	Thousand	Ten Thousand	Hundred Thousand	Million
3,567,248				
6,388,845				
15,573,543				
28,954,274				
856,388,327				

Estimating Sums

Example:

Estimate by rounding before you add.

Nearest Ten	Nearest Hundred	Nearest Thousand

$$\begin{array}{r} 88 \\ +\ 51 \\ \hline 139 \end{array} \longrightarrow \begin{array}{r} 90 \\ +\ 50 \\ \hline 140 \end{array}$$

$$\begin{array}{r} 244 \\ +\ 776 \\ \hline 1{,}020 \end{array} \longrightarrow \begin{array}{r} 200 \\ +\ 800 \\ \hline 1{,}000 \end{array}$$

$$\begin{array}{r} 4{,}566 \\ +\ 3{,}320 \\ \hline 7{,}886 \end{array} \longrightarrow \begin{array}{r} 5{,}000 \\ +\ 3{,}000 \\ \hline 8{,}000 \end{array}$$

Actual = 139
Estimated = 140
Difference = 1

Actual = 1,020
Estimated = 1,000
Difference = 20

Actual = 7,886
Estimated = 8,000
Difference = 114

When you do not have to be exact, estimating can be easy and close to the actual sum.

Directions: Estimate the sums. Round numbers to the highest place value of the smaller number.

1. $\begin{array}{r} 52 \\ +\ 66 \end{array} \longrightarrow \begin{array}{r} 50 \\ +\ 70 \end{array}$

2. $\begin{array}{r} 618 \\ +\ 384 \end{array}$

3. $\begin{array}{r} 3{,}477 \\ +\ 8{,}611 \end{array}$

4. $\begin{array}{r} 44 \\ +\ 91 \end{array}$

5. $\begin{array}{r} 222 \\ +\ 479 \end{array}$

6. $\begin{array}{r} 1{,}190 \\ +\ 7{,}625 \end{array}$

7. $\begin{array}{r} 36 \\ +\ 19 \end{array}$

8. $\begin{array}{r} 566 \\ +\ 818 \end{array}$

9. $\begin{array}{r} 4{,}533 \\ +\ 7{,}498 \end{array}$

Estimating Differences

To estimate differences, round the numbers and then subtract. This skill can be used daily. An example of this would be when you travel by car. If you have a distance of 862 miles to travel and you've gone 381, you can round and subtract in your head— 900 – 400 leaves approximately 500 more miles to go.

Nearest Ten	Nearest Hundred	Nearest Thousand

48 → 50	841 → 800	6,780 → 7,000
– 13 → – 10	– 289 → – 300	– 1,912 → – 2,000
35 40	552 500	4,868 5,000
Actual = 35	Actual = 552	Actual = 4,868
Estimated = 40	Estimated = 500	Estimated = 5,000
Difference = 5	Difference = 52	Difference = 132

Keep in mind that these answers are approximate, so this method should not be used if you want an exact answer.

Directions: Subtract by estimating.

1. $\begin{array}{r} 93 \to 90 \\ - 68 \to - 70 \\ \hline \end{array}$

2. $\begin{array}{r} 571 \\ - 139 \\ \hline \end{array}$

3. $\begin{array}{r} 4,899 \\ - 1,916 \\ \hline \end{array}$

4. $\begin{array}{r} 88 \\ - 19 \\ \hline \end{array}$

5. $\begin{array}{r} 912 \\ - 778 \\ \hline \end{array}$

6. $\begin{array}{r} 8,211 \\ - 5,928 \\ \hline \end{array}$

7. $\begin{array}{r} 71 \\ - 28 \\ \hline \end{array}$

8. $\begin{array}{r} 622 \\ - 266 \\ \hline \end{array}$

9. $\begin{array}{r} 6,935 \\ - 2,899 \\ \hline \end{array}$

Name _____

Prime Numbers

Example: 3 is a **prime number.** 3 ÷ 1 = 3 and 3 ÷ 3=1

Any other divisor will result in a mixed number or fraction.

Example:

11 can be divided only by 1 and 11.
It is a prime number.

Directions: Write the first 15 prime numbers.

A prime number is a positive whole number that can be divided evenly only by itself or one.

Prime Numbers:

_____   _____   _____   _____   _____

_____   _____   _____   _____   _____

_____   _____   _____   _____   _____

How many prime numbers are there between 0 and 100?   ___

Prime Numbers

Directions: Circle the prime numbers.

71	3	82	20	43	69
128	97	23	111	75	51
13	44	137	68	171	83
61	21	77	101	34	16
2	39	92	17	52	29
19	156	63	99	27	147
121	25	88	12	87	55
57	7	139	91	9	37
67	183	5	59	11	95

Multiples

A **multiple** is the product of a specific number and any other number. When you multiply two numbers, the answer is called the **product**.

Example:

The multiples of 2 are 2 (2 x 1), 4 (2 x 2), 6, 8, 10, 12, and so on.
The **least common multiple** (LCM) of two or more numbers is the smallest number other than 0 that is a multiple of each number.

Example:

Multiples of 3 are 3, 6, 9, 12, 15, 18, 21, 24, etc.
Multiples of 6 are 6, 12, 18, 24, 30, 36, 42, etc.
Multiples that 3 and 6 have in common are 6, 12, 18, 24.
The LCM of 3 and 6 is 6.

Directions: Write the first nine multiples of 3, 4, and 6. Write the LCM.

3: _____ , _____ , _____ , _____ , _____ , _____ , _____ , _____ , _____
4: _____ , _____ , _____ , _____ , _____ , _____ , _____ , _____ , _____
6: _____ , _____ , _____ , _____ , _____ , _____ , _____ , _____ , _____

LCM = _____

Directions: Write the first nine multiples of 2 and 5. Write the LCM.

2: _____ , _____ , _____ , _____ , _____ , _____ , _____ , _____ , _____
5: _____ , _____ , _____ , _____ , _____ , _____ , _____ , _____ , _____

LCM = _____

Directions: Find the LCM for each pair of numbers.

7 and 3 _____ 4 and 6 _____ 6 and 9 _____
5 and 15 _____ 5 and 4 _____ 3 and 18 _____

Directions: Fill in the missing numbers.

30 has multiples of 5 and ____ , of 2 and _____ , of 3 and _____ .

Factors

Factors are the numbers multiplied together to give a product. The **greatest common factor** (GCF) is the largest number for a set of numbers that divides evenly into each number in the set.

Example:

The factors of 12 are 3 x 4, 2 x 6 and 1 x 12.
We can write the factors like this: 3, 4, 2, 6, 12, 1.
The factors of 8 are 2, 4, 8, 1.
The common factors of 12 and 8 are 2 and 4 and 1.
The GCF of 12 and 8 is 4.

Directions: Write the factors of each pair of numbers. Then write the common factors and the GCF.

12:_____ , _____ , _____ , _____ , _____ , _____
15:_____ , _____ , _____ , _____

The common factors of 12 and 15 are _____ , _____ .

The GCF is _____ .

20:_____ , _____ , _____ , _____ , _____ , _____
10:_____ _____ , _____ , _____

The common factors of 10 and 20 are _____ , _____ , _____ , _____ .

The GCF is _____ .

32:_____ , _____ , _____ , _____ , _____ , _____
24:_____ _____ , _____ , _____ , _____ , _____ , _____

The common factors of 24 and 32 are _____ , _____ , _____ , _____ .

The GCF is _____ .

Directions: Write the GCF for the following pairs of numbers.

28 and 20 _____   42 and 12 _____
36 and 12 _____   20 and 5 _____

Factor Trees

A **factor tree** shows the prime factors of a number. A prime number, such as 7, has for its factors only itself and 1.

Example:

30
6 x 5
3   2   5

30 = 3 x 2 x 5.
3, 2, and 5 are prime numbers.

Directions: Fill in the numbers in the factor trees.

Factor Trees

Directions: Fill in the numbers in the factor trees. The first one has been done for you.

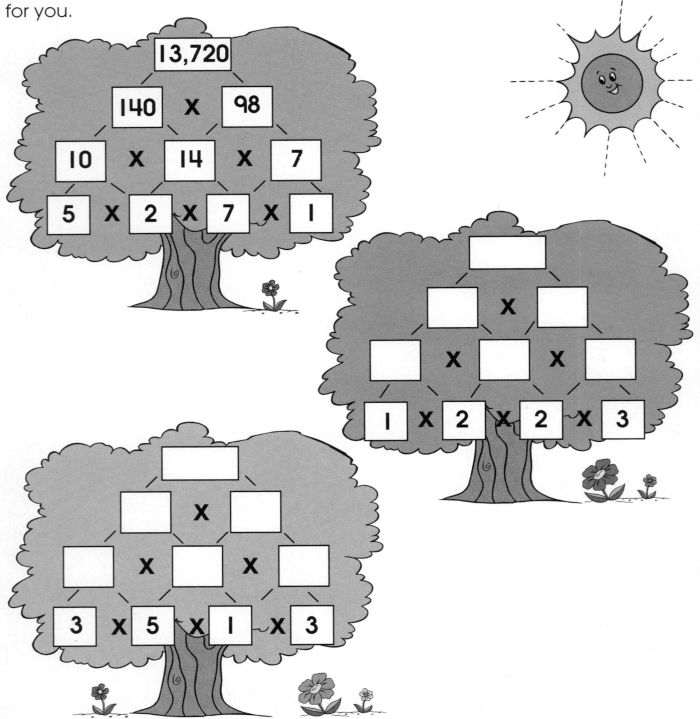

Tree 1:
13,720
140 X 98
10 X 14 X 7
5 X 2 X 7 X 1

Tree 2:
1 X 2 X 2 X 3

Tree 3:
3 X 5 X 1 X 3

Greatest Common Factor

Directions: Write the greatest common factor for each set of numbers.

10 and 35 _____

2 and 10 _____

42 and 63 _____

16 and 40 _____

25 and 55 _____

12 and 20 _____

14 and 28 _____

8 and 20 _____

6 and 27 _____

15 and 35 _____

18 and 48 _____

Name _____

Least Common Multiple

Directions: Write the least common multiple for each pair of numbers.

12 and 7 _____

2 and 4 _____

22 and 4 _____

6 and 10 _____

3 and 7 _____

6 and 8 _____

5 and 10 _____

8 and 12 _____

9 and 15 _____

7 and 5 _____

3 and 8 _____

9 and 4 _____

Deep Blue Sea

An **integer** is any positive or negative whole number, or zero. Negative integers are numbers less than zero. The opposite of any number is found the same distance from 0 on a number line.

Example:

-5 -4 -3 -2 -1 0 1 2 3 4 5

35 below zero can be written as –35.
The opposite of 6 is –6.
The opposite of –41 is 41.
The opposite of 0 is 0.

Directions: Write a number for each description.

1. 5 feet below sea level _____
2. 14 degrees below zero _____
3. a loss of $10 _____
4. climbing down 9 feet into a cave _____
5. a 2 yard gain in a football game _____
6. 3 fewer fish than the day before _____
7. no change _____
8. driving a car 11 feet in reverse _____

Directions: Write a description for each integer.

–6 _____   –14 _____
–3 _____   –7 _____
 0 _____   8 _____
 4 _____   –4 _____

Directions: Write the opposite number.

6 _____   0 _____
4 _____   –14 _____
–9 _____   –7 _____
5 _____   25 _____

Name _____

Add Integers

Example:

A number line can be used to add integers. To add positive integers, move to the right. To add negative integers, move to the left.

$4 + (-5) = (-1)$
Find 4 on the number line. Move 5 spaces to the left.

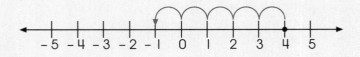

$(-3) + 4 = 1$

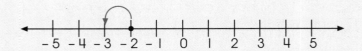

$(-2) + (-1) = (-3)$

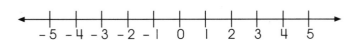

Directions: Add. Use the number lines to help you.

$2 + (-4) =$ _____

$(-3) + (-1) =$ _____

$(-1) + 4 =$ _____

$(-2) + 2 =$ _____

$4 + (-7) =$ _____

$0 + (-4) =$ _____

Integers   **44**   Total Math Grade 5

Subtract Integers

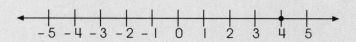
$2 - 4 = 2 + (^-4) = ^-2$

Example:

Steps:

To subtract integers, change the subtraction problem to an addition problem. Then, change the second number in the problem to its opposite. (A **–2** will be a **2**; a **2** will be a **–2**.) Use a number line to solve the problem.

```
←——+——+——+——+——+——+——+——+——+——+——+——→
   -5  -4  -3  -2  -1   0   1   2   3   4   5
```

$2 - 4 = 2 + (–4) = –2$ $3 - (–1) = 3 + 1 = 4$ $(–3) - 1 = (–3) + (–1) = –4$

$(–1) - (–3) = (–1) + 3 = 2$ $(–4) - (–4) = (–4) + 4 = 0$

Directions: Subtract. Show the addition problem that was used.

$1 - 5 =$ _____ $2 - (–2) =$ _____ $(–1) - (–6) =$ _____

$0 - 4 =$ _____ $(–1) - 2 =$ _____ $(–1) - (–1) =$ _____

$(–3) - (–5) =$ _____ $(–3) - 0 =$ _____ $4 - (–1) =$ _____

$2 - 3 =$ _____ $0 - (–2) =$ _____ $(–3) - 3 =$ _____

Directions: Write the + sign or – sign to make each problem true.

$–3 \square –2 = –5$ $1 \square 4 = –3$ $–1 \square –3 = 2$

$–2 \square –2 = 0$ $–4 \square 5 = 1$ $–3 \square –2 = –1$

Timed Multiplication

Directions: Have someone time you as you multiply the following problems.

1	9	4	8	2	5	7	12
x 1	x 3	x 10	x 3	x 10	x 7	x 4	x 3

10	12	10	4	7	11	6	3
x 3	x 9	x 5	x 9	x 5	x 2	x 6	x 2

5	10	9	3	5	9	8	6
x 8	x 4	x 4	x 3	x 9	x 6	x 5	x 7

4	11	12	1	7	10	2	4
x 8	x 3	x 5	x 4	x 7	x 6	x 7	x 7

3	6	9	5	11	3	10	1
x 4	x 8	x 5	x 10	x 9	x 5	x 7	x 5

2	8	9	4	9	8	7	4
x 6	x 7	x 2	x 6	x 8	x 8	x 9	x 5

10	3	6	11	9	2	12	7
x 8	x 6	x 10	x 6	x 7	x 5	x 10	x 10

Fast Facts

Directions: See how many problems you can solve in 90 seconds.

4 x 3 =	11 x 9 =	6 x 6 =	10 x 3 =	2 x 8 =	2 x 1 =
5 x 0 =	3 x 3 =	6 x 7 =	7 x 3 =	12 x 7 =	6 x 10 =
4 x 5 =	8 x 9 =	4 x 8 =	12 x 5 =	7 x 5 =	11 x 7 =
0 x 9 =	12 x 4 =	2 x 5 =	11 x 11 =	9 x 6 =	8 x 6 =
4 x 7 =	5 x 9 =	10 x 12 =	3 x 9 =	5 x 5 =	8 x 5 =
7 x 2 =	11 x 6 =	4 x 10 =	12 x 11 =	6 x 4 =	7 x 9 =
10 x 1 =	9 x 10 =	2 x 4 =	5 x 6 =	1 x 6 =	12 x 2 =
9 x 12 =	2 x 9 =	3 x 1 =	4 x 11 =	7 x 8 =	4 x 4 =
10 x 2 =	4 x 1 =	7 x 10 =	6 x 12 =	8 x 0 =	5 x 10 =
12 x 3 =	10 x 10 =	6 x 3 =	8 x 11 =	3 x 8 =	12 x 1 =
7 x 7 =	9 x 4 =	11 x 10 =	7 x 1 =	9 x 9 =	6 x 2 =
8 x 12 =	2 x 11 =	5 x 3 =	11 x 3 =	2 x 2 =	1 x 1 =
2 x 3 =	9 x 1 =	4 x 0 =	11 x 5 =	10 x 8 =	1 x 11 =

How many problems did you complete correctly? _____

Multiplication (One-Digit Multiplier)

Example A (no regrouping)	234 x 2 468	**Step 1** Multiply ones. 2 x 4 = 8 **Step 2** Multiply tens. 2 x 3 = 6 **Step 3** Multiply hundreds. 2 x 2 = 4

Example B (regrouping)

2 1
563
x   4
2,252

Step 1 Multiply ones. 4 x 3 = 12 ones = 1 ten 2 ones. Carry the 1.
Step 2 Multiply tens. 4 x 6 + 1 = 25 tens = 2 hundreds 5 tens. Carry the 2.
Step 3 Multiply hundreds. 4 x 5 + 2 = 22 hundreds = 2 thousands 2 hundreds

Example C (regrouping and zeros)

7 5
7,086
x   9
63,774

Step 1 Multiply ones. 9 x 6 = 54 ones = 5 tens 4 ones. Carry the 5.
Step 2 Multiply tens. 9 x 8 + 5 = 77 tens = 7 hundreds 7 tens. Carry the 7.
Step 3 Multiply hundreds. 9 x 0 + 7 = 7 hundreds.
Step 4 Multiply thousands. 9 x 7 = 63 thousands = 6 ten-thousands 3 thousands.

Directions: Multiply.

1.   323
   x   8

2.   1,132
   x   2

3.   789
   x   5

4.   4,008
   x   7

5.   2,580
   x   3

6.   888
   x   6

7.   4,234
   x   4

8.   589
   x   9

9.   3,211
   x   3

Multiplication (Two-Digit Multiplier)

Example A
(no regrouping)

$$\begin{array}{r} 21 \\ \times \ 44 \\ \hline 84 \\ + \ 840 \\ \hline 924 \end{array}$$

Step 1 Multiply by ones.
$4 \times 1 = 4$
$4 \times 2 = 8$

Step 2 Multiply by tens.
Add zero in the ones column.
$4 \times 1 = 4$
$4 \times 2 = 8$

Step 3 Add.
$84 + 840 = 924$

Example B
(regrouping)

$$\begin{array}{r} 67 \\ \times \ 58 \\ \hline 536 \\ + \ 3,350 \\ \hline 3,886 \end{array}$$

Step 1 Multiply by ones.
$8 \times 7 = 56$ (Carry the 5.)
$8 \times 6 + 5 = 53$

Step 2 Multiply by tens.
Add zero in the ones column.
$5 \times 7 = 35$ (Carry the 3.)
$5 \times 6 + 3 = 33$

Step 3 Add.
$536 + 3,350 = 3,886$

Directions: Multiply.

1. $\begin{array}{r} 43 \\ \times \ 33 \\ \hline \end{array}$

2. $\begin{array}{r} 55 \\ \times \ 46 \\ \hline \end{array}$

3. $\begin{array}{r} 78 \\ \times \ 68 \\ \hline \end{array}$

4. $\begin{array}{r} 39 \\ \times \ 27 \\ \hline \end{array}$

5. $\begin{array}{r} 21 \\ \times \ 87 \\ \hline \end{array}$

6. $\begin{array}{r} 77 \\ \times \ 24 \\ \hline \end{array}$

7. $\begin{array}{r} 44 \\ \times \ 16 \\ \hline \end{array}$

8. $\begin{array}{r} 80 \\ \times \ 71 \\ \hline \end{array}$

9. $\begin{array}{r} 65 \\ \times \ 49 \\ \hline \end{array}$

One-Digit Multiplication With Regrouping

Example:

Here's how to do 1-digit multiplication with regrouping.

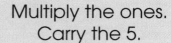

Multiply the ones. Carry the 5.	Multiply the tens. Add the 5. Carry the 2.	Multiply the hundreds and thousands.
5 4, 1 3 7 x 8 6	2 5 4, 1 3 7 x 8 9 6	1 2 5 4, 1 3 7 x 8 3 3, 0 9 6

Directions: Multiply.

216	415	311	738	129	561
x 6	x 8	x 5	x 4	x 3	x 9

1,857	4,286	8,134	3,629	6,295	14,526
x 2	x 7	x 6	x 3	x 4	x 7

Directions: Write a numeral in each box to make the multiplication problem true.

□□□	□□□	□□□	□□□
x □	x □	x □	x □
1, 2 5 4	1, 2 8 8	1, 9 0 2	3, 2 4 4

□□□	□, □□□	□, □□□	□, □□□
x □	x □	x □	x □
2, 3 1 6	8, 1 8 4	3 4, 8 8 8	1 0, 2 4 8

Name _____

Two-Digit Multiplication With Regrouping

Example:

Steps:

Multiply by the ones. Carry numbers as needed.	Multiply by the tens. Carry numbers as needed. Put a zero in the ones place.	Add.

```
      5 3
   6, 0 7 4
  x       3 8
  4 8, 5 9 2
```

```
      2 1 1
   6, 0 7 4
  x       3 8
  4 8, 5 9 2
  1 8 2, 2 2 0
```

```
   6, 0 7 4
  x       3 8
  4 8, 5 9 2
 +1 8 2, 2 2 0
  2 3 0, 8 1 2
```

Directions: Multiply along each diagonal of the square. Write the answer in the oval.

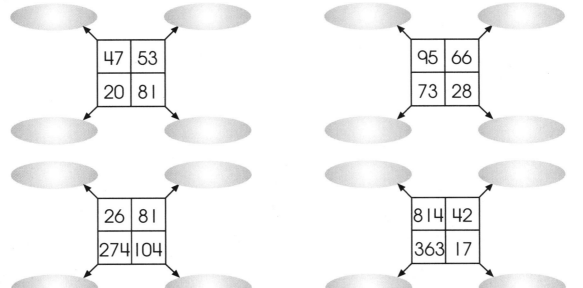

47	53
20	81

95	66
73	28

26	81
274	104

814	42
363	17

Directions: What is the pattern of the answers on opposite corners? Why is that so?

_____

Name _____

Multiplication Maze

Directions: These multiplication problems have already been done, but some of them are wrong. Check each problem. Connect the problems with correct answers to make a path for Zerpo to get back to his ship. Then, correct each wrong answer.

```
   863          904        6,520                          199
 x  24        x  93       x   74                        x  98
 21,712       85,072      582,480                       19,502

   663                      485
 x  54          392       x  53          925           4,516
 53,802       x  28       24,605       x  68          x   22
              11,976                   62,900          98,352

   566                      466
 x  74        2,576       x  18                         534
 35,884       x   92       8,388       1,530          x  34
              236,992                  x   93          28,156
                                       152,290

 5,563                                                        
 x   35         719         239          329
 194,705      x  82       x  15        x  16                  
              69,958       4,585       5,624

 1,344                                                 861
 x  49          671         793                      x  57
 65,856       x  68       x  81                       50,077
              45,628       64,233        651
                                       x  83
                                       34,738        819
                            1,524                   x  76
                          x   43                     52,244
             2,316         64,532
           x   27                      4,110
            62,532                   x   28
                                     125,080
```

Multiplication Riddle

Directions: Answer the riddle at the bottom of the page by solving the problems and writing the matching letters.

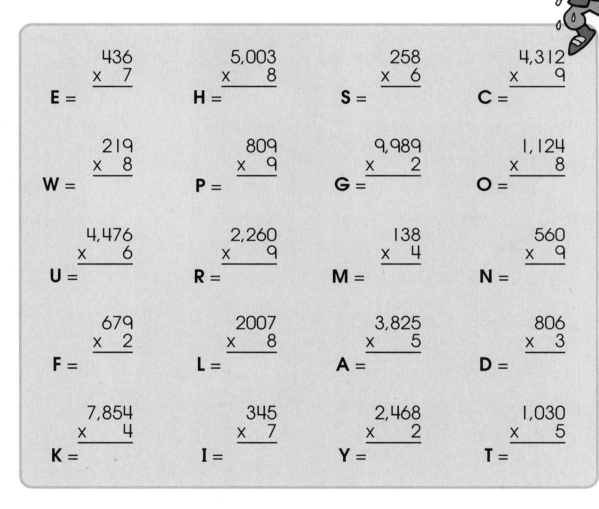

$$
\begin{array}{r} 436 \\ \times\ \ 7 \\ \hline \end{array}
$$
E =

$$
\begin{array}{r} 5{,}003 \\ \times\ \ 8 \\ \hline \end{array}
$$
H =

$$
\begin{array}{r} 258 \\ \times\ \ 6 \\ \hline \end{array}
$$
S =

$$
\begin{array}{r} 4{,}312 \\ \times\ \ 9 \\ \hline \end{array}
$$
C =

$$
\begin{array}{r} 219 \\ \times\ \ 8 \\ \hline \end{array}
$$
W =

$$
\begin{array}{r} 809 \\ \times\ \ 9 \\ \hline \end{array}
$$
P =

$$
\begin{array}{r} 9{,}989 \\ \times\ \ 2 \\ \hline \end{array}
$$
G =

$$
\begin{array}{r} 1{,}124 \\ \times\ \ 8 \\ \hline \end{array}
$$
O =

$$
\begin{array}{r} 4{,}476 \\ \times\ \ 6 \\ \hline \end{array}
$$
U =

$$
\begin{array}{r} 2{,}260 \\ \times\ \ 9 \\ \hline \end{array}
$$
R =

$$
\begin{array}{r} 138 \\ \times\ \ 4 \\ \hline \end{array}
$$
M =

$$
\begin{array}{r} 560 \\ \times\ \ 9 \\ \hline \end{array}
$$
N =

$$
\begin{array}{r} 679 \\ \times\ \ 2 \\ \hline \end{array}
$$
F =

$$
\begin{array}{r} 2007 \\ \times\ \ 8 \\ \hline \end{array}
$$
L =

$$
\begin{array}{r} 3{,}825 \\ \times\ \ 5 \\ \hline \end{array}
$$
A =

$$
\begin{array}{r} 806 \\ \times\ \ 3 \\ \hline \end{array}
$$
D =

$$
\begin{array}{r} 7{,}854 \\ \times\ \ 4 \\ \hline \end{array}
$$
K =

$$
\begin{array}{r} 345 \\ \times\ \ 7 \\ \hline \end{array}
$$
I =

$$
\begin{array}{r} 2{,}468 \\ \times\ \ 2 \\ \hline \end{array}
$$
Y =

$$
\begin{array}{r} 1{,}030 \\ \times\ \ 5 \\ \hline \end{array}
$$
T =

What is the only kind of coat that goes on wet?

____ ____ ____ ____ ____   ____ ____
19,125 38,808 8,992 19,125 5,150 8,992 1,358

____ ____ ____ ____ ____!
7,281 19,125 2,415 5,040 5,150

Crossing the Dragon

Directions: Multiply.

32 x 52	612 x 23	1,243 x 11	408 x 39
2,573 x 30	809 x 27	76 x 25	1,607 x 41
3,505 x 45	6,399 x 47	5,007 x 17	62 x 40
7,042 x 53	640 x 99	623 x 86	473 x 33
94 x 19	782 x 52	4,000 x 44	87 x 78
638 x 10	540 x 85	38 x 56	865 x 73

Puzzling Cross Number

Directions: Solve the multiplication problems below. Write the answers in the puzzle.

Across

1.	462	5.	234	7.	926
	x 212		x 101		x 815

8.	624	11.	832
	x 783		x 458

13.	336	14.	801
	x 817		x 101

Down

2.	634	3.	208	4.	672
	x 755		x 422		x 833

6.	547	9.	926
	x 900		x 950

10.	698	12.	111
	x 741		x 111

Multiplication

Be certain to keep the proper place value when multiplying by tens and hundreds.

Examples:

```
   143            250
 x 262          x 150
   286            000
   858           1250
   286           250
 37,466         37,500
```

Directions: Multiply.

```
    701            621            348            597
  x 308          x 538          x 200          x 424
```

```
    537            416            682            180
  x 189          x 727          x 472          x 340
```

```
    878            267            893            907
  x 638          x 196          x 214          x 428
```

An airplane flies 720 trips a year between the cities of Chicago and Columbus. Each trip is 375 miles. How many miles does the airplane fly each year?

_____

Problem Solving

Directions: Solve each problem.

1. There are 6 rows of desks in the office. Each row has 8 desks. How many desks are in the office?

   There are _____ rows of desks.
   There are _____ desks in each row.
   There are _____ desks in all.

2. There are 9 rows of trees. There are 7 trees in each row. How many trees are there in all?

   There are _____ rows of trees.
   There are _____ trees in each row.
   There are _____ trees in all.

3. The people at the park were separated into teams of 8 people each. Nine teams were formed. How many people were in the park?

   Each team had _____ people.
   There were _____ teams formed.
   There were _____ people in the park.

4. There were 6 people in each car. There were 7 cars. How many people were there in all?

   There were _____ people in each car.
   There were _____ cars.
   There were _____ people in all.

5. How many cents would you need to buy eight 8-cent pencils?

   You would need _____ cents.

1.

2.

3.

4.

5.

57

Problem Solving

Directions: Solve each problem

1. Each club member works 3 hours each month. There are 32 members. What is the total number of hours worked each month by all club members?

   There are _____ club members.
   Each member works _____ hours.
   The club members work _____ hours in all.

2. Mrs. Robins drives 19 miles every working day. How many miles does she drive in a five-day work-week?

   She drives _____ miles every working day.
   She works _____ days a week.
   She drives _____ miles in a five-day work-week.

3. It takes 54 minutes to make one gizmo. How long will it take to make 3 gizmos?

   It takes _____ minutes to make one gizmo.
   There are _____ gizmos.
   It takes _____ minutes to make 3 gizmos.

4. Each box weighs 121 kilograms. There are 4 boxes. What is the total weight of the 4 boxes?

   Each box weighs _____ kilograms.
   There are _____ boxes.
   The total weight of the 4 boxes is _____ kilograms.

5. There are 168 hours in a week. How many hours are there in 6 weeks?

   There are _____ hours in 6 weeks.

1.

2.

3.

4.

5.

Problem Solving

Directions: Solve each problem.

1. There are 60 minutes in one hour. How many minutes are there in 24 hours?

   There are _____ minutes in 24 hours.

2. Forty-eight toy boats are packed in each box. How many boats are there in 16 boxes?

   There are _____ boats in 16 boxes.

3. Seventy-three new cars can be assembled in one hour. At that rate, how many cars could be assembled in 51 hours?

   _____ cars could be assembled in 51 hours.

4. A truck is hauling 36 bags of cement. Each bag weighs 94 pounds. How many pounds of cement are being hauled?

   _____ pounds of cement are being hauled.

5. To square a number means to multiply the number by itself. What is the square of 68?

   The square of 68 is _____ .

6. Sixty-five books are packed in each box. How many books are there in 85 boxes?

   There are _____ books in 85 boxes .

| 1. |
| 2. |
| 3. |
| 4. |
| 5. |
| 6. |

Problem Solving

Directions: Solve each problem.

1. A machine can produce 98 parts in one hour. How many parts could it produce in 72 hours?

   It could produce _____ parts in 72 hours.

2. Each new bus can carry 66 passengers. How many passengers can ride on 85 new buses?

   _____ passengers can ride on 85 buses.

3. A gross is twelve dozen or 144. The school ordered 21 gross of pencils. How many pencils were ordered?

   The school ordered _____ pencils.

4. How many hours are there in a year (365 days)?

   There are _____ hours in a year.

5. Each of 583 people worked a 40-hour week. How many hours of work was this?

   It was _____ hours of work.

6. The highway mileage between New York and Chicago is 840 miles. How many miles would a bus travel in making 68 one-way trips between New York and Chicago?

   The bus would travel _____ miles .

1.

2.

3.

4.

5.

6.

Problem Solving

Directions: Solve each problem.

1. Each crate the men unloaded weighed 342 pounds. They unloaded 212 crates. How many pounds did they unload?

   The men unloaded _____ pounds.

2. The school cafeteria expects to serve 425 customers every day. At that rate, how many meals will be served if the cafeteria is open 175 days a year?

   _____ meals will be served.

3. There are 168 hours in one week. How many hours are there in 260 weeks?

   There are _____ hours in 260 weeks.

4. There are 3,600 seconds in one hour and 168 hours in one week. How many seconds are there in one week?

   There are _____ seconds in one week.

5. A jet carrying 128 passengers flew 2,574 miles. How many passenger-miles (number of passengers times number of miles traveled) would this be?

   It would be _____ passenger miles.

6. How many passenger-miles would be flown by the jet in problem 5, if it flew from Seattle to New Orleans, a distance of 2,098 miles?

   It would be _____ passenger-miles.

| 1. |
| 2. |
| 3. |
| 4. |
| 5. |
| 6. |

Multiplication's Opposite

Directions: Use the multiplication problem to help solve the division problems.

Example:
6 × 7 = 42
42 ÷ 7 = 6
42 ÷ 6 = 7

1. 4 × 8 = 32
32 ÷ _____ = 4
32 ÷ _____ = 8

2. 9 × 9 = 81
81 ÷ 9 = _____

3. 7 × 8 = 56
_____ ÷ 8 = 7
56 ÷ _____ = 8

4. 22 × 12 = 264
_____ ÷ 12 = 22
264 ÷ 22 = _____

5. 37 × 19 = 703
_____ ÷ 37 = 19
703 ÷ 19 = _____

Directions: Solve the following problems and write two related division problems for each.

6. 22 × 17 = _____

7. 45 × 29 = _____

8. 19 × 82 = _____

9. 671 × 63 = _____

10. 663 × 54 = _____

11. 719 × 73 = _____

Division Facts

Directions: Solve the division problems.

3)24	9)81	8)40	4)4	9)90	8)56	6)24
7)14	7)49	5)20	6)36	9)72	4)16	3)27
8)64	9)36	5)25	9)45	2)18	4)24	8)8
3)9	2)14	6)54	7)21	8)32	5)30	1)6
2)4	9)81	6)30	4)8	5)50	5)15	2)20
1)10	7)7	2)16	3)15	7)49	1)4	9)63
8)16	2)12	8)72	3)30	9)63	3)18	7)56
9)9	7)63	2)8	8)80	7)28	6)12	3)6
7)42	3)12	7)35	9)27	6)42	5)10	5)45
2)10	9)54	4)20	8)48	9)18	6)6	2)6

Division

Division is the reverse of multiplication. It is the process of dividing a number into equal groups of smaller numbers.

Directions: Divide.

Greg had 936 marbles to share with his two brothers. If the boys divided them evenly, how many will each one get? _____

The marbles Greg kept were four different colors: blue, green, red, and orange. He had the same number of each color. He divided them into two groups. One group had only orange marbles. The rest of the marbles were in the other group. How many marbles did he have in each group?

orange _____ others _____

The **dividend** is the number to be divided by another number. In the problem 28 ÷ 7 = 4, 28 is the dividend.

The **divisor** is the number by which another number is divided. In the problem 28 ÷ 7 = 4, 7 is the divisor.

The **quotient** is the answer in a division problem. In the problem 28 ÷ 7 = 4, 4 is the quotient.

The **remainder** is the number left over in the quotient of a division problem. In the problem 29 ÷ 7 = 4 r1, 1 is the remainder.

Directions: Write the answers.

In the problem 25 ÷ 8 = 3 r1 . . .

What is the divisor? _____ What is the remainder?_____

What is the quotient? _____ What is the dividend?_____

Directions: Divide.

$9\overline{)2,025}$ $6\overline{)2,508}$ $3\overline{)225}$ $5\overline{)400}$ $2\overline{)1,156}$

Division

The remainder in a division problem must always be less than the divisor.

Example:

```
         244 r 23
    26 | 6,367
         52
         116
         104
          127
          104
           23
```

Directions: Divide.

53 | 1,220   37 | 1,528   83 | 6,270   26 | 3,618

14 | 389   29 | 2,645   60 | 8,010   57 | 5,406

35 | 2,546   43 | 492   83 | 4,608   19 | 185

The Oregon Trail is 2,197 miles long. How long would it take a covered wagon traveling 20 miles a day to complete the trip?

_____

Name _____

Checking Division

Answers in division problems can be checked by multiplying.

Example:

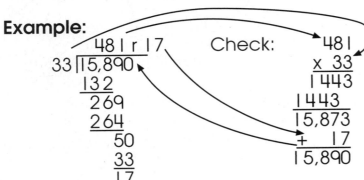

$$\begin{array}{r} 481 \text{ r } 17 \\ 33\overline{)15{,}890} \\ \underline{132} \\ 269 \\ \underline{264} \\ 50 \\ \underline{33} \\ 17 \end{array}$$

Check:

$$\begin{array}{r} 481 \\ \times\ 33 \\ \hline 1443 \\ \underline{1443} \\ 15{,}873 \\ +\ \ \ 17 \\ \hline 15{,}890 \end{array}$$

Add the remainder

Directions: Divide and check your answers.

$61\overline{)2{,}736}$ Check:	$73\overline{)86{,}143}$ Check:
$59\overline{)9{,}390}$ Check:	$43\overline{)77{,}141}$ Check:
$33\overline{)82{,}050}$ Check:	$93\overline{)84{,}039}$ Check:

Denny has a baseball card collection. He has 13,789 cards. He wants to put the cards in a scrapbook that holds 15 cards on a page. How many pages does Denny need in his scrapbook? _____

Car Division

Example:

2 2 6

62 ÷ 2 = 31

8 6 5

56 ÷ 8 = 7

Directions: Write the numerals in the correct part of the equation to get the given answer.

9 1 8

____ ÷ ____ = 2

5 5 0

____ ÷ ____ = 10

7 4 8

____ ÷ ____ = 12

2 3 8

____ ÷ ____ = 4

1 3 2 6

____ ÷ ____ = 3

2 7 4

____ ÷ ____ = 6

1 0 0 4

____ ÷ ____ = 4

5 9 4

____ ÷ ____ = 5

8 4 6

____ ÷ ____ = 8

1 1 2

____ ÷ ____ = 12

6 9 3

____ ÷ ____ = 7

1 1 0

____ ÷ ____ = 0

Crisscross

Some problems with 2-digit divisors have a zero in the quotient.

$$9{,}126 \div 38 \longrightarrow 38\overline{)9{,}126}$$

$$
\begin{array}{r}
240\text{R}6 \\
38\overline{)9{,}126} \\
-76\downarrow \\
\hline
152 \\
-152\downarrow \\
\hline
06 \\
-\ 0 \\
\hline
6 \\
\end{array}
$$

Notice that 38 does not divide into 6.

Across

2. 5,875 ÷ 18
4. 8,206 ÷ 41
7. 9,155 ÷ 27
8. 8,165 ÷ 68
12. 9,956 ÷ 11
14. 6,256 ÷ 45
16. 12,183 ÷ 60
17. 8,362 ÷ 22
18. 17,684 ÷ 36
19. 7,534 ÷ 15

Directions: Solve the problems. Write the answers in the puzzle. Write **R** in its own square when needed.

Down

1. 7,689 ÷ 18
3. 38,061 ÷ 42
5. 6,382 ÷ 10
6. 8,661 ÷ 39
9. 10,001 ÷ 20
10. 7,200 ÷ 17
11. 7,564 ÷ 12
13. 5,078 ÷ 47
15. 9,621 ÷ 52

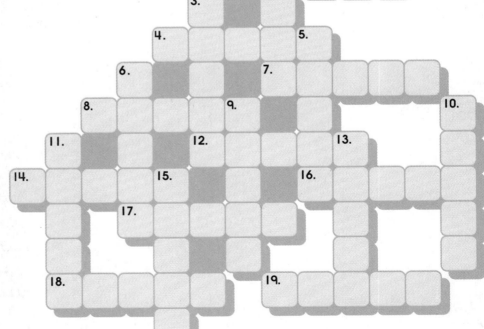

Check It Out

Check the answer to a division problem using multiplication and addition.

$$\begin{array}{r} 89R5 \\ 37\overline{)\,3,298} \end{array} \longrightarrow 3,298 \div 37 = 89R5 \longrightarrow \text{quotient}$$

dividend divisor

Steps:

1. Multiply the quotient by the divisor: $89 \times 37 = 3,293$
2. Add the remainder: $3,293 + 5 = 3,298$
3. The total should equal the dividend: $3,298 = 3,298$

Directions: Check these division problems using multiplication and addition. Circle the four incorrect answers on this page. Then, find the correct answers.

$$\begin{array}{r} 36R2 \\ 48\overline{)\,1,730} \end{array} \qquad \begin{array}{r} 74 \\ 121\overline{)\,8,954} \end{array} \qquad \begin{array}{r} 81R5 \\ 104\overline{)\,8,543} \end{array}$$

$$\begin{array}{r} 30R22 \\ 85\overline{)\,2,572} \end{array} \qquad \begin{array}{r} 42 \\ 253\overline{)\,10,373} \end{array} \qquad \begin{array}{r} 56 \\ 56\overline{)\,3,136} \end{array}$$

$12,726 \div 202 = 64R3$ $2,701 \div 73 = 37$ $8,009 \div 9 = 889R8$

$7,684 \div 44 = 174R28$ $5,459 \div 483 = 10R97$ $15,853 \div 8 = 1,981R5$

Problem Solving

Directions: Solve each problem.

1. There are 18 chairs and 6 tables in the room. There are the same number of chairs at each table. How many chairs are at each table?

There are _____ chairs.
There are _____ tables.
There are _____ chairs at each table.

2. Each box takes 3 minutes to fill. It took 18 minutes to fill all the boxes. How many boxes are there?

It took _____ minutes to fill all the boxes.
It takes _____ minutes to fill 1 box.
There are _____ boxes.

3. Rob, Jose, Jay, Tom, Alex, and Jim share 6 sandwiches. How many sandwiches does each boy get?

There are _____ sandwiches in all.
The sandwiches are shared among _____ boys.
Each boy gets _____ sandwich.

4. Bill and 8 friends each sold the same number of tickets. They sold 72 tickets in all. How many tickets were sold by each person?

Each person sold _____ tickets .

5. Forty-eight oranges are in a crate. The oranges are to be put into bags of 6 each. How many bags can be filled?

_____ bags can be filled.

1.

2.

3.

4.

5.

Problem Solving

Directions: Solve each problem.

1. There are 84 scouts in all. Six will be assigned to each tent. How many tents are there?

   There are _____ scouts in all.
   There are _____ scouts in each tent.
   There are _____ tents.

2. Seven people each worked the same number of hours. They worked 91 hours in all. How many hours were worked by each person?

   _____ hours were worked.
   _____ people worked these hours.
   _____ hours were worked by each person.

3. A group of three is a trio. How many trios could be formed with 72 people?

   _____ trios could be formed.

4. A factory shipped 848 cars to 4 cities. Each city received the same number of cars. How many cars were shipped to each city?

   _____ cars were shipped.
   _____ cities received the cars.
   _____ cars were shipped to each city.

5. Malcolm, his brother, and sister have 702 stamps in all. Suppose each takes the same number of stamps. How many will each get?

   Each will get_____ stamps.

1.

2.

3.

4.

5.

Problem Solving

Directions: Solve each problem.

1. There are 160 packages on 4 large carts. Each cart holds the same number of packages. How many packages are on each cart?

   Each cart has _____ packages.

2. There are 160 packages. To deliver most of the packages, it will take 3 small planes. Each plane will take the same number of packages. How many packages will each plane take? How many packages will be left over?

   Each plane will take _____ packages.
   There will be _____ package(s) left over.

1.

2.

Problem Solving

Directions: Solve each problem.

1. How many bags of 7 oranges each can be filled from a shipment of 341 oranges? How many oranges will be left over?

   _____ bags can be filled.
   _____ oranges will be left over.

2. Beverly has $2.38 (238 cents) to buy pencils for 8¢ each. How many pencils can she buy? How many cents will she have left?

   She can buy _____ pencils.
   She will have _____ cents left over.

3. There are 6 stamps in each row. How many complete rows can be filled with 1,950 stamps? How many stamps will be left over?

   _____ row will be filled.
   _____ stamps will be left over.

4. Daphne had 958 pennies. She exchanged them for nickels. How many nickels did she get? How many pennies did she have left over?

   She got _____ nickels.
   She had _____ pennies left over.

5. Last year Mr. Gomez worked 1,983 hours. How many 8-hour days was this? How many hours are left over?

   It was _____ 8-hour days.
   _____ hours are left over.

1.

2.

3.

4.

5.

Problem Solving

Directions: Solve each problem.

1. The pet store has 84 birds. They have 14 large cages. There are the same number of birds in each cage. How many birds are in each cage?

_____ birds are in each cage.

2. The pet store also has 63 kittens. There are 12 cages with the same number of kittens in each. The rest of the kittens are in the display window. How many kittens are in each cage? How many kittens are in the display window?

_____ kittens are in each cage.
_____ kittens are in the display window.

3. There are 60 guppies in a large tank. If the pet store puts 15 guppies each in smaller tanks, how many smaller tanks will be needed?

_____ smaller tanks will be needed.

4. There are 72 boxes of pet food on a shelf. The boxes are in rows of 13 each. How many full rows of boxes are there? How many boxes are left over?

There are _____ full rows of boxes.
There are _____ boxes left over.

5. There are 52 puppies. There are 13 cages. If each cage contains the same number of puppies, how many puppies are in each cage?

There are _____ puppies in each cage.

| 1. |
| 2. |
| 3. |
| 4. |
| 5. |

What Is the Number?

Directions: Read the clues and solve each riddle.

1. This number will tell how many dots there are on a pair of dice. This number times 29 is 1,218. What is it?   _____

2. This is the average weight in pounds of the ostrich, the heaviest bird on the earth. This number times 11 is 3,795. What is it?   _____

3. This is the number of hours an elephant sleeps each day. This number times 2,604 is 5,208. What is it?   _____

4. This is the speed in miles per hour of the Australian dragonfly—the fastest insect. This number times 53 is 1,855. What is the number?   _____

5. This is how many feet the oceans would rise if all of Antarctica melted. This number times 21 is 4,830. What is it?   _____

6. This number is the body temperature in degrees Fahrenheit that a butterfly needs to be able to fly. This number times 92 is 7,912. What is it?   _____

7. This number will tell how many grooves there are on a quarter. This number times 44 is 5,236. What is the number?   _____

8. This is the average number of gallons of water needed to take a shower. This number times 78 is 936. What is it?   _____

9. This number is the weight in pounds of the largest freshwater fish. This number times 12 is 8,100. What is it?   _____

10. This is the top speed in miles per hour of the cheetah, the world's fastest land animal. This number times 43 is 3,010. What is the number?   _____

Name _____

In the Money

Hamburger $2.95 (cheese: add $0.30)
Grilled Cheese $1.85
Fries: small $0.75 large $1.25
Onion rings $1.00
Soda pop $0.95
Milkshake $1.99
Slice of pie $1.15

Directions: Suppose you are eating at this diner. You have the money shown here. List the combination of bills and coins you would use to pay for the following items exactly (and receive no change).

1. Hamburger _____

2. Pie _____

3. Small fries _____

4. Milkshake _____

5. Onion rings and grilled cheese _____

6. 2 slices of pie _____

7. Cheeseburger and milkshake _____

8. Cheeseburger, large fries, soda pop _____

Adding Money

Example:

Steps:

1. Align the decimal points.
2. Add.

$4.32
+ $2.19
$6.51

$10.43
$ 4.25
+ $12.04
$26.72

Directions: Rewrite the problems and align the decimal points. Then, add.

$1.15 + $2.25 =

$2.09 + $1.46 =

$1.11 + $5.35 =

$3.87 + $2.95 =

$10.42 + $2.54 =

$8.12 + $3.29 =

$11.13 + $10.26 =

$4.03 + $2.99 =

$42.80 + $103.25 + $32.54 =

$3.64 + $49.39 + $1.00 =

Subtracting Money

Example:

Steps:

1. Align the decimal points.
2. Subtract.

$$
\begin{array}{r}
\$14.32 \\
- \ \$ \ 5.43 \\
\hline
\$ \ 8.89
\end{array}
$$

Directions: Rewrite the problems and align the decimal points. Then, subtract.

$4.15 - $2.25 = $2.09 - $1.46 =

$3.93 - $0.44 = $6.06 - $3.85 =

$7.83 - $2.17 = $26.32 - $12.88 =

$11.13 - $10.26 = $4.03 - $2.99 =

$43.76 - $0.94 = $104.65 - $4.87 =

Big Bucks for You!

Directions: Solve the problems on another sheet of paper.

		Answer Space

1. You receive your first royalty check for $1,000.00 and deposit it in your checking account. You go directly to the music store and spend $234.56 on new CDs. What is your balance?

2. You naturally treat all your friends to pizza, which costs you $47.76. You pay with a check. What is your balance now?

3. You decide to restock your wardrobe and buy $389.99 worth of new clothes. What is your balance?

4. Your next royalty check arrives, and you deposit $1,712.34. You also treat yourself to a new 15-speed bicycle, which costs $667.09. What is your balance?

5. You buy your mother some perfume for a present. You write a check for $37.89. What is your balance?

6. You need a tennis racket and some other sports equipment. The bill comes to $203.45. What is your new balance?

7. You treat your family to dinner at Snails in a Pail, where the check comes to $56.17. What is your new balance?

8. You join a health club, and the first payment is $150.90. What is your new balance?

9. You deposit your latest royalty check, which amounts to $4,451.01. What is your new balance?

10. To celebrate this good fortune, you take your entire peewee football team to a professional football game. The bill comes to $4,339.98. What is your new balance?

Total Math Grade 5　　　　　79　　　　　Money

At the Science Store

Directions: Solve. Remember to align the decimal points.

1. Mr. Fargas buys 2 books. How much does he spend?

   $19.98

   ```
        1 1
      $  9.99
    + $  9.99
      $ 19.98
   ```

Telescope	$75.15
Geode	$13.50
Rock set	$ 5.95
Book	$ 9.99
Chemistry set	$26.59
Fossils small	$ 8.79
large	$12.89
Star chart	$21.47
Pendulum	$18.64

Tax included in prices!

2. Janice buys a star chart and a pendulum. How much does she spend?

   _____

3. Can Troy buy a chemistry set and a rock set for less than $30?

   _____

4. Jack buys a rock set and pendulum. He pays with a $20 bill and a $10 bill. How much change does he receive?

   _____

5. Oliver buys *Dinosaurs, The Great Ice Age,* and *Rocks of Hawaii*. How much will his books cost?

   _____

6. Find the price of a large fossil, the chemistry set, and a telescope.

   _____

Multiplying Money

Example:

Joey buys 14 paperback books for $1.95 each.
How much does he spend?

```
   $1.95
 x    14
    780
 + 1950
 $27.30  ←── set decimal point two numbers in from the right
```

Directions: Rewrite the problems and multiply.

$1.55 x 7 = $10.85 x 19 =

$ 3.06 x 9 = $5.35 x 12 =

$10.00 x 15 = $1.25 x 105 =

$9.87 x 13 = $4.95 x 22 =

1. Lauren buys wood for bookshelves at a cost of $0.58 per foot. If she buys 27 feet, how much does she spend?

   _____

2. Which costs more: 5 new books for $5.97 each or 12 used books for $2.50 each?

   _____

Dividing Money

Example:

Six friends earn $63.90 shoveling driveways on a snowy day. If they divide the money evenly, how much does each one earn?

```
        $10.65
    6 ⟌ $63.90
      -6
        3 9
       -3 6
          30
         -30
           0
```

Directions: Rewrite the problems and divide.

$33.72 ÷ 4 = $98.56 ÷ 8 =

$0.96 ÷ 6 = $22.70 ÷ 10 =

$120.96 ÷ 12 = $49.68 ÷ 18 =

1. Jeremy shovels snow for 4 days and earns the same amount each day. If he earns a total of $23, how much does he earn each day?

   _____

2. Randy is one of 8 people who shares $127.76. Can he buy a poster that costs $16?

   _____

Snails in a Pail

Sly Me Slugg, world-famous French chef, has made his fast-food business, Snails in a Pail, the most popular restaurant in the whole area. This is his menu:

Slime Soup	$.49
Slugburger	$1.69
Chicken-Fried Snails	$2.99
Slimy Slush	$.89
Snailcream Shake	$1.49
Snailbits Salad	$1.09

Directions: Solve the problems on another sheet of paper.

Answer Space

1. Sly Me Slugg sold 60 Slimy Slushes and 40 Snailcream Shakes on Friday. How much did he make on drinks that day?

2. A coach treated 15 of his team players to Slugburgers. How much change did he receive from $40.00?

3. Your brother was so hungry that he ordered one of everything on the menu. How much change did he get from a $10.00 bill?

4. Sly Me Slugg sold $43.61 in Slime Soup orders on Wednesday and $38.22 in soup orders on Thursday. How many orders of Slime Soup did he sell in those 2 days?

5. You had a party at Snails in a Pail and bought 9 Slugburgers, 3 orders of Chicken-Fried Snails, 2 Snailbits Salads, 5 Snailcream Shakes, and 10 Slimy Slushes. What was the total cost for the party?

6. In one week, Sly Me Slugg sold 200 Slugburgers and 79 orders of Chicken-Fried Snails. How much money did he earn from these 2 items?

7. You ordered 10 Slugburgers, 10 Snailcream Shakes, and 10 Slimy Slushes. What was your total cost?

8. On Friday, Sly Me earned $1,252. On Saturday, he earned $1,765. On Sunday, he earned $2,998. What was his average daily earnings for those 3 days?

Name _____

Calculator Basics

A calculator cannot figure out how to solve a problem, but it can make doing computations easier—especially when the numbers are large or difficult. Here are some tips for using one.

1. Estimate answers first to check if the calculated answer makes sense.
2. Enter problems into the calculator twice. It is easy to make a mistake pressing keys.
3. Clear the display before starting a new problem.
4. Hit the = key at the end of each problem.
5. Do not enter commas.
6. Enter numbers in the order you want the calculator to perform the operations.

Directions: Each calculator may be a little different, but all calculators have certain things in common. These keys perform basic operations on almost any calculator. Look at your calculator and find out what these keys mean.

ON/OFF This key turns the calculator on and off.

AC This key means "all clear." It will clear the display and the memory.

C/CE This key means "clear" or "clear entry." It will clear the display only.

The number keys enter the digits of a number. Enter numbers from left to right. For example, enter 3,840 by pressing 3 8 4 0

The operation keys add, subtract, multiply, or divide.
+ Add. – Subtract. x Multiply. ÷ Divide.

The = gives the answer after entering all of the operations and numbers.

Using a Calculator

Here are some examples of how to enter problems into a calculator.

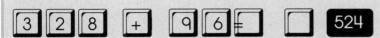

| 3 | 2 | 8 | + | 9 | 6 | = | ☐ | **524** |

| 5 | 4 | + | 7 | 8 | + | 3 | 8 | + | 1 | 2 | 3 | = | **293** |

| 9 | 8 | 3 | – | 2 | 3 | 1 | = | **752** |

| 3 | 2 | x | 5 | 4 | = | **1,728** |

| 1 | , | 8 | 9 | 2 | ÷ | 4 | = | **473** |

Directions: Use a calculator to solve these problems.

404,992 ÷ 452 = _____

35 x 28 x 81 x 10 = _____

4,906 x 659 = _____

239,476 – 20,395 = _____

436,284 + 1,293,058 = _____

33,482 x 2,338 = _____

498 + 298 + 3,904 + 637 + 1,293 = _____

284 x 47 + 1,842 = _____

45,337 – 28,493 = _____

63,856 + 283,447 – 143,396 = _____

2,004 x 742 = _____

2,184,396 ÷ 4 + 5,693 = _____

763,100 ÷ 325 = _____

493 x 329 – 32,058 = _____

Does anything happen if you divide 1,024 ÷ 2 and hit the = key over and over? If so, what? _____

Name _____

Calculator Fun

Directions: Use a calculator to solve these puzzles. If the display is too small for all the digits, use the calculator on a computer instead of a hand-held one.

1. Follow these steps:
   a. Choose a number of hours. (try 2, 8, 24, or 72)
   b. Add 10.
   c. Multiply by 2.
   d. Add 100.
   e. Divide by 2.
   f. Subtract the original number.

   What do you notice about the answer for each? _____

2. Find 4 consecutive numbers that have a product of 83,156,160. _____

3. An ancient story tells of a young girl who asks the king for 1 grain of rice on the first day, 2 on the second, 4 on the third, 8 on the fourth, and so on for a total of 30 days. The king offers her 1 million grains. Which is a better deal? By how much? _____

4. Find 12,345,679 x 9. _____

5. Find:

   11 x 11 _____

   111 x 111 _____

   1,111 x 1,111 _____

   11,111 x 11,111 _____

   111,111 x 111,111 _____

6. If you count one number each second, how long will it take to count to

   1 million? _____

   1 billion? _____

Name _____

Keeping Track

Rob is training for the javelin throw at a big track meet. He wants to know how he is doing, so he records the distances of 10 throws he makes during practice. What is Rob's average distance?

Throw	Distance	Throw	Distance
1	23 feet	6	20 feet
2	26 feet	7	24 feet
3	21 feet	8	23 feet
4	23 feet	9	22 feet
5	25 feet	10	22 feet

The average of a group of numbers tells something about the main trend of the data. The three most important kinds of averages are called the **mode**, the **median**, and the **mean**.

The **mode** is the number in the data that occurs most often. The mode of the javelin distances is 23 feet, since that number appears three times—more often than any other does.

If the data do not have a number that appears more than once, there is no mode. For example, the numbers 6, 4, 8, 7, 5, 3, and 9 have no mode.

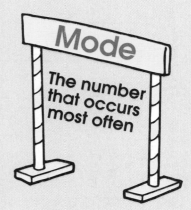

A group of numbers can also have more than one mode. For example, the numbers 2, 5, 4, 3, 2, 3, and 6 have two modes since 2 and 3 both occur twice.

If a group of numbers does have a mode, the mode will always be one of the numbers in the list.

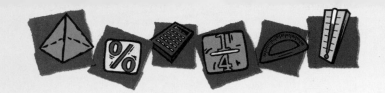

Name _____

Keeping Track

Directions: Find the mode.

3, 6, 9, 5, 12, 5, 7, 8 _____   11, 7, 9, 11, 3, 8, 9, 10, 11 _____

8, 5, 6, 4, 7, 11, 10, 9 _____   5, 7, −2, 4, −5 , −2, 0, 2, 1 _____

4, 7, 5, 6, 7, 4, 3, 4, 8, 4, 7, 7 _____   3, 4, 3, 2, 0, 0, 1, 2, 0, 1 _____

3, 3, 3, 3, 3, 3, 3, 3, 3, 3 _____   1, 2, 3, 4, 5, 6, 7, 8, 9 _____

1, 2, 3, 1, 2, 3, 1, 2, 3, 1, 2, 3 _____   13, 12, 10, 15, 12, 14, 12, 11 _____

Directions: Solve.

1. All of Jill's throws landed 24 feet away. What is the mode? _____

2. On page 87, look at Rob's data for his first ten throws.
   How far would he have to throw the javelin on the
   11th throw so that the data would have two modes? _____

3. Write a list of 6 numbers that have no mode. _____

4. Which javelin thrower below had a higher mode? _____

Kate	Adam
22 feet	21 feet
23	20
24	23
24	24
21	21
22	22
22	25

Name _____

Jumping the Median

The **median** is another kind of average.
When ordering a list of numbers from least to greatest, the median is the number that falls in the middle. Look at Anna's maximum high jumps for the last week.

Day	Height
Monday	62 inches
Tuesday	64 inches
Wednesday	62 inches
Thursday	64 inches
Friday	60 inches
Saturday	61 inches
Sunday	64 inches

Order the numbers: 60, 61, 62, **62**, 64, 64, 64. The number 62 falls in the middle. It is the median.

The mode is 64 inches. In some cases, the median and mode are the same number.

Median
The middle number in an ordered list of numbers

If there is an even number of heights, there will be two numbers in the middle. To find the median, add the two middle numbers and divide the sum by 2.

Example: 2, 2, 3, 4, 6, 6, 7, 9

The numbers 4 and 6 are both in the middle.
= 10; 10 ÷ 2 = 5. The median is 5. The median does not have to be a number in the list.

Directions: Find the median.

3, 6, 9, 5, 12, 5, 8 _____

11, 6, 4, 7, 5, 9, 11, 10 _____

7, 5, 6, 4, 7, 11, 10, 9 _____

3, 3, 3, 3, 3, 3, 3, 3, 3, 3 _____

55, 34, 67, 39, 47, 18, 46, 55, 61 _____

11, 7, 9, 11, 3, 8, 9, 10 _____

–4, 2, –3, –1, 1, –1, –2 _____

2, 4, 6, 8, 10, 12, 14, 16 _____

0, 1, 4, –2, 3, –1, –2 _____

2, –2, 1, –1, 3, –4 _____

What Do You Mean?

Probably the most common average is the **mean.** To find the mean, add all the numbers in the list, then divide the sum by the total number of addends.

Suppose a hurdler completes his trials in the following times. Find the mean.

Trial	Time in Seconds
1	35
2	29
3	34
4	30
5	31
6	33

Mean

The sum of all the numbers divided by the number of addends

Add the numbers: 35 + 29 + 34 + 30 + 31 + 33 = 192
Divide 192 by 6 because there are 6 numbers in the list: 192 ÷ 6 = 32.
The mean is 32 seconds.

The mean may or may not be a number in the list. The mean may also be different from the median and/or the mode.

Directions: Find the mean.

3, 6, 9, 5, 12 _____   11, 5, 9, 11, 3, 7, 9, 9 _____

3, 1, 0, 2, 0, 0 _____   4, 6, –1, –1 _____

–3, –2, –3, –1, –1 _____   2, –1, 1, –2 _____

3, 3, 3, 3, 3, 3, 3, 3, 3, 3 _____   5, 9, 6, 2, 7, 9, 12, 4, 8, 8 _____

9, 4, 5, 2, 6, 0, 3, 4, 3 _____   6, 7, 3, 6, 4, 2, 7, 5 _____

Field Day

Directions: The winners of the 800-meter relay want to know their winning times. Help them fill in their scores. First, find the mean, mode, and median for each list of numbers. Then, follow the directions below.

9, 10, 2, 5, 8, 8, 6, 8 _____   4, 6, 2, 8, 7, 5, 3 _____

12, 9, 10, 7, 9, 11, 12 _____   33, 37, 27, 35, 33 _____

3, 3, 2, 5, 4, 7, 6, 4, 3, 2, 5, 4 _____   7, −2, 3, −1, 1, −1, 0 _____

6, 4, 6, 4, 6, 4, 6, 4, 6, 4 _____   8, 14, 16, 17, 15, 14, 16, 16, 19 _____

24, 26, 28, 30 _____   −4, 3, 6, −3, −4, −1, 3 _____

7, 5, 10, 8, 6, 7, 7, 7, 6 _____   23, 26, 19, 27, 27, 28, 18 _____

The winning team had a time in seconds equal to the mean of the last problem. The second-place team had a time equal to the median. The third-place team had a time equal to the mode. Write the times on the cards.

Adding and Subtracting Like Fractions

A **fraction** is a number that names part of a whole. Examples of fractions are $\frac{1}{2}$ and $\frac{1}{3}$. **Like fractions** have the same **denominator**, or bottom number. Examples of like fractions are $\frac{1}{4}$ and $\frac{3}{4}$.

To add or subtract fractions, the denominators must be the same. Add or subtract only the **numerators,** the numbers above the line in fractions.

Example:

numerators
denominators $\quad \frac{5}{8} - \frac{1}{8} = \frac{4}{8}$

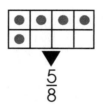 $\quad - \quad$  $\quad = \quad$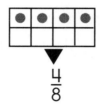

$$\frac{5}{8} \qquad\qquad \frac{1}{8} \qquad\qquad \frac{4}{8}$$

Directions: Add or subtract these fractions.

$\frac{6}{12} - \frac{3}{12} = \frac{3}{12}$	$\frac{4}{9} + \frac{1}{9} = \frac{5}{9}$	$\frac{1}{3} + \frac{1}{3} = \frac{2}{3}$	$\frac{5}{11} + \frac{4}{11} = \frac{9}{11}$
$\frac{3}{5} - \frac{1}{5} = \frac{2}{5}$	$\frac{5}{6} - \frac{2}{6} = \frac{3}{6}$	$\frac{3}{4} - \frac{2}{4} = \frac{1}{4}$	$\frac{5}{10} + \frac{3}{10} = \frac{8}{10}$
$\frac{3}{8} + \frac{2}{8} = \frac{3}{8}$	$\frac{1}{7} + \frac{4}{7} = \frac{5}{7}$	$\frac{2}{20} + \frac{15}{20} = \frac{17}{20}$	$\frac{11}{15} - \frac{9}{15} = \frac{2}{15}$

Directions: Color the part of each pizza that equals the given fraction.

$$\frac{2}{4} \qquad + \qquad \frac{1}{4} \qquad = \qquad \frac{3}{4}$$

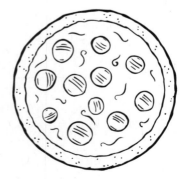  

Adding and Subtracting Unlike Fractions

Unlike fractions have different denominators. Examples of unlike fractions are $\frac{1}{4}$ and $\frac{2}{5}$. To add or subtract fractions, the denominators must be the same.

Example:

Step 1: Make the denominators the same by finding the least common denominator. The LCD of a pair of fractions is the same as the least common multiple (LCM) of their denominators.

$$\frac{1}{3} + \frac{1}{4} =$$

Multiples of 3 are 3, 6, 9, 12, 15.
Multiples of 4 are 4, 8, 12, 16.
LCM (and LCD) = 12

Step 2: Multiply by a number that will give the LCD. The numerator and denominator must be multiplied by the same number.

A. $\frac{1}{3} \times \frac{4}{4} = \frac{4}{12}$ **B.** $\frac{1}{4} \times \frac{3}{3} = \frac{3}{12}$

Step 3: Add the fractions. $\frac{1}{3} + \frac{1}{4} = \frac{4}{12} + \frac{3}{12} = \frac{7}{12}$

Directions: Follow the above steps to add or subtract unlike fractions. Write the LCM.

$\frac{2}{4} + \frac{3}{8} = \frac{7}{8}$ LCM = __18__	$\frac{3}{6} + \frac{1}{3} = \frac{5}{6}$ LCM = __6__	$\frac{4}{5} - \frac{1}{4} = \frac{11}{20}$ LCM = __20__
$\frac{2}{3} + \frac{2}{9} = \frac{8}{9}$ LCM = __9__	$\frac{4}{7} - \frac{2}{14} = \frac{6}{14}$ LCM = __14__	$\frac{7}{12} - \frac{2}{4} = \frac{1}{12}$ LCM = __12__

The basketball team ordered two pizzas.
They left $\frac{1}{3}$ of one $\frac{1}{4}$ and of the other.
How much pizza was left?

Reducing Fractions

A fraction is in lowest terms when the GCF of both the numerator and denominator is 1. These fractions are in lowest possible terms: $\frac{2}{3}$, $\frac{5}{8}$, and $\frac{99}{100}$.

Example: Write $\frac{4}{8}$ in lowest terms.

Step 1: Write the factors of 4 and 8.
Factors of 4 are **4**, 2, 1.
Factors of 8 are 1, 8, 2, **4**.

Step 2: Find the GCF: 4.

Step 3: Divide both the numerator and denominator by 4.

$$\frac{4}{8} \div \frac{4}{4} = \frac{1}{2}$$

Directions: Write each fraction in lowest terms.

$\frac{6}{8} =$ _____ lowest terms $\frac{9}{12} =$ _____ lowest terms

factors of 6: 6, 1, 2, 3 factors of 9: _____ , _____ , _____   _____ GCF

factors of 8: 8, 1, 2, 4 factors of 12: ____ , ____ , ____ , ____ , ____ , ____   _____ GCF

$\frac{2}{6} =$	$\frac{10}{15} =$	$\frac{8}{32} =$	$\frac{4}{10} =$
$\frac{12}{18} =$	$\frac{6}{8} =$	$\frac{4}{6} =$	$\frac{3}{9} =$

Directions: Color the pizzas to show that $\frac{4}{6}$ in lowest terms is $\frac{2}{3}$.

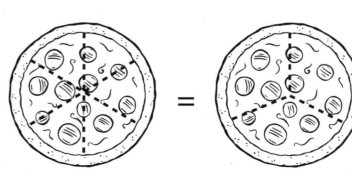

Improper Fractions

An improper fraction has a numerator that is greater than its denominator. An example of an improper fraction is $\frac{7}{6}$. An improper fraction should be reduced to its lowest terms.

Example: $\frac{5}{4}$ is an improper fraction because its numerator is greater than its denominator.

Step 1: Divide the numerator by the denominator: $5 \div 4 = 1, r1$

Step 2: Write the remainder as a fraction: $\frac{1}{4}$

$\frac{5}{4} = 1\frac{1}{4}$ $1\frac{1}{4}$ is a mixed number—a whole number and a fraction.

Directions: Follow the steps above to change the improper fractions to mixed numbers.

$\frac{9}{8} =$	$\frac{11}{5} =$	$\frac{5}{3} =$	$\frac{7}{6} =$	$\frac{8}{7} =$	$\frac{4}{3} =$
$\frac{21}{5} =$	$\frac{9}{4} =$	$\frac{3}{2} =$	$\frac{9}{6} =$	$\frac{25}{4} =$	$\frac{8}{3} =$

Sara had 29 duplicate stamps in her stamp collection. She decided to give them to four of her friends. If she gave each of them the same number of stamps, how many duplicates will she have left? _____

Name the improper fraction in this problem. _____

What step must you do next to solve the problem? _____

_____

Write your answer as a mixed number._____

_____

How many stamps could she give each of her friends?_____

Equivalent Fractions

Directions: Match the pairs of equivalent fractions to find which line is longest—
A, **B**, or **C**.

Line A

$\frac{2}{4}$ •----------------• $\frac{1}{2}$

$\frac{3}{8}$ •   • $\frac{6}{10}$

Line B

$\frac{6}{16}$ •   • $\frac{3}{5}$

$\frac{2}{3}$ •   • $\frac{4}{6}$

$\frac{5}{6}$ •   • $\frac{2}{7}$

• $\frac{6}{14}$

$\frac{10}{12}$ • $\frac{2}{8}$ • $\frac{1}{2}$ •   Line C   • $\frac{1}{3}$ • $\frac{2}{6}$

$\frac{6}{8}$ •   • $\frac{3}{4}$

$\frac{5}{8}$ •   • $\frac{1}{5}$

$\frac{9}{16}$ •   • $\frac{1}{10}$

Directions: Circle the longest line. **A**, **B**, or **C?**

Line A

$\frac{2}{3}$ • $\frac{2}{16}$ •   • $\frac{1}{3}$ • $\frac{1}{2}$

$\frac{2}{6}$ •   • $\frac{3}{4}$

Line B

• $\frac{5}{8}$ • $\frac{3}{8}$

$\frac{10}{17}$ •   • $\frac{6}{16}$

$\frac{9}{12}$ •   Line C   • $\frac{1}{8}$

$\frac{4}{6}$ • $\frac{3}{12}$ •   • $\frac{1}{4}$ • $\frac{5}{10}$

Name _____

Conversion

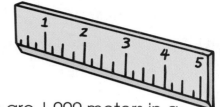

Directions: Find the number of units in each fraction described.

1. If there are 12 eggs in a dozen, how many eggs are in . . .

$\frac{1}{2}$ dozen? _____

$\frac{1}{4}$ dozen? _____

$\frac{1}{3}$ dozen? _____

2. If there are 100 centimeters (cm) in a meter, how many cm are in . . .

$\frac{1}{2}$ meter? _____

$\frac{1}{4}$ meter? _____

$\frac{1}{10}$ meter? _____

3. If there are 16 ounces in a pound, how many ounces are in . . .

$\frac{1}{2}$ pound? _____

$\frac{1}{4}$ pound? _____

$\frac{3}{8}$ pound? _____

4. If there are 4 quarts in a gallon, how many quarts are in . . .

$\frac{1}{2}$ gallon? _____

$\frac{1}{4}$ gallon? _____

$\frac{3}{4}$ gallon? _____

5. If there are 60 seconds in a minute, how many seconds are in . . .

$\frac{1}{2}$ minute? _____

$\frac{1}{4}$ minute? _____

$\frac{3}{4}$ minute? _____

6. If there are 1,000 meters in a kilometer, how many meters are in . . .

$\frac{1}{10}$ kilometer? _____

$\frac{1}{2}$ kilometer? _____

$\frac{1}{4}$ kilometer? _____

7. If there are 30 days in most months, how many days are in . . .

$\frac{1}{3}$ month? _____

$\frac{1}{6}$ month? _____

$\frac{1}{10}$ month? _____

8. If there are 24 hours in a day, how many hours are in . . .

$\frac{1}{3}$ day? _____

$\frac{2}{3}$ day? _____

$\frac{1}{4}$ day? _____

9. If there are 36 inches in a yard, how many inches are in . . .

$\frac{2}{3}$ yard? _____

$\frac{1}{4}$ yard? _____

$\frac{1}{2}$ yard? _____

10. If there are 2,000 pounds in a ton, how many pounds are in . . .

$\frac{1}{2}$ ton? _____

$\frac{1}{4}$ ton? _____

$\frac{1}{20}$ ton? _____

Tic-Tac-Toe Fractions

Directions: Solve each problem. Then, look in the boxes below for the answers to the problems. Draw an **X** over each correct answer. Circle the other numbers.

1. $\dfrac{7}{8} - \dfrac{5}{8}$

2. $\dfrac{8}{10} - \dfrac{3}{10}$

3. $2\dfrac{1}{2} - \dfrac{1}{2}$

4. $\dfrac{7}{9} - \dfrac{4}{9}$

5. $\dfrac{5}{3} - \dfrac{4}{3}$

6. $\dfrac{6}{7} - \dfrac{3}{7}$

7. $\dfrac{4}{5} - \dfrac{2}{5}$

8. $\dfrac{9}{11} - \dfrac{5}{11}$

9. $\dfrac{11}{12} - \dfrac{5}{12}$

10. $\dfrac{11}{6} - \dfrac{7}{6}$

11. $\dfrac{3}{4} - \dfrac{1}{4}$

12. $\dfrac{3}{3} - \dfrac{1}{3}$

$\dfrac{5}{8}$	$\dfrac{1}{7}$	$\dfrac{1}{3}$
$\dfrac{2}{4}$	$\dfrac{5}{10}$	$\dfrac{3}{4}$
2	$\dfrac{3}{5}$	$\dfrac{2}{9}$

$\dfrac{4}{5}$	$\dfrac{3}{7}$	$\dfrac{1}{9}$
$\dfrac{5}{6}$	$\dfrac{1}{2}$	$\dfrac{3}{11}$
$\dfrac{2}{5}$	$\dfrac{2}{3}$	$\dfrac{4}{6}$

$\dfrac{1}{5}$	$\dfrac{6}{12}$	$\dfrac{2}{8}$
$\dfrac{3}{8}$	$\dfrac{4}{11}$	$\dfrac{6}{7}$
$\dfrac{2}{7}$	$\dfrac{1}{10}$	$\dfrac{3}{9}$

Mixed Numbers

A **mixed number** is a whole number and a fraction together. An example of a mixed number is $2\frac{3}{4}$. A mixed number can be changed to an improper fraction.

Example: $2\frac{3}{4}$

Step 1: Multiply the denominator by the whole number: $4 \times 2 = 8$

Step 2: Add the numerator: $8 + 3 = 11$

Step 3: Write the sum over the denominator: $\frac{11}{4}$

Directions: Follow the steps above to change the mixed numbers to improper fractions.

$3\frac{2}{3} =$	$6\frac{1}{5} =$	$4\frac{7}{8} =$	$2\frac{1}{2} =$
$1\frac{4}{5} =$	$5\frac{3}{4} =$	$7\frac{1}{8} =$	$9\frac{1}{9} =$
$8\frac{1}{2} =$	$7\frac{1}{6} =$	$5\frac{3}{5} =$	$9\frac{3}{8} =$
$12\frac{1}{5} =$	$25\frac{1}{2} =$	$10\frac{2}{3} =$	$14\frac{3}{8} =$

Adding Mixed Numbers

Directions: To add mixed numbers, first find the least common denominator. Always reduce the answer to lowest terms.

Example:

$$5\frac{1}{4} \longrightarrow 5\frac{3}{12}$$
$$+ 6\frac{1}{3} \longrightarrow + 6\frac{4}{12}$$
$$11\frac{7}{12}$$

Directions: Add. Reduce the answers to lowest terms.

$$8\frac{1}{2}$$
$$+7\frac{1}{4}$$

$$5\frac{1}{4}$$
$$+2\frac{3}{8}$$

$$9\frac{3}{10}$$
$$+7\frac{1}{5}$$

$$8\frac{1}{5}$$
$$+6\frac{7}{10}$$

$$4\frac{4}{5}$$
$$+3\frac{3}{10}$$

$$3\frac{1}{2}$$
$$+7\frac{1}{4}$$

$$4\frac{1}{2}$$
$$+1\frac{1}{3}$$

$$6\frac{1}{12}$$
$$+3\frac{3}{4}$$

$$5\frac{1}{3}$$
$$+2\frac{3}{9}$$

$$6\frac{1}{3}$$
$$+2\frac{2}{5}$$

$$2\frac{2}{7}$$
$$+4\frac{1}{14}$$

$$3\frac{1}{2}$$
$$+3\frac{1}{4}$$

The boys picked $3\frac{1}{2}$ baskets of apples. The girls picked $5\frac{1}{2}$ baskets. How many baskets of apples did the boys and girls pick in all? _____

Subtracting Mixed Numbers

Directions: To subtract mixed numbers, first find the least common denominator. Reduce the answer to its lowest terms.

Directions: Subtract. Reduce to lowest terms.

Example:

$$6 \tfrac{5}{8} \rightarrow 6 \tfrac{10}{16}$$
$$- 3 \tfrac{4}{16} \rightarrow - 3 \tfrac{4}{16}$$
$$\overline{ 3 \tfrac{6}{16}} = 3 \tfrac{3}{8}$$

$$2 \tfrac{3}{7}$$
$$- 1 \tfrac{1}{14}$$

$$7 \tfrac{2}{3}$$
$$- 5 \tfrac{1}{8}$$

$$6 \tfrac{3}{4}$$
$$- 2 \tfrac{3}{12}$$

$$9 \tfrac{5}{12}$$
$$- 5 \tfrac{9}{24}$$

$$5 \tfrac{1}{2}$$
$$- 3 \tfrac{1}{3}$$

$$7 \tfrac{3}{8}$$
$$- 5 \tfrac{1}{6}$$

$$8 \tfrac{3}{8}$$
$$- 6 \tfrac{5}{12}$$

$$11 \tfrac{5}{6}$$
$$- 7 \tfrac{1}{12}$$

$$9 \tfrac{3}{5}$$
$$- 7 \tfrac{1}{15}$$

$$4 \tfrac{4}{5}$$
$$- 2 \tfrac{1}{4}$$

$$9 \tfrac{2}{3}$$
$$- 4 \tfrac{1}{6}$$

$$13 \tfrac{3}{8}$$
$$- 9 \tfrac{3}{16}$$

The Rodriguez Farm has $9 \tfrac{1}{2}$ acres of corn. The Johnson Farm has $7 \tfrac{1}{3}$ acres of corn. How many more acres of corn does the Rodriguez Farm have? _____

Name _____

A Trip to the Ocean

Maria's girls' club earned enough money from their cookie sale to go on a camping trip by the ocean. Read about their trip.

Directions: Write your answers in complete sentences.

1. The bus started with $6\frac{1}{2}$ gallons of gasoline. When the driver added $9\frac{1}{2}$ more gallons of gasoline, how much gasoline did the bus have in it?

   _____

2. The girls and their leaders stopped for a picnic after driving $58\frac{1}{5}$ miles. After the picnic, they drove another $43\frac{4}{5}$ miles before reaching the ocean. How far were they from home?

   _____

3. Before leaving home, the girls made sandwiches for their lunch. They had $7\frac{1}{2}$ tuna sandwiches, $4\frac{1}{4}$ cheese sandwiches, $2\frac{3}{4}$ peanut butter sandwiches and $5\frac{1}{2}$ beef sandwiches. How many total sandwiches did they bring?

   _____

4. The leader cut a watermelon into 16 slices for lunch. The girls ate 8 of the slices. What fraction of the watermelon did they eat?

   _____

5. When they arrived, they took $1\frac{1}{3}$ hours to set up the tents. They spent another $\frac{2}{3}$ hour getting their bedrolls ready. How long did they work before they could play in the ocean?

   _____

6. The girls swam and played in the water for $1\frac{3}{4}$ hours. Then, they sat in the sun for $\frac{3}{4}$ hour. How many hours did they play and sunbathe?

   _____

7. After dinner, they had a campfire. First, they sang for $1\frac{1}{3}$ hours. Then, they told ghost stories for $\frac{2}{3}$ hour. If they put out the fire and went to sleep at 10:30 P.M., what time did they begin the campfire?

   _____

Name _____

Comparing Fractions

Directions: Use the symbol **>** (greater than), **<** (less than), or **=** (equal to) to show the relationship between each pair of fractions.

$\frac{1}{2}$ _____ $\frac{1}{3}$ $\frac{2}{5}$ _____ $\frac{3}{7}$ $\frac{3}{8}$ _____ $\frac{2}{4}$

$\frac{3}{4}$ _____ $\frac{6}{8}$ $\frac{2}{3}$ _____ $\frac{4}{5}$ $\frac{3}{9}$ _____ $\frac{1}{3}$

$\frac{3}{12}$ _____ $\frac{1}{4}$ $\frac{2}{14}$ _____ $\frac{1}{7}$ $\frac{5}{15}$ _____ $\frac{2}{3}$

If Kelly gave $\frac{1}{3}$ of a pizza to Holly and $\frac{1}{5}$ to Diane, how much did she have left?

_____

Holly decided to share $\frac{1}{2}$ of her share of the pizza with Deb. How much did each of them actually get?

_____

Ordering Fractions

Directions: When putting fractions in order from smallest to largest or largest to smallest, it helps to find a common denominator first.

Example:

$\frac{1}{3}$, $\frac{1}{2}$ changed to $\frac{2}{6}$, $\frac{3}{6}$

Directions: Put the following fractions in order from least to largest value.

				Least			Largest
$\frac{1}{5}$	$\frac{6}{15}$	$\frac{4}{5}$	$\frac{1}{3}$	_____	_____	_____	_____
$\frac{3}{12}$	$\frac{3}{6}$	$\frac{1}{3}$	$\frac{3}{4}$	_____	_____	_____	_____
$\frac{2}{5}$	$\frac{4}{15}$	$\frac{3}{5}$	$\frac{5}{15}$	_____	_____	_____	_____
$3\frac{4}{5}$	$3\frac{2}{5}$	$\frac{9}{5}$	$3\frac{1}{5}$	_____	_____	_____	_____
$9\frac{1}{3}$	$9\frac{2}{3}$	$9\frac{9}{12}$	$8\frac{2}{3}$	_____	_____	_____	_____
$5\frac{8}{12}$	$5\frac{5}{12}$	$5\frac{4}{24}$	$5\frac{3}{6}$	_____	_____	_____	_____
$4\frac{3}{5}$	$5\frac{7}{15}$	$6\frac{2}{5}$	$5\frac{1}{5}$	_____	_____	_____	_____

Four dogs were selected as finalists at a dog show. They were judged in four separate categories. One received a perfect score in each area. The dog with a score closest to four is the winner. Their scores are listed below. Which dog won the contest? ___

Dog A $3\frac{4}{5}$ Dog B $3\frac{2}{3}$ Dog C $3\frac{5}{15}$ Dog D $3\frac{9}{12}$

Adding Unlike Fractions

Directions: Solve the problems. Shade in your answers on the pizzas below to show which pieces have been eaten.

$$\frac{1}{10} \\ + \frac{4}{5}$$ $$\frac{3}{12} \\ + \frac{1}{6}$$ $$\frac{1}{2} \\ + \frac{1}{3}$$ $$\frac{3}{4} \\ + \frac{1}{5}$$ $$\frac{1}{5} \\ + \frac{1}{3}$$

$$\frac{2}{3} \\ + \frac{1}{4}$$ $$\frac{5}{12} \\ + \frac{1}{6}$$ $$\frac{2}{5} \\ + \frac{9}{20}$$ $$\frac{1}{3} \\ + \frac{2}{9}$$ $$\frac{3}{5} \\ + \frac{1}{10}$$

$$\frac{1}{10} \\ + \frac{1}{5}$$ $$\frac{2}{3} \\ + \frac{1}{5}$$ $$\frac{1}{8} \\ + \frac{1}{3}$$ $$\frac{3}{8} \\ + \frac{1}{5}$$ $$\frac{1}{5} \\ + \frac{1}{9}$$

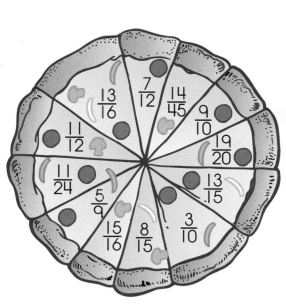

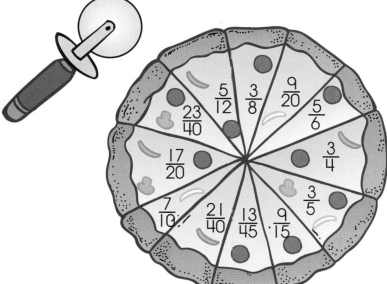

Fractions

Name _____

Sandwich Solutions

Directions: Solve the following subtraction problems to find out who invented the sandwich. Write the letter next to each problem above its answer at the bottom. Reduce the answer to its lowest terms.

A. $\dfrac{3}{5} - \dfrac{1}{4}$

A. $\dfrac{5}{6} - \dfrac{1}{3}$

E. $\dfrac{9}{16} - \dfrac{1}{4}$

I. $\dfrac{7}{10} - \dfrac{3}{5}$

D. $\dfrac{1}{2} - \dfrac{5}{12}$

C. $\dfrac{7}{8} - \dfrac{3}{4}$

W. $\dfrac{13}{18} - \dfrac{1}{6}$

N. $\dfrac{2}{3} - \dfrac{1}{12}$

H. $\dfrac{19}{20} - \dfrac{4}{5}$

F. $\dfrac{18}{25} - \dfrac{2}{5}$

L. $\dfrac{8}{9} - \dfrac{1}{6}$

R. $\dfrac{5}{8} - \dfrac{3}{16}$

O. $\dfrac{4}{5} - \dfrac{2}{3}$

S. $\dfrac{1}{7} - \dfrac{1}{14}$

$\dfrac{5}{16}$ $\dfrac{7}{20}$ $\dfrac{7}{16}$ $\dfrac{13}{18}$ $\dfrac{2}{15}$ $\dfrac{8}{25}$ $\dfrac{1}{14}$ $\dfrac{1}{2}$ $\dfrac{7}{12}$ $\dfrac{1}{12}$ $\dfrac{5}{9}$ $\dfrac{1}{10}$ $\dfrac{1}{8}$ $\dfrac{3}{20}$

Name _____

Fractions: Mixed to Improper

Directions: Change the fractions to mixed numbers. Shade in each answer to find the path to the pot of gold.

1. $\dfrac{11}{9}$ = 2. $\dfrac{8}{3}$ = 3. $\dfrac{8}{7}$ = 4. $\dfrac{11}{6}$ =

5. $\dfrac{7}{3}$ = 6. $\dfrac{7}{6}$ = 7. $\dfrac{9}{4}$ = 8. $\dfrac{8}{5}$ =

9. $\dfrac{4}{3}$ = 10. $\dfrac{7}{2}$ = 11. $\dfrac{3}{2}$ = 12. $\dfrac{6}{5}$ =

13. $\dfrac{7}{4}$ = 14. $\dfrac{9}{2}$ = 15. $\dfrac{11}{8}$ = 16. $\dfrac{5}{2}$ =

17. $\dfrac{9}{7}$ = 18. $\dfrac{11}{4}$ = 19. $\dfrac{17}{12}$ = 20. $\dfrac{13}{12}$ =

$1\dfrac{3}{5}$ $1\dfrac{1}{7}$ $1\dfrac{3}{4}$ $3\dfrac{1}{2}$ $1\dfrac{3}{8}$ $2\dfrac{3}{4}$ $1\dfrac{4}{7}$

$1\dfrac{5}{8}$ $2\dfrac{1}{3}$ $7\dfrac{3}{8}$ $2\dfrac{11}{12}$ $3\dfrac{7}{8}$ $2\dfrac{5}{6}$ $1\dfrac{4}{5}$ $2\dfrac{2}{3}$ $2\dfrac{1}{6}$

$1\dfrac{7}{12}$ $2\dfrac{1}{2}$ $1\dfrac{5}{6}$ $1\dfrac{2}{7}$ $2\dfrac{1}{4}$ $1\dfrac{1}{12}$ $1\dfrac{1}{2}$ $1\dfrac{11}{12}$ $1\dfrac{5}{7}$

$1\dfrac{1}{5}$ $4\dfrac{2}{3}$ $3\dfrac{1}{6}$ $1\dfrac{3}{7}$ $1\dfrac{4}{9}$ $2\dfrac{1}{5}$ $3\dfrac{1}{3}$ $4\dfrac{1}{3}$ $2\dfrac{6}{7}$

$2\dfrac{3}{11}$ $1\dfrac{2}{9}$ $1\dfrac{1}{3}$ $1\dfrac{5}{12}$ $2\dfrac{1}{3}$ $4\dfrac{1}{2}$ $1\dfrac{1}{6}$

x - denominator by whole #. then
+ numerator

Fractions: Mixed to Improper

Directions: Solve the problems. Connect the dots in the order of the answers.

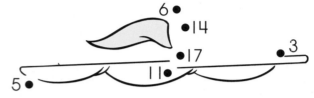

1. $1\frac{+2}{5} = \frac{7}{5}$ 2. $1\frac{1}{3} = \frac{4}{3}$

3. $1\frac{5}{7} = \frac{}{7}$ 4. $2\frac{2}{3} = \frac{}{3}$

5. $2\frac{5}{8} = \frac{}{8}$ 6. $2\frac{1}{2} = \frac{}{2}$

7. $1\frac{5}{6} = \frac{}{6}$ 8. $1\frac{1}{5} = \frac{}{5}$

9. $2\frac{4}{5} = \frac{}{5}$ 10. $1\frac{1}{16} = \frac{}{16}$

11. $1\frac{1}{2} = \frac{}{2}$ 12. $3\frac{1}{5} = \frac{}{5}$

13. $1\frac{11}{12} = \frac{}{12}$ 14. $1\frac{7}{8} = \frac{}{8}$

15. $1\frac{6}{7} = \frac{}{7}$ 16. $2\frac{1}{4} = \frac{}{4}$

17. $1\frac{7}{12} = \frac{}{12}$ 18. $1\frac{3}{7} = \frac{}{7}$

19. $6\frac{2}{3} = \frac{}{3}$ 20. $3\frac{3}{5} = \frac{}{5}$

21. $1\frac{5}{21} = \frac{}{21}$ 22. $1\frac{7}{36} = \frac{}{36}$

23. $1\frac{9}{20} = \frac{}{20}$ 24. $1\frac{13}{24} = \frac{}{24}$

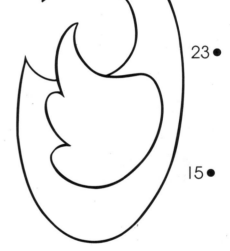

Name _____

Fractions: Addition and Subtraction

Directions: Identify the shaded part.

1. _____

2. 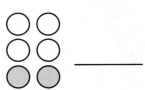 _____

3.  _____

Directions: Reduce to lowest terms.

4. $\dfrac{10}{15}$ = _____

5. $\dfrac{9}{12}$ = ___

6. $\dfrac{18}{54}$ = ___

Directions: Compare using **>** or **<**.

7. $\dfrac{13}{27}$ $\quad$ $\dfrac{12}{27}$

8. $\dfrac{5}{6}$ $\quad$ $\dfrac{3}{4}$

9. $2\dfrac{3}{4}$ $\quad$ $\dfrac{13}{4}$

Directions: Add or subtract.

10. $\dfrac{1}{5}$ + $\dfrac{2}{5}$ = _____

11. $\dfrac{3}{8}$ − $\dfrac{2}{8}$ = _____

12. $\dfrac{3}{4}$ + $\dfrac{1}{2}$ = _____

13. $\dfrac{7}{8}$ − $\dfrac{3}{4}$ = _____

14. $5\dfrac{1}{2}$ + $2\dfrac{1}{2}$ = _____

15. $2\dfrac{1}{8}$ − $1\dfrac{5}{8}$ = _____

16. $\dfrac{21}{5}$ − $\dfrac{21}{10}$ _____

17. $5\dfrac{1}{6}$ + $3\dfrac{2}{4}$ = _____

18. $\dfrac{5}{3}$ + $\dfrac{2}{5}$ = _____

Directions: Draw a model to show each fraction.

19. $3\dfrac{1}{4}$

20. $\dfrac{10}{3}$

Multiplying Fractions

To multiply fractions, follow these steps:

$\dfrac{1}{2}$ x $\dfrac{3}{4}$ =   **Step 1:** Multiply the numerators. $1 \times 3 = \underline{3}$
     Step 2: Multiply the denominators. $2 \times 4 = 8$

When multiplying a fraction by a whole number, first change the whole number to a fraction.

Example:

$\dfrac{1}{2}$ x 8 = $\dfrac{1}{2}$ x $\dfrac{8}{1}$ = $\dfrac{8}{2}$ = 4 reduced to lowest terms

Directions: Multiply. Reduce your answers to lowest terms.

$\dfrac{3}{4}$ x $\dfrac{1}{6}$ =	$\dfrac{1}{2}$ x $\dfrac{5}{8}$ =	$\dfrac{2}{3}$ x $\dfrac{1}{6}$ =	$\dfrac{2}{3}$ x $\dfrac{1}{2}$ =
$\dfrac{5}{6}$ x 4 =	$\dfrac{3}{8}$ x $\dfrac{1}{16}$ =	$\dfrac{1}{5}$ x 5 =	$\dfrac{7}{8}$ x $\dfrac{3}{4}$ =
$\dfrac{7}{11}$ x $\dfrac{1}{3}$ =	$\dfrac{2}{9}$ x $\dfrac{9}{4}$ =	$\dfrac{1}{3}$ x $\dfrac{1}{3}$ x $\dfrac{1}{3}$ =	$\dfrac{1}{8}$ x $\dfrac{1}{4}$ x $\dfrac{1}{2}$ =

Jennifer has 10 pets. Two-fifths of the pets are cats, one-half are fish and one-tenth are dogs. How many of each pet does she have?

_____

_____

_____

Multiplying Mixed Numbers

Multiply mixed numbers by first changing them to improper fractions. Always reduce your answers to lowest terms.

Example:

$$2\frac{1}{3} \times 1\frac{1}{8} = \frac{7}{3} \times \frac{9}{8} = \frac{63}{24} = 2\frac{15}{24} = 2\frac{5}{8}$$

Directions: Multiply. Reduce to lowest terms.

$4\frac{1}{4} \times 2\frac{1}{5} =$	$1\frac{1}{3} \times 3\frac{1}{4} =$	$1\frac{1}{9} \times 3\frac{3}{5} =$
$1\frac{6}{7} \times 4\frac{1}{2} =$	$2\frac{3}{4} \times 2\frac{3}{5} =$	$4\frac{2}{3} \times 3\frac{1}{7} =$
$6\frac{2}{5} \times 2\frac{1}{8} =$	$3\frac{1}{7} \times 4\frac{5}{8} =$	$7\frac{3}{8} \times 2\frac{1}{9} =$

Sunnyside Farm has two barns with 25 stalls in each barn. Cows use $\frac{3}{5}$ of the stalls, and horses use the rest.

How many stalls are for cows? _____

How many are for horses? _____

(Hint: First, find how many total stalls are in the two barns.)

Name _____

Puzzling Fractions

Directions: Multiply to solve the problems.

$7 \times \dfrac{1}{5} =$ _____ $9 \times \dfrac{1}{10} =$ _____ $8 \times \dfrac{1}{8} =$ _____ $8 \times \dfrac{1}{7} =$ _____

$7 \times \dfrac{1}{11} =$ _____ $9 \times \dfrac{1}{3} =$ _____ $3 \times \dfrac{1}{6} =$ _____ $12 \times \dfrac{1}{5} =$

$\dfrac{1}{5} \times 4 =$ _____ $\dfrac{1}{6} \times 9 =$ _____ $\dfrac{1}{5} \times 20 =$ _____ $\dfrac{1}{6} \times 12 =$ _____

$\dfrac{1}{10} \times \dfrac{1}{100} =$ _____ $\dfrac{1}{6} \times \dfrac{1}{10} =$ _____ $\dfrac{1}{12} \times \dfrac{1}{3} =$ _____ $\dfrac{1}{6} \times \dfrac{1}{6} =$ _____

$\dfrac{1}{9} \times \dfrac{1}{8} =$ _____ $\dfrac{1}{9} \times \dfrac{1}{10} =$ _____ $\dfrac{1}{10} \times \dfrac{1}{10} =$ _____ $\dfrac{1}{20} \times \dfrac{1}{5} =$ _____

$8 \times \dfrac{1}{10} =$ _____ $\dfrac{1}{5} \times \dfrac{1}{8} =$ _____ $\dfrac{1}{6} \times \dfrac{1}{7} =$ _____ $\dfrac{1}{100} \times \dfrac{1}{100} =$ _____

$\dfrac{1}{9} \times 9 =$ _____ $\dfrac{1}{8} \times 7 =$ _____ $\dfrac{1}{7} \times 6 =$ _____ $12 \times \dfrac{1}{4} =$ _____

$\dfrac{1}{15} \times \dfrac{1}{13} =$ _____ $\dfrac{1}{3} \times \dfrac{1}{7} =$ _____ $\dfrac{1}{8} \times 3 =$ _____ $\dfrac{1}{7} \times 21 =$ _____

Fractions

Total Math Grade 5

Multiplication With Mixed Numbers

When multiplying by a mixed number, change the mixed number to an improper fraction. Cancel if possible. Multiply the numerators, then the denominators. Write the improper fractions as mixed numbers.

Example A: $\dfrac{3}{4} \times 1\dfrac{1}{2} = \dfrac{3}{4} \times \dfrac{3}{2} = \dfrac{9}{8} = 1\dfrac{1}{8}$

multiply

multiply

Example B: $2\dfrac{4}{7} \times \dfrac{5}{9} = \dfrac{2\ \cancel{18}}{7} \times \dfrac{5}{\cancel{9}_1} = \dfrac{10}{7} = 1\dfrac{3}{7}$

multiply

multiply

Directions: Multiply.

1. $\dfrac{1}{2} \times 8\dfrac{3}{4} = \dfrac{1}{2} \times \dfrac{35}{4} =$

2. $5\dfrac{1}{3} \times \dfrac{6}{7} =$

3. $\dfrac{11}{12} \times 11\dfrac{1}{3} =$

4. $7\dfrac{1}{2} \times \dfrac{8}{9} =$

5. $\dfrac{2}{5} \times 2\dfrac{1}{12} =$

6. $8\dfrac{2}{3} \times \dfrac{1}{4} =$

Dividing Fractions

To divide fractions, follow these steps:

$$\frac{3}{4} \div \frac{1}{4} =$$

Step 1: "Invert" the divisor. That means to turn it upside down.

$$\frac{3}{4} \div \frac{4}{1}$$

Step 2: Multiply the two fractions:

$$\frac{3}{4} \times \frac{4}{1} = \frac{12}{4}$$

Step 3: Reduce the fraction to lowest terms by dividing the denominator into the numerator.

$$12 \div 4 = 3$$
$$\frac{3}{4} \div \frac{1}{4} = 3$$

Directions: Follow the above steps to divide fractions.

$\frac{1}{4} \div \frac{1}{5} =$	$\frac{1}{3} \div \frac{1}{12} =$	$\frac{3}{4} \div \frac{1}{3} =$
$\frac{5}{12} \div \frac{1}{3} =$	$\frac{3}{4} \div \frac{1}{6} =$	$\frac{2}{9} \div \frac{2}{3} =$
$\frac{3}{7} \div \frac{1}{4} =$	$\frac{2}{3} \div \frac{4}{6} =$	$\frac{1}{8} \div \frac{2}{3} =$
$\frac{4}{5} \div \frac{1}{3} =$	$\frac{4}{8} \div \frac{1}{2} =$	$\frac{5}{12} \div \frac{6}{8} =$

Dividing Fractions

When dividing fractions, change the problem to multiplication. Invert the divisor. Cancel if possible. Multiply the numerators, then the denominators. Write improper fractions as mixed numbers.

Example A: $\dfrac{3}{10} \div \dfrac{4}{5} = \dfrac{3}{10} \times \dfrac{5}{4} = {}_2\dfrac{3}{10} \times \dfrac{5^1}{4} = \dfrac{3}{8}$

multiply

multiply

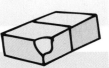

Example B: $\dfrac{5}{12} \div \dfrac{3}{8} = \dfrac{5}{12} \times \dfrac{8}{3} = {}_3\dfrac{5}{12} \times \dfrac{8^2}{3} = \dfrac{10}{9} = 1\dfrac{1}{9}$

multiply

multiply

Directions: Divide.

1. $\dfrac{1}{2} \div \dfrac{3}{10} = \dfrac{1}{2} \times \dfrac{10}{3} =$

2. $\dfrac{3}{8} \div \dfrac{1}{4} =$

3. $\dfrac{4}{9} \div \dfrac{2}{3} =$

4. $\dfrac{3}{8} \div \dfrac{5}{12} =$

5. $\dfrac{1}{10} \div \dfrac{2}{5} =$

6. $\dfrac{5}{6} \div \dfrac{11}{12} =$

7. $\dfrac{14}{15} \div \dfrac{2}{3} =$

8. $\dfrac{4}{5} \div \dfrac{3}{10} =$

Name _____

Stump the Teacher

Directions: The students in Ms. Davidson's class were playing "Stump the Teacher." See if you can solve their problems.

1. If baseball cards are worth $\frac{1}{10}$ of a dollar each, how much are Brad's 54 cards worth? _____

2. If $\frac{6}{8}$ of Sally's 8 puppies are female and $\frac{1}{2}$ of the female puppies have been sold, how many female puppies have been sold?_____

3. Felipe used $\frac{2}{3}$ cup of cheese for each pizza. If he made 4 pizzas, how much cheese did he need to buy? _____

4. Francis bought $\frac{15}{16}$ of a yard of fabric. She used $\frac{1}{2}$ of it to make a dress for her doll. What fraction of a yard did she use? _____

5. If a lot is $\frac{5}{8}$ of an acre, and the house covers $\frac{1}{2}$ of it, what fraction of an acre is covered by the house?_____

6. At the track meet, Rick entered 5 sprint contests. If each race was $\frac{1}{4}$ mile long, how many miles did Rick sprint in all?_____

7. The class had $\frac{1}{4}$ of an hour to take a math quiz. Nate used only $\frac{1}{3}$ of the time. What fraction of an hour did Nate use for the quiz?

_____

8. Lisa and Kim live $\frac{3}{8}$ of a mile apart. If they each walked $\frac{1}{2}$ of the way and met in the middle, what part of a mile did each walk?

_____

9. This year's summer vacation was $\frac{1}{6}$ of the year. How many months long was the summer vacation this year?_____

10. Paul's dog was asleep $\frac{2}{3}$ of the day. How many hours was it awake?

_____

Fractions: Multiplication and Division

Directions: Solve.

1. $\dfrac{7}{9} \times \dfrac{1}{4} =$ _____

2. $\dfrac{5}{6} \times \dfrac{1}{10} =$ _____

3. $\dfrac{9}{10} \times \dfrac{2}{3} =$ _____

4. $8 \times \dfrac{1}{4} =$ _____

5. $\dfrac{1}{3} \times 15 =$ _____

6. Jaime sat in his chair for $\dfrac{5}{6}$ of an hour. For $\dfrac{1}{3}$ of this time, he worked on this assignment. What fraction of an hour did he work on this assignment?

7. $\dfrac{1}{2} \div \dfrac{1}{5} =$ _____

8. $\dfrac{1}{5} \div \dfrac{1}{2} =$ _____

9. $\dfrac{3}{4} \div \dfrac{3}{8} =$ _____

10. $\dfrac{7}{16} \div \dfrac{4}{7} =$ _____

Dividing Whole Numbers by Fractions

Follow these steps to divide a whole number by a fraction:

$$8 \div \frac{1}{4} =$$

Step 1: Write the whole number as a fraction:

$$\frac{8}{1} \div \frac{1}{4} =$$

Step 2: Invert the divisor.

$$\frac{8}{1} \div \frac{4}{1} =$$

Step 3: Multiply the two fractions:

$$\frac{8}{1} \times \frac{4}{1} = \frac{32}{1}$$

Step 4: Reduce the fraction to lowest terms by dividing the denominator into the numerator: $32 \div 1 = 32$

Directions: Follow the above steps to divide a whole number by a fraction.

$6 \div \frac{1}{3} =$	$4 \div \frac{1}{2} =$	$21 \div \frac{1}{3} =$
$8 \div \frac{1}{2} =$	$3 \div \frac{1}{6} =$	$15 \div \frac{1}{7} =$
$9 \div \frac{1}{5} =$	$4 \div \frac{1}{9} =$	$12 \div \frac{1}{6} =$

Three-fourths of a bag of popcorn fits into one bowl.
How many bowls do you need if you have six bags of popcorn? _____

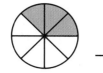

Name _____

Fraction Review

Directions: Identify the shaded fraction and simplify to lowest terms.

1. 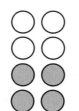 _____

2. ○○ _____
   ○○
   ●○
   ●○

3. △△△△△ _____
   △△△△△
   △△△△△
   △△△△△

Directions: Compare using **>** or **<**.

4. $\dfrac{3}{5}$ $\dfrac{4}{5}$

5. $\dfrac{5}{8}$ $\dfrac{5}{11}$

6. 1 $\dfrac{7}{8}$

Directions: Add or subtract. Reduce to lowest terms.

7. $\dfrac{1}{9} + \dfrac{5}{9} =$ ____

8. $\dfrac{2}{5} + \dfrac{1}{10} =$ ____

9. $\dfrac{3}{8} + \dfrac{1}{6} =$ ____

10. $3\dfrac{1}{4} + 2\dfrac{1}{3} =$ ____

11. $\dfrac{7}{9} - \dfrac{2}{3} =$ ____

12. $11\dfrac{7}{8} - 4\dfrac{5}{12} =$ ____

13. Change $\dfrac{17}{4}$ into a mixed number. ___

14. Change $3\dfrac{2}{5}$ into an improper fraction. ____

Directions: Multiply or divide.

15. $\dfrac{3}{4} \times \dfrac{1}{2} =$ ____

16. $\dfrac{11}{12} \times \dfrac{4}{5} =$ ____

17. $\dfrac{2}{3} \div \dfrac{1}{3} =$ ____

18. $\dfrac{1}{2} \div \dfrac{1}{4} =$ ____

Decimals

A **decimal** is a number with one or more places to the right of a decimal point.

Examples: 6.5 and 2.25

Fractions with denominators of 10 or 100 can be written as decimals.

Examples:

$\frac{7}{10}$ = 0.7

$\underline{\quad 0 \quad}$	.	$\underline{\quad 7 \quad}$	$\underline{\quad 0 \quad}$
ones		tenths	hundredths

$1\frac{52}{100}$ = 1.52

$\underline{\quad 1 \quad}$	.	$\underline{\quad 5 \quad}$	$\underline{\quad 2 \quad}$
ones		tenths	hundredths

1/2   0.50

Directions: Write the fractions as decimals.

$\frac{1}{2} = \overline{10} = 0.\underline{\quad}$

$\frac{2}{5} = \overline{10} = 0.\underline{\quad}$

$\frac{1}{5} = \overline{10} = 0.\underline{\quad}$

$\frac{3}{5} = \overline{10} = 0.\underline{\quad}$

$\frac{1}{2}$	$\frac{1}{4}$	$\frac{1}{5}$	1/10
			1/10
	$\frac{1}{4}$	$\frac{1}{5}$	1/10
			1/10
$\frac{1}{2}$	$\frac{1}{4}$	$\frac{1}{5}$	1/10
			1/10
		$\frac{1}{5}$	1/10
	$\frac{1}{4}$		1/10
		$\frac{1}{5}$	1/10
			1/10

$\frac{63}{100}$ =	$2\frac{8}{10}$ =	$38\frac{4}{100}$ =	$6\frac{13}{100}$ =
$\frac{1}{4}$ =	$\frac{2}{5}$ =	$\frac{1}{50}$ =	$\frac{100}{200}$ =
$5\frac{2}{100}$ =	$\frac{4}{25}$ =	$15\frac{3}{5}$ =	$\frac{3}{100}$ =

Name _____

Decimal Drawings

Decimals represent numbers that include a part of a whole. With decimals, the part that is less than 1 is always separated into 10, or a power of 10, parts.

one	one tenth	one hundredth
1	0.1	0.01

Examples:

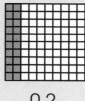

| 0.2 | 0.75 | 1.00 |

Directions: Write the decimal number that shows the part that is shaded.

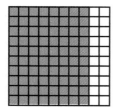   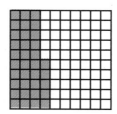   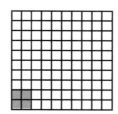   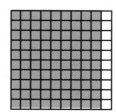

_____   _____   _____   _____

Directions: Shade the diagrams to show the decimal number.

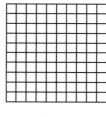   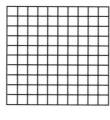   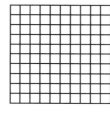   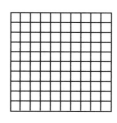

0.50   0.02   0.93   0.15

That's the Point

When writing a decimal, place the decimal point between the ones column and the tenths column. Here are some place values to the right and left of the decimal point:

| hundreds | tens | ones | tenths | hundredths | thousandths |

Steps:

1. Read the whole number.
2. Say the word "and" or "point."
3. Read the number after the decimal point.
4. Say the decimal place of the last digit to the right.

Examples:

45.91 is read "forty-five and ninety-one hundredths"
222.1 is read "two hundred twenty-two point one"
10.004 is read "ten and four thousandths"

Directions: Fill in the numbers or write the names to complete the place-value chart.

Hundreds Tens Ones Tenths Hundredths Thousandths

1	1	.	8			eleven and eight tenths
	3	.			1	three and one hundred forty-one thousandths
		.				two and fifteen hundredths
4	0	5	.				four hundred five and fifty-six thousandths
		.				forty-eight hundredths
5	6	.	1	1	1	_____
		.				ninety-eight and three hundredths

More Puzzling Problems

Directions: Solve the crossword puzzle.

Across

3. 7.333 = seven and three hundred thirty-three _____
5. 67.02 = sixty-seven and _____ hundredths
6. 490.1 = four hundred _____ and one tenth
7. 0.512 = five _____ twelve thousandths
9. 8.06 = eight and _____ hundredths
10. 0.007 = _____ thousandths
12. 11.3 = _____ and three tenths
13. 300.12 = _____ hundred and twelve hundredths
15. 62.08 = sixty-two and _____ hundredths
18. 70.009 = _____ and nine thousandths
19. 9.3 = _____ and three tenths
20. 10.51 = _____ and fifty-one hundredths
21. 1,000.02 = one thousand and two __

Down

1. 6.5 = six and five _____
2. 0.428 = four hundred _____ thousandths
3. 8,100.1 = eight _____ one hundred and one tenth
4. 3.02 = three and two _____
8. 0.685 = six hundred _____ thousandths
11. 50.19 = fifty and _____ hundredths
14. 0.015 = _____ thousandths
16. 430.7 = four hundred thirty and seven _____
17. 73.4 = seventy-three and four _____

Missing Train

Directions: Circle the . . .

1.	smallest number	0.31 (A)	0.05 (F)	0.20 (R)
2.	greatest number	0.001 (R)	0.137 (O)	0.100 (A)
3.	greatest number	9.910 (L)	9.010 (C)	9.909 (T)
4.	smallest number	0.110 (A)	0.09 (L)	0.3 (R)
5.	greatest number	0.090 (S)	0.10 (P)	0.12 (O)
6.	smallest number	0.131 (H)	0.2 (T)	0.08 (W)
7.	greatest number	1.310 (E)	1.03 (H)	1.33 (T)
8.	smallest number	2.001 (H)	2.9 (F)	2.010 (A)
9.	greatest number	0.3 (E)	0.03 (A)	0.003 (R)
10.	greatest number	1.01 (U)	1.001 (R)	1.1 (T)
11.	greatest number	3.04 (R)	3.009 (U)	3.039 (N)
12.	smallest number	6.01 (A)	6.11 (C)	6.030 (O)
13.	greatest number	0.001 (T)	0.100 (C)	0.090 (N)
14.	smallest number	1.027 (K)	1.270 (R)	1.207 (P)
15.	smallest number	9.909 (N)	9.09 (G)	9.009 (S)

Directions: Fill in the circled letters to solve the riddle below.

How do you search for a missing train?

$\overline{}\ \overline{}\ \overline{}\ \overline{}\ \overline{}\ \overline{}\quad \overline{}\ \overline{}\ \overline{}\quad \overline{}\ \overline{}\ \overline{}\ \overline{}\ \overline{}\ \overline{}$
 1   2   3   4   5   6   7   8   9   10 11 12 13 14 15

The Missing Piece

Directions: Each puzzle piece on this page is missing its match. Cut out the pieces below. Match the word name with its decimal and tape the two pieces together along the broken lines. When complete, there should be a square, a triangle, a rectangle, a circle, a parallelogram, and a pentagon.

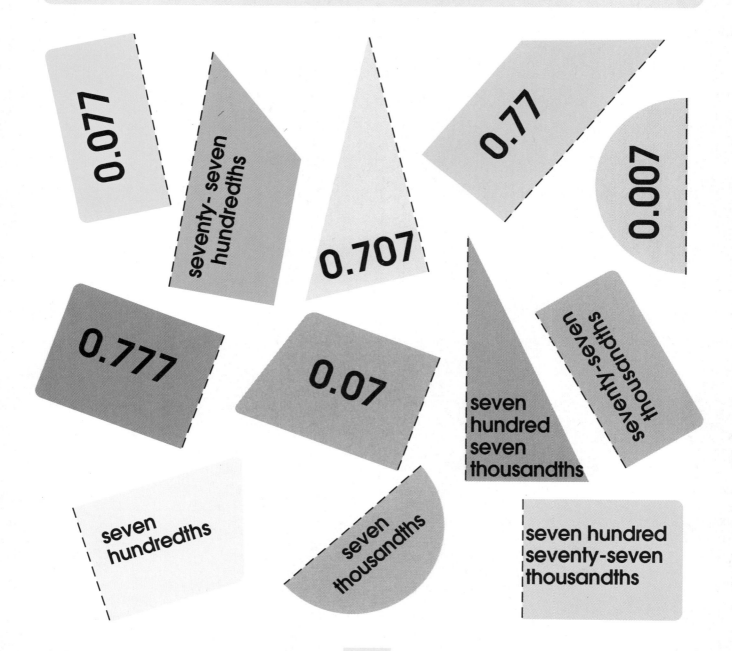

0.077

seventy-seven hundredths

0.707

0.77

0.007

0.777

0.07

seventy-seven thousandths

seven hundred seven thousandths

seven hundredths

seven thousandths

seven hundred seventy-seven thousandths

This page was left
intentionally blank.

Decimals and Fractions

Directions: Write the letter of the fraction that is equal to the decimal.

0.25= _____

0.5 = _____

0.7 = _____

0.8 = _____

0.37= _____

0.2 = _____

0.65= _____

0.75= _____

0.6 = _____

0.12= _____

0.33= _____

0.95= _____

0.24= _____

0.3 = _____

0.4 = _____

A. $\dfrac{33}{100}$

B. $\dfrac{3}{4}$

C. $\dfrac{13}{20}$

D. $\dfrac{3}{5}$

E. $\dfrac{3}{25}$

F. $\dfrac{19}{20}$

G. $\dfrac{1}{4}$

H. $\dfrac{2}{5}$

I. $\dfrac{3}{10}$

J. $\dfrac{37}{100}$

K. $\dfrac{1}{5}$

L. $\dfrac{1}{2}$

M. $\dfrac{6}{25}$

N. $\dfrac{4}{5}$

O. $\dfrac{7}{10}$

Adding and Subtracting Decimals

Add and subtract with decimals the same way you do with whole numbers. Keep the decimal points lined up so that you work with hundreths, then tenths, then ones, and so on.

Directions: Add or subtract. Remember to keep the decimal point in the proper place.

$$
\begin{array}{r} 0.5 \\ +\ 0.8 \\ \hline \end{array}
\qquad
\begin{array}{r} 0.35 \\ +\ 0.25 \\ \hline \end{array}
\qquad
\begin{array}{r} 47.5 \\ -\ 32.7 \\ \hline \end{array}
\qquad
\begin{array}{r} 85.7 \\ -\ 9.8 \\ \hline \end{array}
$$

$$
\begin{array}{r} 13.90 \\ +\ 4.23 \\ \hline \end{array}
\qquad
\begin{array}{r} 9.53 \\ -\ 8.16 \\ \hline \end{array}
\qquad
\begin{array}{r} 72.8 \\ -\ 63.9 \\ \hline \end{array}
\qquad
\begin{array}{r} 6.43 \\ +\ 4.58 \\ \hline \end{array}
$$

$$
\begin{array}{r} 638.07 \\ -\ 19.34 \\ \hline \end{array}
\qquad
\begin{array}{r} 811.060 \\ +\ 78.430 \\ \hline \end{array}
\qquad
\begin{array}{r} 521.09 \\ -\ 148.75 \\ \hline \end{array}
$$

$$
\begin{array}{r} 916.635 \\ +\ 172.136 \\ \hline \end{array}
\qquad
\begin{array}{r} 287.768 \\ -\ 63.951 \\ \hline \end{array}
\qquad
\begin{array}{r} 467.05 \\ -\ 398.19 \\ \hline \end{array}
$$

Sean ran a 1-mile race in 5.58 minutes. Carlos ran it in 6.38 minutes. How much less time did Sean need?

_____

Name _____

Decimals

Directions: Solve.

1. Write out 36.124 in words. _____

2. Write two hundred thirty-seven and twenty-six hundredths in numerals.
   _____

3. Use **>** or **<** to indicate which decimal fraction is greater.

   3.147_____3.205   3.06_____3.059

4. Round 87.658 to the nearest whole number. _____

5. Round 87.658 to the nearest tenth. _____

6. Round 87.658 to the nearest hundredth. _____

7. Write 0.5 as a fraction in lowest terms. _____

8. Write 0.69 as a fraction in lowest terms. _____

9. Write 7.85 as a fraction in lowest terms. _____

10. Draw a model of 0.3.

Name _____

Blast Off!

Directions: Solve the crossword puzzle.

Hint: Decimal points take up their own square. Do not use a zero before the decimal.

Across

3. $\begin{array}{r} 8.237 \\ -\ 2.083 \end{array}$ 4. $\begin{array}{r} 2.23 \\ -\ 1.256 \end{array}$ 5. $\begin{array}{r} 1{,}376.33 \\ -\ 542.13 \end{array}$

6. 8.538 – 0.228   8. 3.099 – 2.406

12. 124.107 – 45.642   14. 465.52 – 104.1

15. 0.732 – 0.633   16. 67.549 – 55.412

Down

1. $\begin{array}{r} 33.333 \\ +\ 0.896 \end{array}$ 2. $\begin{array}{r} 2.587 \\ +\ 3.191 \end{array}$ 3. $\begin{array}{r} 5.78 \\ +\ 1.09 \end{array}$

7. 22.05 + 15.91   9. 2.057 + 0.008

10. 0.531 + .19   11. 7.852 + 1.489

13. 3.012 + 1.025

Decimal Delight

Directions: Kooky Claude Clod, the cafeteria cook, has some strange ideas about cooking. He does not understand fractions—only decimals. Help Claude convert these measurements to decimals so he can get cooking!

Kooky Soup

Mix together and sauté:

$\frac{9}{20}$ cup minced cat whiskers
$\frac{7}{8}$ cup crushed snails
$\frac{3}{5}$ cup toothpaste
$\frac{3}{4}$ tablespoon vinegar
$\frac{11}{25}$ cup pig slop

Simmer $93\frac{1}{2}$ days.

Gradually fold in:

$\frac{1}{5}$ teaspoon soot
$\frac{3}{8}$ cup motor oil
$\frac{9}{10}$ tablespoon lemon juice
$\frac{11}{20}$ cup chopped poison ivy
$6\frac{1}{4}$ rotten eggs

Brew for $1,500\frac{24}{25}$ years. Enjoy!

Mix together and sauté:

_____ cup minced cat whiskers

_____ cup crushed snails

_____ cup toothpaste

_____ tablespoon vinegar

_____ cup pig slop

Simmer _____ days.

Gradually fold in:

_____ teaspoon soot

_____ cup motor oil

_____ tablespoon lemon juice

_____ cup chopped poison ivy

_____ rotten eggs

Brew for _____ years. Enjoy!

Historical Harry

Directions: What were the large cannons that were used by Germany in World War I? Solve the following subtraction problems and find the answers in the cannon. Write the corresponding letter above the problem's number at the bottom of the page to spell out the answer to this historical trivia question.

A = 8.01
E = 0.28
B = 8.57
I = 11.92
B = 19.46
R = 33.75
S = 1.98
G = 11.38
H = 0.33
T = 5.998

1. 9 – 0.43

2. 12 – 0.08

3. 15 – 3.62

4. 20 – 0.54

5. 1 – 0.72

6. 46 – 12.25

7. 6 – 0.002

8. 21 – 20.67

9. 9 – 0.99

10. 4 – 2.02

___ ___ ___   ___ ___ ___ ___ ___   ___ ___
 1   2   3   4   5   6   7   8   9   10

Name _____

Multiplying Decimals

Directions: Multiply with decimals the same way you do with whole numbers. The decimal point moves in multiplication. Count the number of decimal places in the problem and use the same number of decimal places in your answer.

Example:

```
  3.5
x 1.5
  175
 35
 5.25
```

Directions: Multiply.

2.5	67.4	83.7	13.35
x .9	x 2.3	x 9.8	x 3.06

9.06	28.97	33.41	28.7
x 2.38	x 5.16	x .93	x 11.9

The jet flies 1.5 times faster than the plane with a propeller. The propeller plane flies 165.7 miles per hour. How fast does the jet fly?

_____

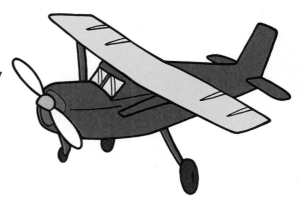

Multiple Design

Directions: Solve the problems on a separate sheet of paper. Find the answers in the design and color correctly.

green
0.463
x   82

blue
28.5
x   7.4

red
6.51
x   6.9

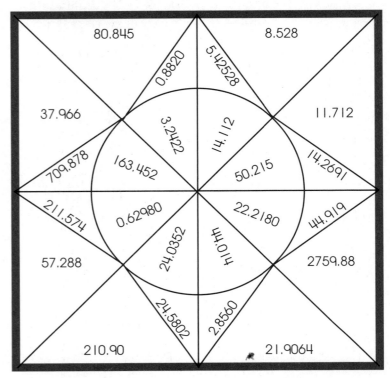

yellow
39.2
x 0.36

purple
7.54
x 0.43

purple
0.670
x   0.94

yellow
64.9
x 3.26

yellow
0.592
x   40.6

purple
7.46
x   5.9

green
92.4
x 0.62

blue
32.8
x 0.26

blue
85.1
x 0.95

green
7.32
x   1.6

purple
6.05
x   8.3

green
3.27
x 844

blue
5.56
x 3.94

yellow
80.5
x 0.276

red
5.77
x 4.26

red
95.8
x 7.41

red
0.784
x   6.92

yellow
2.57
x 63.6

yellow
29.3
x 0.487

yellow
6.80
x 0.42

yellow
0.245
x   3.6

Dividing With Decimals

Directions: When the dividend has a decimal, place the decimal point for the answer directly above the decimal point in the dividend. The first one has been done for you.

$$
\begin{array}{r}
12.5 \\
3 \overline{)37.5} \\
-3 \\
\hline
07 \\
-6 \\
\hline
15 \\
-15 \\
\hline
0
\end{array}
$$

$4 \overline{)34.4}$ $2 \overline{)31.6}$ $3 \overline{)131.4}$

$5 \overline{)187.5}$ $7 \overline{)181.3}$ $6 \overline{)340.8}$ $9 \overline{)294.3}$

$3 \overline{)135.6}$ $5 \overline{)264.5}$ $2 \overline{)134.6}$ $8 \overline{)754.4}$

$5 \overline{)35.25}$ $7 \overline{)79.45}$ $9 \overline{)28.71}$ $36 \overline{)199.44}$

The Perfect Sweet-Treat Solution

Directions: Solve each division problem on a separate sheet of paper. Draw a line from the popcorn (problem) to the correct drink (answer).

$3\overline{)7.95}$

6.84

$1\overline{)3.322}$

$5\overline{)0.31}$

2.65

0.905

$9\overline{)2.196}$

0.395

0.302

$2\overline{)0.016}$

$7\overline{)47.88}$

0.063

$5\overline{)11.4}$

0.244

$4\overline{)15.48}$

1.135

$8\overline{)7.24}$

0.008

3.87

$2\overline{)0.79}$

2.28

$8\overline{)0.504}$

0.062

$6\overline{)6.81}$

Dividing Decimals by Decimals

Directions: When the divisor has a decimal point you must eliminate it before dividing. You can do this by moving the decimal point to the right to create a whole number. You must also move the decimal point the same number of spaces to the right in the dividend.

Sometimes you need to add zeros to do this.

Example:

$$0.25\overline{)85.50} \quad \text{changes to}$$

$$
\begin{array}{r}
342 \\
25\overline{)8550} \\
-\underline{75} \\
105 \\
-\underline{100} \\
50 \\
\underline{50} \\
0
\end{array}
$$

Directions: Divide.

$0.3\overline{)27.9}$ $0.6\overline{)42.6}$ $0.9\overline{)81.9}$ $0.7\overline{)83.3}$

$0.4\overline{)23.2}$ $0.7\overline{)56.7}$ $1.2\overline{)10.8}$ $2.2\overline{)138.6}$

$12.6\overline{)5,670}$ $4.7\overline{)564}$ $8.6\overline{)842.8}$ $3.7\overline{)2,009.1}$

$5.9\overline{)1,917.5}$ $4.3\overline{)1,376}$ $2.9\overline{)922.2}$ $2.7\overline{)5613.3}$

Name _____

Working With Decimals

Directions: Solve.

1. Write 207.426 in words.

   _____

2. Write forty-seven and thirteen thousandths in numerals. _____

3. Use > or < to indicate which decimal fraction is greater.
   17.35_____17.295

Directions: Fill in the blanks.

4. Round 12.836 to the nearest whole number. _____

5. Round 12.836 to the nearest tenth. _____

6. Round 12.836 to the nearest hundredth. _____

7. Write 0.36 as a fraction in lowest terms. _____

8. Write 0.25 as a fraction in lowest terms. _____

9. Write $\frac{3}{4}$ as a decimal number. _____

Directions: Solve.

10. 36.2 + 27.325 = _____

11. 87.36 − 84.95 = _____

12. 4.6 x 1.2 = _____

13. 3.46 x 10 = _____

14. 11.55 ÷ 7 = _____

15. 39 ÷ 12 = _____

16. 367.52 ÷ 10 = _____

Giving 100%

Example:

The word **percent** means "for each hundred."
A test score of 95% means that 95 out of 100
answers are correct.

There are 100 squares in this grid. Each square
represents one hundredth. Since 63 squares
are shaded, 63% is shaded.

Directions: Write the percent of
squares shaded.

Shade each grid to show the
percent.

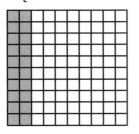

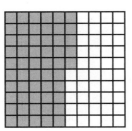

_____

_____

45%

10%

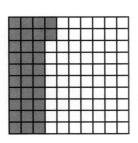

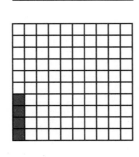

_____

_____

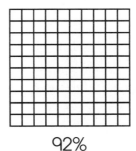

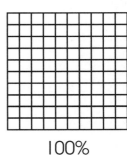

92%

100%

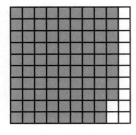

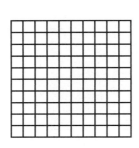

_____

_____

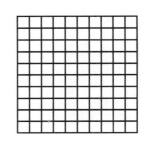

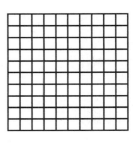

8%

67%

Name _____

tenth = 0.1
hundredth = 0.16 = 100
thousandth =
        0.163

$0.16 = \frac{16}{100}$ 1.24 $\frac{124}{100}$

Decimals, Fractions, and Percents

Decimals, fractions, and percents are different ways of representing the same number.

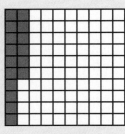   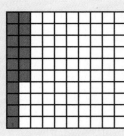   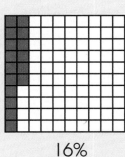

0.16 $\frac{16}{100}$ 16%
(sixteen hundredths)
                (or 4/25 in simplest form)

Directions: Write the amount shaded as a decimal, a fraction in the simplest form, and a percent.

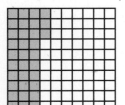   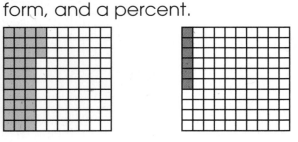

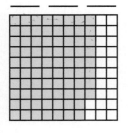   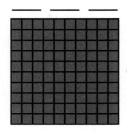   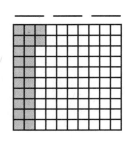   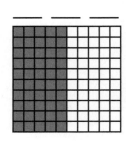

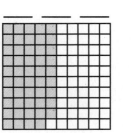   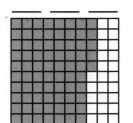   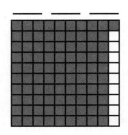   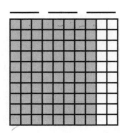

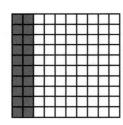   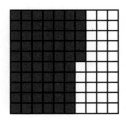

___ ___ ___   ___ ___ ___   ___ ___ ___   ___ ___ ___

Percents and Fractions

Directions: Write the fraction and percent represented in each situation.

Situation	Fraction	Percent
30 marbles out of 100 marbles are red	$\frac{30}{100}$	30%
29 people out of 100 people voted.		
10 fish out of 100 fish are tropical.		
7 cats out of 100 cats live indoors.		
4 turtles out of 100 turtles laid eggs.		
7 out of 10 puppies had spots.	$\frac{7}{10} = \overline{100}$	
5 out of 10 baskets were made.		
6 out of 25 rocks in my yard are igneous.	$\frac{6}{25} = \overline{100}$	
17 out of 25 rulers are metric.		
18 out of 20 goldfish are orange.		
The dress was reduced $5 from $20.		

Models

Directions: Draw the model and fill in the missing fraction, percent or decimal.

Draw	Fraction	Percent	Decimal
			0.25
	$\frac{37}{100}$		
		18%	
	$\frac{7}{10}$		
		4%	

Percents and Fractions

Example:

Steps to change a percent to a fraction, or a fraction to a percent:

Percent $\longrightarrow$ Fraction

$67\% = 0.67 = \dfrac{67}{100}$

$8\% = 0.08 = \dfrac{8}{100} = \dfrac{2}{25}$

$125\% = 1.25 = \dfrac{125}{100} = \dfrac{5}{4} = 1\dfrac{1}{4}$

Fraction $\longrightarrow$ Percent

$\dfrac{4}{5} = 4 \div 5 = 0.8 = 80\%$

$\dfrac{1}{3} = 1 \div 3 = 0.333\ldots = 33.3\%$

$1\dfrac{1}{2} = \dfrac{3}{2} = 3 \div 2 = 1.5 = 150\%$

Directions: Match the percent with the fraction in simplest form. Write the letter on the line.

1. _____ 5%	A. $\dfrac{3}{25}$	B. $\dfrac{11}{20}$	2. _____ 12%	
3. _____ 17%	C. $\dfrac{1}{3}$	D. $1\dfrac{1}{5}$	4. _____ 20%	
5. _____ 25%	E. $\dfrac{1}{2}$	F. $\dfrac{5}{6}$	6. _____ 33.3%	
7. _____ 48%	G. $\dfrac{1}{5}$	H. $\dfrac{1}{20}$	8. _____ 50%	
9. _____ 55%	I. $\dfrac{7}{10}$	J. $\dfrac{47}{50}$	10. _____ 70%	
11. _____ 75%	K. $\dfrac{1}{4}$	L. $1\dfrac{11}{25}$	12. _____ 83.3%	
13. _____ 94%	M. $\dfrac{17}{100}$	N. $\dfrac{3}{4}$	14. _____ 120%	
15. _____ 144%	O. $\dfrac{12}{25}$			

Percents and Decimals

Examples:

Steps to change a percent to a decimal, or a decimal to a percent:

Percent → Decimal

60% = 60 hundredths = 0.60
3% = 3 hundredths = 0.03
155% = 155 hundredths = 1.55

Decimal → Percent

0.35 = 35 hundredths = 35%
0.9 = 90 hundredths = 90%
1.24 = 124 hundredths = 124%

Directions: Write the equivalent decimal or percent.

1. 0.54 =

2. 0.07 =

3. 0.8 =

4. 1.35 =

5. 35% =

6. 125% =

7. 50% =

8. 2% =

9. 2.44 =

10. 0.85 =

11. 23% =

12. 0.5 =

13. 105% =

14. 0.02 =

15. 8% =

16. 10% =

3.00 =

2.08 =

0.05 =

0.89 =

120% =

43% =

3% =

90% =

1.85 =

2.5 =

0.4 =

Name _____

Percent of a Number

Example ✗

Find 30% of 12.

Method 1
Use a fraction.

Method 2
Use a decimal.

$\frac{30}{100} \times 12 = \frac{360}{100} = \frac{36}{10} = \frac{18}{5} = 3\frac{3}{5}$ $0.3 \times 12 = 3.6$

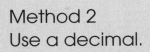

$\frac{30}{100} \times \frac{12}{1} = \frac{360}{100}$

30% of 12 is $3\frac{3}{5}$ or 3.6.

Directions: ✗

Find 25% of:

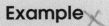16 _____

20 _____

64 _____

140 _____

10 _____

35 _____ ✓

120 _____ ✓

630 _____ ✓

Find 4% of:

10 _____

96 _____

150 _____

200 _____

20 _____

35 _____

90 _____

140 _____

Find 60% of:

15 _____

60 _____

100 _____

125 _____

7 _____

32 _____

110 _____

297 _____

Sale!

Sale!
All items 20% off

Example:

What is the sale price of the bat?

$34 x 20% = $34 x 0.2 = $6.80
$34 – $6.80 = $27.20

or

100% – 20% = 80%
$34 x 80% = $34 x 0.8 = $27.20

The sale price is $27.20.

Directions: Solve.

1. What is the sale price of the bike helmet? _____

2. What is the sale price of the running socks? _____

3. How much will Tara save if she buys the soccer ball on sale? _____

4. How much will it cost to buy the baseball cap and the glove? _____

5. How much will it cost to buy the racket and tennis balls? _____

6. Patti buys the football jersey and pays with $30. How much change does she receive? _____

7. Darren has $13. Can he buy the baseball cap on sale? _____

8. Which costs less on sale, the tennis racket or the track shoes ? _____

Name _____

Percent

Directions: Percent is a ratio meaning "per hundred." It is written with a % sign. 20% means 20 percent or 20 per hundred.

Example:

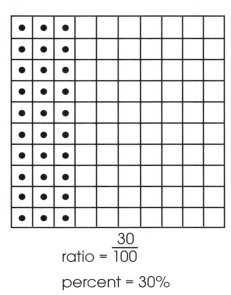

ratio = $\frac{30}{100}$

percent = 30%

ratio = _____

percent = _____

Directions: Write the percent for each ratio.

Book Sale

$\frac{7}{100} =$	$\frac{38}{100} =$
$\frac{63}{100} =$	$\frac{3}{100} =$
$\frac{40}{100} =$	$\frac{1}{5} =$

The school received 100 books for the Book Fair. It sold 43 books.

What is the percent of books sold to books received? _____

Name _____

Using Calculators to Find Percent

A calculator is a machine that rapidly does addition, subtraction, multiplication, division, and other mathematical functions.

Example:

Carlos got 7 hits in 20 "at bats."

$$\frac{7}{20} = \frac{35}{100} = 35\%$$

To use a calculator:
Step 1: Press 7.
Step 2: Press the ÷ symbol.
Step 3: Press 20.
Step 4: Press the = symbol.
Step 5: 0.35 appears.
       0.35 = 35%.

Directions: Use a calculator to find the percent of hits to the number of "at bats" for each baseball player. Round your answer to two digits. If your calculator displays the answer 0.753, round it to 0.75 or 75%.

Player	Hits	At Bats	Percent
Carlos	7	20	35%
Troy	3	12	_____
Sasha	4	14	_____
Dan	8	18	_____
Jaye	5	16	_____
Keesha	9	17	_____
Martin	11	16	_____
Robi	6	21	_____
Devan	4	15	_____

Who is most likely to get a hit? _____

✓ Finding Percents

Find percent by dividing the number you have by the number possible.

Example:

15 out of 20 possible: $\dfrac{0.75}{20 \overline{)15.00}}$ = 75%
$\quad\quad\quad\quad\quad\quad -\underline{140}$
$\quad\quad\quad\quad\quad\quad\quad 100$
$\quad\quad\quad\quad\quad\quad\quad \underline{100}$

Annie has been keeping track of the scores she earned on each spelling test during the grading period.

Directions: Find out each percentage grade she earned. The first one has been done for you.

Week	Number Correct		Total Number of Words	Score in Percent
1	14	(out of)	20	70%
2	16		20	_____
3	18		20	_____
4	12		15	_____
5	16		16	_____
6	17		18	_____
Review Test	51		60	_____

If Susan scored 5% higher than Annie on the review test,   _____
how many words did she get right?

Carrie scored 10% lower than Susan on the review test.   _____
How many words did she spell correctly?

Of the 24 students in Annie's class, 25% had the same score as Annie.
Only 10% had a higher score. What percent had a lower score? _____

Is that answer possible? _____

Why? _____

Name _____

Ratio

A **ratio** is a comparison of two quantities.

Ratios can be written three ways: 2 to 3 or 2 : 3 or. $\frac{2}{3}$
Each ratio is read: two to three.

Example:

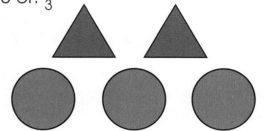

The ratio of triangles to circles is 2 to 3.
The ratio of circles to triangles is 3 to 2.

Directions: Write the ratio that compares these items.

ratio of tulips to cacti _____

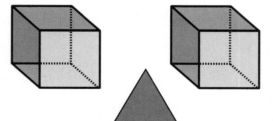

ratio of cubes to triangles _____

ratio of pens to pencils _____

Name _____

Ratios

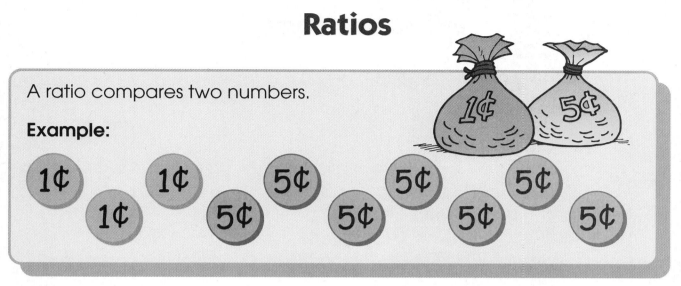

A ratio compares two numbers.

Example:

Directions: Put 10 pennies and 10 nickels in a bag. Without looking, pull out a small handful of coins. Draw the coins in a box below. Write each ratio. Return the coins to the bag and repeat 4 more times. The first example is shown.

pennies to nickels	**3:5**	coins to pennies	**8:3**
nickels to pennies	**5:3**	nickels to coins	**5:8**
pennies to coins	**3:8**	coins to nickels	**8:5**

pennies to nickels _____	coins to pennies _____
nickels to pennies _____	nickels to coins _____
pennies to coins _____	coins to nickels _____

pennies to nickels _____	coins to pennies _____
nickels to pennies _____	nickels to coins _____
pennies to coins _____	coins to nickels _____

pennies to nickels _____	coins to pennies _____
nickels to pennies _____	nickels to coins _____
pennies to coins _____	coins to nickels _____

pennies to nickels _____	coins to pennies _____
nickels to pennies _____	nickels to coins _____
pennies to coins _____	coins to nickels _____

pennies to nickels _____	coins to pennies _____
nickels to pennies _____	nickels to coins _____
pennies to coins _____	coins to nickels _____

Proportions

Another way of writing a ratio is as a fraction. 3:7 is the same as $\frac{3}{7}$. $\overset{8}{\underset{2}{1}}\times\overset{8}{\underset{8}{4}}$
Remember what you have learned about cross multiplication.

Because the products of cross multiplication are the same, the fractions are equivalent. When two ratios or fractions are equivalent, they form a proportion.

Example:

Steps to find an unknown term of a proportion:

Lisa uses 2 pots to plant 8 seeds.
How many pots will she need to plant 24 seeds?

1. Write a proportion. $\dfrac{2 \text{ pots}}{8 \text{ seeds}} = \dfrac{n \text{ pots}}{24 \text{ seeds}}$

2. Cross multiply. $\dfrac{2}{8} \times \dfrac{n}{24}$

$8 \times n = 48$
$n = 6$ (Divide both sides of the proportion by 8.)
Lisa needs 6 pots to plant 24 seeds.

Directions: If the ratios form a proportion, write **yes** on the line. If not, write **no**.

$\dfrac{4}{5} = \dfrac{24}{30}$ _____

$\dfrac{1}{2} = \dfrac{36}{72}$ _____

$\dfrac{3}{7} = \dfrac{20}{35}$ _____

$\dfrac{1}{23} = \dfrac{8}{184}$ _____

$\dfrac{6}{13} = \dfrac{75}{156}$ _____

$\dfrac{9}{5} = \dfrac{171}{95}$ _____

$\dfrac{4}{21} = \dfrac{40}{210}$ _____

$\dfrac{11}{12} = \dfrac{154}{168}$ _____

Directions: Find the unknown term in each of these proportions.

$\dfrac{4}{5} = \dfrac{n}{15}$ _____

$\dfrac{n}{104} = \dfrac{5}{13}$ _____

$\dfrac{5}{6} = \dfrac{45}{n}$ _____

Probability

Probability is the ratio of favorable outcomes to possible outcomes of an experiment.

Vehicle	Number Sold
4 door	26
2 door	18
Sport	7
Van	12
Wagon	7
Compact	5
Total	75

Example:

This table records vehicle sales for 1 month. What is the probability of a person buying a van?

number of vans sold = 12   total number of cars = 75

The probability that a person will choose a van is 12 in 75 or $\frac{12}{75}$.

Directions: Look at the chart of flowers sold in a month. What is the probability that a person will buy each?

Roses _____

Tulips _____

Violets _____

Orchids _____

Flowers	Number Sold
Roses	48
Tulips	10
Violets	11
Orchids	7
Total	76

How would probability help a flower store owner keep the correct quantity of each flower in the store?

_____

_____

_____

Name _____

What Are the Chances?

Probability is the chance that something will happen.

Example:

This spinner has 8 equal-sized spaces. What is the probability, or chance, that a person would spin:

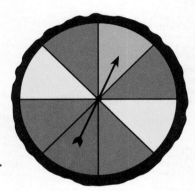

Blue? $\frac{4}{8}$ or 4:8, because 4 of 8 sections are blue.
Red? $\frac{1}{8}$ or 1:8, because 1 of 8 sections is red.
Yellow? $\frac{2}{8}$ or 2:8, because 2 of 8 sections are yellow.
Green? $\frac{1}{8}$ or 1:8, because 1 of 8 sections is green.

Directions: Use the spinner to the right to answer the questions.

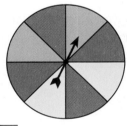

1. What is the probability of spinning blue? _____

2. What is the probability of spinning yellow? _____

3. What is the probability of spinning green? _____

4. What is the probability of spinning yellow or red? _____

Directions: Use the spinner to the right to answer the questions.

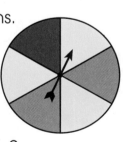

1. What is the probability of spinning purple? _____

2. What is the probability of spinning orange? _____

3. What is the probability of spinning yellow? _____

4. What is the probability of spinning yellow, orange or purple? _____

Directions: Use the spinner to the right to answer the questions.

1. What is the probability of spinning a 4? _____

2. What is the probability of spinning a 1? _____

3. What is the probability of spinning a 3? _____

4. What is the probability of spinning 3, 4, or 6? _____

Name _____

Likely and Unlikely

The probability of an event happening can be written as a fraction between 0 and 1.

Example:

Certain if the probability is 1.

The probability of spinning red, blue, or green is $\frac{6}{6}$ or 1.

More likely if its probability is greater than another.

It is more likely to spin green ($\frac{3}{6}$) than red ($\frac{2}{6}$).

Less likely if its probability is less than another.

It is less likely to spin red ($\frac{2}{6}$) than blue ($\frac{1}{6}$).

Equally likely if the probabilities are the same.

It is equally likely to spin red or blue ($\frac{3}{6}$) or green ($\frac{3}{6}$).

Impossible if the probability is 0.

It is impossible to spin white ($\frac{0}{6}$ = 0).

Directions: Look at the spinner. Write the probability for each event below. Write **certain** or **impossible,** where appropriate.

spinning a 6 _____   spinning a 4 _____

spinning a 2 _____   spinning a 4 or 5 _____

spinning an even number _____   spinning a prime number _____

spinning a number < 10 _____   spinning a zero _____

Directions: Look at the spinner to find which is **more likely, less likely,** or **equally likely.**

Spinning a 4 is _____ than spinning a 5.

Spinning a 4 is _____ than spinning a 1.

Spinning an even number is _____ than spinning an odd number.

Name _____

Flying Forks

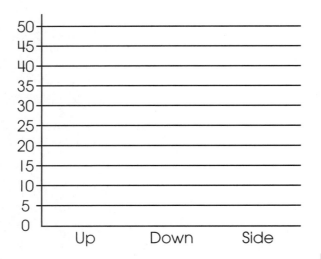

Look at a plastic fork. What do you think will happen if you drop the fork—will it land faceup, facedown, or on its side? What is the probability of each position?

Directions: Write your answers below.

Predict:
Imagine dropping the fork 50 different times.
Predict how many times the fork will land:

Faceup: _____

Facedown: _____

On its side: _____

Experiment:
Drop the fork 50 times. Record how many times it lands in each position.

Faceup: _____

Facedown: _____

On its side: _____

Organize the Data:
Graph the results.

Interpret the Data:
Explain what the results mean. Why might these results have occurred?

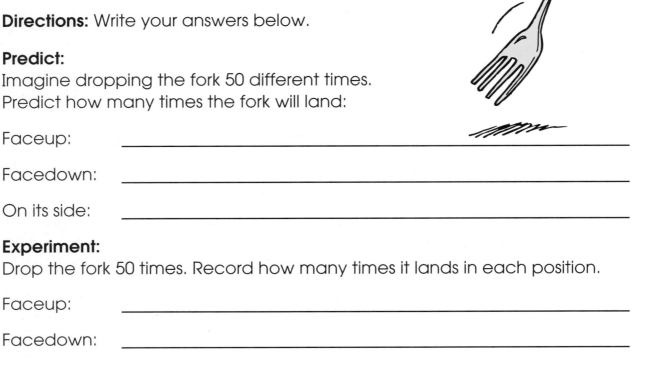

_____

_____

_____

_____

Lines and Segments

A **line** has no endpoints.

To name a line, name any two points on the line.

J   W

line JW   or   line WJ

A **line segment** has two endpoints.

A line segment is part of a line. The line segment consists of the endpoints and all points on the line between the endpoints. To name a line segment, name the endpoints.

G   S

line segment GS   or   line segment SG

Directions: Circle the correct name for each figure.

1.   B   A   line AB   line segment BA   line CA

2.   G   F   line segment FG   line GF   line FG

3.   C   E   line CD   line segment CE   line CE

4.   M   N   line segment MN   line MM   line MN

5.   R   S   line RS   line segment RS   line SR

6.   K   I   line segment KI   line KI   line IK

7.   Z   X   line LZ   line segment ZX   line ZX

8.   E   P   line segment PE   line EP   line EE

9.   T   V   line V   line segment VT   line VT

Directions: Draw and label the following

10. line segment HQ

Lines

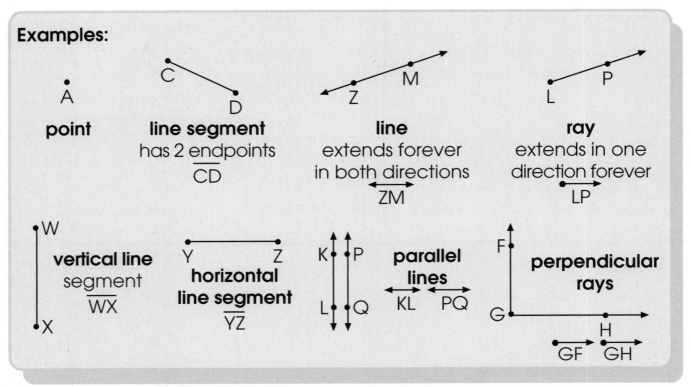

Examples:

point

line segment
has 2 endpoints
$\overline{CD}$

line
extends forever
in both directions
ZM

ray
extends in one
direction forever
LP

vertical line
segment
$\overline{WX}$

horizontal
line segment
$\overline{YZ}$

parallel
lines
KL   PQ

perpendicular
rays
GF GH

Directions: Describe each object using words and symbols.

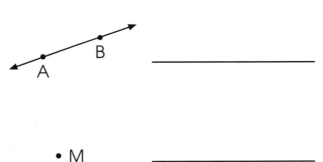

_____

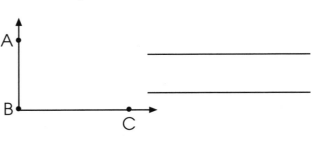

_____

_____

• M   _____

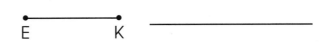

_____

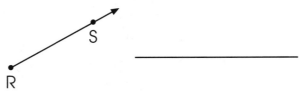

_____

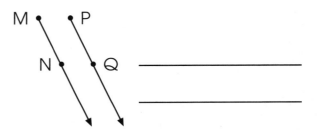

_____

_____

Geometric Figures

Directions: Write the correct letter in the box next to each figure.

Point S = •S   Ray XY = $\overrightarrow{XY}$
Line CD = $\overleftrightarrow{CD}$ Line segment BC = $\overline{BC}$

1. 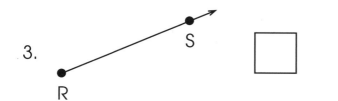 L   M □

2. Q □

3.  S R □

4. Y — Z □

5.  N M □

6. 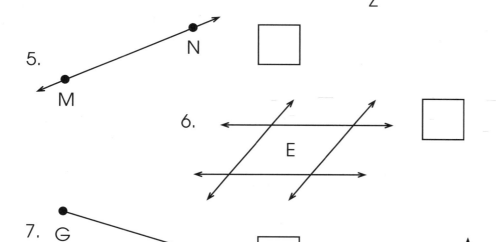 E □

7. G H □

9. •A □

10. P O □

8. H I □

11. J K  □

A. $\overrightarrow{GH}$

B. Point Q

C. Plane E

D. Point A

E. $\overrightarrow{OP}$

F. $\overleftrightarrow{LM}$

G. $\overline{YZ}$

H. $\overleftrightarrow{MN}$

I. $\overleftrightarrow{HI}$

J. $\overrightarrow{JK}$

K. $\overrightarrow{RS}$

Angles

An **angle** has two sides and a **vertex**.

Angle GHB (denoted ∠GHB) has a vertex of H. When naming an angle, use the vertex as the middle letter.

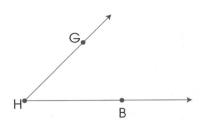

To use a protractor to measure an angle:

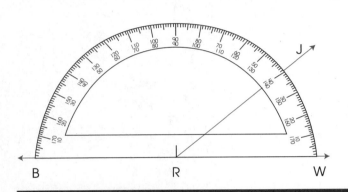

Place the center of the protractor at the vertex of the angle. Align one side of the angle with the base of the protractor. Use the scale starting at 0 and read the measure of the angle.

The measurement of ∠JRW is 40°
The measurement of ∠JRB is 140°

Directions: Name each angle. Then use a protractor to measure each angle.

1.

∠___ ; ___°

∠___ ; ___°

∠___ ; ___°

2.

∠___ ; ___°

∠___ ; ___°

∠___ ; ___°

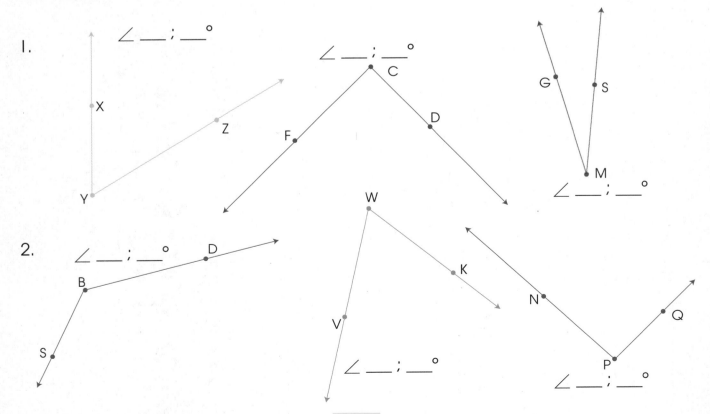

SMILE

TOTALLY!

WOW!

AWESOME!

COOL!

SA

Angle Measurement

The **degree** is the unit used to measure angles.

Directions: Measure the following angles using a protractor.

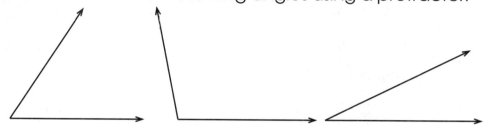

1. _____   2. _____   3. _____   4. _____

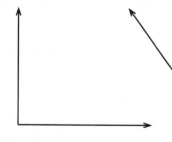

5. _____   6. _____   7. _____   8. _____

Directions: Draw the angles given using a protractor.

1. 70°   2. 120°   3. 40°

4. 90°   5. 150°   6. 110°

Polygons

Polygons are named for the number of sides they have.

Triangle   Quadrilateral   Pentagon   Hexagon   Heptagon   Octagon

_3_ sides   ___sides   ___sides   ___sides   ___sides   ___sides

Look at the hexagon at the right.
All of the sides are the same length.
All of the angles have the same measure.
This is a regular hexagon.

Directions: On the line after each name, write the letter(s) of the figure(s) it describes.
Some names will have more than one letter. Some figures have more than one name.

1. pentagon ____b.,h.____

2. hexagon _____

3. octagon _____

4. triangle _____

5. heptagon _____

6. quadrilateral _____

7. regular triangle _____

8. regular hexagon _____

9. regular pentagon _____

a.   b.   c.   d.   e.   f.   g.   h.   i.

Directions: Answer the following questions.

10. What is another name for a regular quadrilateral?_____

11. What of the triangles show below are regular triangles? _____

a.   b.   c.   d.   e.   f.

Polygons

The word **polygon** means "many angles" and describes a shape that:

a) starts and stops at the same place (making it "closed").
b) can be traced without lifting the pencil or crosssing or retracing any part.
c) is made of at least three line segments.

A **regular polygon** has sides that are all the same length.

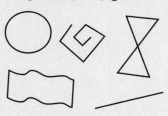

shapes

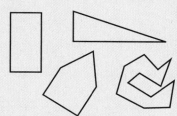

polygons

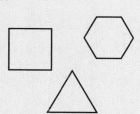

regular polygons

Directions: Circle any shape that is a polygon. Color any shape that is a regular polygon. If the shape if not a polygon, explain why.

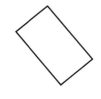 

_____ _____ _____ _____

_____ _____ _____ _____

_____ _____ _____ _____

163

Name _____

Polygons and Circles

To name a polygon, use the letters of the vertices (plural of vertex).

Figure ABCDE or Pentagon ABCDE

A line segment that connects two vertices, but is not a side is called a diagonal.

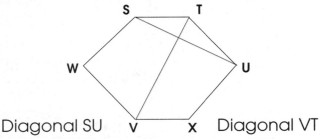

Diagonal SU   Diagonal VT

To name a circle, use the letters of the circle.

A line segment from the center of the circle to a point on the circle is a **radius**. A line segment that has endpoints on the circle and passes through the center of the circle is c **diameter.**

Radius LM

Diameter KN

Note that KL and LN are also radii (plural of radius).

Directions: Answer the following questions.

1. Draw and name all of the diagonals of figure FGHIJ

_____

2. Are all of the diagonals of figure FGHIJ the same length?_____

3. Name a radius of circle P. _____

4. Name a diameter of circle P. _____

5. In the circle P, draw a diameter that goes through point N.

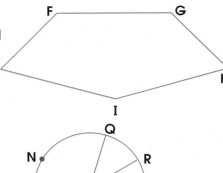

6. Is figure RSTUVW a regular hexagon? _____

7. Draw all the diagonals for figure RSTUVW.

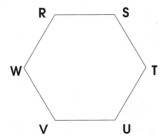

8. How many diagonals does figure RSTUVW have?_____

9. Are all of the diagonals of figure RSTUVW the same length?_____

Name _____

Three-Dimensional Objects

 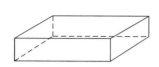

Cube **Rectangular Prism** **Triangular Pyramid** **Square Pyramid**

Each of these objects has faces, edges, and vertices.
Each of the faces of these objects is a polygon.

This is a *face*.   This is an *edge*.   This is a *vertex*.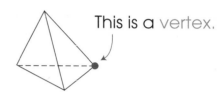

edge	face	rectangle	square	triangle	vertex
edges	faces	rectangles	squares	triangles	vertices

Directions: Choose from the list above to complete each sentence. You might use some words more than once. You might not use all the words.

1. All of the faces of a cube are _____.

2. All of the faces of a retangular prism are _____ .

3. The bottom face of a triangular pyramid is a _____ .

4. The colored part of object A below is a(n) _____ .

5. The colored part of object B below is a(n) _____ .

6. The colored part of object C below is a(n) _____ .

A    **B**    **C**

Directions: Answer each question with **yes** or **no**.

7. Are all squares rectangles? _____

8. Are all faces of a cube rectangles? _____

9. Is a cube a rectangular prism? _____

Name _____

Geometry

Geometry is the branch of mathematics that has to do with points, lines, and shapes.

Directions: Use the Glossary on pages 237-239 if you need help. Write the word from the box that is described below.

triangle	square	cube	angle
line	ray	segment	rectangle

a collection of points on a straight path
that goes on and on in opposite directions _____

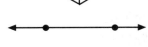

a figure with three sides and three corners _____

a figure with four equal sides and
four corners _____

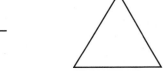

part of a line that has one end point
and goes on and on in one direction _____

part of a line having two end points _____

a space figure with six square faces _____

two rays with a common end point _____

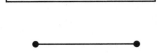

a figure with four corners and four sides _____

Geometry

Review the definitions on the previous page before completing the problems below.

Directions: Identify the labeled section of each of the following diagrams.

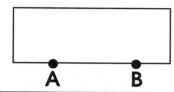

AB = _____

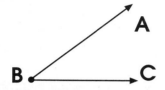

ABC = _____

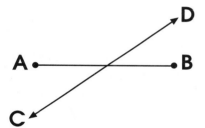

AB = _____

CD = _____

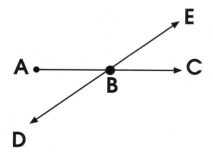

AC = _____

AB = _____

EBC = _____

BC = _____

Name _____

Geometric Patterns

Directions: Draw the next three shapes in the pattern.

Directions: Draw a pattern that uses shapes. Have another person draw the next three shapes in the pattern.

_____ _____ _____ _____ _____

_____ _____ _____ _____ _____

Identify the Quadrilateral

Directions: Cut out and sort the shapes. Make your own categories and name them.

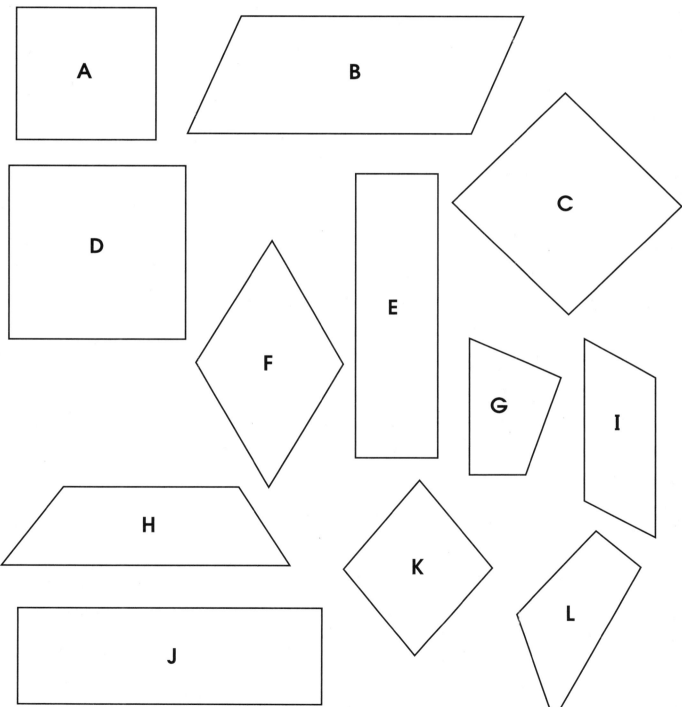

This page was left
intentionally blank.

Shapes in Hiding

Directions: Shade triangles to make each shape.

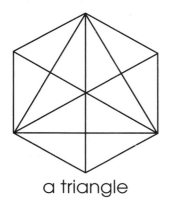

a triangle

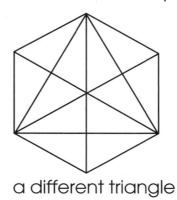

a different triangle

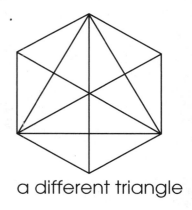

a different triangle

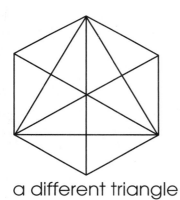

a different triangle

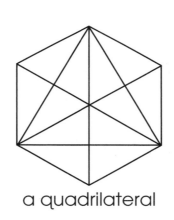

a quadrilateral

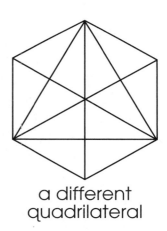

a different
quadrilateral

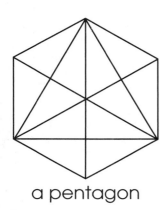

a pentagon

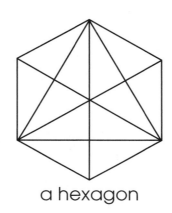

a hexagon

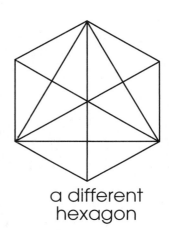

a different
hexagon

The Rocketangular Puzzle

Directions: Take an $8\frac{1}{2}$" x 11" piece of paper. Fold it in half, half again, half again and half again. Open it up. It should look like this:

Directions: Draw in the two diagonals using a ruler and fold on them. Trace over all the fold lines on both sides. Cut on the dashed lines.

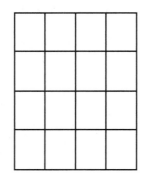

Fold Lines
_____

Cut Lines
- - - - - - - - - - - -

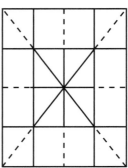

Directions: Fold the piece of paper flat to make each shape below. Calculate the area of each shape and write it on the blank.

1.
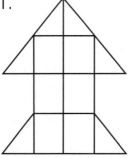
_____

2.
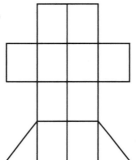
_____

3.
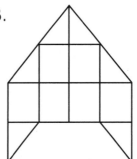
_____

4.

_____

5.
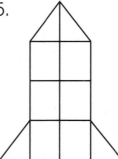
_____

6.
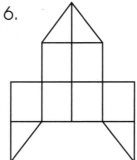
_____

7.
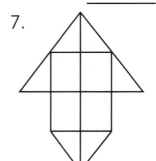
_____

8.
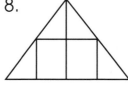
_____

Name _____

Similar, Congruent, and Symmetrical Figures

Similar figures have the same shape but have varying sizes.

Figures that are **congruent** have identical shapes but different orientations. That means they face in different directions.

Symmetrical figures can be divided equally into two identical parts.

Directions: Cross out the shape that does not belong in each group. Label the two remaining shapes as similiar, congruent, or symmetrical.

_____   _____   _____

_____   _____   _____

_____   _____   _____

_____   _____   _____

Perimeter and Area

The **perimeter (P)** of a figure is the distance around it. To find the perimeter, add the lengths of the sides.

The **area (A)** of a figure is the number of units in a figure. Find the area by multiplying the length of a figure by its width.

Example:

P = 16 units
A = 16 units

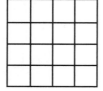

Directions: Find the perimeter and area of each figure.

P = _____
A = _____

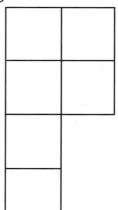

P = _____
A = _____

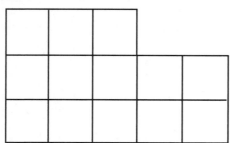

9 Yards

9 Yards

P = _____
A = _____

2 Miles

45 Miles

P = _____
A = _____

Perimeter and Area

Directions: Use the formulas for finding perimeter and area to solve these problems.

Julie's family moved to a new house. Her parents said she could have the largest bedroom. Julie knew she would need to find the area of each room to find which one was largest.

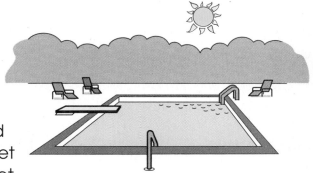

One rectangular bedroom is 7 feet wide and 12 feet long. Another is 11 feet long and 9 feet wide. The third bedroom is a square. It is 9 feet wide and 9 feet long. Which one should she select to have the largest room?

_____

The new home also has a swimming pool in the backyard. It is 32 feet long and 18 feet wide. What is the perimeter of the pool?

_____

Julie's mother wants to plant flowers on each side of the new house. She will need three plants for every foot of space. The house is 75 feet across the front and back and 37.5 feet along each side. Find the perimeter of the house.

_____

How many plants should she buy? _____

The family decided to buy new carpeting for several rooms. Complete the necessary information to determine how much carpeting to buy.

Den: 12 ft. x 14 ft. = _____ sq. ft.

Master Bedroom: 20 ft. x _____ = 360 sq. ft.

Family Room: _____ x 25 ft. = 375 sq. ft.

Total square feet of carpeting: _____

Volume

The formula for finding the **volume** (depth) of a box is length times width times height **(L x W x H).** The answer is given in cubic units.

Directions: Solve the problems.

Example:

Height 8 ft.
Length 8 ft.
Width   8 ft. **L** x **W** x **H** = volume
        8' x 8' x 8' = 512 cubic ft. or 512 ft.^{3}

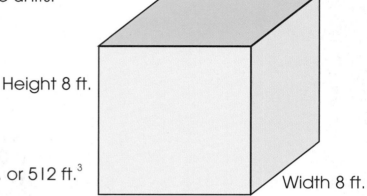

Height 8 ft.

Length 8 ft.

Width 8 ft.

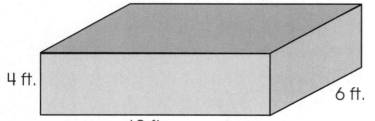

4 ft.

12 ft.

6 ft.

V = _____

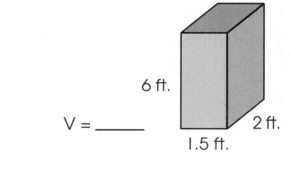

6 ft.

V = _____   2 ft.

1.5 ft.

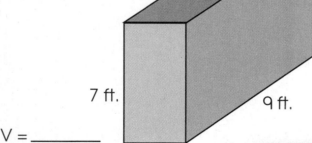

7 ft.

9 ft.

3 ft.

V = _____

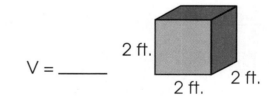

2 ft.

V = _____

2 ft.   2 ft.

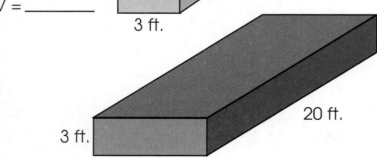

3 ft.

6 ft.

20 ft.

V = _____

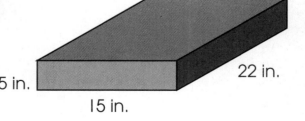

5 in.

15 in.

22 in.

V = _____ in.^{3} V = _____ ft.^{3}

Cut and Paste

What is the area of a parallelogram?
Do this activity and find out.

1. Cut out the parallelogram at the bottom of the page.

2. Cut out the triangle along the dotted line.

3. Slide the triangle to make the parallelogram into a rectangle.

4. Use the formula for the area of a rectangle to find the area of a parallelogram.

Area of a parallelogram = base x height = bh

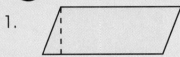

1.

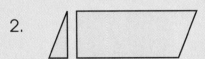

2.

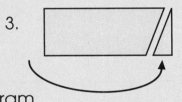

3.

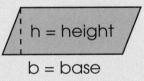

h = height

b = base

Directions: On a separate sheet of paper, draw a parrallelogram with a base of 4 inches and a height of 2 inches. Find the area. _____

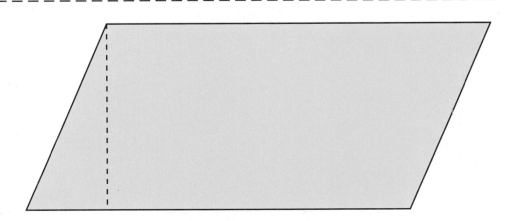

This page was left
intentionally blank.

Perimeter, Area, and Volume

Name _____

Directions: Find the perimeter and area.

1. Length = 8 ft.
   Width   = 11 ft.
   P = _____ A = _____

2. Length = 12 ft.
   Width   = 10 ft.
   P = _____ A = _____

3. Length = 121 ft.
   Width   = 16 ft.
   P = _____ A = _____

4. Length = 72 in.
   Width   = 5 ft.
   P = _____ A = _____

Directions: Find the perimeter, area, and volume.

5. Length = 7 ft.
   Width = 12 ft.
   Height = 10 ft.
   P = _____
   A = _____
   V = _____

7. Length = 12 in.
   Width = 15 in.
   Height = 20 in.
   P = _____
   A = _____
   V = _____

6. Length = 48 in.
   Width = 7 ft.
   Height = 12 in.
   P = _____
   A = _____
   V = _____

8. Length = 22 ft.
   Width = 40 ft.
   Height = 10 ft.
   P = _____
   A = _____
   V = _____

Circumference

Circumference is the distance around a circle. The **diameter** is a line segment that passes through the center of a circle and has both end points on the circle.

To find the circumference of any circle, multiply 3.14 times the diameter. The number 3.14 represents **pi** (pronounced "pie") and is often written by this Greek symbol, π.

The formula for circumference is C = π x d

    C = circumference

    d = diameter

    π = 3.14

Example:

Circle A
d = 2 in.
C = 3.14 x 2 in.
C = 6.28 in.

Directions: Find the circumference of each circle.

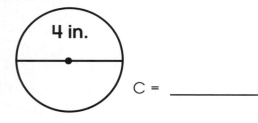

C = _____

C = _____

d = 10 in.
C = _____

d = 14 in.
C = _____

d = 3 yd.
C = _____

d = 4 ft.
C = _____

d = 8 ft.
C = _____

d = 12 ft.
C = _____

Circumference

The **radius** of a circle is the distance from the center of the circle to its outside edge. The diameter equals two times the radius.

Find the circumference by multiplying π (3.14) times the diameter or by multiplying π (3.14) times 2r (2 times the radius).

C = π x d or C = π x 2r

Directions: Write the missing radius, diameter, or circumference.

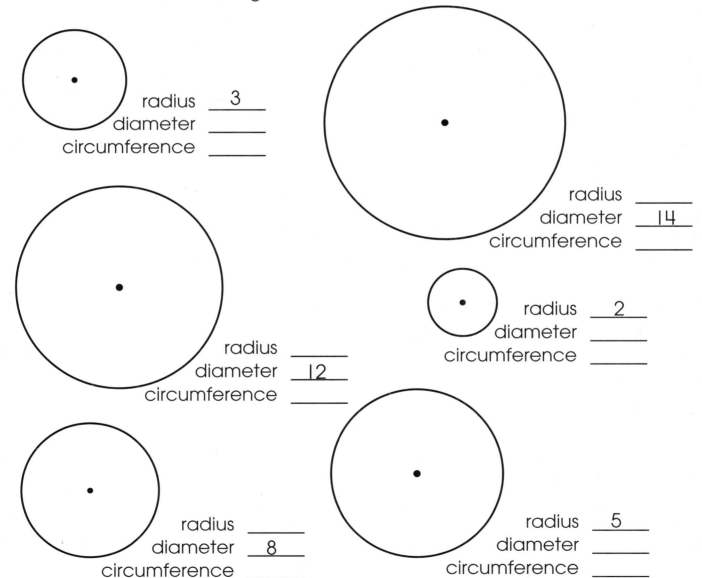

radius ___3___
diameter _____
circumference _____

radius _____
diameter ___14___
circumference _____

radius _____
diameter ___12___
circumference _____

radius ___2___
diameter _____
circumference _____

radius _____
diameter ___8___
circumference _____

radius ___5___
diameter _____
circumference _____

The Circle Game

The perimeter of a circle is called the circumference. There is a formula for finding the circumference of a circle. The formula uses this special number, 3.14. We call this number pi (π). To find the circumference of a circle, use this formula:

Circumference = π x diameter
Circumference = π d

or

Circumference = π x 2 x radius
Circumference = 2πr

Examples:

C = πd   C = 2πr
C = 3.14 x 4   C = 2 x 3.14 x 2
C = 12.56   C = 12.56

Directions: Find the circumference for each circle.

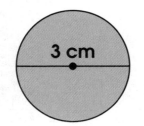

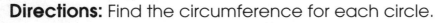

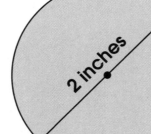

_____

_____

_____

Diameter, Radius, and Circumference

$C = \pi \times d$ or $C = \pi \times 2r$

Directions: Write the missing radius, diameter or circumference.

Katie was asked to draw a circle on the playground for a game during recess. If the radius of the circle needed to be 14 inches, how long is the diameter?

_____

What is the circumference? _____

A friend told her that more kids could play the game if they enlarged the circle. She had a friend help her. They made the diameter of the circle 45 inches long.

What is the radius? _____

What is the circumference? _____

Jamie was creating an art project. He wanted part of it to be a sphere. He measured 24 inches for the diameter.

What would the radius of the sphere be?_____

Find the circumference. _____

Unfortunately, Jamie discovered that he didn't have enough material to create a sphere that large, so he cut the dimensions in half. What are the new dimensions for his sphere?

Radius _____

Diameter _____

Circumference _____

Triangle Angles

A triangle is a figure with three corners and three sides. Every triangle contains three angles. The sum of the angles is always 180°, regardless of the size or shape of the triangle.

If you know two of the angles, you can add them together, then subtract the total from 180 to find the number of degrees in the third angle.

Directions: Find the number of degrees in the third angle of each triangle.

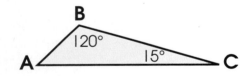

C = _____

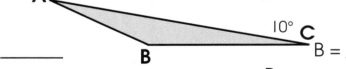

A = _____

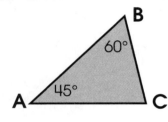

B = _____

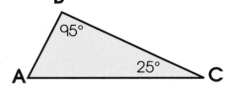

B = _____

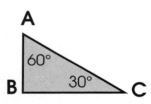

A = _____

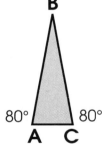

B = _____

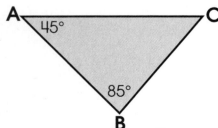

C = _____

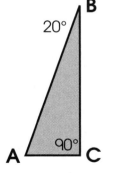

A = _____

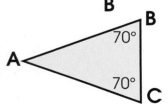

A = _____

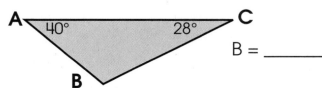

B = _____

Area of a Triangle

The area of a triangle is found by multiplying $\frac{1}{2}$ times the base times the height. $A = \frac{1}{2} \times b \times h$

Example:

$\overline{CD}$ is the height.   4 in.

$\overline{AB}$ is the base.   8 in.

Area $= \frac{1}{2} \times 4 \times 8 = \frac{32}{2} = 16$ sq. in.

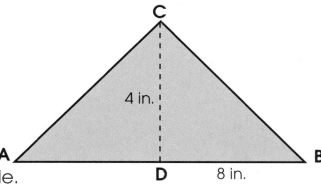

Directions: Find the area of each triangle.

A = _____

A = _____

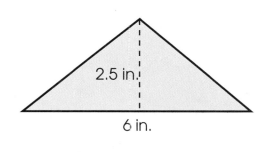

A = _____

A = _____

Name _____

I'm Hungry

Directions: Someone has already found the area for each triangle, but some are incorrect. Check each problem. Connect the problems with correct areas to make a path for the giraffe to the tree. Then, correct each wrong area.

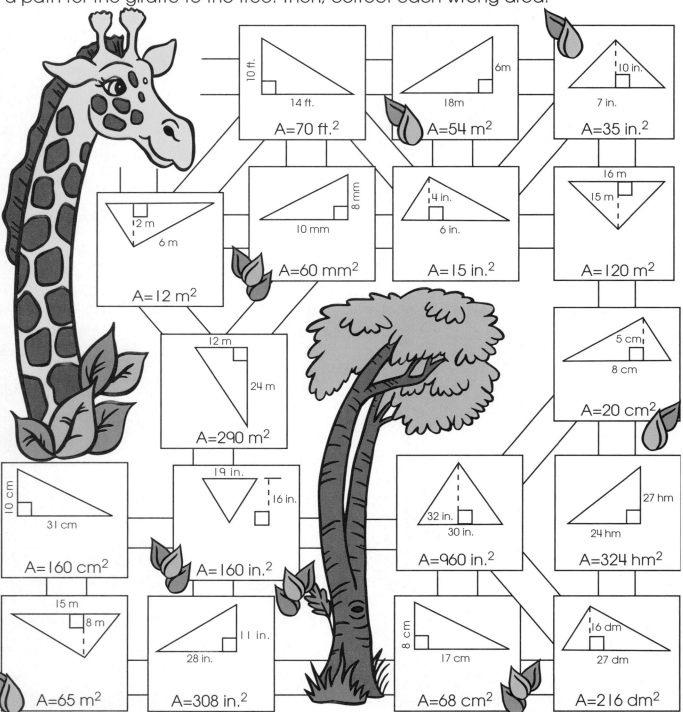

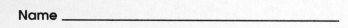

Lines Across a Triangle

Directions: Draw the given number of straight lines to divide each triangle into the shapes listed. The first one has been done for you.

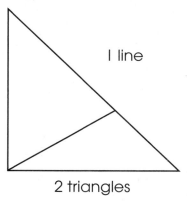

1 line

2 triangles

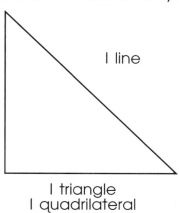

1 line

1 triangle
1 quadrilateral

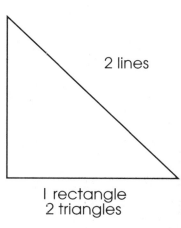

2 lines

1 rectangle
2 triangles

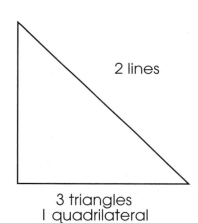

2 lines

3 triangles
1 quadrilateral

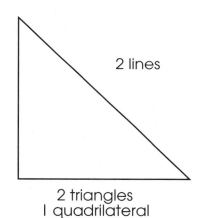

2 lines

2 triangles
1 quadrilateral

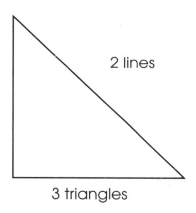

2 lines

3 triangles

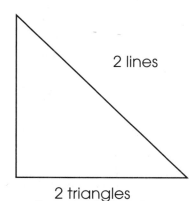

2 lines

2 triangles
2 quadrilaterals

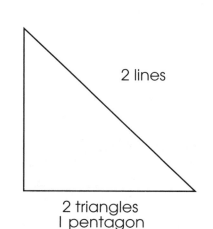

2 lines

2 triangles
1 pentagon

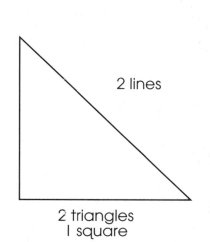

2 lines

2 triangles
1 square

Name _____

Try a Triangle

Directions: A triangle is a three-sided polygon. It has three sides and three angles. Write the number of triangles there are in each drawing.

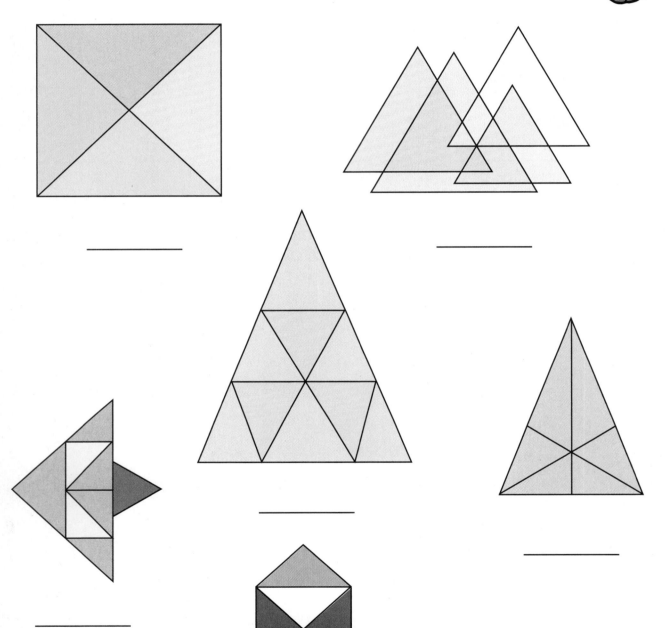

Geometry: Triangles

188

Total Math Grade 5

Space Figures

Space figures are figures whose points are in more than one plane. Cubes and cylinders are space figures.

  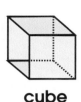 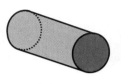

rectangular prism   **cone**   **cube**   **cylinder**   **sphere**   **pyramid**

A **prism** has two identical, parallel bases.

All of the faces on a **rectangular prism** are rectangles.

A **cube** is a prism with six identical, square faces.

A **pyramid** is a space figure whose base is a polygon and whose faces are triangles with a common vertex—the point where two rays meet.

A **cylinder** has a curved surface and two parallel bases that are identical circles.

A **cone** has one circular, flat face and one vertex.

A **sphere** has no flat surface. All points are an equal distance from the center.

Directions: Circle the name of the figure you see in each of these familiar objects.

cone   sphere   cylinder

cone   sphere   cylinder

cube   rectangular prism   pyramid

cone   pyramid   cylinder

A Unit of My Own

Example:

Steps to make a nonstandard ruler:

1. Fold a sheet of paper in half along the longest side. Fold in that direction again, and once again.
2. Unfold the paper. Draw lines and labels like the ones shown here.
3. Name the units after yourself. For example, Julie's ruler measures 8 Julies long.
4. Use the ruler to measure objects in your units.

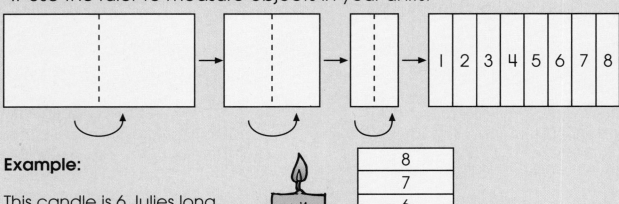

Example:

This candle is 6 Julies long.

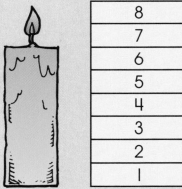

Directions: On another sheet of paper, set up a chart like the one below. Then measure 10 different objects with your ruler and record their lengths.

Object	Length

Standard Length

Standardized units are units that are agreed upon all over the world, so that measurements made in India are the same as measurements made in Iceland, Israel, or Italy. The two main systems are **customary** and **metric.**

Examples:

The customary units for measuring length are **inch (in.), foot (ft.), yard (yd.),** and **mile (mi.).**

A paper clip is about 1 inch long.

A notebook is about 1 foot wide.

A baseball bat is about 1 yard long.

A mile is the distance 4 times around a running track.

Directions: Circle the most reasonable length.

The height of a refrigerator:

      2 inches   2 feet   2 yards   2 miles

The distance from New York to Los Angeles:

      3,000 inches   3,000 feet   3,000 yards   3,000 miles

The width of a butterfly:

      3 inches   3 feet   3 yards   3 miles

The length of a car:

      8 inches   8 feet   8 yards   8 miles

The thickness of a cookie:

      $\frac{1}{4}$ inch $\frac{1}{4}$ foot $\frac{1}{4}$ yard $\frac{1}{4}$ mile

Length

Inches, feet, yards, and miles are used to measure length in the United States.

12 inches = 1 foot (ft.)
3 feet   = 1 yard (yd.)
36 inches = 1 yard
1,760 yards = 1 mile (mi.)

Directions: Circle the best unit to measure each object. The first one has been done for you.

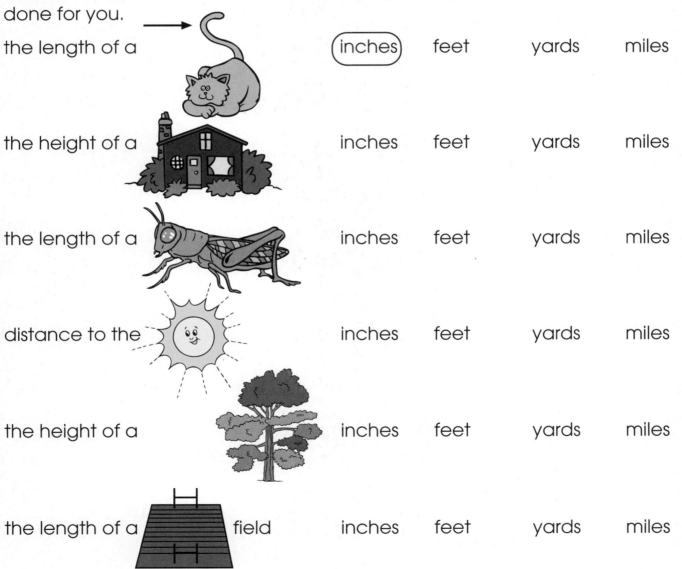

	inches	feet	yards	miles
the length of a	(inches)	feet	yards	miles
the height of a	inches	feet	yards	miles
the length of a	inches	feet	yards	miles
distance to the	inches	feet	yards	miles
the height of a	inches	feet	yards	miles
the length of a ___ field	inches	feet	yards	miles

Name _____

Length

Directions: Use a ruler to find the shortest paths. Round your measurement to the nearest quarter inch. Then convert to yards using the scale.

Scale: 1 inch = 100 yards

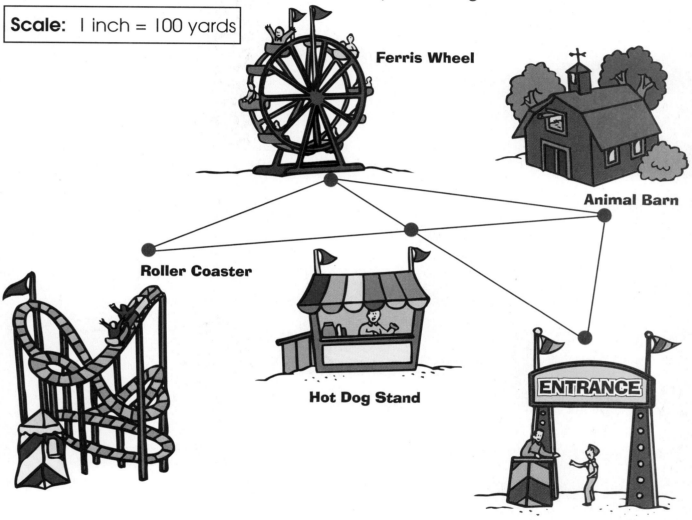

Ferris Wheel

Animal Barn

Roller Coaster

Hot Dog Stand

ENTRANCE

Hot dog stand to the roller coaster . . . _____

The Ferris wheel to the animal barn . . . _____

Entrance to roller coaster . . . _____

Animal barn to hot dog stand . . . _____

Ferris wheel to roller coaster to entrance . . . _____

Measuring Perimeter

Directions: Use a ruler to measure and find the perimeter of each shape. Use inches.

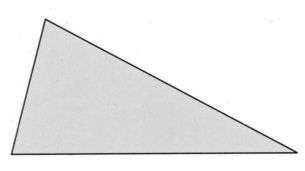

_____

_____

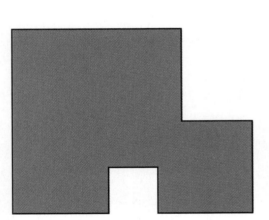

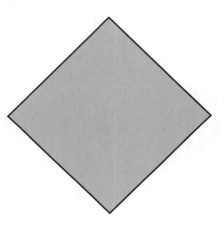

_____

_____

_____

_____

Name _____

Weight

Ounces, pounds, and **tons** are used to measure weight in the United States.

> **16 ounces = 1 pound (lb.)**
>
> **2,000 pounds = 1 ton (tn.)**

Directions: Circle the most reasonable estimate for the weight of each object. The first one has been done for you.

10 ounces	(10 pounds)	10 tons
6 ounces	6 pounds	6 tons
2 ounces	2 pounds	2 tons
3 ounces	3 pounds	3 tons
1,800 ounces	1,800 pounds	1,800 tons
20 ounces	20 pounds	20 tons
1 ounce	1 pound	1 ton

Capacity

The **fluid ounce, cup, pint, quart,** and **gallon** are used to measure capacity in the United States.

| I cup | I pint | I quart | I half gallon | I gallon |

8 fluid ounces (fl. oz.) = I cup (c.)
2 cups = I pint (pt.)
2 pints = I quart (qt.)
2 quarts = I half gallon ($\frac{1}{2}$ gal.)
4 quarts = I gallon (gal.)

Directions: Convert the units of capacity.

13 gal. = ____ qt.   10 pt. = ____ c.   12 c. = ____ pt.

4 gal. = ____ qt.   16 qt. = ____ gal.   5 c. = ____ pt.

36 pt. = ____ gal.   12 qt. = ____ pt.   6 gal. = ____ pt.

16 c. = ____ qt.   32 oz. = ____ c.   16 oz. = ____ pt.

Name _____

Length: Metric

Millimeters, centimeters, meters, and **kilometers** are used to measure length in the metric system.

> **1 meter = 39.37 inches**
> **1 kilometer = about $\frac{5}{8}$ mile**
> **10 millimeters = 1 centimeter (cm)**
> **100 centimeters = 1 meter (m)**
> **1,000 meters = 1 kilometer (km)**

Directions: Circle the best unit to measure each object. The first one has been done for you.

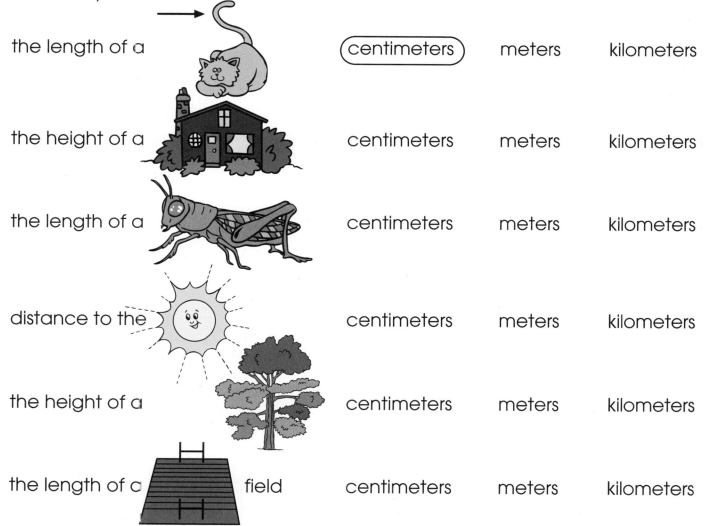

the length of a   (centimeters)   meters   kilometers

the height of a   centimeters   meters   kilometers

the length of a   centimeters   meters   kilometers

distance to the   centimeters   meters   kilometers

the height of a   centimeters   meters   kilometers

the length of a   field   centimeters   meters   kilometers

Name _____

Weight: Metric

Grams and **kilograms** are units of weight in the metric system. A paper clip weighs about 1 gram. A kitten weighs about 1 kilogram.

1 kilogram (kg) = about 2.2 pounds
1,000 grams (g) = 1 kilogram

Directions: Circle the best unit to weigh each object.

kilogram
gram

kilogram
gram

kilogram
gram

kilogram
gram

kilogram
gram

kilogram
gram

kilogram
gram

kilogram
gram

kilogram
gram

kilogram
gram

Capacity: Metric

Milliliters and **liters** are units of capacity in the metric system. A can of soda contains about 350 milliliters of liquid. A large plastic bottle contains 1 liter of liquid. A liter is about a quart.

1,000 milliliters (mL) = 1 liter (L)

Directions: Circle the best unit to measure each liquid.

milliliters
liters

milliliters
liters

milliliters
liters

milliliters
liters

milliliters
liters

milliliters
liters

milliliters
liters

milliliters
liters

milliliters
liters

milliliters
liters

Name _____

Comparing Measurements

Directions: Use the symbols greater than (>), less than (<), or equal to (=) to complete each statement.

10 inches _____ 10 centimeters

40 feet _____ 120 yards

25 grams _____ 25 kilograms

16 quarts _____ 4 gallons

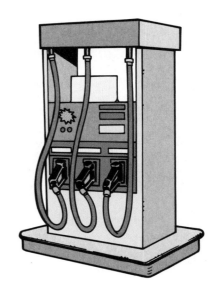

2 liters _____ 2 milliliters

16 yards _____ 6 meters

3 miles _____ 3 kilometers

20 centimeters _____ 20 meters

85 kilograms _____ 8 grams

2 liters _____ 1 gallon

Will It Fit?

1 cup = 8 fluid ounces
1 pint = 2 cups = 16 fluid ounces
1 quart = 2 pints = 4 cups = 32 fluid ounces
1 gallon = 4 quarts = 8 pints = 16 cups = 128 ounces

Directions: Complete the following table.

	fl. ounces	cups	pints	quarts	gallons
1 fl. ounce =	1	$\frac{1}{8}$			
1 cup =		1			
1 pint =			1		
1 quart =				1	
1 gallon =					1

Directions: Write **yes** or **no**.

1. Will 6 cups fit in a 1-quart container? _____

2. Will 8 ounces fit in a 1-cup container? _____

3. Will 16 pints fit in a 2-gallon container? _____

4. Will 3 quarts fit in a 5-pint container? _____

5. Will 64 ounces fit in a $\frac{1}{2}$-gallon container? _____

6. Will 18 cups fit in an 8-pint container? _____

7. Will 12 quarts fit in a 4-gallon container? _____

8. Will 8 gallons fit in a 16-quart container? _____

Weights and Measures

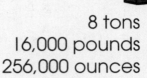

Example:

8 tons
16,000 pounds
256,000 ounces

1 pound = 16 ounces
1 ton = 2,000 pounds = 32,000 ounces

Steps to convert one customary unit of weight to another:

Multiply to change a larger unit to a smaller one.

3 pounds = _____ ounces
3 pounds x 16 = 48 ounces

Divide to change a smaller unit to a larger one.

10,000 pounds = _____ tons
10,000 pounds ÷ 2000 = 5 tons

Directions: Change each measurement to tons.

6,000 pounds _____   192,000 ounces _____   14,000 pounds _____

9,000 pounds _____   128,000 ounces _____   1,000 pounds _____

Directions: Change each measurement to pounds.

5 tons _____   160 ounces _____ $3\frac{1}{2}$ tons _____

192 ounces _____   2,160 ounces _____   92 ounces _____

Directions: Change each measurement to ounces.

8 pounds _____   4.5 pounds _____   2 tons _____

43 pounds _____   0.6 tons _____   101 pounds _____

Renaming Lengths

Example:

4 miles
7,040 yards
21,120 feet
253,440 inches

1 foot = 12 inches
1 yard = 3 feet = 36 inches
1 mile = 5,280 feet = 1,760 yards = 63,360 inches

Steps to convert, or change, one customary unit of length to another:

Multiply to change a larger unit to a smaller one.

8 yards = _____ feet
8 yards x 3 = 24 feet

Divide to change a smaller unit to a larger one.

36 inches = _____ feet
36 inches ÷ 12 = 3 feet

Directions: Find the missing number in each problem.

4 feet = _____ inches   144 inches = _____ feet   237 yards = _____ inches

78 yards = _____ feet   3 miles = _____ yards   180 inches = _____ yards

2 miles = _____ yards   6 yards = _____ inches   10,560 feet = _____ miles

10 yards = _____ inches   8,800 yards = _____ miles   30 feet = _____ yards

72 feet = _____ yards   360 inches = _____ yards   5,280 yards = _____ miles

7 miles = _____ feet   18 inches = _____ feet   45 yards = _____ feet

Measurement Review

Directions: Write the best unit to measure each item: inch, foot, yard, mile, ounce, pound, ton, fluid ounce, cup, pint, quart, or gallon.

distance from New York to Chicago _____

weight of a goldfish _____

height of a building _____

water in a large fish tank _____

glass of milk _____

weight of a whale _____

length of a pencil _____

distance from first base to second base _____

distance traveled by a space shuttle _____

length of a soccer field _____

amount of paint needed to cover a house _____

material needed to make a dress _____

Temperature: Fahrenheit

Degrees **Fahrenheit** (°F) is a unit for measuring temperature.

Directions: Write the temperature in degrees Fahrenheit (°F).

Example:

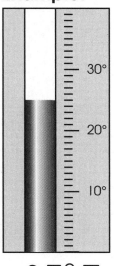

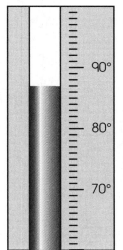

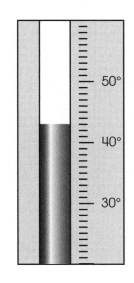

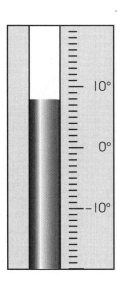

25°F

_____

_____

_____

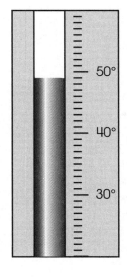

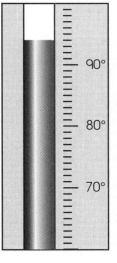

_____

_____

_____

_____

Temperature: Celsius

Degrees **Celsius** (°C) is a unit for measuring temperature in the metric system.

Directions: Write the temperature in degrees Celsius (°C).

Example:

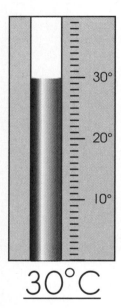

30°C

_____

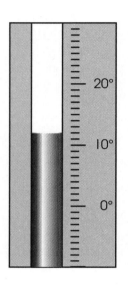

_____

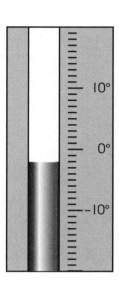

_____

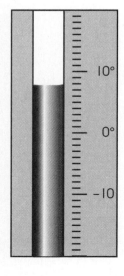

_____

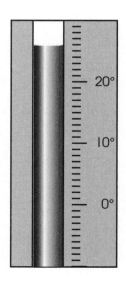

_____

_____

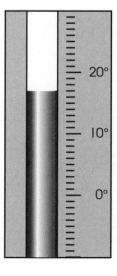

_____

Temperature

The customary unit of temperature is the degree Fahrenheit (°F). A thermometer is used to measure temperature.

Examples:

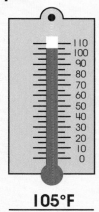 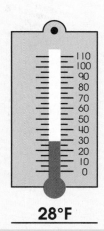 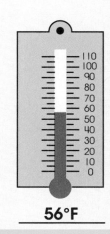 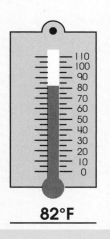

| 105°F | 28°F | 56°F | 82°F |

Directions: Write the temperature shown on each thermometer.

 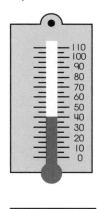  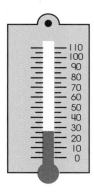

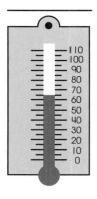 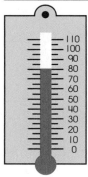 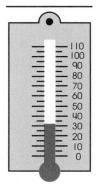 

Name _____

Heat Wave

Example:

Water freezes at 32°F. It boils at 212°F.

30°F is cold   70°F is warm
50°F is cool   90°F is hot

Directions: Circle the most reasonable temperature for each item. The first one is done for you.

hot cocoa	30°F	70°F	(180°F)	300°F
snowy day	–60°F	10°F	65°F	80°F
iced tea	0°F	10°F	20°F	40°F
swimming pool	40°F	75°F	110°F	145°F
inside a refrigerator	45°F	60°F	75°F	90°F
room temperature	25°F	45°F	70°F	212°F
the air on a hot day	20°F	32°F	55°F	90°F
body temperature	60°F	80°F	100°F	120°F
top of a ski mountain	0°F	50°F	100°F	150°F
oven for baking cookies	75°F	200°F	350°F	500°F
spring day in Ohio	20°F	40°F	60°F	90°F
highest recorded shade temperature on Earth	95°F	100°F	135°F	180°F

Name _____

Metric Temperature

The metric unit of temperature is the degree Celsius (°C). A thermometer is used to measure temperature.

Example:

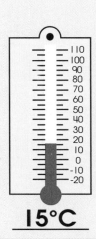 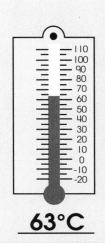 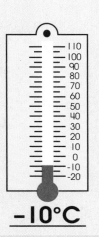

0°C **15°C** **63°C** **–10°C**

Directions: Write the temperature shown on each thermometer.

 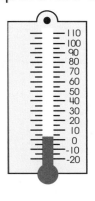 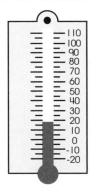 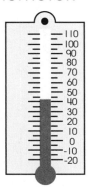

_____ _____ _____ _____

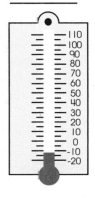 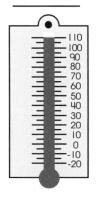 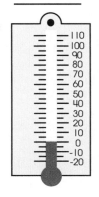 

_____ _____ _____ _____

Name _____

Blowing Hot and Cold

Water freezes at 0°C. It boils at 100°C.

0°C is cold.
10°C is cool.
20°C is warm.
30°C is hot.

Directions: Circle the most reasonable temperature.

soup	10°C	20°C	(85°C)	110°C
snowy day	–30°C	0°C	30°C	60°C
iced tea	–10°C	10°C	30°C	40°C
swimming pool	15°C	25°C	35°C	45°C
inside a refrigerator	5°C	15°C	20°C	25°C
room temperature	10°C	15°C	20°C	25°C
the air on a hot day	10°C	15°C	20°C	25°C
body temperature	20°C	25°C	30°C	35°C
top of a ski mountain	–100°C	–10°C	20°C	30°C
oven for baking cookies	160°C	300°C	350°C	1,000°C
a spring day in Ohio	–10°C	–5°C	5°C	15°C
average July temperature in Texas	10°C	20°C	35°C	60°C

Temperature Change

This equation shows how Celsius and Fahrenheit are related.

°F = 1.8 x °C + 32

Examples:

Steps to find the Fahrenheit temperature, given a Celsius temperature:

1. Multiply by 1.8.
2. Add 32°.

    15°C = _____°F
    (15 x 1.8) + 32 = 27 + 32 = 59°F

Steps to find Celsius temperature, given a Fahrenheit temperature:

1. Subtract 32.
2. Divide by 1.8.

    50°F = _____°C
    (50 – 32) ÷ 1.8 = 18 ÷ 1.8 = 10°C

°F   °C
212 —— —— 100
194 —— —— 90
176 —— —— 80
158 —— —— 70
140 —— —— 60
122 —— —— 50
104 —— —— 40
86 —— —— 30
68 —— —— 20
50 —— —— 10
32 —— —— 0
–1 —— —— –10
–2 —— —— –20

Directions: The Safe and Sound Bank sign showed these pairs of temperatures. If the pairs of temperatures are equal, circle them. If not, find the correct Fahrenheit temperature.

0°C   32°F _____   14°F   –10°C_____   25°C   77°F _____

58°F   15°C _____   5°C   41°F _____   40.5°F   10°C _____

20°C   68°F _____   12°C   53.6°F_____   44.6°F   7°C _____

–3°C   26.6°F_____   14°C   53°F _____   71.6°F   22°C _____

Graphs

A **graph** is a drawing that shows information about changes in numbers.

Directions: Use the graph to answer the questions.

Line Graph   **Temperatures for 1 Year**

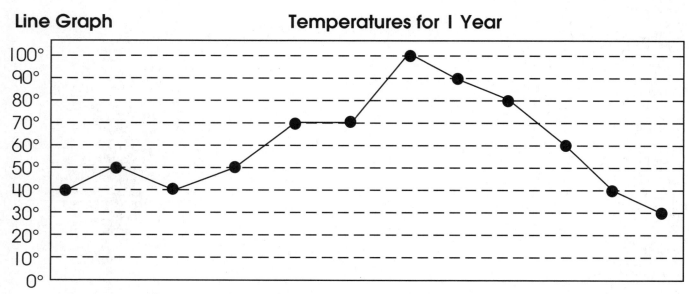

Which month was the coldest?   _____
Which month was the warmest?   _____
Which three months were 40 degrees?   _____
How much warmer was it in May than October? _____

Bar Graph

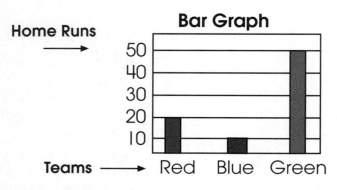

How many home runs did the Green team hit? _____

How many more home runs did the Green team
hit than the Red team and Blue team combined? _____

Graphs

Directions: Read each graph and follow the directions.

List the names of the students from the shortest to the tallest.

1. _____   4. _____

2. _____   5. _____

3. _____   6. _____

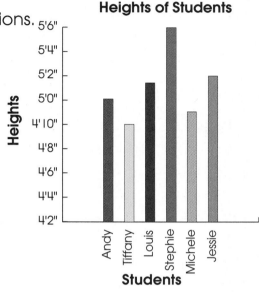

Heights of Students

Lunches Bought

List how many lunches the students bought each day, from the day the most were bought to the least.

1. _____   4. _____

2. _____   5. _____

3. _____

List the months in the order of the most number of outside recesses to the least number.

1. _____   6. _____

2. _____   7. _____

3. _____   8. _____

4. _____   9. _____

5. _____   10. _____

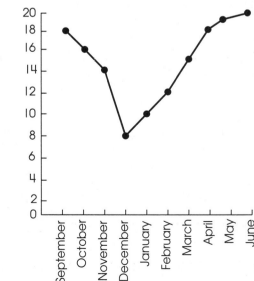

Days of Outside Recess

Graphs

Directions: Complete the graph using the information in the table.

Student	Books Read in February
Sue	20
Joe	8
Peter	12
Cindy	16
Dean	15
Carol	8

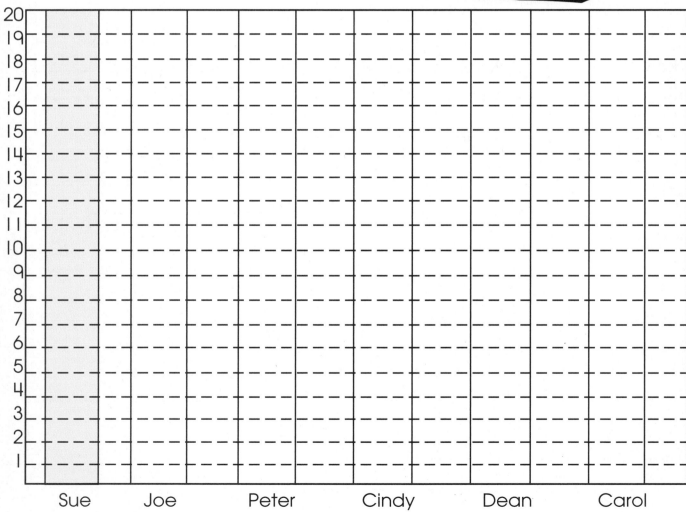

Locating Points on a Grid

To locate points on a grid, read the first coordinate and follow it to the second coordinate.

Example: C, 3

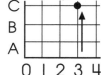

Directions: Maya is new in town. Help her learn the way around her new neighborhood. Place the following locations on the grid below.

Grocery	C, 10
Home	B, 2
School	A, 12
Playground	B, 13
Library	D, 6
Bank	G, 1
Post Office	E, 7
Ice-Cream Shop	D, 3

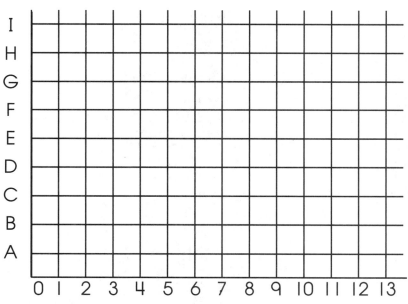

Is her home closer to the bank or the grocery? _____

Does she pass the playground on her way to school? _____

If she needs to stop at the library after school, will she be closer to home or farther away? _____

Name _____

Dog and Jog Graphs

Directions: Answer the questions using the graphs indicated.

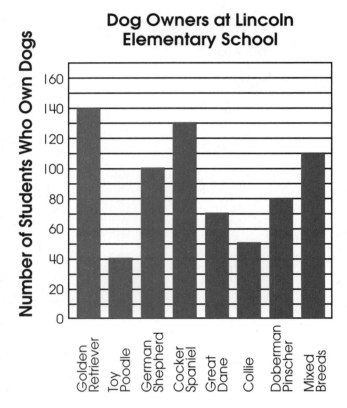

Dog Owners at Lincoln Elementary School

Number of Students Who Own Dogs

Golden Retriever, Toy Poodle, German Shepherd, Cocker Spaniel, Great Dane, Collie, Doberman Pinscher, Mixed Breeds

1. How many students own Great Danes at Lincoln Elementary School? _____

2. Which breed of dog is owned by the fewest students? _____

3. Which breed is owned by the most students? _____

4. How many students own Doberman pinschers? _____

5. How many more students own German shepherds than collies?

_____

1. What class jogged the most during a one-week period? _____

2. Which class jogged the most miles during this four-week period? _____ What was the difference between classes? _____

3. Which week had the greatest range between the two classes? _____

4. Which week had the smallest range? _____

5. What was the range for Mr. Halverson's class during these four weeks?

_____

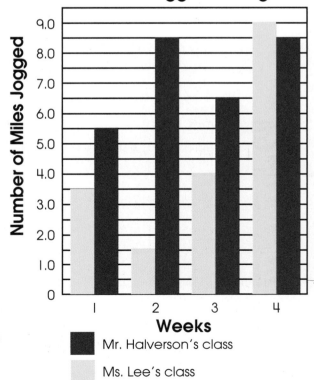

Distance Jogged During P.E.

Number of Miles Jogged

Weeks

■ Mr. Halverson's class

□ Ms. Lee's class

Circle Graph

Ned earns an allowance of $10.00 each week. He created this circle graph on his computer to show his parents how he spends the money.

Directions: Refer to the graph to answer each question below.

Ned's Allowance

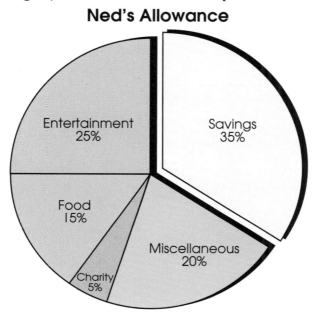

1. Ned highlighted the savings segment of the circle graph because his family believes that having a savings account is very important.
    If Ned saves $3.50 each week, how much will he have left for other things?

    _____

2. Ned spends all of his entertainment allowance on movies. How much does he spend each week on movies?

    _____

3. How much does Ned spend each week on miscellaneous expenses? Name some things he might buy which would fall into this category.

    _____

4. If you have an allowance, create your own circle graph detailing your spending habits. If you don't have an allowance, write two sentences describing how you would spend $10.00 differently than Ned.

    _____

    _____

Summer Fun

A **pictograph** uses pictures to show information.

Example:

Favorite Summer Activities	
Pool	🏐 🏐
Beach	🏐 🏐 ◗
Sports	🏐 🏐 🏐 🏐 🏐
Picnic	🏐

Key: 1 🏐 = 2 people

Directions: Use this pictograph to answer the questions.

1. What is this graph about? _____

2. How many people does each 🏐 represent? _____

3. How many people like sports best? _____

4. How many people like the beach best? _____

5. Which activity is the least popular? _____

6. How many more people like the beach than the pool? _____

7. How many more people like the pool than a picnic? _____

8. How many people in all were asked about their favorite activities? _____

Making Pictographs

Example:
Steps to use data, or information, to make a pictograph:

1. Choose a picture for the graph.
2. Decide how many people each will represent. Since many of the numbers are divisible by 4, let each ☺ = 4 people.
3. Divide to find how many ☺ are needed for each category.
    Examples: $16 ÷ 4 = 4$; $10 ÷ 4 = 2\frac{1}{2}$
4. Draw the graph. Add a title and a key.

Club Members	
Soccer	16
French	12
Science	10
Band	20

Club Members	
Soccer	☺☺☺☺
French	☺☺☺
Science	☺☺◖
Band	☺☺☺☺☺

Key: ☺ = 4 people

Directions: Use the data to make a pictograph. Add a key.

Baseball Team Wins	
April	2
May	8
June	8
July	12
August	6

Baseball Team Wins	
April	
May	
June	
July	
August	

Key:

Bar Graphs

Bar graphs use bars to show information. They are good for showing information that can be easily counted.

Example:

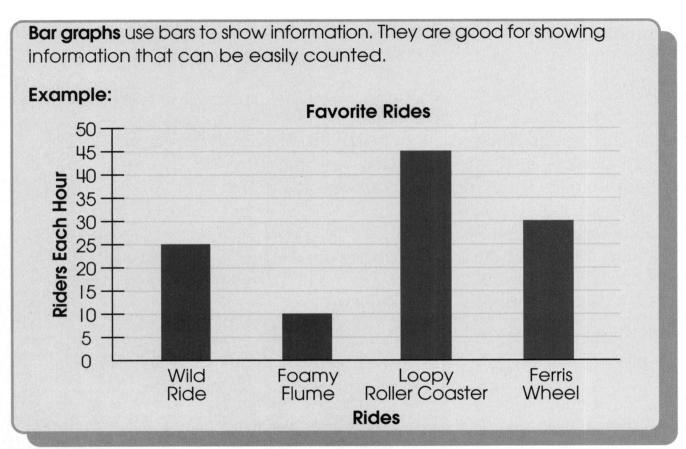

Directions: Use the bar graph to answer the questions.

1. What is this graph about? _____

2. How many rides are included in the graph? _____

3. How many rode the Wild Ride in one hour? _____

4. How many rode the Foamy Flume in one hour? _____

5. Which ride is the most popular? _____

6. How many more rode the Ferris Wheel than the Wild Ride? _____

7. How many more rode the Loopy Roller Coaster than the Foamy Flume?_____

8. How many altogether rode the rides in one hour? _____

Name _____

Making Bar Graphs

Example:

Steps to use data to make a bar graph:

1. Choose how to space the numbers. Since the numbers are large multiples of 10, use 10. (5 would also work, but the graph would be much taller.)
2. Label both sides of the graph.
3. Draw the bars and add a title.

Park Visitors	
Reston State Park	110
Brambell Reservoir	50
Fallen Oak Campground	90
Granger Trail	40

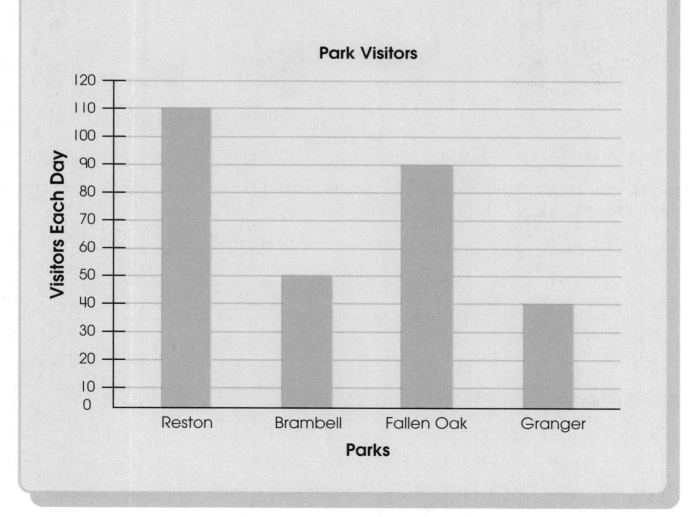

Double Bar Graphs

Double bar graphs use different colored bars to compare two sets of data. They are similar to bar graphs, and they include a key to show what the different bars mean.

Example:

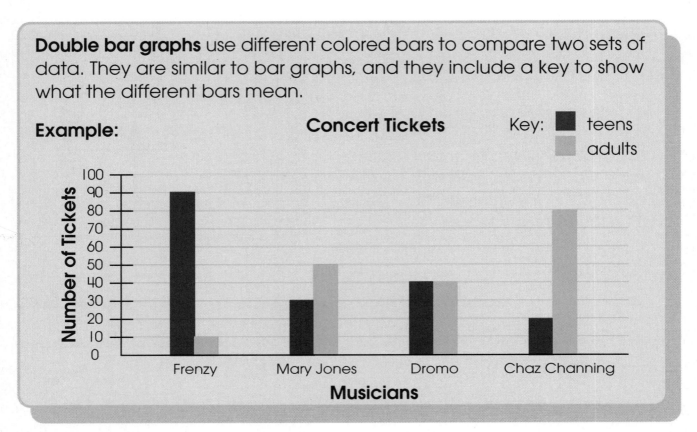

Concert Tickets

Key: ■ teens
     ▨ adults

Directions: On another sheet of paper, use the data to make a double bar graph. Then, answer the questions.

1. How many more sixth graders play baseball than fifth graders? _____

2. Which group is the largest? _____
   How does the graph show this? _____
   _____

3. Which sport has an equal number of fifth and sixth graders? _____ How does the graph show this? _____
   _____

4. How many people play baseball altogether? _____

Number of Members		
	Grade 5	Grade 6
Baseball	12	16
Soccer	20	14
Tennis	8	8

Pie in the Sky

A **circle graph,** or pie chart, shows how parts relate to a whole. It makes it easy to see the data quickly.

Example:

This graph shows that pepperoni was the most popular topping.

Favorite Pizza Toppings

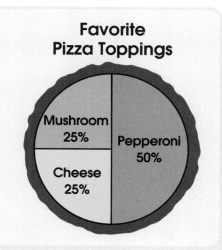

Favorite Pizza Toppings

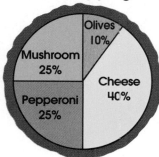

Directions: Use the circle graphs to answer the questions.

1. What percent of people like cheese best? _____

2. What is the least popular topping? _____

3. Which toppings are equally popular? _____

4. What percent of people like cheese or olives best?

    _____

Favorite Pizza Toppings

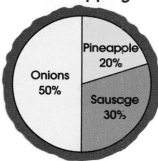

1. Which topping is the most popular? _____

2. What percent of people like sausage more than pineapple?

    _____

3. If 2 people like pineapple, how many people like onion?

    _____

4. If 4 people like pineapple, how many people voted in all?

    _____

Color Wheels

Example:

Steps to use data to make a circle graph:

Favorite Colors	
Red	1
Green	4
Purple	10
Yellow	5

1. Find the total: 20.

2. Find what percent of the total each part is.

$1 \div 20 = 0.05 = 5\%$
$4 \div 20 = 0.20 = 20\%$
$10 \div 20 = 0.20 = 50\%$
$5 \div 20 = 0.25 = 25\%$

3. Divide the circle into the different parts.

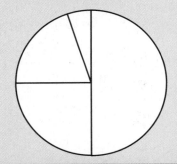

4. Label the graph and give it a title.

Favorite Colors

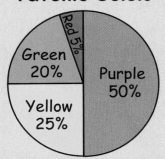

Directions: Use the data to make your own circle graphs.

Favorite Colors	
Red	6
Green	3
Blue	3

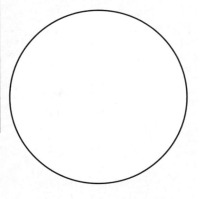

Favorite Ice Cream Flavors	
Rocky Road	8
Cherry	2
Cookie Dough	30

Braille Numbers

A **number line** is a simple kind of graph.
It shows how numbers are ordered.

Example:

This number line shows the numbers 0 to 9.

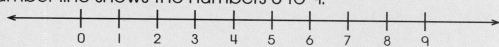

Blind people can read letters and numbers by touching raised dots on paper. The dots are formed into patterns on a 2 x 3 grid. This system of raised dots is called Braille.

Braille symbols for the numbers and the comma:

, =   1 =   2 =   3 =

4 =   5 =   6 =   7 =

8 =   9 =   0 =

These symbols can be combined to write any number.

Example: 39

Example: 1,276

Directions: Write the number for each of these Braille numerals.

Total Math Grade 5

225

Graphs and Charts

Line Graphs

A **line graph** is a good way to show data that changes over time. This graph shows the company sales for Wacky Water Slides from 1994 to 2001.

Example:

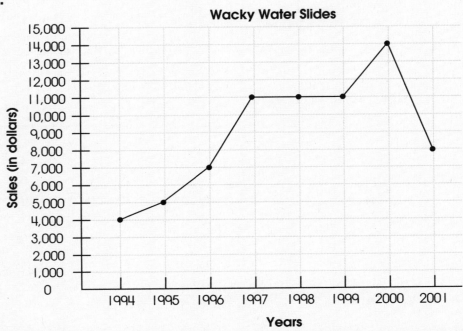

Directions: Use the line graph to answer the questions.

1. How many years are covered in the graph? _____

2. How much did the company earn in 1996? _____

3. During which year did the company earn $8,000? _____

4. What was the most money the company ever earned? In what year did this happen? _____

5. How much more did the company earn in 1997 than 1994? _____

6. During which years did sales increase? How does the graph show this? _____
   _____

7. During which years did sales stay the same? How does the graph show this?
   _____

Hot and Cold

Directions: Use the data to make line graphs. Remember to include titles. Use abbreviations for the days and months.

Temperatures Week of March 7

Day	Temperature
Sunday	11°C
Monday	12°C
Tuesday	8°C
Wednesday	9°C
Thursday	8°C
Friday	10°C
Saturday	12°C

High Temperatures

Day	Temperature
January 1	6°C
February 1	4°C
March 1	10°C
April 1	16°C
May 1	16°C
June 1	23°C
July 1	27°C
August 1	27°C
September 1	23°C
October 1	20°C
November 1	14°C
December 1	9°C

Surveys

A **survey** is a way to collect data by asking people questions.

Directions: Follow these steps to conduct your own survey:

1. Decide what question to ask.

   _____

   _____

2. Decide who will be surveyed.

   _____

   _____

3. Do the survey and record the data. (In other words, ask lots of people your question, and write down what each person says.)

Surveys

Directions: Show the results of your survey by summarizing your data.

4. Choose a kind of graph to show the data, then make the graph.

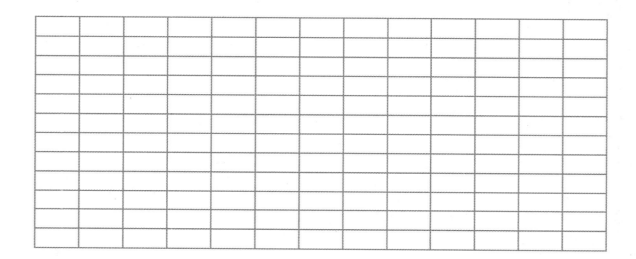

Circle Graph

5. Explain the results.

_____

_____

_____

Tree Diagrams

A **tree diagram** shows the possible results of a group of events. It is very helpful in organizing probabilities and combinations.

Example:

A candy company offers white, milk, and dark chocolate candy shells with raspberry or caramel fillings. How many different candies do they make and what are they?

Shells	Fillings	Combinations
	R	White/Raspberry
W	C	White/Caramel
	R	Milk/Raspberry
M	C	Milk/Caramel
	R	Dark/Raspberry
D	C	Dark/Caramel

Directions: On another sheet of paper, make a tree diagram to answer each question.

1. List all the possible outcomes of flipping a coin and rolling one die. (Hint: There are 12 possible outcomes.)

2. Tuna, turkey, and egg salad sandwiches can be made on white, wheat, or rye bread. List all the possible combinations.

3. Roma's makes pizzas in 3 sizes—small, medium, and large. They come in red (with sauce) or white (without). Each pizza can be made with regular or Sicilian crust. How many different ways can the pizzas be made? What are they?

Name _____

Pennies From Heaven

Directions: On another sheet of paper, make a tree diagram to answer each question.

1. List all the combinations of heads and tails that are possible from flipping 1 penny. How many possible outcomes are there? _____

2. List all the combinations of heads and tails that are possible from flipping 2 pennies. How many possible outcomes are there? _____

3. List all the combinations of heads and tails that are possible from flipping 3 pennies. How many possible outcomes are there? _____

4. List all the combinations of heads and tails that are possible from flipping 4 pennies. How many possible outcomes are there? _____

5. List all the combinations of heads and tails that are possible from flipping 5 pennies. How many possible outcomes are there? _____

Is there a pattern? If so, write it. _____

_____

6. Find:

$2^1 =$ _____ $2^2 =$ _____ $2^3 =$ _____ $2^4 =$ _____ $2^5 =$ _____

How are the solutions to the exponents related to the results above?

_____

_____

Use the pattern, not a tree diagram, to find the number of possible outcomes from flipping 10 pennies.

_____

Name _____

Coordinate Graphs

Coordinate graphs are line graphs that use ordered pairs to name the points. An **ordered pair** tells how many units to the right and up from the origin a point is located. It is written like this:

Example: (2, 1)

Move this many units to the right. ↗ ↖ Move this many units up.

Example: Plot the point (4, 3).
What is the location of point H?
Point H is located at (2, 5).

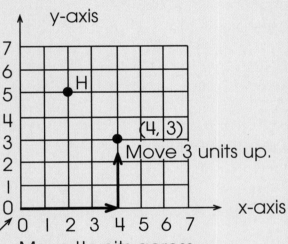

(0, 0) is the origin   Move 4 units across.

Directions: Plot and label the ordered pairs.

G (2, 3)
N (4, 0)
Q (5, 1)
E (0, 3)
L (0, 0)

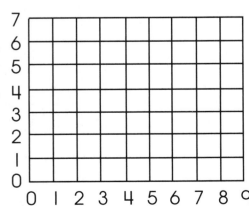

Name the ordered pair for each point.

K _____

R _____

C _____

A _____

M _____

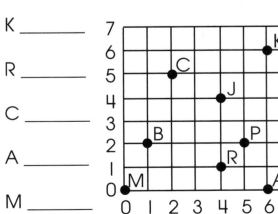

Graph Shapes

Example:

These four ordered pairs form a rectangle.

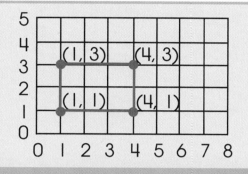

Directions: Plot the ordered pairs. Name the shape created.

(3, 2); (5, 2); (3, 4); (5, 4)

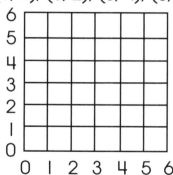

_____

(4, 1); (2, 6); (0, 4); (4, 4); (0, 1)

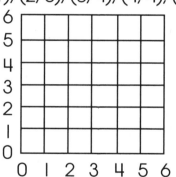

_____

(0, 0); (6, 0); (3, 3)

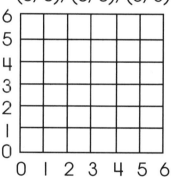

_____

Directions: Plot and list a group of ordered pairs that makes each shape.

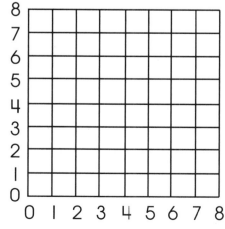

Rectangle

_____

Parallelogram

_____

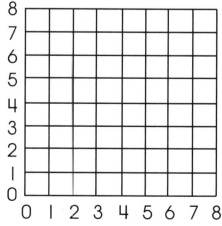

Scalene Triangle

_____

Flying Experiment

Example:

Sally and Frank did an experiment with their flying disks. They threw disks of different sizes and measured how far they flew.

Disk Diameter (inches)	Distance (feet)
5	6
6	10
8	12
9	12
10	16

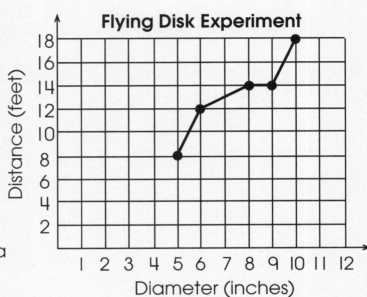

Steps to use data to make a coordinate graph:

1. Draw and label the grid.
2. Plot the ordered pairs.
3. Connect the points with straight lines and add a title.

Directions: Graph the data.

Tomato Plant Growth

Day	Height (inches)
1	0
2	0
3	1
4	1
6	2
7	4
9	7

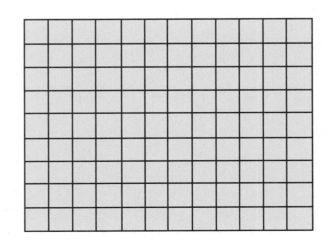

The Four Corners

Using negative numbers extends the coordinate graph into 4 quadrants, or sections. A positive number means move right or up. A negative number means move left or down.

Example:

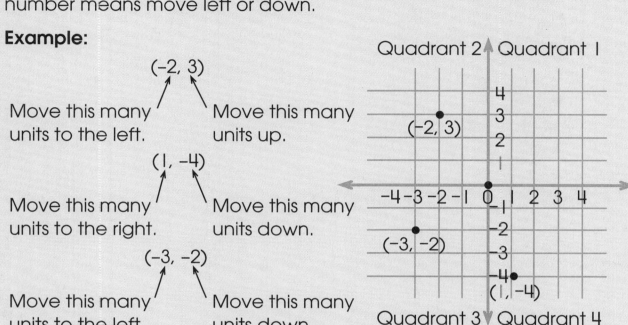

(-2, 3)

Move this many units to the left.

Move this many units up.

(1, -4)

Move this many units to the right.

Move this many units down.

(-3, -2)

Move this many units to the left.

Move this many units down.

Directions: Play this game with a friend.

Rules:
1. Write the numbers 0, 1, 2, 3, 4, 5, -1, -2, -3, -4, -5 on index cards, one number for each card.
2. Put the cards in a paper bag.
3. Use the grid as a gameboard.
4. The first player draws one card from the bag. Use this number as the first number of an ordered pair. Return the card to the bag and draw another card. That number is the second number of the ordered pair. Plot the point and label it with your initials.
5. Take turns. The first player to plot an ordered pair in each quadrant wins.

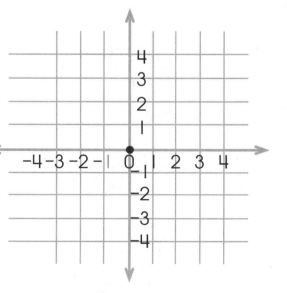

What's My Line?

Example:

A line on a graph can represent an equation. The table on the left lists some possible values for x and y in the equation y = 2x + 1. Each ordered pair is plotted and the points are joined to form a line.

Example: y = 2x + 1

x	y
–2	–3
–1	–1
0	1
1	3
2	5
___	___

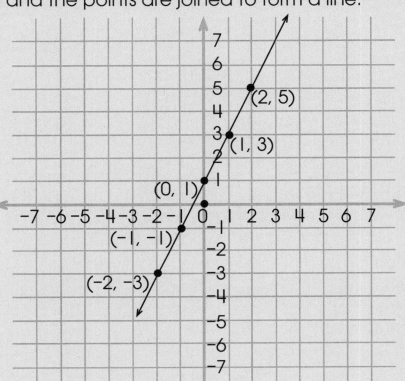

Directions: Study this graph.
In the chart, fill in the next ordered pair for quadrant 1, and then plot the point on the graph.

Glossary

Addition: The process of "putting together" two or more numbers to find the sum.

Angle: The shape formed by two rays with the same end point.

Area: The number of square units in a figure.

Bar Graph: A type of graph that uses bars to display the data.

Calculator: A machine that rapidly does addition, subtraction, multiplication, division, and other mathematical functions.

Celsius: A measurement of temperature in the metric system using units called *degrees Celsius.*

Centimeter (cm): A metric measurement of length equal to $\frac{1}{100}$ of a meter. There are 2.54 centimeters in an inch.

Circle Graph: A graph that show data as parts of a circle.

Circumference: The distance around a circle.

Cone: A space figure having one circular surface, one flat face, and one vertex.

Congruent Figures: Figures having identical shapes but different orientations, that is, facing in different directions.

Coordinate Graph: A graph that uses ordered pairs to name the points.

Cube: A space figure with six square faces.

Cup (c.): A measurement of capacity equal to 8 fluid ounces.

Cylinder: A space figure with a curved surface and two parallel bases that are identical circles.

Decimal: A number with one or more places to the right of a decimal point, such as 6.5 or 2.25.

Degree: The unit used to measure angles.

Denominator: The number below the fraction bar in a fraction.

Diameter: A line segment that passes through the center of a circle and has both end points on the circle.

Dividend: The number that is divided by another number (the divisor) in a division problem. In the problem 28 ÷ 7 = 4, 28 is the dividend.

Division: The process of dividing a number into equal groups of smaller numbers.

Divisor: The number by which another number (the dividend) is divided in a division problem. In the problem 28 − 7 = 4, 7 is the divisor.

Double Bar Graph: A bar graph that compares two related sets of data.

Estimate: To give an approximate rather than an exact answer.

Exponent: A number that tells how many times a base is to be multiplied.

Factor Tree: It shows the prime factors of a number

Factors: The numbers multiplied together to give a product.

Fahrenheit: A measurement of temperature using units called *degrees Fahrenheit.*

Fluid Ounce (fl. oz.): A measure of capacity equal to $\frac{1}{8}$ of a cup.

Foot (ft.): A measurement of length equal to 12 inches.

Fraction: A number that names part of a whole. It is usually shown as one number (the part) above a second number (the whole), with a horizontal line between. Examples: $\frac{1}{2}$ and $\frac{1}{4}$

Gallon (gal.): A measurement of capacity equal to 4 quarts.

Geometry: The branch of mathematics that has to do with points, lines, and shapes.

Gram (g): A metric measurement of weight. 1,000 grams = 1 kilogram.

Graph: A drawing that shows information about changes in numbers.

Greatest Common Factor (GCF): The largest number that is a factor of every number in a given set of numbers. Example: The greatest common factor of 9, 15, and 27 is 3 (3 x 3 = 9, 3 x 5 = 15, and 3 x 9 = 27), while the GCF of 9, 15, and 25 is 1.

Improper Fraction: A fraction in which the numerator is greater than its denominator.

Inch: A measurement of length. 12 inches = 1 foot.

Integer: Any positive or negative whole number, or zero.

Kilogram (kg): A metric measurement of weight equal to 1,000 grams. 1 kilogram = about 2.2 pounds.

Kilometer (km): A metric measure of distance equal to 1,000 meters or about 5/8 mile.

Least Common Denominator (LCD): The least common multiple of the denominators in a given set of fractions.

Least Common Multiple (LCM): The smallest number other than 0 that is a multiple of each number in a given set of more numbers. Example: The least common multiple of 3, 5, and 6 is 30 (3 x 10, 5 x 6, 6 x 5).

Like Fractions: Fractions with the same denominator, or bottom number.

Line: A collection of points on a straight path that goes on and on in opposite directions.

Line Graph: A graph that uses connected line segments to show how the data changes.

Line Segment: A line that has two endpoints.

Liter (L): A metric measurement of capacity equal to about 1 quart.

Mean: A type of average found by adding all of the data and dividing by the number of addends.

Median: A type of average found by ordering numbers in a set of data and finding the middle number.

Meter (m): A metric measurement of length equal to 39.37 inches.

Metric System: A standard system of units based on the number 10.

Mile (mi.): A measurement of distance equal to 1,760 yards.

Milliliter (mL): A metric measurement of capacity. 1,000 milliliters = 1 liter.

Millimeter (mm): A metric measurement of length equal to 1/1000 of a meter. 10 millimeters = 1 centimeter.

Mixed Number: A number written as a whole number and a fraction.

Mode: A type of average that selects the most common number in the data.

Multiple: The product of a specific number and any other number.
Example: The multiples of 2 are 2 (2 x 1), 4 (2 x 2), 6, 8, 10, 12, and so on.

Multiplication: The process of quick addition of a number a certain number of times.

Number Line: A simple kind of graph that shows how numbers are ordered.

Numerator: The number above the fraction bar in a fraction.

Ounce (oz.): A measurement of weight. 16 ounces = 1 pound.

Percent: A ratio that means "per hundred."

Perimeter: The distance around an object found by adding the lengths of the sides.

Pi (π): A symbol representing a number equal to approximately 3.14.

Pictograph: A graph that uses pictures to represent data.

Pint (pt.): A measurement of capacity equal to 2 cups.

Place Value: The value of a digit as representing ones, tens, hundreds, and so on, according to its position, or place, in a number.

Polygon: A closed shape made of line segments that can be made without lifting the pencil or crossing another line.

Pound (lb.): A measurement of weight equal to 16 ounces.

Prime Number: A positive whole number that can be divided evenly only by itself or one.

Prism: A space figure with two identical, parallel bases.

Probability: The ratio of favorable outcomes to possible outcomes of an experiment.

Product: The quantity that results from multiplying two or more numbers.

Pyramid: A space figure whose base is a polygon and whose faces are triangles with a common vertex—the point where two rays meet.

Quart (qt.): A measurement of capacity equal to 4 cups or 2 pints.

Quotient: The answer found by dividing one number by another number.

Radius: A line segment with one end point on the circle and the other end point at the center.

Ratio: A comparison of two quantities.

Ray: A part of a line with one end point that goes on and on in one direction.

Rectangle: A figure with four equal angles and four sides, having the sides opposite each other of equal length.

Rectangular Prism: A space figure with six sides, or faces, all of which are rectangles.

Remainder: The number left over in the quotient of a division problem.

Roman Numerals: A number system used in ancient Rome that used letters to represent the numbers 1, 5, 10, 50, 100, 500, and 1,000.

Rounding: Expressing a number to the nearest ten, hundred, thousand, and so on. Examples: round 18 up to 20; round 113 down to 100.

Segment: A part of a line having two end points.

Similar Figures: Figures having the same shape but different sizes.

Space Figures: Figures whose points are in more than one plane.

Sphere: A space figure with no flat surface. All points are an equal distance from the center.

Square: A figure with four equal sides and four equal angles.

Standardized Units: Units that are agreed upon all over the world.

Subtraction: The process of "taking away" one number from another. It is used to find the difference between two numbers.

Survey: A way to collect data by asking people questions.

Symmetrical Figure: A figure that can be divided equally into two identical parts.

Ton (tn.): A measurement of weight equal to 2,000 pounds.

Tree Diagram: A diagram that shows the possible results of a group of events.

Triangle: A figure with three sides and three angles.

Unlike Fractions: Fractions with different denominators, or bottom numbers.

Vertex: A point where two line segments or rays meet to form an angel or where three edges of a three-dimensional object meet.

Volume: The number of cubic units inside a space figure.

Yard (yd.): A measurement of distance equal to 3 feet.

Page 4

Coin Crossword

Directions: Complete the puzzle. The answer to **A. Across** tells the month and day that the first U.S. coin was minted. The answer to **A. Down** gives the year.

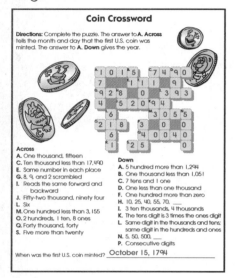

Across
A. One thousand, fifteen
C. Ten thousand less than 17,490
E. Same number in each place
G. 8, 9, and 2 scrambled
I. Reads the same forward and backward
J. Fifty-two thousand, ninety four
L. Six
M. One hundred more than 3,155
O. 2 hundreds, 1 ten, 8 ones
Q. Forty thousand, forty
S. Five more than twenty

Down
A. 5 hundred more than 1,294
B. One thousand less than 1,051
C. 7 tens and 1 one
D. One less than one thousand
F. One hundred more than zero
H. 10, 25, 40, 55, 70, ___
I. 3 ten thousands, 4 thousands
K. The tens digit is 3 times the ones digit
L. Same digit in the thousands and tens; same digit in the hundreds and ones
N. 5, 50, 500, ___
P. Consecutive digits

When was the first U.S. coin minted? __October 15, 1794__

Page 5

Roman Numerals

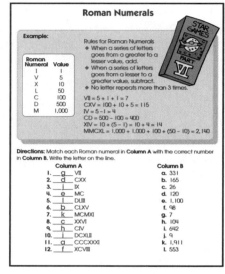

Example:

Roman Numeral	Value
I	1
V	5
X	10
L	50
C	100
D	500
M	1,000

Rules for Roman Numerals
♦ When a series of letters goes from a greater to a lesser value, add.
♦ When a series of letters goes from a lesser to a greater value, subtract.
♦ No letter repeats more than 3 times.

VII = 5 + 1 + 1 = 7
CXV = 100 + 10 + 5 = 115
IV = 5 − 1 = 4
CD = 500 − 100 = 400
XIV = 10 + (5 − 1) = 10 + 4 = 14
MMCXL = 1,000 + 1,000 + 100 + (50 − 10) = 2,140

Directions: Match each Roman numeral in Column A with the correct number in Column B. Write the letter on the line.

Column A		Column B
1. __g__	VII	a. 331
2. __d__	CXX	b. 165
3. __j__	IX	c. 26
4. __e__	MC	d. 120
5. __l__	DLIII	e. 1,100
6. __b__	CLXV	f. 98
7. __k__	MCMXI	g. 7
8. __c__	XXVI	h. 104
9. __h__	CIV	i. 642
10. __i__	DCXLII	j. 9
11. __a__	CCCXXXI	k. 1,911
12. __f__	XCVIII	l. 553

Page 6

Egyptian Numerals

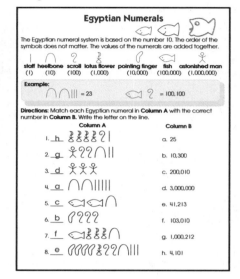

The Egyptian numeral system is based on the number 10. The order of the symbols does not matter. The values of the numerals are added together.

	∩	𝟮	scroll	pointing finger	fish	astonished man
staff	heelbone	scroll	lotus flower	pointing finger	fish	astonished man
(1)	(10)	(100)	(1,000)	(10,000)	(100,000)	(1,000,000)

Example: ∩∩III = 23   = 100,100

Directions: Match each Egyptian numeral in Column A with the correct number in Column B. Write the letter on the line.

Column A	Column B
1. __h__	a. 25
2. __g__	b. 10,300
3. __d__	c. 200,010
4. __a__	d. 3,000,000
5. __c__	e. 41,213
6. __b__	f. 103,010
7. __f__	g. 1,000,212
8. __e__	h. 4,101

Page 7

Place Value

The **place value** of a digit or numeral is shown by where it is in the number. In the number 1,234, 1 has the place value of thousands, 2 is hundreds, 3 is tens and 4 is ones.

Example: 1,250,000,000
Read: One billion, two hundred fifty million
Write: 1,250,000,000

Billions	Millions	Thousands	Ones
h t o	h t o	h t o	h t o
1,	2 5 0,	0 0 0,	0 0 0

Directions: Read the words. Then write the numbers.

twenty million, three hundred four thousand __20,304,000__

five thousand, four hundred twenty-three __5,423__

one hundred fifty billion, eight million, one thousand, five hundred __150,008,001,500__

sixty billion, seven hundred million, one thousand, three hundred twelve __60,700,100,312__

four hundred million, fifteen thousand, seven hundred one __400,015,701__

six hundred ninety-nine million, four thousand, nine hundred forty-two __699,004,942__

Here's a game to play with a partner.

Write a ten-digit number using each digit, 0 to 9, only once. Do not show the number to your partner. Give clues like: "There is a five in the hundreds place." The clues can be given in any order. See if your partner can write the same number you have written.

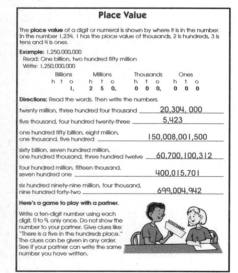

Page 8

Place Value

Directions: Draw a line to connect each number to its correct written form.

1. 791,000 — Three hundred fifty thousand
2. 350,000 — Seventeen million, five hundred thousand
3. 17,500,000 — Seven hundred ninety-one thousand
4. 3,500,000 — Seventy thousand, nine hundred ten
5. 70,910 — Three million, five hundred thousand
6. 35,500,000 — Seventeen billion, five hundred thousand
7. 17,000,500,000 — Thirty-five million, five hundred thousand

Directions: Look carefully at this number: 2,071,463,548. Write the numeral for each of the following places:

8. __6__ ten thousands
9. __1__ millions
10. __5__ hundreds
11. __2__ billions
12. __4__ hundred thousands
13. __7__ ten millions
14. __3__ one thousands
15. __0__ hundred millions

2,342

Page 9

Powers of 10

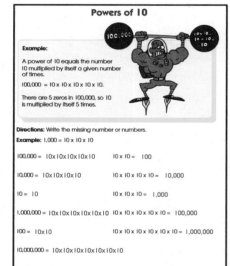

Example:

A power of 10 equals the number 10 multiplied by itself a given number of times.

100,000 = 10 x 10 x 10 x 10 x 10.

There are 5 zeros in 100,000, so 10 is multiplied by itself 5 times.

Directions: Write the missing number or numbers.

Example: 1,000 = 10 x 10 x 10

100,000 = 10x10x10x10x10   10 x 10 = 100

10,000 = 10x10x10x10   10 x 10 x 10 x 10 = 10,000

10 = 10   10 x 10 x 10 = 1,000

1,000,000 = 10x10x10x10x10x10   10 x 10 x 10 x 10 = 100,000

100 = 10x10   10 x 10 x 10 x 10 x 10 = 1,000,000

10,000,000 = 10x10x10x10x10x10x10

Page 10

Tens Trivia

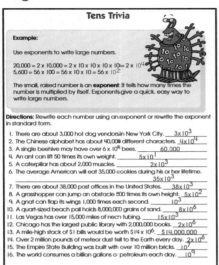

Example:

Use exponents to write large numbers.

$20,000 = 2 \times 10,000 = 2 \times 10 \times 10 \times 10 \times 10 = 2 \times 10^4$
$5,600 = 56 \times 100 = 56 \times 10 \times 10 = 56 \times 10^2$

The small, raised number is an **exponent**. It tells how many times the number is multiplied by itself. Exponents give a quick, easy way to write large numbers.

Directions: Rewrite each number using an exponent or rewrite the exponent in standard form.

1. There are about 3,000 hot dog vendors in New York City. 3×10^3
2. The Chinese alphabet has about 40,000 different characters. 4×10^4
3. A single beehive may have about 6 × 10⁴ bees. 60,000
4. An ant can lift 50 times its own weight. 5×10^1
5. A caterpillar has about 2,000 muscles. 2×10^3
6. The average American will eat 35,000 cookies during his or her lifetime. 35×10^3
7. There are about 38,000 post offices in the United States. 38×10^3
8. A grasshopper can jump an obstacle 500 times its own height. 5×10^2
9. A gnat can flap its wings 1,000 times each second. 10^3
10. A quart-sized beach pail holds 8,000,000 grains of sand. 8×10^6
11. Las Vegas has over 15,000 miles of neon tubing. 15×10^3
12. Chicago has the largest public library with 2,000,000 books. 2×10^6
13. A mile-high stack of $1 bills would be worth $14 × 10⁶. $14,000,000
14. Over 2 million pounds of meteor dust fall to the Earth every day. 2×10^6
15. The Empire State Building was built with over 10 million bricks. 10^7
16. The world consumes a billion gallons of petroleum each day. 10^9

Page 11

Addition

Teachers of an Earth Science class planned to take 50 students on an overnight hiking and camping experience. After planning the menu, they went to the grocery store for supplies.

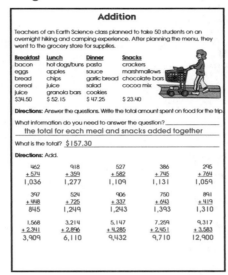

Breakfast	Lunch	Dinner	Snacks
bacon	hot dogs/buns	pasta	crackers
eggs	apples	sauce	marshmallows
bread	chips	garlic bread	chocolate bars
cereal	juice	salad	cocoa mix
juice	granola bars	cookies	
$34.50	$52.15	$47.25	$23.40

Directions: Answer the questions. Write the total amount spent on food for the trip.

What information do you need to answer the question? the total for each meal and snacks added together

What is the total? $157.30

Directions: Add.

462 +574 1,036	918 +359 1,277	527 +582 1,109	386 +745 1,131	295 +764 1,059
397 +448 845	524 +725 1,249	906 +337 1,243	750 +643 1,393	891 +419 1,310
1,568 +2,341 3,909	3,214 +2,896 6,110	5,147 +4,285 9,432	7,259 +2,451 9,710	9,317 +3,583 12,900

Page 12

Addition

Directions: Add.

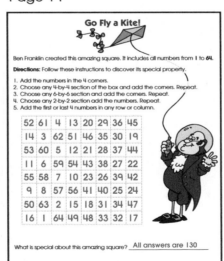

1. Tourists travel to national parks to see the many animals that live there. Park Rangers estimate 384 buffalo, 282 grizzly bears, and 426 deer in the park. What is the total number of buffalo, bears, and deer estimated in the park? 1,092 buffalo, bears, and deer

2. Last August, 2,248 visitors drove motor homes into the campgrounds for overnight camping. 647 set up campsites with tents. How many campsites were there altogether in August? 2,895 campsites

3. During a 3-week camping trip, Tom and his family hiked 42 miles, took a 126-mile long canoeing trip, and drove their car 853 miles. How many miles did they travel in all? 1,021 miles

4. Old Faithful is a geyser that spouts water high into the air. 10,000 gallons of water burst into the air regularly. Two other geysers spout 2,400 gallons of water during each eruption. What is the amount of water thrust into the air during one cycle? 14,800 gallons

5. Yellowstone National Park covers approximately 2,221,772 acres of land. Close by, the Grand Tetons cover approximately 310,350 acres. How many acres of land are there in these two parks? 2,532,122 acres

6. Hiking trails cover 486 miles, motor routes around the north rim total 376 miles, and another 322 miles of road allow visitors to follow a loop around the southern part of the park. How many miles of trails and roadways are there? 1,184 miles

Page 13

Addition

Bob the butcher is popular with the dogs in town. He was making a delivery this morning when he noticed he was being followed by two dogs. Bob tried to climb a ladder to escape from the dogs.

Directions: Solve the following addition problems and shade in the answers on the ladder. If all the numbers are shaded when the problems have been solved, Bob made it up the ladder. Some answers may not be on the ladder.

Ladder: 1,319,046 / 2,803,757 / 5,743,665 / 3,118,356 / 56,597 / 4,079,553 / 1,807,485 / 2,943,230 / 18,344,666 / 1,735,063 / 5,752,163 / 896,316 / 3,841,672 / 5,646,339

1. 986,145
621,332
+200,008
1,807,485

2. 1,873,402
925,666
+4,689
2,803,757

3. 506,328
886,510
+342,225
1,735,063

4. 43,015
2,811,604
+987,053
3,841,672

5. 18,443
300,604
+999,999
1,319,046

6. 8,075
14,608
+33,914
56,597

7. 9,162
7,804
+755,122
772,088

8. 88,714
213,653
+5,441,298
5,743,665

9. 3,244,662
1,986,114
+521,387
5,752,163

10. 4,581
22,983
+5,618,775
5,646,339

11. 818,623
926
+3,260,004
4,079,553

12. 80,436
9,159
+3,028,761
3,118,356

Does Bob make it? no

Page 14

Go Fly a Kite!

Ben Franklin created this amazing square. It includes all numbers from 1 to 64.

Directions: Follow these instructions to discover its special property.

1. Add the numbers in the 4 corners.
2. Choose any 4-by-4 section of the box and add the corners. Repeat.
3. Choose any 6-by-6 section and add the corners. Repeat.
4. Choose any 2-by-2 section and add the numbers. Repeat.
5. Add the first or last 4 numbers in any row or column.

52	61	4	13	20	29	36	45
14	3	62	51	46	35	30	19
53	60	5	12	21	28	37	44
11	6	59	54	43	38	27	22
55	58	7	10	23	26	39	42
9	8	57	56	41	40	25	24
50	63	2	15	18	31	34	47
16	1	64	49	48	33	32	17

What is special about this amazing square? All answers are 130

Page 15

Mount Rushmore

Which four presidents are carved into Mount Rushmore?

Directions: To find out, solve these problems. Then, use the key.

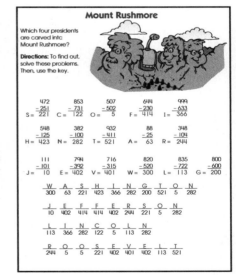

472 −251 S= 221	853 −731 C= 122	507 −502 O= 5	644 −230 F= 414	999 −633 I= 366
548 −125 H= 423	382 −100 N= 282	932 −411 T= 521	88 −25 A= 63	348 −104 R= 244
111 −101 J= 10	794 −392 E= 402	716 −315 V= 401	820 −520 W= 300	835 −722 L= 113	800 −600 G= 200

W A S H I N G T O N
300 63 221 423 396 282 200 521 5 282

J E F F E R S O N
10 402 414 414 402 244 221 5 282

L I N C O L N
113 366 282 122 5 113 282

R O O S E V E L T
244 5 5 221 402 401 402 113 521

Subtraction Squares

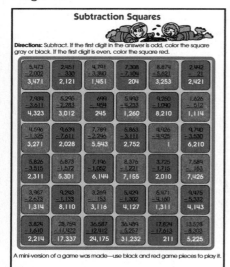

Directions: Subtract. If the first digit in the answer is odd, color the square gray or black. If the first digit is even, color the square red.

5,473 − 2,002 = 3,471	2,451 − 330 = 2,121	4,791 − 3,340 = 1,451	7,308 − 7,104 = 204	8,874 − 5,621 = 3,253	2,442 − 21 = 2,421
7,934 − 3,611 = 4,323	5,295 − 2,283 = 3,012	699 − 454 = 245	5,493 − 4,233 = 1,260	9,250 − 1,040 = 8,210	1,626 − 512 = 1,114
4,596 − 1,325 = 3,271	9,639 − 7,611 = 2,028	7,789 − 2,246 = 5,543	5,863 − 3,111 = 2,752	4,926 − 4,925 = 1	9,740 − 3,530 = 6,210
5,826 − 3,515 = 2,311	6,873 − 1,572 = 5,301	7,196 − 1,052 = 6,144	8,376 − 1,221 = 7,155	3,725 − 1,715 = 2,010	7,589 − 163 = 7,426
3,967 − 2,653 = 1,314	9,243 − 1,133 = 8,110	3,269 − 153 = 3,116	5,429 − 1,302 = 4,127	5,471 − 4,160 = 1,311	9,475 − 5,332 = 4,143
3,824 − 1,610 = 2,214	28,759 − 11,422 = 17,337	36,587 − 12,412 = 24,175	36,489 − 5,257 = 31,232	17,824 − 17,613 = 211	13,528 − 8,303 = 5,225

A mini-version of a game was made—use black and red game pieces to play it.

Subtraction

When working with larger numbers, it is important to keep the numbers lined up according to place value.

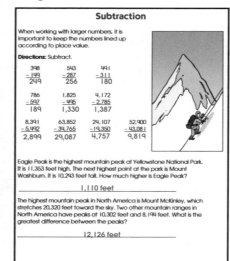

Directions: Subtract.

398 − 149 = 249	543 − 287 = 256	491 − 311 = 180
786 − 597 = 189	1,825 − 495 = 1,330	4,172 − 2,785 = 1,387
8,391 − 5,492 = 2,899	63,852 − 34,765 = 29,087	24,107 − 19,350 = 4,757
		52,900 − 43,081 = 9,819

Eagle Peak is the highest mountain peak at Yellowstone National Park. It is 11,353 feet high. The next highest point at the park is Mount Washburn. It is 10,243 feet tall. How much higher is Eagle Peak?

1,110 feet

The highest mountain peak in North America is Mount McKinley, which stretches 20,320 feet toward the sky. Two other mountain ranges in North America have peaks at 10,302 feet and 8,194 feet. What is the greatest difference between the peaks?

12,126 feet

What's in a Name?

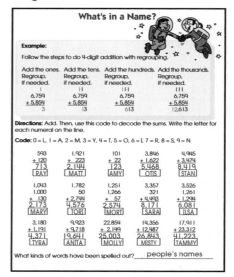

Example:

Follow the steps to do 4-digit addition with regrouping.

Add the ones. Regroup, if needed.	Add the tens. Regroup, if needed.	Add the hundreds. Regroup, if needed.	Add the thousands. Regroup, if needed.
1 6,759 + 5,854 = 3	11 6,759 + 5,854 = 13	111 6,759 + 5,854 = 613	111 6,759 + 5,854 = 12,613

Directions: Add. Then, use this code to decode the sums. Write the letter for each numeral on the line.

Code: 0 = L, 1 = A, 2 = M, 3 = Y, 4 = T, 5 = O, 6 = I, 7 = R, 8 = S, 9 = N

593 + 120 = 713 RAY	1,921 + 223 = 2,144 MATT	101 + 22 = 123 AMY	3,846 + 1,622 = 5,468 OTIS	4,945 + 3,474 = 8,419 STAN
1,043 1,000 + 130 = 2,173 MARY	1,782 50 + 2,744 = 4,576 TORI	1,251 1,266 + 57 = 2,574 MORT	3,357 321 + 4,493 = 8,171 SARA	3,526 1,261 + 1,294 = 6,081 ILSA
3,180 + 1,191 = 4,371 TYRA	9,923 + 9,718 = 19,641 ANITA	22,854 + 2,149 = 25,003 MOLLY	14,356 + 12,487 = 26,843 MISTY	17,911 + 23,312 = 41,223 TAMMY

What kinds of words have been spelled out? people's names

Subtraction Search

The Dead Sea is the lowest place on the earth.

Directions: To find how many feet below sea level it is, subtract. Then, find and circle each answer in the puzzle. Numbers can read forward, backward, up, down, or diagonally. Finally, read the four uncircled numbers from left to right to find the number of feet.

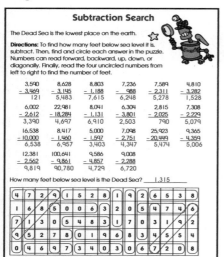

3,590 − 3,469 = 121	8,628 − 3,145 = 5,483	8,803 − 1,188 = 7,615	7,236 − 988 = 6,248	7,589 − 2,311 = 5,278	4,810 − 3,282 = 1,528
6,002 − 2,612 = 3,390	22,981 − 18,284 = 4,697	8,041 − 1,131 = 6,910	6,304 − 3,801 = 2,503	2,815 − 2,025 = 790	7,308 − 2,229 = 5,079
16,538 − 10,000 = 6,538	8,417 − 1,460 = 6,957	5,000 − 1,597 = 3,403	7,098 − 2,751 = 4,347	25,923 − 20,449 = 5,474	9,365 − 4,359 = 5,006
12,381 − 2,562 = 9,819	100,641 − 9,861 = 90,780	9,586 − 4,857 = 4,729	9,008 − 2,288 = 6,720		

How many feet below sea level is the Dead Sea? 1,315

4	7	2	9	1	5	2	8	1	9	2	6	5	3	8
1	6	8	5	0	0	6	3	2	0	5	4	7	4	6
7	1	3	0	5	4	8	3	1	7	0	3	1	9	2
9	5	2	7	8	0	1	9	6	3	4	5	5	4	1
0	4	6	9	7	3	4	0	3	0	6	7	2	0	8

Batting a Thousand

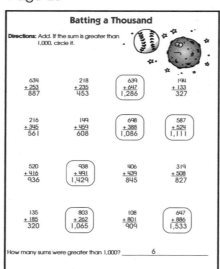

Directions: Add. If the sum is greater than 1,000, circle it.

634 + 253 = 887	218 + 235 = 453	639 + 647 = 1,286	194 + 133 = 327
216 + 345 = 561	149 + 459 = 608	698 + 388 = 1,086	587 + 524 = 1,111
520 + 416 = 936	938 + 491 = 1,429	406 + 439 = 845	319 + 508 = 827
135 + 185 = 320	803 + 262 = 1,065	108 + 801 = 909	647 + 886 = 1,533

How many sums were greater than 1,000? 6

Checking Subtraction

You can check your subtraction by using addition.

Example: 34,436 − 12,264 = 22,172 → Check: 22,172 + 12,264 = 34,436

Directions: Subtract. Then check your answers by adding.

	Check:			Check:	
15,326 − 11,532 = 3,794		3,794 + 11,532 = 15,326	28,615 − 25,329 = 3,286		3,286 + 25,329 = 28,615
96,521 − 47,378 = 49,143	Check:	49,143 + 47,378 = 96,521	46,496 − 35,877 = 10,619	Check:	10,619 + 35,877 = 46,496
77,911 − 63,783 = 14,128	Check:	14,128 + 63,783 = 77,911	156,901 − 112,732 = 44,169	Check:	44,169 + 112,732 = 156,901
395,638 − 187,569 = 208,069		208,069 + 187,569 = 395,638	67,002 − 53,195 = 13,807	Check:	13,807 + 53,195 = 67,002
16,075 − 15,896 = 179	Check:	179 + 15,896 = 16,075	39,678 − 19,769 = 19,909		19,909 + 19,769 = 39,678
84,654 − 49,997 = 34,657	Check:	34,657 + 49,997 = 84,654	12,335 − 10,697 = 1,638	Check:	1,638 + 10,697 = 12,335

During the summer, 158,941 people visited Yellowstone National Park. During the fall, there were 52,397 visitors. How many more visitors went to the park during the summer than the fall?

106,544 visitors

Page 22

Making the Grade

Example:

A subtraction problem can be checked with addition.

502
− 347
155

If the answer is correct, then 155 + 347 must equal 502.

Directions: Grade this test paper. Check each problem. Write a ✔ if it is correct and an X if it is incorrect. Then, use the key at the bottom to give yourself a grade.

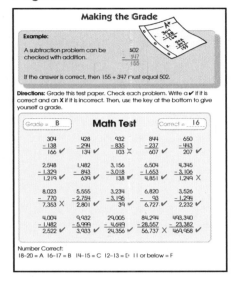

Grade = **B**   **Math Test**   Correct = **16**

304 − 138 166 ✔	428 − 294 134 ✔	932 − 835 103 X	844 − 237 607 ✔	650 − 443 207 ✔
2,548 − 1,329 1,219 ✔	1,482 − 843 639 ✔	3,156 − 3,018 138 ✔	6,504 − 1,653 4,851 ✔	4,345 − 3,106 1,249 X
8,023 − 770 7,353 X	5,555 − 2,754 2,801 ✔	3,234 − 3,195 39 ✔	6,820 − 93 6,727 ✔	3,526 − 1,294 2,232 ✔
4,004 − 1,482 2,522 X	9,932 − 5,999 3,933 ✔	29,005 − 4,649 24,356 ✔	84,294 − 28,557 56,737 X	493,340 − 23,382 469,958 ✔

Number Correct:
18–20 = A   16–17 = B   14–15 = C   12–13 = D   11 or below = F

Page 23

Addition and Subtraction

Directions: Check the answers. Write **T** if the answer is true and **F** if it is false.

Example: 48,973   Check: 35,856
− 35,856   + 13,118
13,118   **F**   48,974

18,264 + 17,893 36,157	Check: **T**	36,157 − 17,893 18,264	458,342 − 297,652 160,680	Check: **F**	160,680 + 297,652 458,332
39,854 + 52,713 92,577	Check: **F**	92,577 − 52,713 39,864	631,928 − 457,615 174,313	Check: **T**	174,313 + 457,615 631,928
14,389 + 93,587 107,976	Check: **T**	107,976 − 93,587 14,389	554,974 − 376,585 178,389	Check: **T**	178,389 + 376,585 554,974
87,321 − 62,348 24,973	Check: **T**	24,973 + 62,348 87,321	109,568 + 97,373 206,941	Check: **T**	206,941 − 97,373 109,568

Directions: Read the story problem. Write the equation and check the answer.

A camper hikes 53,741 feet out into the wilderness. On his return trip he takes a shortcut, walking 36,752 feet back to his cabin. The shortcut saves him 16,998 feet of hiking. True or (False)

53,741   16,989
− 36,752   + 36,752
16,989   53,741

Page 24

Addition and Subtraction

Directions: Add or subtract to find the answers.

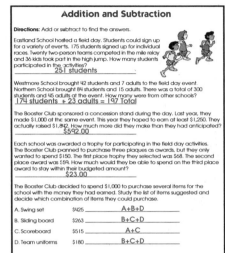

Eastland School hosted a field day. Students could sign up for a variety of events. 175 students signed up for individual races. Twenty two-person teams competed in the mile relay and 36 kids took part in the high jump. How many students participated in the activities?
251 students

Westmore School brought 42 students and 7 adults to the field day event. Northern School brought 84 students and 15 adults. There was a total of 300 students and 45 adults at the event. How many were from other schools?
174 students + 23 adults = 197 Total

The Booster Club sponsored a concession stand during the day. Last year, they made $1,000 at the same event. This year they hoped to earn at least $1,250. They actually raised $1,842. How much more did they make than they had anticipated?
$592.00

Each school was awarded a trophy for participating in the field day activities. The Booster Club planned to purchase three plaques as awards, but they only wanted to spend $150. The first place trophy they selected was $68. The second place award was $59. How much would they be able to spend on the third place award to stay within their budgeted amount?
$23.00

The Booster Club decided to spend $1,000 to purchase several items for the school with the money they had earned. Study the list of items suggested and decide which combination of items they could purchase.

A. Swing set	$425	**A+B+D**
B. Sliding board	$263	**B+C+D**
C. Scoreboard	$515	**A+C**
D. Team uniforms	$180	**B+C+D**

Page 25

Rounding

Rounding a number means to express it to the nearest ten, hundred, thousand, and so on. When rounding a number, if the number has five or more ones, round up. Round down if the number has four or fewer ones.

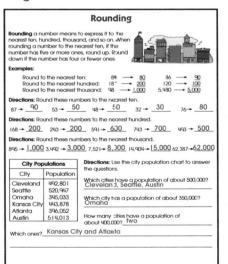

Examples:

Round to the nearest ten: 84 → 80   86 → 90
Round to the nearest hundred: 187 → 200   120 → 100
Round to the nearest thousand: 98 → 1,000   5,480 → 5,000

Directions: Round these numbers to the nearest ten.

87 → **90**   53 → **50**   48 → **50**   32 → **30**   76 → **80**

Directions: Round these numbers to the nearest hundred.

168 → **200**   243 → **200**   591 → **600**   743 → **700**   443 → **500**

Directions: Round these numbers to the nearest thousand.

895 → **1,000**   3,492 → **3,000**   7,521 → **8,000**   14,904 → **15,000**   62,387 → **62,000**

City Populations	
City	Population
Cleveland	492,801
Seattle	520,947
Omaha	345,033
Kansas City	443,878
Atlanta	396,052
Austin	514,013

Directions: Use the city population chart to answer the questions.

Which cities have a population of about 500,000?
Cleveland, Seattle, Austin

Which city has a population of about 350,000?
Omaha

How many cities have a population of about 400,000? **two**

Which ones? **Kansas City and Atlanta**

Page 26

Getting Around to Rounding

Example:

Round 36,528 to the nearest hundred.	Round 36,528 to the nearest thousand.	Round 36,528 to the nearest ten thousand.
36,528 2 is less than 5. Do not change the 5. 36,500	36,528 5 = 5. Round the 6 to 7. 37,000	36,528 6 is greater than 5. Round the 3 to 4. 40,000

Directions: Round each number to the nearest hundred, thousand, and ten thousand.

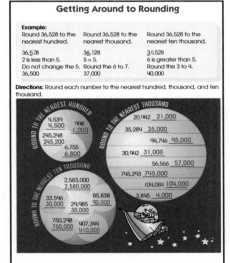

ROUND TO THE NEAREST HUNDRED
4,539   **4,500**
998   **1,000**
245,248   **245,200**
6,755   **6,800**

ROUND TO THE NEAREST THOUSAND
20,942   **21,000**
35,284   **35,000**
94,746   **95,000**
30,942   **31,000**
56,566   **57,000**
745,293   **745,000**
104,084   **104,000**
3,845   **4,000**

ROUND TO THE NEAREST TEN THOUSAND
2,583,000   **2,580,000**
85,838   **90,000**
33,596   **30,000**
29,985   **30,000**
750,298   **750,000**
407,344   **410,000**

Page 27

Rounding

Follow these steps to round numbers to a given place.

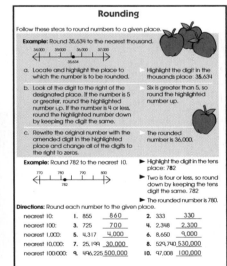

Example: Round 35,634 to the nearest thousand.

34,000   35,000   36,000   37,000
35,634

a. Locate and highlight the place to which the number is to be rounded.
► Highlight the digit in the thousands place: 35,634

b. Look at the digit to the right of the designated place. If the number is 5 or greater, round the highlighted number up. If the number is 4 or less, round the highlighted number down by keeping the digit the same.
► Six is greater than 5, so round the highlighted number up.

c. Rewrite the original number with the amended digit in the highlighted place and change all of the digits to the right to zeros.
► The rounded number is 36,000.

Example: Round 782 to the nearest 10.

770   780   790   800
782

► Highlight the digit in the tens place: 782
► Two is four or less, so round down by keeping the tens digit the same. 782
► The rounded number is 780.

Directions: Round each number to the given place.

nearest 10:	1. 855	**860**	2. 333	**330**
	3. 725	**700**	4. 2,348	**2,300**
nearest 1,000:	5. 4,317	**4,000**	6. 8,650	**9,000**
nearest 10,000:	7. 25,199	**30,000**	8. 529,740	**530,000**
nearest 100,000:	9. 496,225	**500,000**	10. 97,008	**100,000**

Page 28

Number-line Rounding

Directions: Label the endpoints. Plot the given number. Circle the closer endpoint. The first three have been done for you.

1. Round 87 to the nearest ten. (80, 87, 90 — 90 circled)

2. Round 1,322 to the nearest hundred. (1,300, 1,322, 1,400 — 1,300 circled)

3. Round 1,475 to the nearest ten. (1,470, 1,475, 1,480 — 1,480 circled)

4. Round 8,274 to the nearest ten. (8,270, 8,274, 8,280 — 8,270 circled)

5. Round 8,274 to the nearest hundred. (8,200, 8,274, 8,300 — 8,300 circled)

6. Round 1,452 to the nearest thousand. (1,000, 1,452, 2,000 — 1,000 circled)

7. Round 1,452 to the nearest ten. (1,450, 1,452, 1,460 — 1,450 circled)

8. Round 6,937 to the nearest thousand. (6,000, 6,937, 7,000 — 7,000 circled)

9. Round 8,485 to the nearest thousand. (8,000, 8,485, 9,000 — 8,000 circled)

10. Round 25,683 to the nearest ten thousand. (20,000, 25,683, 30,000 — 30,000 circled)

Page 29

Rounding And Estimating

Rounding numbers and estimating answers is an easy way of finding the approximate answer without writing out the problem or using a calculator.

Directions: Circle the correct answer.

Round to the nearest ten:

73 → (70) 80   48 → 40 (50)   65 → 60 (70)

85 → 80 (90)   92 → (90) 100   37 → 30 (40)

Round to the nearest hundred:

139 → (100) 200   782 → 700 (800)   390 → (300) 400

640 → (600) 700   525 → (500) 600   457 → 400 (500)

Round to the nearest thousand:

1,375 → (1,000) 2,000   21,800 → 21,000 (22,000)   36,240 → (36,000) 37,000

Sam wanted to buy a new computer. He knew he had only about $1,200 to spend. Which of the following ones could he afford to buy?

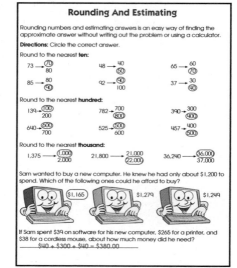

$1,165 $1,279 $1,249

If Sam spent $39 on software for his new computer, $265 for a printer, and $38 for a cordless mouse, about how much money did he need?

$40 + $300 + $40 = $380.00

Page 30

Estimating

To **estimate** means to give an approximate rather than an exact answer. Rounding each number first makes it easy to estimate an answer.

Example:

93 → 90	321 → 300	1,859 → 2,000
+ 48 → + 50	+ 597 → + 600	− 997 → − 1,000
140	900	1,000

Directions: Estimate the sums and differences by rounding the numbers first.

68 → 70	12 → 10	89 → 90
+ 34 → + 30	+ 98 → + 100	+ 23 → + 20
100	110	110

638 → 600	281 → 300	271 → 300
− 395 → − 400	− 69 → − 70	− 126 → − 100
200	230	200

1,532 → 2,000	8,312 → 8,000	6,341 → 6,000
− 998 → − 1,000	− 4,789 → − 5,000	+ 9,286 → + 9,000
1,000	3,000	15,000

Bonnie has $50 to purchase tennis shoes, a tennis racquet, and tennis balls. Does she have enough money?

yes

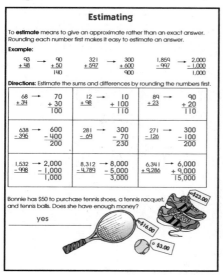

$23.00 $16.00 $3.00

Page 31

What Do You Think?

Directions: Estimate the answer to each question. Use a timer, watch, or clock that measures seconds to time the activity. Then, record the actual answer. How close was the estimate?

Question	Estimate	Actual Number
1. How many jumping jacks can you do in 15 seconds?		
2. How many seconds does it take to say the alphabet backwards?		
3. How many light bulbs are there in your home?		
4. How many seconds does it take to tie both shoes?		
5. How many times does the letter **p** appear on this page?		
6. How many spoonfuls of water does it take to fill a small drinking glass?		
7. How high can you count out loud in 15 seconds?		
8. How many steps does it take to walk around the edge of the largest room in your home?		
9. How many numbers between 1 and 99 have the numeral 2 in them?		
10. How many seconds does it take to sing "Happy Birthday to You"?		

Answers will vary.

Page 32

The Missing Link

Directions: Round each number to the nearest thousand, ten thousand, hundred thousand, and million.

	Thousand	Ten Thousand	Hundred Thousand	Million
3,567,248	3,567,000	3,570,000	3,600,000	4,000,000
6,388,845	6,389,000	6,390,000	6,400,000	6,000,000
15,573,543	15,574,000	15,570,000	15,600,000	16,000,000
28,954,274	28,954,000	28,950,000	29,000,000	29,000,000
856,388,327	856,388,000	856,390,000	856,400,000	856,000,000

Page 33

Estimating Sums

Example:

Estimate by rounding before you add.

Nearest Ten	Nearest Hundred	Nearest Thousand
88 → 90	244 → 200	4,566 → 5,000
+ 51 → + 50	+ 776 → + 800	+ 3,320 → + 3,000
139 → 140	1,020 → 1,000	7,886 → 8,000
Actual = 139	Actual = 1,020	Actual = 7,886
Estimated = 140	Estimated = 1,000	Estimated = 8,000
Difference = 1	Difference = 20	Difference = 114

When you do not have to be exact, estimating can be easy and close to the actual sum.

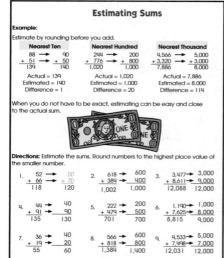

Directions: Estimate the sums. Round numbers to the highest place value of the smaller number.

1. 52 → 50 / + 66 → + 70 / 118 → 120

2. 618 → 600 / + 384 → + 400 / 1,002 → 1,000

3. 3,477 → 3,000 / + 8,611 → + 9,000 / 12,088 → 12,000

4. 44 → 40 / + 91 → + 90 / 135 → 130

5. 222 → 200 / + 479 → + 500 / 701 → 700

6. 1,190 → 1,000 / + 7,625 → + 8,000 / 8,815 → 9,000

7. 36 → 40 / + 19 → + 20 / 55 → 60

8. 566 → 600 / + 818 → + 800 / 1,384 → 1,400

9. 4,533 → 5,000 / + 7,498 → + 7,000 / 12,031 → 12,000

Page 34

Estimating Differences

To estimate differences, round the numbers and then subtract. This skill can be used daily. An example of this would be when you travel by car. If you have a distance of 862 miles to travel and you've gone 381, you can round and subtract in your head—900 – 400 leaves approximately 500 more miles to go.

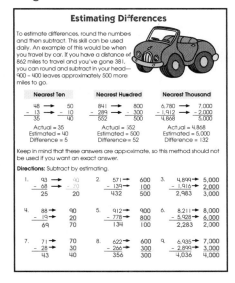

Nearest Ten	Nearest Hundred	Nearest Thousand
48 → 50	841 → 800	6,780 → 7,000
– 13 → – 10	– 289 → – 300	– 1,912 → – 2,000
35 40	552 500	4,868 5,000
Actual = 35	Actual = 552	Actual = 4,868
Estimated = 40	Estimated = 500	Estimated = 5,000
Difference = 5	Difference = 52	Difference = 132

Keep in mind that these answers are approximate, so this method should not be used if you want an exact answer.

Directions: Subtract by estimating.

1. 93 → 90
   – 68 → – 70
   25   20

2. 571   600
   – 139   100
   432   500

3. 4,899   5,000
   – 1,916   2,000
   2,983   3,000

4. 88 → 90
   – 19 → 20
   69   70

5. 912   900
   – 778   800
   134   100

6. 8,211   8,000
   – 5,928   6,000
   2,283   2,000

7. 71 → 70
   – 28 → 30
   43   40

8. 622   600
   – 266   300
   356   300

9. 6,935   7,000
   – 2,899   3,000
   4,036   4,000

Page 35

Prime Numbers

Example: 3 is a **prime number.** 3 ÷ 1 = 3 and 3 ÷ 3 = 1

Any other divisor will result in a mixed number or fraction.

Example:

11 can be divided only by 1 and 11.
It is a prime number.

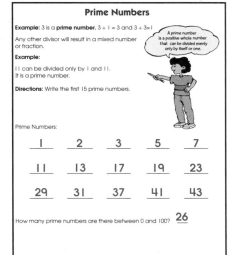

A prime number is a positive whole number that can be divided evenly only by itself or one.

Directions: Write the first 15 prime numbers.

Prime Numbers:

1	2	3	5	7
11	13	17	19	23
29	31	37	41	43

How many prime numbers are there between 0 and 100? __26__

Page 36

Prime Numbers

Directions: Circle the prime numbers.

(71)	(3)	82	20	(43)	69
128	(97)	(23)	111	75	51
(13)	44	(137)	68	171	(83)
(61)	21	77	(101)	34	16
(2)	39	92	(17)	52	(29)
(19)	156	63	99	27	147
121	25	88	12	87	55
57	(7)	(139)	91	9	(37)
(67)	183	(5)	(59)	(11)	95

Page 37

Multiples

A **multiple** is the product of a specific number and any other number. When you multiply two numbers, the answer is called the **product**.

Example:

The multiples of 2 are 2 (2 x 1), 4 (2 x 2), 6, 8, 10, 12, and so on. The **least common multiple** (LCM) of two or more numbers is the smallest number other than 0 that is a multiple of each number.

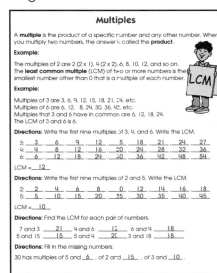

LCM

Example:

Multiples of 3 are 3, 6, 9, 12, 15, 18, 21, 24, etc.
Multiples of 6 are 6, 12, 8, 24, 30, 36, 42, etc.
Multiples that 3 and 6 have in common are 6, 12, 18, 24.
The LCM of 3 and 6 is 6.

Directions: Write the first nine multiples of 3, 4, and 6. Write the LCM.

3: 3, 6, 9, 12, 15, 18, 21, 24, 27
4: 4, 8, 12, 16, 20, 24, 28, 32, 36
6: 6, 12, 18, 24, 30, 36, 42, 48, 54

LCM = 12

Directions: Write the first nine multiples of 2 and 5. Write the LCM.

2: 2, 4, 6, 8, 10, 12, 14, 16, 18
5: 5, 10, 15, 20, 25, 30, 35, 40, 45

LCM = 10

Directions: Find the LCM for each pair of numbers.

7 and 3 __21__ 4 and 6 __12__ 6 and 9 __18__
5 and 15 __15__ 5 and 4 __20__ 3 and 18 __18__

Directions: Fill in the missing numbers.

30 has multiples of 5 and __6__, of 2 and __15__, of 3 and __10__.

Page 38

Factors

Factors are the numbers multiplied together to give a product. The **greatest common factor** (GCF) is the largest number for a set of numbers that divides evenly into each number in the set.

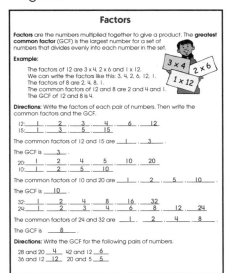

3 x 4 2 x 6 1 x 12

Example:

The factors of 12 are 3 x 4, 2 x 6 and 1 x 12.
We can write the factors like this: 3, 4, 2, 6, 12, 1.
The factors of 8 are 2, 4, 8, 1.
The common factors of 12 and 8 are 2 and 4 and 1.
The GCF of 12 and 8 is 4.

Directions: Write the factors of each pair of numbers. Then write the common factors and the GCF.

12: 1, 2, 3, 4, 6, 12
15: 1, 3, 5, 15

The common factors of 12 and 15 are __1__, __3__.

The GCF is __3__.

20: 1, 2, 4, 5, 10, 20
10: 1, 2, 5, 10

The common factors of 10 and 20 are __1__, __2__, __5__, __10__.

The GCF is __10__.

32: 1, 2, 4, 8, 16, 32
24: 1, 2, 3, 4, 6, 8, 12, 24

The common factors of 24 and 32 are __1__, __2__, __4__, __8__.

The GCF is __8__.

Directions: Write the GCF for the following pairs of numbers.

28 and 20 __4__ 42 and 12 __6__
36 and 12 __12__ 20 and 5 __5__

Page 39

Factor Trees

A **factor tree** shows the prime factors of a number. A prime number, such as 7, has for its factors only itself and 1.

Example:

30
6 x 5
3 2 5

30 = 3 x 2 x 5.
3, 2, and 5 are prime numbers.

Directions: Fill in the numbers in the factor trees.

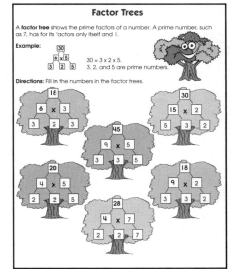

18
6 x 3
3 2 3

30
15 x 2
5 3 2

45
9 x 5
3 3 5

20
4 x 5
2 2 5

18
9 x 2
3 3 2

28
4 x 7
2 2 7

Page 40

Factor Trees

Directions: Fill in the numbers in the factor trees. The first one has been done for you.

Tree 1: 13,720
- 140 x 98
- 10 x 14 x 7
- 5 x 2 x 7 x 1

Tree 2: 192
- 8 x 24
- x 4 x 6
- 1 x 2 x 2 x 3

Tree 3: 1,125
- 75 x 15
- 15 x 5 x 3
- 3 x 5 x 1 x 3

Page 41

Greatest Common Factor

Directions: Write the greatest common factor for each set of numbers.

10 and 35 ___5___
2 and 10 ___2___
42 and 63 ___21___
16 and 40 ___8___
25 and 55 ___5___
12 and 20 ___4___
14 and 28 ___14___
8 and 20 ___4___
6 and 27 ___3___
15 and 35 ___5___
18 and 48 ___6___

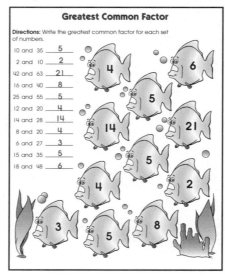

Page 42

Least Common Multiple

Directions: Write the least common multiple for each pair of numbers.

12 and 7 ___84___
2 and 4 ___4___
22 and 4 ___44___
6 and 10 ___30___
3 and 7 ___21___
6 and 8 ___24___
5 and 10 ___10___
8 and 12 ___24___
9 and 15 ___45___
7 and 5 ___35___
3 and 8 ___24___
9 and 4 ___36___

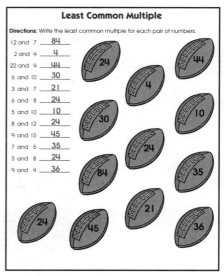

Page 43

Deep Blue Sea

An **integer** is any positive or negative whole number, or zero. Negative integers are numbers less than zero. The opposite of any number is found the same distance from 0 on a number line.

Example:
35 below zero can be written as –35.
The opposite of 6 is –6.
The opposite of –41 is 41.
The opposite of 0 is 0.

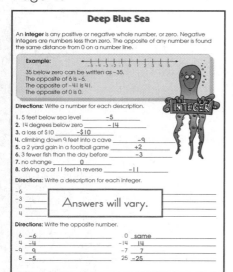

Directions: Write a number for each description.

1. 5 feet below sea level ___–5___
2. 14 degrees below zero ___–14___
3. a loss of $10 ___–$10___
4. climbing down 9 feet into a cave ___–9___
5. a 2 yard gain in a football game ___+2___
6. 3 fewer fish than the day before ___–3___
7. no change ___0___
8. driving a car 11 feet in reverse ___–11___

Directions: Write a description for each integer.

–6 ___
–3 ___
0 ___
4 ___

Answers will vary.

Directions: Write the opposite number.

6 ___–6___   0 ___same___
4 ___–4___   –14 ___14___
–9 ___9___   –7 ___7___
5 ___–5___   25 ___–25___

Page 44

Add Integers

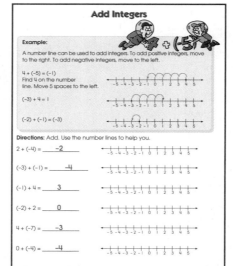

Example:
A number line can be used to add integers. To add positive integers, move to the right. To add negative integers, move to the left.

4 + (–5) = (–1)
Find 4 on the number line. Move 5 spaces to the left.

(–3) + 4 = 1

(–2) + (–1) = (–3)

Directions: Add. Use the number lines to help you.

2 + (–4) = ___–2___

(–3) + (–1) = ___–4___

(–1) + 4 = ___3___

(–2) + 2 = ___0___

4 + (–7) = ___–3___

0 + (–4) = ___–4___

Page 45

Subtract Integers

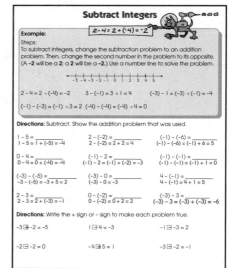

2 – 4 = 2 + (–4) = –2

Example:
Steps:
To subtract integers, change the subtraction problem to an addition problem. Then, change the second number in the problem to its opposite. (A –2 will be a 2; a 2 will be a –2.) Use a number line to solve the problem.

2 – 4 = 2 + (–4) = –2   3 – (–1) = 3 + 1 = 4   (–3) – 1 = (–3) + (–1) = –4

(–1) – (–3) = (–1) + 3 = 2   2 – (–4) – (–4) = (–4) + 4 = 0

Directions: Subtract. Show the addition problem that was used.

1 – 5 = ___
1 – 5 = 1 + (–5) = –4

2 – (–2) = ___
2 – (–2) = 2 + 2 = 4

(–1) – (–6) = ___
(–1) – (–6) = (–1) + 6 = 5

0 – 4 = ___
0 – 4 = 0 + (–4) = –4

(–1) – 2 = ___
(–1) – 2 = (–1) + (–2) = –3

(–1) – (–1) = ___
(–1) – (–1) = (–1) + 1 = 0

(–3) – (–5) = ___
–3 – (–5) = –3 + 5 = 2

(–3) – 0 = ___
(–3) – 0 = –3

4 – (–1) = ___
4 – (–1) = 4 + 1 = 5

2 – 3 = ___
2 – 3 = 2 + (–3) = –1

0 – (–2) = ___
0 – (–2) = 0 + 2 = 2

(–3) – 3 = ___
(–3) – 3 = (–3) + (–3) = –6

Directions: Write the + sign or – sign to make each problem true.

–3 ⊟ –2 = –5   1 ⊟ 4 = –3   –1 ⊟ 3 = 2

–2 ⊟ –2 = 0   –4 ⊞ 5 = 1   –3 ⊟ –2 = –1

Page 46

Timed Multiplication

Directions: Have someone time you as you multiply the following problems.

1	9	4	8	2	5	7	12
× 1	× 3	× 10	× 3	× 10	× 7	× 4	× 3
1	27	40	24	20	35	28	36

10	12	10	4	7	11	6	3
× 3	× 9	× 5	× 9	× 5	× 2	× 6	× 2
30	108	50	36	35	22	36	6

5	10	9	3	5	9	8	6
× 8	× 4	× 4	× 3	× 9	× 6	× 5	× 7
40	40	36	9	45	54	40	42

4	11	12	1	7	10	2	4
× 8	× 3	× 5	× 4	× 7	× 6	× 7	× 7
32	33	60	4	49	60	14	28

3	6	9	5	11	3	10	1
× 4	× 8	× 5	× 10	× 9	× 5	× 7	× 5
12	48	45	50	99	15	70	5

2	8	9	4	9	8	7	4
× 6	× 7	× 2	× 6	× 8	× 8	× 9	× 5
12	56	18	24	72	64	63	20

10	3	6	11	9	2	12	7
× 8	× 6	× 10	× 6	× 7	× 5	× 10	× 10
80	18	60	66	63	10	120	70

Page 47

Fast Facts

Directions: See how many problems you can solve in 90 seconds.

4 × 3 = 12	11 × 9 = 99	6 × 6 = 36	10 × 3 = 30	2 × 8 = 16	2 × 1 = 2
5 × 0 = 0	3 × 3 = 9	6 × 7 = 42	7 × 3 = 21	12 × 7 = 84	6 × 10 = 60
4 × 5 = 20	8 × 9 = 72	4 × 8 = 32	12 × 5 = 60	7 × 5 = 35	11 × 7 = 77
0 × 9 = 0	12 × 4 = 48	2 × 5 = 10	11 × 11 = 121	9 × 6 = 54	8 × 6 = 48
4 × 7 = 28	5 × 9 = 45	10 × 12 = 120	3 × 9 = 27	5 × 5 = 25	8 × 5 = 40
7 × 2 = 14	11 × 6 = 66	4 × 10 = 40	12 × 1 = 132	6 × 4 = 24	7 × 9 = 63
10 × 1 = 10	9 × 10 = 90	2 × 4 = 8	5 × 6 = 30	1 × 6 = 6	12 × 2 = 24
9 × 12 = 108	2 × 9 = 18	3 × 1 = 3	4 × 11 = 44	7 × 8 = 56	4 × 4 = 16
10 × 2 = 20	4 × 1 = 4	7 × 10 = 70	6 × 12 = 72	8 × 0 = 0	5 × 10 = 50
12 × 3 = 36	10 × 10 = 100	6 × 3 = 18	8 × 11 = 88	3 × 8 = 24	12 × 1 = 12
7 × 7 = 49	9 × 4 = 36	11 × 10 = 110	7 × 1 = 7	9 × 9 = 81	6 × 2 = 12
8 × 12 = 96	2 × 11 = 22	5 × 3 = 15	11 × 3 = 33	2 × 2 = 4	1 × 1 = 1
2 × 3 = 6	9 × 1 = 9	4 × 0 = 0	11 × 5 = 55	10 × 8 = 80	1 × 11 = 11

How many problems did you complete correctly? _____

Page 48

Multiplication (One-Digit Multiplier)

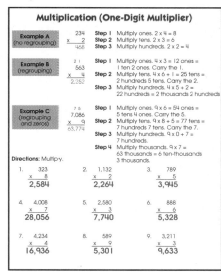

Example A (no regrouping)

234
× 2
468

Step 1 Multiply ones. 2 × 4 = 8
Step 2 Multiply tens. 2 × 3 = 6
Step 3 Multiply hundreds. 2 × 2 = 4

Example B (regrouping)

2 1
563
× 4
2,252

Step 1 Multiply ones. 4 × 3 = 12 ones = 1 ten 2 ones. Carry the 1.
Step 2 Multiply tens. 4 × 6 + 1 = 25 tens = 2 hundreds 5 tens. Carry the 2.
Step 3 Multiply hundreds. 4 × 5 + 2 = 22 hundreds = 2 thousands 2 hundreds

Example C (regrouping and zeros)

7 5
7,086
× 9
63,774

Step 1 Multiply ones. 9 × 6 = 54 ones = 5 tens 4 ones. Carry the 5.
Step 2 Multiply tens. 9 × 8 + 5 = 77 tens = 7 hundreds 7 tens. Carry the 7.
Step 3 Multiply hundreds. 9 × 0 + 7 = 7 hundreds.
Step 4 Multiply thousands. 9 × 7 = 63 thousands = 6 ten-thousands 3 thousands.

Directions: Multiply.

1. 323 × 8 = **2,584**	2. 1,132 × 2 = **2,264**	3. 789 × 5 = **3,945**
4. 4,008 × 7 = **28,056**	5. 2,580 × 3 = **7,740**	6. 888 × 6 = **5,328**
7. 4,234 × 4 = **16,936**	8. 589 × 9 = **5,301**	9. 3,211 × 3 = **9,633**

Page 49

Multiplication (Two-Digit Multiplier)

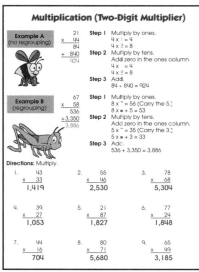

Example A (no regrouping)

21
× 44
84
+ 840
924

Step 1 Multiply by ones.
4 × 1 = 4
4 × 2 = 8
Step 2 Multiply by tens. Add zero in the ones column.
4 × 1 = 4
4 × 2 = 8
Step 3 Add.
84 + 840 = 924

Example B (regrouping)

67
× 58
536
+3,350
3,886

Step 1 Multiply by ones.
8 × 7 = 56 (Carry the 5.)
8 × 6 + 5 = 53
Step 2 Multiply by tens. Add zero in the ones column.
5 × 7 = 35 (Carry the 3.)
5 × 6 + 3 = 33
Step 3 Add.
536 + 3,350 = 3,886

Directions: Multiply.

1. 43 × 33 = **1,419**	2. 55 × 46 = **2,530**	3. 78 × 68 = **5,304**
4. 39 × 27 = **1,053**	5. 21 × 87 = **1,827**	6. 77 × 24 = **1,848**
7. 44 × 16 = **704**	8. 80 × 71 = **5,680**	9. 65 × 49 = **3,185**

Page 50

One-Digit Multiplication With Regrouping

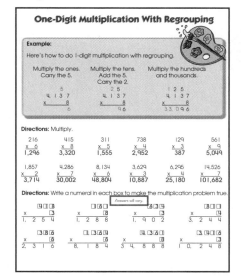

Example:

Here's how to do 1-digit multiplication with regrouping.

Multiply the ones. Carry the 5.

5
4,137
× 8
6

Multiply the tens. Add the 5. Carry the 2.

2 5
4,137
× 8
96

Multiply the hundreds and thousands.

1 2 5
4,137
× 8
33,096

Directions: Multiply.

216 × 6 = **1,296**	415 × 8 = **3,320**	311 × 5 = **1,555**	738 × 4 = **2,952**	129 × 3 = **387**	561 × 9 = **5,049**
1,857 × 2 = **3,714**	4,286 × 7 = **30,002**	8,134 × 6 = **48,804**	3,629 × 3 = **10,887**	6,295 × 4 = **25,180**	14,526 × 7 = **101,682**

Directions: Write a numeral in each box to make the multiplication problem true.

Answers will vary.

Page 51

Two-Digit Multiplication With Regrouping

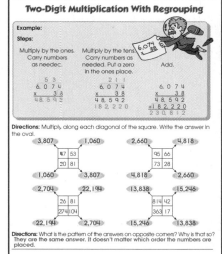

Example:

Steps:

Multiply by the ones. Carry numbers as needed.

5 3
6,074
× 8
48,592

Multiply by the tens. Carry numbers as needed. Put a zero in the ones place.

2 1 1
6,074
× 3 8
48,592
182,220

Add.

6,074
× 3 8
48,592
+182,220
230,812

Directions: Multiply, along each diagonal of the square. Write the answer in the oval.

3,807	1,060		2,660	4,818
	47 53			95 66
	20 81			73 28
1,060	3,807		4,818	2,660

2,704	22,194		13,838	15,246
	26 81			814 42
	274 104			363 17
22,194	2,704		15,246	13,838

Directions: What is the pattern of the answers on opposite corners? Why is that so? They are the same answer. It doesn't matter which order the numbers are placed.

Page 52

Multiplication Maze

Directions: These multiplication problems have already been done, but some of them are wrong. Check each problem. Connect the problems with correct answers to make a path for Zerpo to get back to his ship. Then, correct each wrong answer.

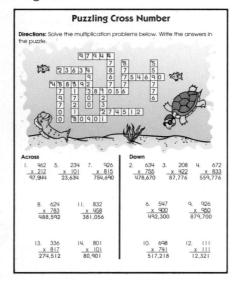

```
  863          904        6,520
  x 24         x 93       x 74
 21,712       (93)       582,480
(20,712)                (482,480)

  663          392        485
  x 54         x 28       x 53              99
 53,802       11,976     24,605            x 98
(38,802)     (10,976)   (25,705)          19,502
                          925

  566         2,576       466                   4,516
  x 74         x 36       x 18                  x 22
 35,884      236,992      8,388                98,352
(41,884)                                      (99,352)

 5,565         719        239            534
  x 35         x 82       x 15           x 34
194,705      63,958      4,565          28,156
            (58,958)    (3,585)        (18,156)

 1,044         671        793           329
 65,856        x 68       x 81          x 16
              45,628     64,233         5,624
                                       (5,264)

                          1,524           861
                           x 43           x 57
                          64,532        50,077
                         (65,532)      (49,077)

                                         651        819
                                         x 83       x 76
                          2,316         (54,033)   52,244
                           x 27                    (62,244)
                          62,532
                                         4,110
                                         x 28
                                       125,080
                                      (115,080)
```

Page 53

Multiplication Riddle

Directions: Answer the riddle at the bottom of the page by solving the problems and writing the matching letters.

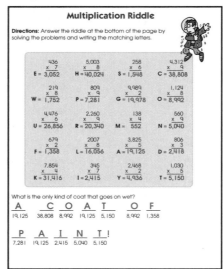

```
   436        5,003        258          4,312
   x 7        x 8         x 6           x 9
E = 3,052  H = 40,024  S = 1,548    C = 38,808

   219         809        9,989         1,124
   x 8         x 9        x 2           x 8
W = 1,752  P = 7,281   G = 19,978   O = 8,992

  4,476       2,260        138           560
   x 6         x 9         x 4           x 9
U = 26,856 R = 20,340   M = 552      N = 5,040

   679        2007        3,825          806
   x 2         x 8         x 5           x 3
F = 1,358  L = 16,056  A = 19,125   D = 2,418

  7,854        345        2,468         1,030
   x 4         x 7         x 2           x 5
K = 31,416 I = 2,415   Y = 4,936    T = 5,150
```

What is the only kind of coat that goes on wet?

<u>A</u> <u>C</u> <u>O</u> <u>A</u> <u>T</u> <u>O</u> <u>F</u>
19,125 38,808 8,992 19,125 5,150 8,992 1,358

<u>P</u> <u>A</u> <u>I</u> <u>N</u> <u>T</u>!
7,281 19,125 2,415 5,040 5,150

Page 54

Crossing the Dragon

Directions: Multiply.

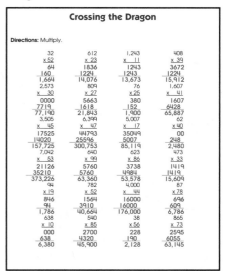

```
    32         612      1,243        408
   x 52        x 23     x 11        x 39
    64        1836      1243        3672
   160        1224      1243        1224
  1,664      14,076    13,673      15,912
  2,573        809        76        1,607
   x 30        x 27      x 25        x 41
  0000        5663       380        1607
  7719        1618       152        6428
 77,190      21,843     1,900      65,887
  3,505       6,399     5,007         62
   x 45        x 47      x 17        x 40
 17525       44793      35049         00
 14020       25596      5007         248
157,725     300,753    85,119      2,480
  7,042        640        623        473
   x 53        x 99       x 86       x 33
    63        5760       3738       1419
 21126       5760       4984       1419
 35210      63,360     53,578     15,609
373,226       782      4,000         87
   x 19        x 52      x 44        x 78
   846        1564      16000        696
    94        3910      16000        609
 1,786      40,664    176,000      6,786
   638         540        38        865
   x 10        x 85      x 56       x 73
   000        2700       228        2595
   638        4320       190        6055
 6,380      45,900     2,128      63,145
```

Page 55

Puzzling Cross Number

Directions: Solve the multiplication problems below. Write the answers in the puzzle.

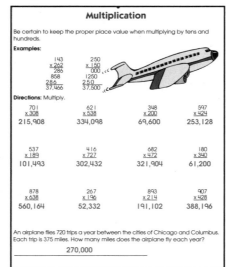

```
  9 7 9 4 6
  2 3 6 3 4       8    5
                  7    5
  4 8 8 5 9 2  7 5 4 6 9 0
  7 1   3 8 0 5 2
  9   7 0 2      7
  7 0 1     2 7 4 5 1 2
  3 8 0 9 0 1
```

Across

1. 462   5. 234   7. 926
   x 212   x 101   x 815
   97,944   23,634   754,690

8. 624   11. 832   6. 547   9. 926
   x 783   x 458   x 900   x 950
   488,592   381,056   492,300   879,700

13. 336   14. 801   10. 698   12. 111
    x 817   x 101   x 741   x 111
    274,512   80,901   517,218   12,321

Down

2. 634   3. 208   4. 672
   x 755   x 422   x 833
   478,670   87,776   559,776

Page 56

Multiplication

Be certain to keep the proper place value when multiplying by tens and hundreds.

Examples:

```
   143           250
  x 262         x 150
   286           000
   858          1250
   286           250
 37,466        37,500
```

Directions: Multiply.

```
   701         621         348         597
  x 308       x 538       x 200       x 424
 215,908     334,098     69,600      253,128

   537         416         682         180
  x 189       x 727       x 472       x 340
 101,493     302,432     321,904     61,200

   878         267         893         907
  x 638       x 196       x 214       x 428
 560,164     52,332      191,102     388,196
```

An airplane flies 720 trips a year between the cities of Chicago and Columbus. Each trip is 375 miles. How many miles does the airplane fly each year?

_____ 270,000

Page 57

Problem Solving

Directions: Solve each problem.

1. There are 6 rows of desks in the office. Each row has 8 desks. How many desks are in the office?

   There are __6__ rows of desks.
   There are __8__ desks in each row.
   There are __48__ desks in all.

2. There are 9 rows of trees. There are 7 trees in each row. How many trees are there in all?

   There are __9__ rows of trees.
   There are __7__ trees in each row.
   There are __63__ trees in all.

3. The people at the park were separated into teams of 8 people each. Nine teams were formed. How many people were in the park?

   Each team had __8__ people.
   There were __9__ teams formed.
   There were __72__ people in the park.

4. There were 6 people in each car. There were 7 cars. How many people were there in all?

   There were __6__ people in each car.
   There were __7__ cars.
   There were __42__ people in all.

5. How many cents would you need to buy eight 8-cent pencils?

   You would need __64__ cents.

1.

2.

3.

4.

5.

Page 58

Problem Solving

Directions: Solve each problem

1. Each club member works 3 hours each month. There are 32 members. What is the total number of hours worked each month by all club members?

There are **32** club members.
Each member works **3** hours.
The club members work **96** hours in all.

2. Mrs. Robins drives 19 miles every working day. How many miles does she drive in a five-day work-week?

She drives **19** miles every working day.
She works **5** days a week.
She drives **95** miles in a five-day work-week.

3. It takes 54 minutes to make one gizmo. How long will it take to make 3 gizmos?

It takes **54** minutes to make one gizmo.
There are **3** gizmos.
It takes **162** minutes to make 3 gizmos.

4. Each box weighs 121 kilograms. There are 4 boxes. What is the total weight of the 4 boxes?

Each box weighs **121** kilograms.
There are **4** boxes.
The total weight of the 4 boxes is **484** kilograms.

5. There are 168 hours in a week. How many hours are there in 6 weeks?

There are **1,008** hours in 6 weeks.

Page 59

Problem Solving

Directions: Solve each problem.

1. There are 60 minutes in one hour. How many minutes are there in 24 hours?

There are **1,440** minutes in 24 hours.

2. Forty-eight toy boats are packed in each box. How many boats are there in 16 boxes?

There are **768** boats in 16 boxes.

3. Seventy-three new cars can be assembled in one hour. At that rate, how many cars could be assembled in 51 hours?

3,723 cars could be assembled in 51 hours.

4. A truck is hauling 36 bags of cement. Each bag weighs 94 pounds. How many pounds of cement are being hauled?

3,384 pounds of cement are being hauled.

5. To square a number means to multiply the number by itself. What is the square of 68?

The square of 68 is **4,624**.

6. Sixty-five books are packed in each box. How many books are there in 85 boxes?

There are **5,525** books in 85 boxes.

Page 60

Problem Solving

Directions: Solve each problem.

1. A machine can produce 98 parts in one hour. How many parts could it produce in 72 hours?

It could produce **7,056** parts in 72 hours.

2. Each new bus can carry 66 passengers. How many passengers can ride on 85 new buses?

5,610 passengers can ride on 85 buses.

3. A gross is twelve dozen or 144. The school ordered 21 gross of pencils. How many pencils were ordered?

The school ordered **3,024** pencils.

4. How many hours are there in a year (365 days)?

There are **8,760** hours in a year.

5. Each of 583 people worked a 40-hour week. How many hours of work was this?

It was **23,320** hours of work.

6. The highway mileage between New York and Chicago is 840 miles. How many miles would a bus travel in making 68 one-way trips between New York and Chicago?

The bus would travel **57,120** miles.

Page 61

Problem Solving

Directions: Solve each problem.

1. Each crate the men unloaded weighed 342 pounds. They unloaded 212 crates. How many pounds did they unload?

The men unloaded **72,504** pounds.

2. The school cafeteria expects to serve 425 customers every day. At that rate, how many meals will be served if the cafeteria is open 175 days a year?

74,375 meals will be served.

3. There are 168 hours in one week. How many hours are there in 260 weeks?

There are **43,680** hours in 260 weeks.

4. There are 3,600 seconds in one hour and 168 hours in one week. How many seconds are there in one week?

There are **604,800** seconds in one week.

5. A jet carrying 128 passengers flew 2,574 miles. How many passenger-miles (number of passengers times number of miles traveled) would this be?

It would be **329,472** passenger miles.

6. How many passenger-miles would be flown by the jet in problem 5, if it flew from Seattle to New Orleans, a distance of 2,098 miles?

It would be **268,544** passenger-miles.

Page 62

Multiplication's Opposite

Directions: Use the multiplication problem to help solve the division problems.

Example:
6 x 7 = 42
42 ÷ 7 = 6
42 ÷ 6 = 7

1. 4 x 8 = 32
32 ÷ **8** = 4
32 ÷ **4** = 8

2. 9 x 9 = 81
81 ÷ 9 = **9**

3. 7 x 8 = 56
56 ÷ 8 = 7
56 ÷ **7** = 8

4. 22 x 12 = 264
264 ÷ 12 = 22
264 ÷ 22 = **12**

5. 37 x 19 = 703
703 ÷ 37 = 19
703 ÷ 19 = **37**

Directions: Solve the following problems and write two related division problems for each.

6. 22 x 17 = **374**
374 ÷ 17 = 22
374 ÷ 22 = 17

7. 45 x 29 = **1,305**
1,305 ÷ 45 = 29
1,305 ÷ 29 = 45

8. 19 x 82 = **1,558**
1,558 ÷ 82 = 19
1,558 ÷ 19 = 82

9. 671 x 63 = **42,273**
42,273 ÷ 63 = 671
42,273 ÷ 671 = 63

10. 663 x 54 = **35,802**
35,802 ÷ 663 = 54
35,802 ÷ 54 = 663

11. 719 x 73 = **52,487**
52,487 ÷ 73 = 719
52,487 ÷ 719 = 73

Page 63

Division Facts

Directions: Solve the division problems.

3)24 **8**	9)81 **9**	8)40 **5**	4)4 **1**	9)90 **10**	8)56 **7**	6)24 **4**
7)14 **2**	7)49 **7**	5)20 **4**	6)36 **6**	9)72 **8**	4)16 **4**	3)27 **9**
8)64 **8**	9)36 **4**	9)45 **5**	9)45 **5**	2)18 **9**	4)24 **6**	8)8 **1**
3)9 **3**	2)14 **7**	6)54 **9**	7)21 **3**	8)32 **4**	5)30 **6**	6)6 **1**
2)4 **2**	9)81 **9**	6)30 **5**	4)8 **2**	5)50 **10**	5)15 **3**	2)20 **10**
1)10 **10**	7)7 **1**	2)16 **8**	3)15 **5**	7)49 **7**	1)4 **4**	9)63 **7**
8)16 **2**	2)12 **6**	8)72 **9**	3)30 **10**	9)63 **7**	3)18 **6**	7)56 **8**
9)9 **1**	7)63 **9**	2)8 **4**	8)80 **10**	7)28 **4**	6)12 **2**	3)6 **2**
7)42 **6**	3)12 **4**	7)35 **5**	9)27 **3**	6)42 **7**	5)10 **2**	5)45 **9**
2)10 **5**	9)54 **6**	4)20 **5**	8)48 **6**	9)18 **2**	6)6 **1**	2)6 **3**

Page 64

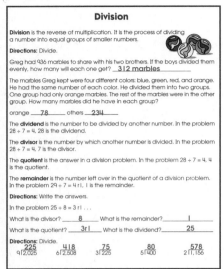

Division

Division is the reverse of multiplication. It is the process of dividing a number into equal groups of smaller numbers.

Directions: Divide.

Greg had 936 marbles to share with his two brothers. If the boys divided them evenly, how many will each one get? **312 marbles**

The marbles Greg kept were four different colors: blue, green, red, and orange. He had the same number of each color. He divided them into two groups. One group had only orange marbles. The rest of the marbles were in the other group. How many marbles did he have in each group?

orange **78**   others **234**

The **dividend** is the number to be divided by another number. In the problem 28 ÷ 7 = 4, 28 is the dividend.

The **divisor** is the number by which another number is divided. In the problem 28 ÷ 7 = 4, 7 is the divisor.

The **quotient** is the answer in a division problem. In the problem 28 ÷ 7 = 4, 4 is the quotient.

The **remainder** is the number left over in the quotient of a division problem. In the problem 29 ÷ 7 = 4 r1, 1 is the remainder.

Directions: Write the answers.

In the problem 25 ÷ 8 = 3 r1 . . .

What is the divisor? **8**   What is the remainder? **1**

What is the quotient? **3 r1**   What is the dividend? **25**

Directions: Divide.

225   **418**   **75**   **80**   **578**
9⟌2,025   6⟌2,508   3⟌225   5⟌400   2⟌1,156

Page 65

Division

The remainder in a division problem must always be less than the divisor.

Example: 244 r23
26⟌6,367
        52
        116
        104
        127
        104
        23

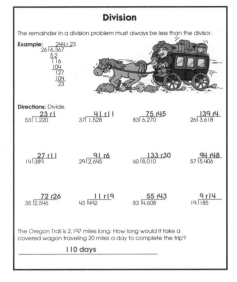

Directions: Divide.

23 r1   **41 r11**   **75 r45**   **139 r4**
53⟌1,220   37⟌1,528   83⟌6,270   26⟌3,618

27 r11   **91 r6**   **133 r30**   **94 r48**
14⟌389   29⟌2,645   60⟌8,010   57⟌5,406

72 r26   **11 r19**   **55 r43**   **9 r14**
35⟌2,546   43⟌492   83⟌4,608   19⟌185

The Oregon Trail is 2,197 miles long. How long would it take a covered wagon traveling 20 miles a day to complete the trip?

110 days

Page 66

Checking Division

Answers in division problems can be checked by multiplying.

Example: 481 r17   Check: 481
33⟌15,890   x 33
        132   1443
        269   1443
        264   15,873
        50   + 17
        33   15,890
        17
    Add the remainder

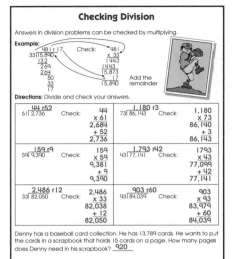

Directions: Divide and check your answers.

44 r52	Check:	44	**1,180 r3**	Check:	1,180
61⟌2,736		x 61	73⟌86,143		86,140
		2,684			+ 3
		+ 52			86,143
		2,736			

159 r9	Check:	159	**1,793 r42**	Check:	1793
59⟌9,390		x 59	43⟌77,141		x 43
		9,381			77,099
		+ 9			+ 42
		9,390			77,141

2,486 r12	Check:	2,486	**903 r60**	Check:	903
33⟌82,050		x 33	93⟌84,039		x 93
		82,038			83,979
		+ 12			+ 60
		82,050			84,039

Denny has a baseball card collection. He has 13,789 cards. He wants to put the cards in a scrapbook that holds 15 cards on a page. How many pages does Denny need in his scrapbook? **920**

Page 67

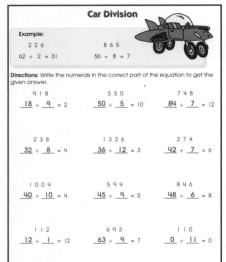

Car Division

Example:

2 2 6   8 6 5
62 ÷ 2 = 31   56 ÷ 8 = 7

Directions: Write the numerals in the correct part of the equation to get the given answer.

9 1 8   5 5 0   7 4 8
18 ÷ **9** = 2   **50** ÷ **5** = 10   **84** ÷ **7** = 12

2 3 8   1 3 2 6   2 7 4
32 ÷ **8** = 4   **36** ÷ **12** = 3   **42** ÷ **7** = 6

1 0 0 4   5 9 4   8 4 6
40 ÷ **10** = 4   **45** ÷ **9** = 5   **48** ÷ **6** = 8

1 1 2   6 9 3   1 1 0
12 ÷ **1** = 12   **63** ÷ **9** = 7   **0** ÷ **11** = 0

Page 68

Crisscross

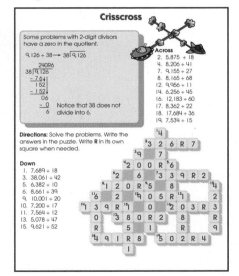

Some problems with 2-digit divisors have a zero in the quotient.

9,126 ÷ 38 → 38⟌9,126

    240 R6
38⟌9,126
    − 76 ↓
    152
    − 152 ↓
    06
    − 0   Notice that 38 does not
    6   divide into 6.

Directions: Solve the problems. Write the answers in the puzzle. Write **R** in its own square when needed.

Across
2. 5,875 ÷ 18
4. 8,206 ÷ 41
7. 9,155 ÷ 27
8. 8,165 ÷ 68
12. 9,956 ÷ 11
14. 6,256 ÷ 45
16. 12,183 ÷ 60
17. 8,362 ÷ 22
18. 17,684 ÷ 36
19. 7,534 ÷ 15

Down
1. 7,689 ÷ 18
3. 38,061 ÷ 42
5. 6,382 ÷ 10
6. 8,661 ÷ 39
9. 10,001 ÷ 20
10. 7,200 ÷ 17
11. 7,564 ÷ 12
13. 5,078 ÷ 47
15. 9,621 ÷ 52

Page 69

Check It Out

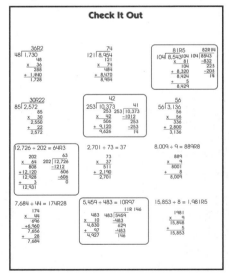

    36R2   74   81R5   82R114
48⟌1,730   121⟌8,954   104⟌8,543 104⟌8543
    48   121   x 81   −832
    288   x 74   104   223
    x 1,440   8,470   + 8,320   −208
    + 1,440   + 8,954   8,424   14
    1,728   + 5
                                            8,429

    30R22   42   56
85⟌2,572   253⟌10,373 253⟌10,373   56⟌3,136
    85   x 42   −1012   56
    x 30   506   253   x 56
    2,550   + 9,120   −253   336
    + 22   9,626   14   + 2,800
    2,572   2,800
                                            3,136

12,726 ÷ 202 = 64R3   2,701 ÷ 73 = 37   8,009 ÷ 9 = 889R8
    202   63   73   889
    x 64   202⟌12,726   x 37   x 9
    808   −1212   511   8001
    + 12,120   606   + 2,190   + 8
    12,928   −606   2,701   8,009
    + 3   0
    12,923

7,684 ÷ 44 = 174R28   5,459 ÷ 483 = 10R97   15,853 ÷ 8 = 1,981R5
    174   11R 146   1981
    x 44   483   483⟌5459   x 8
    696   x 10   −483   15,848
    + 6,960   4,830   629   + 5
    7,656   + 97   −483   15,853
    + 28   4,927   146
    7,684

Page 70

Problem Solving

Directions: Solve each problem.

1. There are 18 chairs and 6 tables in the room. There are the same number of chairs at each table. How many chairs are at each table?

There are __18__ chairs.
There are __6__ tables.
There are __3__ chairs at each table.

2. Each box takes 3 minutes to fill. It took 18 minutes to fill all the boxes. How many boxes are there?

It took __18__ minutes to fill all the boxes.
It takes __3__ minutes to fill 1 box.
There are __6__ boxes.

3. Rob, Jose, Jay, Tom, Alex, and Jim share 6 sandwiches. How many sandwiches does each boy get?

There are __6__ sandwiches in all.
The sandwiches are shared among __6__ boys.
Each boy gets __1__ sandwich.

4. Bill and 8 friends each sold the same number of tickets. They sold 72 tickets in all. How many tickets were sold by each person?

Each person sold __8__ tickets.

5. Forty-eight oranges are in a crate. The oranges are to be put into bags of 6 each. How many bags can be filled?

__8__ bags can be filled.

1.

2.

3.

4.

5.

Page 71

Problem Solving

Directions: Solve each problem.

1. There are 84 scouts in all. Six will be assigned to each tent. How many tents are there?

There are __84__ scouts in all.
There are __6__ scouts in each tent.
There are __14__ tents.

2. Seven people each worked the same number of hours. They worked 91 hours in all. How many hours were worked by each person?

__91__ hours were worked.
__7__ people worked these hours.
__13__ hours were worked by each person.

3. A group of three is a trio. How many trios could be formed with 72 people?

__24__ trios could be formed.

4. A factory shipped 848 cars to 4 cities. Each city received the same number of cars. How many cars were shipped to each city?

__848__ cars were shipped.
__4__ cities received the cars.
__212__ cars were shipped to each city.

5. Malcolm, his brother, and sister have 702 stamps in all. Suppose each takes the same number of stamps. How many will each get?

Each will get __234__ stamps.

1.

2.

3.

4.

5.

Page 72

Problem Solving

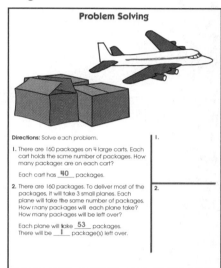

Directions: Solve each problem.

1. There are 160 packages on 4 large carts. Each cart holds the same number of packages. How many packages are on each cart?

Each cart has __40__ packages.

2. There are 160 packages. To deliver most of the packages, it will take 3 small planes. Each plane will take the same number of packages. How many packages will each plane take? How many packages will be left over?

Each plane will take __53__ packages.
There will be __1__ package(s) left over.

1.

2.

Page 73

Problem Solving

Directions: Solve each problem.

1. How many bags of 7 oranges each can be filled from a shipment of 341 oranges? How many oranges will be left over?

__48__ bags can be filled.
__5__ oranges will be left over.

2. Beverly has $2.38 (238 cents) to buy pencils for 8¢ each. How many pencils can she buy? How many cents will she have left?

She can buy __29__ pencils.
She will have __6__ cents left over.

3. There are 6 stamps in each row. How many complete rows can be filled with 1,950 stamps? How many stamps will be left over?

__325__ row will be filled.
__0__ stamps will be left over.

4. Daphne had 958 pennies. She exchanged them for nickels. How many nickels did she get? How many pennies did she have left over?

She got __191__ nickels.
She had __3__ pennies left over.

5. Last year Mr. Gomez worked 1,983 hours. How many 8-hour days was this? How many hours are left over?

It was __247__ 8-hour days.
__7__ hours are left over.

1.

2.

3.

4.

5.

Page 74

Problem Solving

Directions: Solve each problem.

1. The pet store has 84 birds. They have 14 large cages. There are the same number of birds in each cage. How many birds are in each cage?

__6__ birds are in each cage.

2. The pet store also has 63 kittens. There are 12 cages with the same number of kittens in each. The rest of the kittens are in the display window. How many kittens are in each cage? How many kittens are in the display window?

__5__ kittens are in each cage.
__3__ kittens are in the display window.

3. There are 60 guppies in a large tank. If the pet store puts 15 guppies each in smaller tanks, how many smaller tanks will be needed?

__4__ smaller tanks will be needed.

4. There are 72 boxes of pet food on a shelf. The boxes are in rows of 13 each. How many full rows of boxes are there? How many boxes are left over?

There are __5__ full rows of boxes.
There are __7__ boxes left over.

5. There are 52 puppies. There are 13 cages. If each cage contains the same number of puppies, how many puppies are in each cage?

There are __4__ puppies in each cage.

1.

2.

3.

4.

5.

Page 75

What Is the Number?

Directions: Read the clues and solve each riddle.

1. This number will tell how many dots there are on a pair of dice. This number times 29 is 1,218. What is it? __42__

2. This is the average weight in pounds of the ostrich, the heaviest bird on the earth. This number times 11 is 3,795. What is it? __345__

3. This is the number of hours an elephant sleeps each day. This number times 2,604 is 5,208. What is it? __2__

4. This is the speed in miles per hour of the Australian dragonfly—the fastest insect. This number times 53 is 1,855. What is the number? __35__

5. This is how many feet the oceans would rise if all of Antarctica melted. This number times 21 is 4,830. What is it? __230__

6. This number is the body temperature in degrees Fahrenheit that a butterfly needs to be able to fly. This number times 92 is 7,912. What is it? __86__

7. This number will tell how many grooves there are on a quarter. This number times 44 is 5,236. What is the number? __119__

8. This is the average number of gallons of water needed to take a shower. This number times 78 is 936. What is it? __12__

9. This number is the weight in pounds of the largest freshwater fish. This number times 12 is 8,100. What is it? __675__

10. This is the top speed in miles per hour of the cheetah, the world's fastest land animal. This number times 43 is 3,010. What is the number? __70__

Page 76

In the Money

Hamburger $2.95 (cheese: add $0.30)
Grilled Cheese $1.85
Fries: small $0.75 large $1.25
Onion rings $1.00
Soda pop $0.95
Milkshake $1.99
Slice of pie $1.15

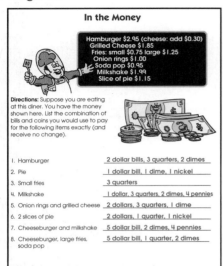

Directions: Suppose you are eating at this diner. You have the money shown here. List the combination of bills and coins you would use to pay for the following items exactly (and receive no change).

1. Hamburger — 2 dollar bills, 3 quarters, 2 dimes
2. Pie — 1 dollar bill, 1 dime, 1 nickel
3. Small fries — 3 quarters
4. Milkshake — 1 dollar, 3 quarters, 2 dimes, 4 pennies
5. Onion rings and grilled cheese — 2 dollars, 1 dime
6. 2 slices of pie — 2 dollars, 1 quarter, 1 nickel
7. Cheeseburger and milkshake — 5 dollar bill, 2 dimes, 4 pennies
8. Cheeseburger, large fries, soda pop — 5 dollar bill, 1 quarter, 2 dimes

Page 77

Adding Money

Example:

Steps:

1. Align the decimal points.
2. Add.

```
 $4.32      $10.43
+$2.19    + $ 4.25
 $6.51    + $12.04
            $26.72
```

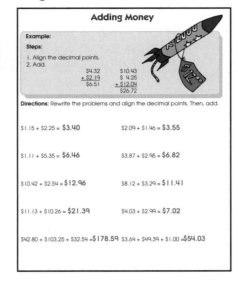

Directions: Rewrite the problems and align the decimal points. Then, add.

$1.15 + $2.25 = **$3.40** $2.09 + $1.46 = **$3.55**

$1.11 + $5.35 = **$6.46** $3.87 + $2.95 = **$6.82**

$10.42 + $2.54 = **$12.96** $8.12 + $3.29 = **$11.41**

$11.13 + $10.26 = **$21.39** $4.03 + $2.99 = **$7.02**

$42.80 + $103.25 + $32.54 = **$178.59** $3.64 + $49.39 + $1.00 = **$54.03**

Page 78

Subtracting Money

Example:

Steps:

1. Align the decimal points.
2. Subtract.

```
 $14.32
- $ 5.43
 $ 8.89
```

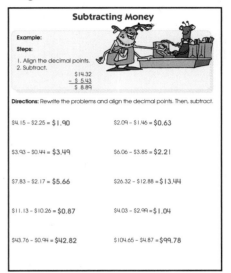

Directions: Rewrite the problems and align the decimal points. Then, subtract.

$4.15 - $2.25 = **$1.90** $2.09 - $1.46 = **$0.63**

$3.93 - $0.44 = **$3.49** $6.06 - $3.85 = **$2.21**

$7.83 - $2.17 = **$5.66** $26.32 - $12.88 = **$13.44**

$11.13 - $10.26 = **$0.87** $4.03 - $2.99 = **$1.04**

$43.76 - $0.94 = **$42.82** $104.65 - $4.87 = **$99.78**

Page 79

Big Bucks for You!

Directions: Solve the problems on another sheet of paper.

	Answer Space
1. You receive your first royalty check for $1,000.00 and deposit it in your checking account. You go directly to the music store and spend $234.56 on new CDs. What is your balance?	$765.44
2. You naturally treat all your friends to pizza, which costs you $47.76. You pay with a check. What is your balance now?	$717.68
3. You decide to restock your wardrobe and buy $389.99 worth of new clothes. What is your balance?	$327.69
4. Your next royalty check arrives, and you deposit $1,712.34. You also treat yourself to a new 15-speed bicycle, which costs $667.09. What is your balance?	$1372.94
5. You buy your mother some new perfume for a present. You write a check for $37.89. What is your balance?	$1335.05
6. You need a tennis racket and some other sports equipment. The bill comes to $203.45. What is your balance?	$1131.60
7. You treat your family to dinner at Snails in a Pail, where the check comes to $56.17. What is your new balance?	$1075.43
8. You join a health club, and the first payment is $150.90. What is your new balance?	$924.53
9. You deposit your latest royalty check, which amounts to $4,451.01. What is your new balance?	$5375.54
10. To celebrate this good fortune, you take your entire peewee football team to a professional football game. The bill comes to $4,339.98. What is your new balance?	$1035.56

Page 80

At the Science Store

Directions: Solve. Remember to align the decimal points.

1. Mr. Fargas buys 2 books. How much does he spend?
   $19.98
   ```
      1 1
      9.99
   + $ 9.99
     $19.98
   ```

2. Janice buys a star chart and a pendulum. How much does she spend?
   $40.11

3. Can Troy buy a chemistry set and a rock set for less than $30?
   no - $32.54

4. Jack buys a rock set and pendulum. He pays with a $20 bill and a $10 bill. How much change does he receive?
   $5.41

Telescope	$75.15
Geode	$13.50
Rock set	$ 5.95
Book	$ 9.99
Chemistry set	$26.59
Fossils small	$ 8.79
large	$12.89
Star chart	$21.47
Pendulum	$18.64

Tax included in prices!

5. Oliver buys *Dinosaurs*, *The Great Ice Age*, and *Rocks of Hawaii*. How much will his books cost?
   $29.97

6. Find the price of a large fossil, the chemistry set, and a telescope.
   $114.63

Page 81

Multiplying Money

Example:

Joey buys 14 paperback books for $1.95 each. How much does he spend?

```
  $1.95
x   14
  780
+1950
$27.30 ← set decimal point two numbers in from the right
```

Directions: Rewrite the problems and multiply.

$1.55 x 7 = **$10.85** $10.85 x 19 = **$206.15**

$3.06 x 9 = **$27.54** $5.35 x 12 = **$64.20**

$10.00 x 15 = **$150.00** $1.25 x 105 = **$131.25**

$9.87 x 13 = **$128.31** $4.95 x 22 = **$108.90**

1. Lauren buys wood for bookshelves at a cost of $0.58 per foot. If she buys 27 feet, how much does she spend?
   $15.66

2. Which costs more: 5 new books for $5.97 each or 12 used books for $2.50 each?
   the used books

Page 82

Dividing Money

Example:

Six friends earn $63.90 shoveling driveways on a snowy day. If they divide the money evenly, how much does each one earn?

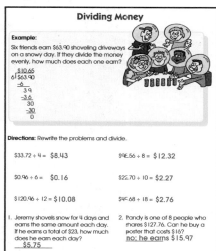

```
     $10.65
6)$63.90
  -6
   3 9
  -3 6
     30
    -30
      0
```

Directions: Rewrite the problems and divide.

$33.72 ÷ 4 = $8.43

$98.56 ÷ 8 = $12.32

$0.96 ÷ 6 = $0.16

$22.70 ÷ 10 = $2.27

$120.96 ÷ 12 = $10.08

$49.68 ÷ 18 = $2.76

1. Jeremy shovels snow for 4 days and earns the same amount each day. If he earns a total of $23, how much does he earn each day? __$5.75__

2. Randy is one of 8 people who shares $127.76. Can he buy a poster that costs $16? __no; he earns $15.97__

Page 83

Snails in a Pail

Sly Me Slugg, world-famous French chef, has made his fast-food business, Snails in a Pail, the most popular restaurant in the whole area. This is his menu:

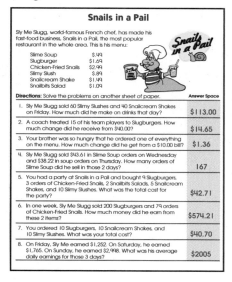

Slime Soup	$.49
Slugburger	$1.69
Chicken-Fried Snails	$2.99
Slimy Slush	$.89
Snailcream Shake	$1.49
Snailbits Salad	$1.09

Directions: Solve the problems on another sheet of paper.

		Answer Space
1.	Sly Me Slugg sold 60 Slimy Slushes and 40 Snailcream Shakes on Friday. How much did he make on drinks that day?	$113.00
2.	A coach treated 15 of his team players to Slugburgers. How much change did he receive from $40.00?	$14.65
3.	Your brother was so hungry that he ordered one of everything on the menu. How much change did he get from a $10.00 bill?	$1.36
4.	Sly Me Slugg sold $43.61 in Slime Soup orders on Wednesday and $38.22 in soup orders on Thursday. How many orders of Slime Soup did he sell in those 2 days?	167
5.	You had a party at Snails in a Pail and bought 9 Slugburgers, 3 orders of Chicken-Fried Snails, 2 Snailbits Salads, 5 Snailcream Shakes, and 10 Slimy Slushes. What was the total cost for the party?	$42.71
6.	In one week, Sly Me Slugg sold 200 Slugburgers and 79 orders of Chicken-Fried Snails. How much money did he earn from these 2 items?	$574.21
7.	You ordered 10 Slugburgers, 10 Snailcream Shakes, and 10 Slimy Slushes. What was your total cost?	$40.70
8.	On Friday, Sly Me earned $1,252. On Saturday, he earned $1,765. On Sunday, he earned $2,998. What was his average daily earnings for those 3 days?	$2005

Page 85

Using a Calculator

Here are some examples of how to enter problems into a calculator.

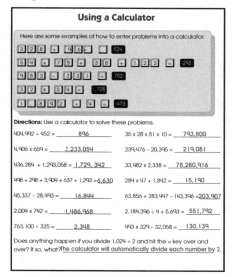

Directions: Use a calculator to solve these problems.

404,992 ÷ 452 = __896__

35 × 28 × 81 × 10 = __793,800__

4,906 × 659 = __3,233,054__

239,476 − 20,395 = __219,081__

436,284 + 1,293,058 = __1,729,342__

33,482 × 2,338 = __78,280,916__

498 + 298 + 3,904 + 637 + 1,293 = __6,630__

284 × 47 + 1,842 = __15,190__

45,337 − 28,493 = __16,844__

63,856 + 283,447 − 143,396 = __203,907__

2,004 × 742 = __1,486,968__

2,184,396 ÷ 4 + 5,693 = __551,792__

763,100 ÷ 325 = __2,348__

493 × 329 − 32,058 = __130,139__

Does anything happen if you divide 1,024 ÷ 2 and hit the = key over and over? If so, what? __The calculator will automatically divide each number by 2.__

Page 86

Calculator Fun

Directions: Use a calculator to solve these puzzles. If the display is too small for all the digits, use the calculator on a computer instead of a hand-held one.

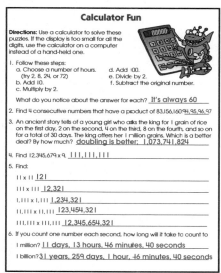

1. Follow these steps:
   a. Choose a number of hours. (try 2, 8, 24, or 72)
   b. Add 10.
   c. Multiply by 2.
   d. Add 100.
   e. Divide by 2.
   f. Subtract the original number.

   What do you notice about the answer for each? __It's always 60__

2. Find 4 consecutive numbers that have a product of 83,156,160. __94, 95, 96, 97__

3. An ancient story tells of a young girl who asks the king for 1 grain of rice on the first day, 2 on the second, 4 on the third, 8 on the fourth, and so on for a total of 30 days. The king offers her 1 million grains. Which is a better deal? By how much? __doubling is better; 1,073,741,824__

4. Find 12,345,679 × 9. __111,111,111__

5. Find:

   11 × 11 __121__

   111 × 111 __12,321__

   1,111 × 1,111 __1,234,321__

   11,111 × 11,111 __123,454,321__

   111,111 × 111,111 __12,345,654,321__

6. If you count one number each second, how long will it take to count to

   1 million? __11 days, 13 hours, 46 minutes, 40 seconds__

   1 billion? __31 years, 259 days, 1 hour, 46 minutes, 40 seconds__

Page 88

Keeping Track

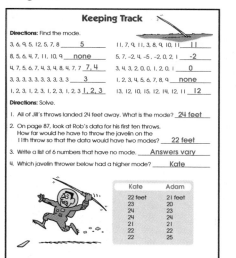

Directions: Find the mode.

3, 6, 9, 5, 12, 5, 7, 8 __5__

11, 7, 9, 11, 3, 8, 9, 10, 11 __11__

8, 5, 6, 4, 7, 11, 10, 9 __none__

5, 7, −2, 4, −5, −2, 0, 2, 1 __−2__

4, 7, 5, 6, 7, 4, 3, 4, 8, 4, 7, 7 __7, 4__

3, 4, 3, 2, 0, 0, 1, 2, 0, 1 __0__

3, 3, 3, 3, 3, 3, 3, 3, 3, 3 __3__

1, 2, 3, 4, 5, 6, 7, 8, 9 __none__

1, 2, 3, 1, 2, 3, 1, 2, 3, 1, 2, 3 __1, 2, 3__

13, 12, 10, 15, 12, 14, 12, 11 __12__

Directions: Solve.

1. All of Jill's throws landed 24 feet away. What is the mode? __24 feet__

2. On page 87, look at Rob's data for his first ten throws. How far would he have to throw the javelin on the 11th throw so that the data would have two modes? __22 feet__

3. Write a list of 6 numbers that have no mode. __Answers vary__

4. Which javelin thrower below had a higher mode? __Kate__

Kate	Adam
22 feet	21 feet
23	20
24	23
24	24
21	21
22	22
22	25

Page 89

Jumping the Median

The **median** is another kind of average.

When ordering a list of numbers from least to greatest, the median is the number that falls in the middle. Look at Anna's maximum high jumps for the last week.

Day	Height
Monday	62 inches
Tuesday	64 inches
Wednesday	64 inches
Thursday	64 inches
Friday	60 inches
Saturday	61 inches
Sunday	64 inches

Order the numbers: 60, 61, 62, **62**, 64, 64, 64. The number 62 falls in the middle. It is the median.

The mode is 64 inches. In some cases, the median and mode are the same number.

If there is an even number of heights, there will be two numbers in the middle. To find the median, add the two middle numbers and divide the sum by 2.

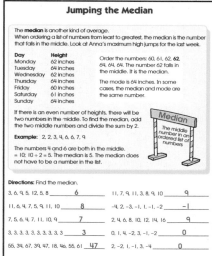

Example: 2, 2, 3, 4, 6, 7, 9

The numbers 4 and 6 are both in the middle. = 10; 10 ÷ 2 = 5. The median is 5. The median does not have to be a number in the list.

Directions: Find the median.

3, 6, 9, 5, 12, 5, 8 __6__

11, 7, 9, 11, 3, 8, 9, 10 __9__

11, 6, 4, 7, 5, 9, 11, 10 __8__

−4, 2, −3, −1, 1, −1, −1, −2 __−1__

7, 5, 4, 7, 11, 10, 9 __7__

2, 4, 6, 8, 10, 12, 14, 16 __9__

3, 3, 3, 3, 3, 3, 3, 3, 3 __3__

0, 1, 4, −2, 3, −1, −2 __0__

55, 34, 67, 39, 47, 18, 46, 55, 61 __47__

2, −2, 1, −1, 3, −4 __0__

Page 90

What Do You Mean?

Probably the most common average is the **mean**. To find the mean, add all the numbers in the list, then divide the sum by the total number of addends.

Suppose a hurdler completes his trials in the following times. Find the mean.

Trial	Time in Seconds
1	35
2	29
3	34
4	30
5	31
6	33

Mean — The sum of all the numbers divided by the number of addends.

Add the numbers: 35 + 29 + 34 + 30 + 31 + 33 = 192
Divide 192 by 6 because there are 6 numbers in the list: 192 ÷ 6 = 32.
The mean is 32 seconds.

The mean may or may not be a number in the list. The mean may also be different from the median and/or the mode.

Directions: Find the mean.

3, 6, 9, 5, 12 _____7_____   11, 5, 9, 11, 3, 7, 9, 9 _____8_____

3, 1, 0, 2, 0, 0 _____1_____   4, 6, -1, -1 _____2_____

-3, -2, -3, -1, -1 _____-2_____   2, -1, 1, -2 _____0_____

3, 3, 3, 3, 3, 3, 3, 3, 3 _____3_____   5, 9, 6, 2, 7, 9, 12, 4, 8, 8 _____7_____

9, 4, 5, 2, 6, 0, 3, 4, 3 _____4_____   6, 7, 3, 6, 4, 2, 7, 5 _____5_____

Page 91

Field Day

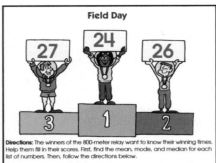

Directions: The winners of the 800-meter relay want to know their winning times. Help them fill in their scores. First, find the mean, mode, and median for each list of numbers. Then, follow the directions below.

9, 10, 2, 5, 8, 8, 6, 8 _**7, 8, 8**_   4, 6, 2, 8, 7, 5, 3 _**5, none, 5**_

12, 9, 10, 7, 9, 11, 12 _**10, 12, and 10**_   23, 37, 27, 35, 33 _**33, 33, 33**_

3, 3, 2, 5, 4, 7, 6, 4, 3, 2, 5, 4 _**4, 3 and 4,**_ 4   7, -2, 3, -1, 1, -1, 0 _**1, -1, 0**_

6, 4, 6, 4, 6, 4, 6, 4, 6, 5 _**5, 4 and 6, 5**_   8, 14, 16, 17, 15, 14, 16, 16, 19 _**5, 16, 16**_

24, 26, 28, 30 _**27, none, 27**_   -4, 3, 6, -3, -4, -1, 30 _**-4 and 3, -1**_

7, 5, 10, 8, 6, 7, 7, 7, 6 _**7, 7, 7**_   23, 26, 19, 27, 27, 28, 18 _**24, 27, 26**_

The winning team had a time in seconds equal to the mean of the last problem. The second-place team had a time equal to the median. The third-place team had a time equal to the mode. Write the times on the cards.

Page 92

Adding and Subtracting Like Fractions

A **fraction** is a number that names part of a whole. Examples of fractions are $\frac{1}{2}$ and $\frac{1}{3}$. **Like fractions** have the same **denominator**, or bottom number. Examples of like fractions are $\frac{1}{4}$ and $\frac{3}{4}$.

To add or subtract fractions, the denominators must be the same. Add or subtract only the **numerators**, the numbers above the line in fractions.

Example:

numerators
denominators $\frac{5}{8} - \frac{1}{8} = \frac{4}{8}$

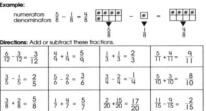

Directions: Add or subtract these fractions.

$\frac{6}{12} - \frac{3}{12} = \frac{3}{12}$	$\frac{4}{9} + \frac{1}{9} = \frac{5}{9}$	$\frac{1}{3} + \frac{1}{3} = \frac{2}{3}$	$\frac{5}{11} + \frac{4}{11} = \frac{9}{11}$
$\frac{3}{5} - \frac{1}{5} = \frac{2}{5}$	$\frac{5}{6} - \frac{2}{6} = \frac{3}{6}$	$\frac{3}{4} - \frac{2}{4} = \frac{1}{4}$	$\frac{5}{10} + \frac{3}{10} = \frac{8}{10}$
$\frac{3}{8} + \frac{2}{8} = \frac{5}{8}$	$\frac{1}{7} + \frac{4}{7} = \frac{5}{7}$	$\frac{2}{20} + \frac{15}{20} = \frac{17}{20}$	$\frac{11}{15} - \frac{9}{15} = \frac{2}{15}$

Directions: Color the part of each pizza that equals the given fraction.

$\frac{2}{4}$ + $\frac{1}{4}$ = $\frac{3}{4}$

Page 93

Adding and Subtracting Unlike Fractions

Unlike fractions have different denominators. Examples of unlike fractions are $\frac{1}{4}$ and $\frac{2}{5}$. To add or subtract fractions, the denominators must be the same.

Example:

Step 1: Make the denominators the same by finding the least common denominator. The LCD of a pair of fractions is the same as the least common multiple (LCM) of their denominators.

$\frac{1}{3} + \frac{1}{4} =$ Multiples of 3 are 3, 6, 9, 12, 15.
Multiples of 4 are 4, 8, 12, 16.
LCM (and LCD) = 12

Step 2: Multiply by a number that will give the LCD. The numerator and denominator must be multiplied by the same number.

A. $\frac{1}{3} \times \frac{4}{4} = \frac{4}{12}$ B. $\frac{1}{4} \times \frac{3}{3} = \frac{3}{12}$

Step 3: Add the fractions. $\frac{1}{3} + \frac{1}{4} = \frac{4}{12} + \frac{3}{12} = \frac{7}{12}$

Directions: Follow the above steps to add or subtract unlike fractions. Write the LCM.

$\frac{2}{4} + \frac{3}{8} = \frac{7}{8}$	$\frac{3}{6} + \frac{1}{3} = \frac{5}{6}$	$\frac{4}{5} - \frac{1}{4} = \frac{11}{20}$
LCM = ___8___	LCM = ___6___	LCM = ___20___
$\frac{2}{3} + \frac{2}{9} = \frac{8}{9}$	$\frac{4}{7} - \frac{2}{14} = \frac{6}{14}$	$\frac{7}{12} - \frac{2}{4} = \frac{1}{12}$
LCM = ___9___	LCM = ___14___	LCM = ___12___

The basketball team ordered two pizzas. They left $\frac{1}{3}$ of one and $\frac{1}{4}$ of the other. How much pizza was left? $\frac{7}{12}$

Page 94

Reducing Fractions

A fraction is in lowest terms when the GCF of both the numerator and denominator is 1. These fractions are in lowest possible terms: $\frac{2}{3}$, $\frac{5}{8}$, and $\frac{99}{100}$.

Example: Write $\frac{4}{8}$ in lowest terms.

Step 1: Write the factors of 4 and 8.
Factors of 4 are 4, 2, 1.
Factors of 8 are 1, 8, 2, 4.

Step 2: Find the GCF: 4.

Step 3: Divide both the numerator and denominator by 4.

   $\frac{4 \div 4}{8 \div 4} = \frac{1}{2}$

Directions: Write each fraction in lowest terms.

$\frac{6}{8} = \frac{3}{4}$ lowest terms $\frac{9}{12} = \frac{3}{4}$ lowest terms

factors of 6: 6, 1, 2, 3 factors of 9: _1_, _3_, _9_ _3_ GCF

factors of 8: 8, 1, 2, 4 factors of 12: _1_, _2_, _3_, _4_, _6_, _12_ _4_ GCF

$\frac{2}{6} = \frac{1}{3}$	$\frac{10}{15} = \frac{2}{3}$	$\frac{8}{32} = \frac{1}{4}$	$\frac{4}{10} = \frac{2}{5}$
$\frac{12}{18} = \frac{2}{3}$	$\frac{6}{8} = \frac{3}{4}$	$\frac{4}{6} = \frac{2}{3}$	$\frac{3}{9} = \frac{1}{3}$

Directions: Color the pizzas to show that $\frac{4}{6}$ in lowest terms is $\frac{2}{3}$.

 =

Page 95

Improper Fractions

An improper fraction has a numerator that is greater than its denominator. An example of an improper fraction is $\frac{7}{4}$. An improper fraction should be reduced to its lowest terms.

Example: $\frac{5}{4}$ is an improper fraction because its numerator is greater than its denominator.

Step 1: Divide the numerator by the denominator: 5 ÷ 4 = 1, r1

Step 2: Write the remainder as a fraction: $\frac{1}{4}$

$\frac{5}{4} = 1\frac{1}{4}$ $1\frac{1}{4}$ is a mixed number—a whole number and a fraction.

Directions: Follow the steps above to change the improper fractions to mixed numbers.

$\frac{9}{8} = 1\frac{1}{8}$	$\frac{11}{5} = 2\frac{1}{5}$	$\frac{5}{3} = 1\frac{2}{3}$	$\frac{7}{6} = 1\frac{1}{6}$	$\frac{8}{7} = 1\frac{1}{7}$	$\frac{4}{3} = 1\frac{1}{3}$
$\frac{21}{5} = 4\frac{1}{5}$	$\frac{9}{4} = 2\frac{1}{4}$	$\frac{3}{2} = 1\frac{1}{2}$	$\frac{9}{8} = 1\frac{1}{2}$	$\frac{25}{4} = 6\frac{1}{4}$	$\frac{8}{3} = 2\frac{2}{3}$

Sara had 29 duplicate stamps in her stamp collection. She decided to give them to four of her friends. If she gave each of them the same number of stamps, how many duplicates will she have left? ___1___

Name the improper fraction in this problem. $\frac{29}{4}$

What step must you do next to solve the problem? **change to a mixed number**

Write your answer as a mixed number. $7\frac{1}{4}$

How many stamps could she give each of her friends? ___7___

Page 96

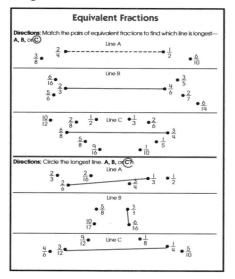

Equivalent Fractions

Directions: Match the pairs of equivalent fractions to find which line is longest— A, B, or **C**

Line A

$\frac{3}{8}$ • ------------------- • $\frac{1}{2}$ • $\frac{6}{10}$

$\frac{2}{4}$ •

Line B

$\frac{6}{16}$ • $\frac{2}{3}$ ————— • $\frac{4}{6}$ • $\frac{3}{5}$

$\frac{5}{6}$ • • $\frac{2}{7}$

• $\frac{6}{14}$

Line C

$\frac{10}{12}$ • $\frac{2}{4}$ • $\frac{1}{2}$ • $\frac{1}{3}$ • $\frac{2}{6}$

$\frac{6}{8}$ • ———— • $\frac{3}{4}$

$\frac{5}{8}$ • $\frac{9}{11}$ • $\frac{1}{10}$

Directions: Circle the longest line. **A, B, or C**

Line A

$\frac{2}{3}$ • $\frac{2}{6}$ • $\frac{1}{3}$ • $\frac{1}{2}$

$\frac{2}{6}$ •

Line B

$\frac{5}{8}$ • $\frac{3}{4}$

$\frac{10}{17}$ • $\frac{6}{16}$

Line C

$\frac{4}{6}$ • $\frac{3}{12}$ • $\frac{9}{12}$ • $\frac{1}{8}$ • $\frac{1}{4}$ • $\frac{5}{10}$

Page 97

Conversion

Directions: Find the number of units in each fraction described.

1. If there are 12 eggs in a dozen, how many eggs are in . . .
$\frac{1}{2}$ dozen? _____6_____
$\frac{1}{4}$ dozen? _____3_____
$\frac{1}{3}$ dozen? _____4_____

2. If there are 100 centimeters (cm) in a meter, how many cm are in . . .
$\frac{1}{2}$ meter? _____50_____
$\frac{1}{4}$ meter? _____25_____
$\frac{1}{10}$ meter? _____10_____

3. If there are 16 ounces in a pound, how many ounces are in . . .
$\frac{1}{2}$ pound? _____8_____
$\frac{1}{4}$ pound? _____4_____
$\frac{3}{8}$ pound? _____6_____

4. If there are 4 quarts in a gallon, how many quarts are in . . .
$\frac{1}{2}$ gallon? _____2_____
$\frac{1}{4}$ gallon? _____1_____
$\frac{3}{4}$ gallon? _____3_____

5. If there are 60 seconds in a minute, how many seconds are in . . .
$\frac{1}{2}$ minute? _____30_____
$\frac{1}{4}$ minute? _____15_____
$\frac{3}{4}$ minute? _____45_____

6. If there are 1,000 meters in a kilometer, how many meters are in . . .
$\frac{1}{10}$ kilometer? _____100_____
$\frac{1}{2}$ kilometer? _____500_____
$\frac{1}{4}$ kilometer? _____250_____

7. If there are 30 days in most months, how many days are in . . .
$\frac{1}{3}$ month? _____10_____
$\frac{1}{6}$ month? _____5_____
$\frac{1}{10}$ month? _____3_____

8. If there are 24 hours in a day, how many hours are in . . .
$\frac{1}{3}$ day? _____8_____
$\frac{2}{3}$ day? _____16_____
$\frac{1}{4}$ day? _____6_____

9. If there are 36 inches in a yard, how many inches are in . . .
$\frac{2}{3}$ yard? _____24_____
$\frac{1}{4}$ yard? _____9_____
$\frac{1}{2}$ yard? _____18_____

10. If there are 2,000 pounds in a ton, how many pounds are in . . .
$\frac{1}{2}$ ton? _____1,000_____
$\frac{1}{4}$ ton? _____500_____
$\frac{1}{20}$ ton? _____100_____

Page 98

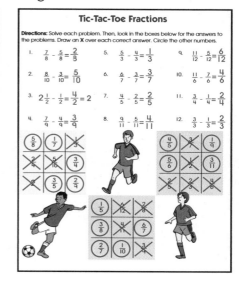

Tic-Tac-Toe Fractions

Directions: Solve each problem. Then, look in the boxes below for the answers to the problems. Draw an X over each correct answer. Circle the other numbers.

1. $\frac{7}{8} - \frac{5}{8} = \frac{2}{8}$

2. $\frac{8}{10} - \frac{3}{10} = \frac{5}{10}$

3. $2\frac{1}{2} - \frac{1}{2} = \frac{4}{2} = 2$

4. $\frac{7}{9} - \frac{4}{9} = \frac{3}{9}$

5. $\frac{5}{3} - \frac{3}{3} = \frac{2}{3}$

6. $\frac{6}{7} - \frac{3}{7} = \frac{3}{7}$

7. $\frac{4}{5} - \frac{2}{5} = \frac{2}{5}$

8. $\frac{9}{11} - \frac{5}{11} = \frac{4}{11}$

9. $\frac{11}{12} - \frac{5}{12} = \frac{6}{12}$

10. $\frac{11}{6} - \frac{5}{6} = \frac{4}{6}$

11. $\frac{3}{4} - \frac{1}{4} = \frac{2}{4}$

12. $\frac{3}{3} - \frac{1}{3} = \frac{2}{3}$

Page 99

Mixed Numbers

A **mixed number** is a whole number and a fraction together. An example of a mixed number is $2\frac{3}{8}$. A mixed number can be changed to an improper fraction.

Example: $2\frac{3}{4}$

Step 1: Multiply the denominator by the whole number: $4 \times 2 = 8$

Step 2: Add the numerator: $8 + 3 = 11$

Step 3: Write the sum over the denominator: $\frac{11}{4}$

Mixed Numbers

Directions: Follow the steps above to change the mixed numbers to improper fractions.

$3\frac{2}{3} = \frac{11}{3}$	$6\frac{1}{5} = \frac{31}{5}$	$4\frac{7}{8} = \frac{39}{8}$	$2\frac{1}{2} = \frac{5}{2}$
$1\frac{4}{5} = \frac{9}{5}$	$5\frac{3}{4} = \frac{23}{4}$	$7\frac{1}{8} = \frac{57}{8}$	$9\frac{1}{9} = \frac{82}{9}$
$8\frac{1}{2} = \frac{17}{2}$	$7\frac{1}{6} = \frac{43}{6}$	$5\frac{3}{5} = \frac{28}{5}$	$9\frac{3}{8} = \frac{75}{8}$
$12\frac{1}{5} = \frac{61}{5}$	$25\frac{1}{2} = \frac{51}{2}$	$10\frac{2}{3} = \frac{32}{3}$	$14\frac{3}{8} = \frac{115}{8}$

Page 100

Adding Mixed Numbers

Directions: To add mixed numbers, first find the least common denominator. Always reduce the answer to lowest terms.

Example:

$5\frac{1}{4} \longrightarrow 5\frac{3}{12}$
$+ 6\frac{1}{3} \longrightarrow + 6\frac{4}{12}$
$\overline{\qquad\quad 11\frac{7}{12}}$

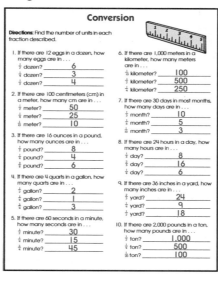

Directions: Add. Reduce the answers to lowest terms.

$8\frac{1}{4}$
$+ 7\frac{1}{4}$
$\overline{15\frac{3}{4}}$

$5\frac{1}{4}$
$+ 2\frac{3}{8}$
$\overline{7\frac{5}{8}}$

$9\frac{3}{10}$
$+ 7\frac{1}{5}$
$\overline{16\frac{1}{2}}$

$8\frac{1}{5}$
$+ 6\frac{7}{10}$
$\overline{14\frac{9}{10}}$

$4\frac{4}{5}$
$+ 3\frac{3}{10}$
$\overline{8\frac{1}{10}}$

$3\frac{1}{8}$
$+ 7\frac{1}{4}$
$\overline{10\frac{3}{8}}$

$4\frac{1}{2}$
$+ 1\frac{1}{3}$
$\overline{5\frac{5}{6}}$

$6\frac{1}{2}$
$+ 3\frac{1}{4}$
$\overline{9\frac{3}{4}}$

$5\frac{1}{3}$
$+ 2\frac{1}{3}$
$\overline{7\frac{2}{3}}$

$6\frac{1}{3}$
$+ 2\frac{1}{3}$
$\overline{8\frac{11}{12}}$

$2\frac{2}{7}$
$+ 4\frac{1}{14}$
$\overline{6\frac{5}{14}}$

$3\frac{1}{2}$
$+ 3\frac{1}{4}$
$\overline{6\frac{3}{4}}$

The boys picked $3\frac{1}{2}$ baskets of apples. The girls picked $5\frac{1}{2}$ baskets. How many baskets of apples did the boys and girls pick in all? _____9_____

Page 101

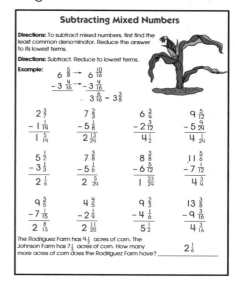

Subtracting Mixed Numbers

Directions: To subtract mixed numbers, first find the least common denominator. Reduce the answer to its lowest terms.

Directions: Subtract. Reduce to lowest terms.

Example:

$6\frac{5}{8} \longrightarrow 6\frac{10}{16}$
$- 3\frac{4}{16} \longrightarrow - 3\frac{4}{16}$
$\overline{\qquad\quad 3\frac{6}{16} = 3\frac{3}{8}}$

$2\frac{3}{7}$
$- 1\frac{1}{14}$
$\overline{1\frac{5}{14}}$

$7\frac{2}{3}$
$- 5\frac{1}{8}$
$\overline{2\frac{13}{24}}$

$6\frac{3}{4}$
$- 2\frac{3}{12}$
$\overline{4\frac{1}{2}}$

$9\frac{5}{12}$
$- 5\frac{9}{24}$
$\overline{4\frac{1}{24}}$

$5\frac{1}{2}$
$- 3\frac{1}{3}$
$\overline{2\frac{1}{6}}$

$7\frac{8}{9}$
$- 5\frac{1}{6}$
$\overline{2\frac{5}{6}}$

$8\frac{3}{8}$
$- 6\frac{5}{12}$
$\overline{1\frac{23}{24}}$

$11\frac{5}{6}$
$- 7\frac{1}{12}$
$\overline{4\frac{3}{4}}$

$9\frac{3}{5}$
$- 7\frac{1}{2}$
$\overline{2\frac{8}{15}}$

$4\frac{4}{5}$
$- 2\frac{1}{4}$
$\overline{2\frac{11}{20}}$

$9\frac{2}{3}$
$- 4\frac{1}{6}$
$\overline{5\frac{1}{2}}$

$13\frac{3}{8}$
$- 9\frac{3}{16}$
$\overline{4\frac{3}{16}}$

The Rodriguez Farm has $9\frac{1}{2}$ acres of corn. The Johnson Farm has $7\frac{1}{3}$ acres of corn. How many more acres of corn does the Rodriguez Farm have? _____$2\frac{1}{6}$_____

Page 102

A Trip to the Ocean

Maria's girls' club earned enough money from their cookie sale to go on a camping trip by the ocean. Read about their trip.

Directions: Write your answers in complete sentences.

1. The bus started with $6\frac{1}{2}$ gallons of gasoline. When the driver added $9\frac{1}{2}$ more gallons of gasoline, how much gasoline did the bus have in it?
   There were 16 gallons of gas in the bus.
2. The girls and their leaders stopped for a picnic after driving $58\frac{1}{5}$ miles. After the picnic, they drove another $43\frac{4}{5}$ miles before reaching the ocean. How far were they from home?
   They were 102 miles from home.
3. Before leaving home, the girls made sandwiches for their lunch. They had $7\frac{1}{2}$ tuna sandwiches, $4\frac{1}{4}$ cheese sandwiches, $2\frac{3}{4}$ peanut butter sandwiches and $5\frac{1}{2}$ beef sandwiches. How many total sandwiches did they bring?
   They brought 20 sandwiches.
4. The leader cut a watermelon into 16 slices for lunch. The girls ate 8 of the slices. What fraction of the watermelon did they eat?
   They ate $\frac{8}{16}$ or $\frac{1}{2}$ of the melon.
5. When they arrived, they took $1\frac{1}{3}$ hours to set up the tents. They spent another $\frac{2}{3}$ hour getting their bedrolls ready. How long did they work before they could play in the ocean?
   They worked 2 hours.
6. The girls swam and played in the water for $1\frac{3}{4}$ hours. Then, they sat in the sun for $\frac{3}{4}$ hour. How many hours did they play and sunbathe?
   They played and sunbathed for $2\frac{1}{2}$ hours.
7. After dinner, they had a campfire. First, they sang for $1\frac{1}{3}$ hours. Then, they told ghost stories for $\frac{2}{3}$ hour. If they put out the fire and went to sleep at 10:30 P.M., what time did they begin the campfire?
   They began the campfire at 8:30 P.M.

Page 103

Comparing Fractions

Directions: Use the symbol > (greater than), < (less than), or = (equal to) to show the relationship between each pair of fractions.

$\frac{1}{2} > \frac{1}{3}$	$\frac{2}{5} < \frac{3}{7}$	$\frac{3}{8} < \frac{2}{4}$
$\frac{3}{4} = \frac{6}{8}$	$\frac{2}{3} < \frac{4}{5}$	$\frac{3}{9} = \frac{1}{3}$
$\frac{3}{12} = \frac{1}{4}$	$\frac{2}{14} = \frac{1}{7}$	$\frac{5}{15} < \frac{2}{3}$

If Kelly gave $\frac{1}{3}$ of a pizza to Holly and $\frac{1}{5}$ to Diane, how much did she have left? $\frac{7}{15}$

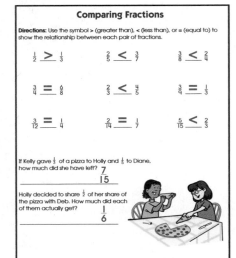

Holly decided to share $\frac{1}{2}$ of her share of the pizza with Deb. How much did each of them actually get? $\frac{1}{6}$

Page 104

Ordering Fractions

Directions: When putting fractions in order from smallest to largest or largest to smallest, it helps to find a common denominator first.

Example:

$\frac{1}{3}$, $\frac{1}{2}$ changed to $\frac{2}{6}$, $\frac{3}{6}$

Directions: Put the following fractions in order from least to largest value.

				Least			Largest
$\frac{1}{5}$	$\frac{6}{15}$	$\frac{4}{5}$	$\frac{1}{3}$	$\frac{1}{5}$	$\frac{1}{3}$	$\frac{6}{15}$	$\frac{4}{5}$
$\frac{3}{12}$	$\frac{3}{6}$	$\frac{1}{3}$	$\frac{3}{4}$	$\frac{3}{12}$	$\frac{1}{3}$	$\frac{3}{6}$	$\frac{3}{4}$
$\frac{2}{5}$	$\frac{4}{15}$	$\frac{3}{5}$	$\frac{5}{15}$	$\frac{4}{15}$	$\frac{5}{15}$	$\frac{2}{5}$	$\frac{3}{5}$
$3\frac{4}{5}$	$3\frac{2}{5}$	$\frac{9}{5}$	$3\frac{1}{5}$	$\frac{9}{5}$	$3\frac{1}{5}$	$3\frac{2}{5}$	$3\frac{4}{5}$
$9\frac{1}{3}$	$9\frac{2}{3}$	$9\frac{9}{12}$	$8\frac{2}{3}$	$8\frac{2}{3}$	$9\frac{1}{3}$	$9\frac{2}{3}$	$9\frac{9}{12}$
$5\frac{8}{12}$	$5\frac{5}{12}$	$5\frac{4}{24}$	$5\frac{3}{6}$	$5\frac{4}{24}$	$5\frac{5}{12}$	$5\frac{3}{6}$	$5\frac{8}{12}$
$4\frac{3}{5}$	$5\frac{7}{15}$	$6\frac{2}{5}$	$5\frac{1}{5}$	$4\frac{3}{5}$	$5\frac{1}{5}$	$5\frac{7}{15}$	$6\frac{2}{5}$

Four dogs were selected as finalists at a dog show. They were judged in four separate categories. One received a perfect score in each area. The dog with a score closest to four is the winner. Their scores are listed below. Which dog won the contest? A

Dog A $3\frac{4}{5}$ (circled) Dog B $3\frac{2}{3}$ Dog C $3\frac{5}{15}$ Dog D $3\frac{9}{12}$

Page 105

Adding Unlike Fractions

Directions: Solve the problems. Shade in your answers on the pizzas below to show which pieces have been eaten.

$\frac{1}{10} + \frac{4}{5} = \frac{9}{10}$	$\frac{3}{12} + \frac{1}{6} = \frac{5}{12}$	$\frac{1}{2} + \frac{1}{3} = \frac{5}{6}$	$\frac{3}{4} + \frac{1}{5} = \frac{19}{20}$	$\frac{1}{5} + \frac{1}{3} = \frac{8}{15}$
$\frac{2}{3} + \frac{1}{4} = \frac{11}{12}$	$\frac{5}{12} + \frac{1}{6} = \frac{7}{12}$	$\frac{2}{5} + \frac{9}{20} = \frac{17}{20}$	$\frac{1}{3} + \frac{2}{9} = \frac{5}{9}$	$\frac{3}{5} + \frac{1}{10} = \frac{7}{10}$
$\frac{1}{10} + \frac{1}{5} = \frac{3}{10}$	$\frac{2}{3} + \frac{1}{5} = \frac{13}{15}$	$\frac{1}{8} + \frac{1}{3} = \frac{11}{24}$	$\frac{3}{8} + \frac{1}{5} = \frac{23}{40}$	$\frac{1}{5} + \frac{1}{9} = \frac{14}{45}$

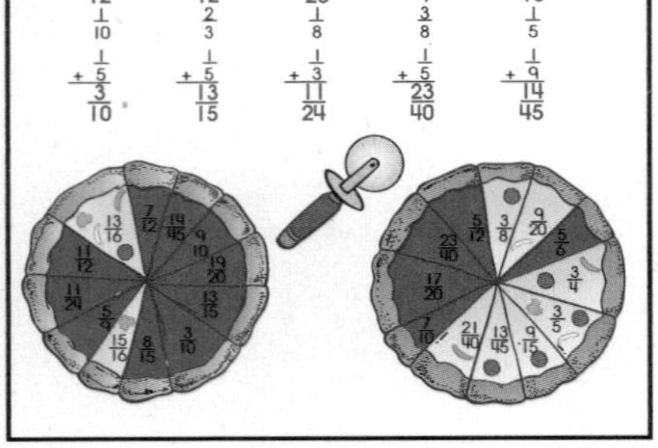

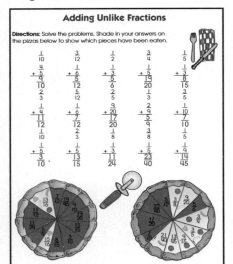

Page 106

Sandwich Solutions

Directions: Solve the following subtraction problems to find out who invented the sandwich. Write the letter next to each problem above its answer at the bottom. Reduce the answer to its lowest terms.

A. $\frac{3}{5} - \frac{1}{4} = \frac{7}{20}$ A. $\frac{5}{6} - \frac{1}{3} = \frac{1}{2}$ E. $\frac{9}{16} - \frac{1}{4} = \frac{5}{16}$

I. $\frac{7}{10} - \frac{3}{5} = \frac{1}{10}$ D. $\frac{1}{2} - \frac{5}{12} = \frac{1}{12}$ C. $\frac{7}{8} - \frac{3}{4} = \frac{1}{8}$

W. $\frac{13}{18} - \frac{1}{6} = \frac{10}{18} = \frac{5}{9}$ N. $\frac{2}{3} - \frac{1}{12} = \frac{7}{12}$ H. $\frac{19}{20} - \frac{4}{5} = \frac{3}{20}$

F. $\frac{18}{25} - \frac{2}{5} = \frac{8}{25}$ L. $\frac{8}{9} - \frac{1}{6} = \frac{13}{18}$ R. $\frac{5}{8} - \frac{3}{16} = \frac{7}{16}$

O. $\frac{4}{5} - \frac{2}{3} = \frac{2}{15}$ S. $\frac{1}{7} - \frac{1}{14} = \frac{1}{14}$

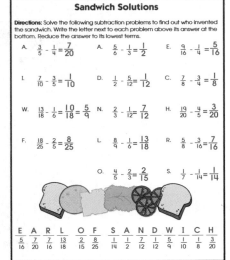

E	A	R	L	O	F	S	A	N	D	W	I	C	H
$\frac{5}{16}$	$\frac{7}{20}$	$\frac{7}{16}$	$\frac{13}{18}$	$\frac{2}{15}$	$\frac{8}{25}$	$\frac{1}{14}$	$\frac{1}{2}$	$\frac{7}{12}$	$\frac{1}{12}$	$\frac{5}{9}$	$\frac{1}{10}$	$\frac{1}{8}$	$\frac{3}{20}$

Page 107

Fractions: Mixed to Improper

Directions: Change the fractions to mixed numbers. Shade in each answer to find the path to the pot of gold.

1. $\frac{11}{9} = 1\frac{2}{9}$	2. $\frac{8}{3} = 2\frac{2}{3}$	3. $\frac{8}{7} = 1\frac{1}{7}$	4. $\frac{11}{6} = 1\frac{5}{6}$
5. $\frac{7}{3} = 2\frac{1}{3}$	6. $\frac{7}{6} = 1\frac{1}{6}$	7. $\frac{9}{4} = 2\frac{1}{4}$	8. $\frac{8}{5} = 1\frac{3}{5}$
9. $\frac{4}{3} = 1\frac{1}{3}$	10. $\frac{7}{2} = 3\frac{1}{2}$	11. $\frac{3}{2} = 1\frac{1}{2}$	12. $\frac{6}{5} = 1\frac{1}{5}$
13. $\frac{7}{4} = 1\frac{3}{4}$	14. $\frac{9}{2} = 4\frac{1}{2}$	15. $\frac{11}{8} = 1\frac{3}{8}$	16. $\frac{5}{2} = 2\frac{1}{2}$
17. $\frac{9}{7} = 1\frac{2}{7}$	18. $\frac{11}{4} = 2\frac{3}{4}$	19. $\frac{17}{12} = 1\frac{5}{12}$	20. $\frac{13}{12} = 1\frac{1}{12}$

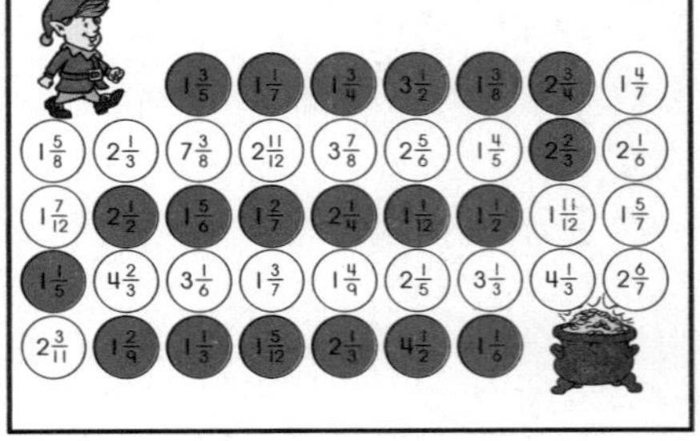

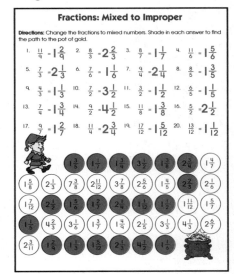

Fractions: Mixed to Improper

Directions: Solve the problems. Connect the dots in the order of the answers.

1. $1\frac{2}{5} = \frac{7}{5}$
2. $1\frac{1}{3} = \frac{4}{3}$
3. $1\frac{5}{7} = \frac{12}{7}$
4. $2\frac{2}{3} = \frac{8}{3}$
5. $2\frac{5}{8} = \frac{21}{8}$
6. $2\frac{1}{2} = \frac{5}{2}$
7. $1\frac{5}{6} = \frac{11}{6}$
8. $1\frac{1}{5} = \frac{6}{5}$
9. $2\frac{4}{5} = \frac{14}{5}$
10. $1\frac{1}{16} = \frac{17}{16}$
11. $1\frac{1}{2} = \frac{3}{2}$
12. $3\frac{1}{5} = \frac{16}{5}$
13. $1\frac{11}{12} = \frac{23}{12}$
14. $1\frac{7}{8} = \frac{15}{8}$
15. $1\frac{6}{7} = \frac{13}{7}$
16. $2\frac{1}{4} = \frac{9}{4}$
17. $1\frac{7}{12} = \frac{19}{12}$
18. $1\frac{3}{7} = \frac{10}{7}$
19. $6\frac{2}{3} = \frac{20}{3}$
20. $3\frac{3}{5} = \frac{18}{5}$
21. $1\frac{5}{21} = \frac{26}{21}$
22. $1\frac{7}{36} = \frac{43}{36}$
23. $1\frac{9}{20} = \frac{29}{20}$
24. $1\frac{13}{24} = \frac{37}{24}$

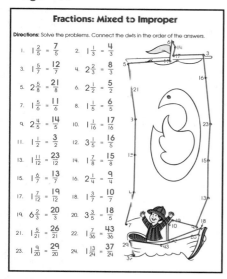

Fractions: Addition and Subtraction

Directions: Identify the shaded part.

1. $\frac{1}{4}$
2. $\frac{2}{6}$
3. $1\frac{1}{8}$

Directions: Reduce to lowest terms.

4. $\frac{10}{15} = \frac{2}{3}$
5. $\frac{9}{12} = \frac{3}{4}$
6. $\frac{18}{54} = \frac{2}{6} = \frac{1}{3}$

Directions: Compare using > or <.

7. $\frac{13}{27} > \frac{12}{27}$
8. $\frac{5}{6} > \frac{3}{4}$
9. $2\frac{3}{4} < \frac{13}{4}$

Directions: Add or subtract.

10. $\frac{1}{5} + \frac{2}{5} = \frac{3}{5}$
11. $\frac{3}{8} - \frac{2}{8} = \frac{1}{8}$
12. $\frac{3}{4} + \frac{1}{2} = \frac{5}{4} = 1\frac{1}{4}$
13. $\frac{7}{8} - \frac{3}{4} = \frac{1}{8}$
14. $5\frac{1}{2} + 2\frac{1}{2} = \frac{16}{2} = 8$
15. $2\frac{1}{8} - 1\frac{5}{8} = \frac{4}{8} = \frac{1}{2}$
16. $\frac{21}{5} - \frac{21}{10} = \frac{21}{10} = 2\frac{1}{10}$
17. $5\frac{5}{8} + 3\frac{2}{4} = 8\frac{8}{12} = 8\frac{2}{12}$
18. $\frac{5}{3} + \frac{2}{5} = \frac{31}{15} = 2\frac{1}{15}$

Directions: Draw a model to show each fraction.

19. $3\frac{1}{4}$
20. $\frac{10}{3}$

Multiplying Fractions

To multiply fractions, follow these steps:

$\frac{1}{2} \times \frac{3}{4} =$ **Step 1:** Multiply the numerators. $1 \times 3 = 3$
Step 2: Multiply the denominators. $2 \times 4 = 8$

When multiplying a fraction by a whole number, first change the whole number to a fraction.

Example:

$\frac{1}{2} \times 8 = \frac{1}{2} \times \frac{8}{1} = \frac{8}{2} = 4$ reduced to lowest terms

Directions: Multiply. Reduce your answers to lowest terms.

$\frac{3}{4} \times \frac{1}{6} = \frac{1}{8}$	$\frac{1}{2} \times \frac{5}{8} = \frac{5}{16}$	$\frac{2}{3} \times \frac{1}{6} = \frac{1}{9}$	$\frac{2}{3} \times \frac{1}{2} = \frac{1}{3}$
$\frac{5}{6} \times 4 = 3\frac{1}{3}$	$\frac{3}{8} \times \frac{1}{16} = \frac{3}{128}$	$\frac{1}{5} \times 5 = 1$	$\frac{7}{8} \times \frac{3}{4} = \frac{21}{32}$
$\frac{7}{11} \times \frac{1}{3} = \frac{7}{33}$	$\frac{2}{9} \times \frac{9}{4} = \frac{1}{2}$	$\frac{1}{3} \times \frac{1}{3} \times \frac{1}{3} = \frac{1}{27}$	$\frac{1}{4} \times \frac{1}{4} \times \frac{1}{2} = \frac{1}{64}$

Jennifer has 10 pets. Two-fifths of the pets are cats, one-half are fish and one-tenth are dogs. How many of each pet does she have?

Cats = 4
Fish = 5
Dogs = 1

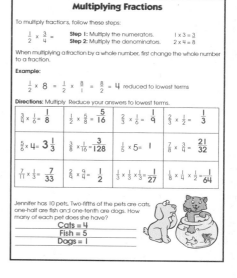

Multiplying Mixed Numbers

Multiply mixed numbers by first changing them to improper fractions. Always reduce your answers to lowest terms.

Example:

$2\frac{1}{3} \times 1\frac{1}{8} = \frac{7}{3} \times \frac{9}{8} = \frac{63}{24} = 2\frac{15}{24} = 2\frac{5}{8}$

Directions: Multiply. Reduce to lowest terms.

$4\frac{1}{4} \times 2\frac{1}{5} = 9\frac{7}{20}$	$1\frac{1}{3} \times 3\frac{1}{4} = 4\frac{1}{3}$	$1\frac{1}{9} \times 3\frac{3}{5} = 4$
$1\frac{6}{9} \times 4\frac{1}{2} = 8\frac{5}{14}$	$2\frac{3}{4} \times 2\frac{3}{5} = 7\frac{3}{20}$	$4\frac{2}{3} \times 3\frac{1}{7} = 14\frac{2}{3}$
$6\frac{2}{3} \times 2\frac{1}{8} = 13\frac{3}{5}$	$3\frac{1}{7} \times 4\frac{5}{8} = 14\frac{15}{28}$	$7\frac{3}{8} \times 2\frac{1}{4} = 15\frac{41}{72}$

Sunnyside Farm has two barns with 25 stalls in each barn. Cows use $\frac{3}{5}$ of the stalls, and horses use the rest.

How many stalls are for cows? 30
How many are for horses? 20

(Hint: First, find how many total stalls are in the two barns.)

Puzzling Fractions

Directions: Multiply to solve the problems.

$7 \times \frac{1}{5} = \frac{7}{5} = 1\frac{2}{5}$ $9 \times \frac{1}{10} = \frac{9}{10}$ $8 \times \frac{1}{8} = \frac{8}{8} = 1$ $8 \times \frac{1}{7} = \frac{8}{7} = 1\frac{1}{7}$

$7 \times \frac{1}{11} = \frac{7}{11}$ $9 \times \frac{1}{3} = \frac{9}{3} = 3$ $3 \times \frac{1}{6} = \frac{3}{6} = \frac{1}{2}$ $12 \times \frac{1}{5} = \frac{12}{5} = 2\frac{2}{5}$

$\frac{1}{5} \times 4 = \frac{4}{5}$ $\frac{1}{6} \times 9 = \frac{9}{6} = 1\frac{1}{2}$ $\frac{1}{5} \times 20 = \frac{20}{5} = 4$ $\frac{1}{6} \times 12 = \frac{12}{6} = 2$

$\frac{1}{10} \times \frac{1}{100} = \frac{1}{1000}$ $\frac{1}{6} \times \frac{1}{10} = \frac{1}{60}$ $\frac{1}{12} \times \frac{1}{3} = \frac{1}{36}$ $\frac{1}{6} \times \frac{1}{6} = \frac{1}{36}$

$\frac{1}{9} \times \frac{1}{8} = \frac{1}{72}$ $\frac{1}{4} \times \frac{1}{10} = \frac{1}{90}$ $\frac{1}{10} \times \frac{1}{10} = \frac{1}{100}$ $\frac{1}{20} \times \frac{1}{5} = \frac{1}{100}$

$8 \times \frac{1}{10} = \frac{8}{10} = \frac{4}{5}$ $\frac{1}{5} \times \frac{1}{8} = \frac{1}{40}$ $\frac{1}{6} \times \frac{1}{7} = \frac{1}{42}$ $\frac{1}{100} \times \frac{1}{100} = \frac{1}{10,000}$

$\frac{1}{9} \times 9 = \frac{9}{9} = 1$ $\frac{1}{8} \times 7 = \frac{7}{8}$ $\frac{1}{7} \times 6 = \frac{6}{7}$ $12 \times \frac{1}{4} = \frac{12}{4} = 3$

$\frac{1}{15} \times \frac{1}{13} = \frac{1}{195}$ $\frac{1}{3} \times \frac{1}{7} = \frac{1}{21}$ $\frac{1}{8} \times 3 = \frac{3}{8}$ $\frac{1}{7} \times 21 = \frac{21}{7} = 3$

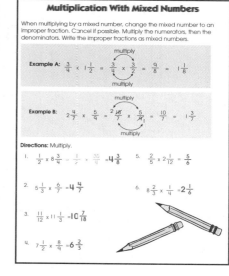

Multiplication With Mixed Numbers

When multiplying by a mixed number, change the mixed number to an improper fraction. Cancel if possible. Multiply the numerators, then the denominators. Write the improper fractions as mixed numbers.

Example A: $\frac{3}{4} \times 1\frac{1}{2} = \frac{3}{4} \times \frac{3}{2} = \frac{9}{8} = 1\frac{1}{8}$

Example B: $2\frac{4}{7} \times \frac{5}{4} = 2\frac{18}{7} \times \frac{5}{4} = \frac{10}{7} = 1\frac{3}{7}$

Directions: Multiply.

1. $\frac{1}{2} \times 8\frac{3}{4} = \frac{35}{4} = 4\frac{3}{8}$
2. $5\frac{1}{3} \times \frac{6}{7} = 4\frac{4}{7}$
3. $\frac{11}{12} \times 11\frac{1}{3} = 10\frac{7}{18}$
4. $7\frac{1}{2} \times \frac{8}{9} = 6\frac{2}{3}$
5. $\frac{2}{5} \times 2\frac{1}{12} = \frac{5}{6}$
6. $8\frac{2}{3} \times \frac{1}{4} = 2\frac{1}{6}$

Page 114

Dividing Fractions

To divide fractions, follow these steps:

$$\frac{3}{4} \div \frac{1}{4} =$$

Step 1: "Invert" the divisor. That means to turn it upside down.

$$\frac{3}{4} \div \frac{4}{1}$$

Step 2: Multiply the two fractions:

$$\frac{3}{4} \times \frac{4}{1} = \frac{12}{4}$$

Step 3: Reduce the fraction to lowest terms by dividing the denominator into the numerator.

$$12 \div 4 = 3$$
$$\frac{3}{4} \div \frac{1}{4} = 3$$

Directions: Follow the above steps to divide fractions.

$\frac{1}{4} \div \frac{1}{5} =$ **1$\frac{1}{4}$**	$\frac{1}{3} \div \frac{1}{12} =$ **4**	$\frac{3}{4} \div \frac{1}{3} =$ **2$\frac{1}{4}$**
$\frac{5}{12} \div \frac{1}{3} =$ **1$\frac{1}{4}$**	$\frac{3}{4} \div \frac{1}{6} =$ **4$\frac{1}{2}$**	$\frac{2}{9} \div \frac{2}{3} =$ **$\frac{1}{3}$**
$\frac{3}{7} \div \frac{1}{4} =$ **1$\frac{5}{7}$**	$\frac{2}{3} \div \frac{4}{6} =$ **1**	$\frac{1}{8} \div \frac{2}{3} =$ **$\frac{3}{16}$**
$\frac{4}{5} \div \frac{1}{3} =$ **2$\frac{2}{5}$**	$\frac{4}{8} \div \frac{2}{1} =$ **1**	$\frac{5}{12} \div \frac{6}{8} =$ **$\frac{5}{9}$**

Page 115

Dividing Fractions

When dividing fractions, change the problem to multiplication. Invert the divisor. Cancel if possible. Multiply the numerators, then the denominators. Write improper fractions as mixed numbers.

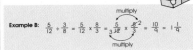

Example A: $\frac{3}{10} \div \frac{4}{5} = \frac{3}{10} \times \frac{5}{4} = \frac{3}{\cancel{10}} \times \frac{\cancel{5}}{4} = \frac{3}{8}$

Example B: $\frac{5}{12} \div \frac{3}{8} = \frac{5}{12} \times \frac{8}{3} = \frac{5}{\cancel{12}} \times \frac{\cancel{8}^{2}}{3} = \frac{10}{9} = 1\frac{1}{9}$

Directions: Divide.

1. $\frac{1}{2} \div \frac{3}{10} = \frac{1}{2} \times \frac{10}{3} = 1\frac{2}{3}$ 5. $\frac{1}{10} \div \frac{2}{5} = \frac{1}{4}$

2. $\frac{3}{8} \div \frac{1}{4} = 1\frac{1}{2}$ 6. $\frac{5}{6} \div \frac{11}{12} = \frac{10}{11}$

3. $\frac{4}{9} \div \frac{2}{3} = \frac{2}{3}$ 7. $\frac{14}{15} \div \frac{2}{3} = 1\frac{2}{5}$

4. $\frac{3}{8} \div \frac{5}{12} = \frac{9}{10}$ 8. $\frac{4}{5} \div \frac{3}{10} = 2\frac{2}{3}$

Page 116

Stump the Teacher

Directions: The students in Ms. Davidson's class were playing "Stump the Teacher." See if you can solve their problems.

1. If baseball cards are worth $\frac{1}{10}$ of a dollar each, how much are Brad's 54 cards worth? **$5.40**

2. If $\frac{6}{8}$ of Sally's 8 puppies are female and $\frac{1}{2}$ of the female puppies have been sold, how many female puppies have been sold? **3 puppies**

3. Felipe used $\frac{2}{3}$ cup of cheese for each pizza. If he made 4 pizzas, how much cheese did he need to buy? **2$\frac{2}{3}$ cups**

4. Francis bought $\frac{15}{16}$ of a yard of fabric. She used $\frac{1}{2}$ of it to make a dress for her doll. What fraction of a yard did she use? **$\frac{15}{32}$ yd.**

5. If a lot is $\frac{5}{8}$ of an acre, and the house covers $\frac{1}{2}$ of it, what fraction of an acre is covered by the house? **$\frac{5}{16}$ acre**

6. At the track meet, Rick entered 5 sprint contests. If each race was $\frac{1}{4}$ mile long, how many miles did Rick sprint in all? **1$\frac{1}{4}$ mi.**

7. The class had $\frac{1}{4}$ of an hour to take a math quiz. Nate used only $\frac{1}{3}$ of the time. What fraction of an hour did Nate use for the quiz? **$\frac{1}{12}$ hr.**

8. Lisa and Kim live $\frac{3}{8}$ of a mile apart. If they each walked $\frac{1}{2}$ of the way and met in the middle, what part of a mile did each walk? **$\frac{3}{16}$ mi.**

9. This year's summer vacation was $\frac{1}{6}$ of the year. How many months long was the summer vacation this year? **2 mo.**

10. Paul's dog was asleep $\frac{2}{3}$ of the day. How many hours was it awake? **8 hrs.**

Page 117

Fractions: Multiplication and Division

Directions: Solve.

1. $\frac{7}{9} \times \frac{1}{4} = \frac{7}{36}$ 2. $\frac{5}{6} \times \frac{1}{10} = \frac{5}{60} = \frac{1}{12}$ 3. $\frac{9}{10} \times \frac{2}{3} = \frac{18}{30} = \frac{3}{5}$

4. $8 \times \frac{1}{4} = \frac{8}{4} = 2$ 5. $\frac{1}{3} \times 15 = \frac{15}{3} = 5$

6. Jaime sat in his chair for $\frac{5}{6}$ of an hour. For $\frac{1}{3}$ of this time, he worked on this assignment. What fraction of an hour did he work on this assignment?

$$\frac{1}{3} \times \frac{5}{6} = \frac{5}{18}$$

7. $\frac{1}{2} \div \frac{1}{5} = \frac{5}{2} = 2\frac{1}{2}$ 8. $\frac{1}{5} \div \frac{1}{2} = \frac{2}{5}$

9. $\frac{3}{4} \div \frac{3}{8} = \frac{24}{12} = 2$ 10. $\frac{7}{16} \div \frac{4}{7} = \frac{49}{64}$

Page 118

Dividing Whole Numbers by Fractions

Follow these steps to divide a whole number by a fraction:

$$8 \div \frac{1}{4} =$$

Step 1: Write the whole number as a fraction:

$$\frac{8}{1} \div \frac{1}{4} =$$

Step 2: Invert the divisor.

$$\frac{8}{1} \div \frac{4}{1} =$$

Step 3: Multiply the two fractions:

$$\frac{8}{1} \times \frac{4}{1} = \frac{32}{1}$$

Step 4: Reduce the fraction to lowest terms by dividing the denominator into the numerator: $32 \div 1 = 32$

Directions: Follow the above steps to divide a whole number by a fraction.

$6 \div \frac{1}{3} =$ **18**	$4 \div \frac{1}{2} =$ **8**	$21 \div \frac{1}{3} =$ **63**
$8 \div \frac{1}{2} =$ **16**	$3 \div \frac{1}{6} =$ **18**	$15 \div \frac{1}{7} =$ **105**
$9 \div \frac{1}{5} =$ **45**	$4 \div \frac{1}{9} =$ **36**	$12 \div \frac{1}{6} =$ **72**

Three-fourths of a bag of popcorn fits into one bowl. How many bowls do you need if you have six bags of popcorn? **8**

Page 119

Fraction Review

Directions: Identify the shaded fraction and simplify to lowest terms.

1. $\frac{3}{8}$ 2. $\frac{4}{8} = \frac{1}{2}$ 3. $\frac{16}{20} = \frac{4}{5}$

Directions: Compare using > or <.

4. $\frac{3}{5} < \frac{4}{5}$ 5. $\frac{5}{8} > \frac{5}{11}$ 6. $1 > \frac{7}{8}$

Directions: Add or subtract. Reduce to lowest terms.

7. $\frac{1}{9} + \frac{5}{9} = \frac{6}{9} = \frac{2}{3}$ 8. $\frac{2}{5} + \frac{1}{10} = \frac{5}{10} = \frac{1}{2}$ 9. $\frac{3}{8} + \frac{1}{6} = \frac{13}{24}$

10. $3\frac{1}{4} + 2\frac{1}{3} = 5\frac{7}{12}$ 11. $\frac{7}{9} - \frac{2}{3} = \frac{1}{9}$ 12. $11\frac{7}{8} - 4\frac{5}{12} = 7\frac{11}{24}$

13. Change $\frac{17}{4}$ into a mixed number. **4$\frac{1}{4}$**   14. Change $3\frac{2}{5}$ into an improper fraction. **$\frac{17}{5}$**

Directions: Multiply or divide.

15. $\frac{3}{4} \times \frac{1}{2} = \frac{3}{8}$ 16. $\frac{11}{12} \times \frac{4}{5} = \frac{44}{60} = \frac{22}{30} = \frac{11}{15}$

17. $\frac{2}{3} \div \frac{1}{3} = 2$ 18. $\frac{1}{2} \div \frac{1}{4} = 2$

Page 120

Decimals

A **decimal** is a number with one or more places to the right of a decimal point.

Examples: 6.5 and 2.25

Fractions with denominators of 10 or 100 can be written as decimals.

Examples:

$\frac{7}{10} = 0.7$

0	.	7	▢
ones		tenths	hundredths

$1\frac{52}{100} = 1.52$

1	.	5	2
ones		tenths	hundredths

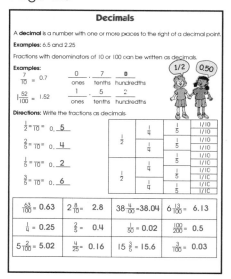

Directions: Write the fractions as decimals.

$\frac{1}{2} = \frac{}{10} = 0.\underline{5}$

$\frac{2}{5} = \frac{}{10} = 0.\underline{4}$

$\frac{1}{5} = \frac{}{10} = 0.\underline{2}$

$\frac{3}{5} = \frac{}{10} = 0.\underline{6}$

			1/5	1/10
	1/2	1/4	1/5	1/10
			1/5	1/10
			1/5	1/10
	1/2	1/4	1/5	1/10
			1/5	1/10
				1/10

$\frac{63}{100} = 0.63$	$2\frac{8}{10} = 2.8$	$38\frac{4}{100} = 38.04$	$6\frac{13}{100} = 6.13$
$\frac{1}{4} = 0.25$	$\frac{2}{5} = 0.4$	$\frac{1}{50} = 0.02$	$\frac{100}{200} = 0.5$
$5\frac{2}{100} = 5.02$	$\frac{4}{25} = 0.16$	$15\frac{3}{5} = 15.6$	$\frac{3}{100} = 0.03$

Page 121

Decimal Drawings

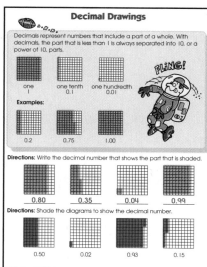

Decimals represent numbers that include a part of a whole. With decimals, the part that is less than 1 is always separated into 10, or a power of 10, parts.

one
1

one tenth
0.1

one hundredth
0.01

Examples:

0.2

0.75

1.00

Directions: Write the decimal number that shows the part that is shaded.

0.80   0.35   0.04   0.99

Directions: Shade the diagrams to show the decimal number.

0.50   0.02   0.93   0.15

Page 122

That's the Point

When writing a decimal, place the decimal point between the ones column and the tenths column. Here are some place values to the right and left of the decimal point:

hundreds	tens	ones		tenths	hundredths	thousandths

Steps:
1. Read the whole number.
2. Say the word "and" or "point."
3. Read the number after the decimal point.
4. Say the decimal place of the last digit to the right.

Examples:

45.91 is read "forty-five and ninety-one hundredths"
222.1 is read "two hundred twenty-two point one"
10.004 is read "ten and four thousandths"

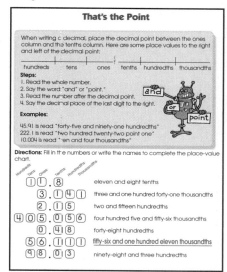

Directions: Fill in the numbers or write the names to complete the place-value chart.

1	1	.	8			eleven and eight tenths
3	.	1	4	1		three and one hundred forty-one thousandths
2	.	1	5			two and fifteen hundredths
4	0	5	.	0	5	6	four hundred five and fifty-six thousandths
0	.	4	8			forty-eight hundredths
5	6	.	1	1	1	fifty-six and one hundred eleven thousandths
9	8	.	0	3		ninety-eight and three hundredths

Page 123

More Puzzling Problems

Directions: Solve the crossword puzzle.

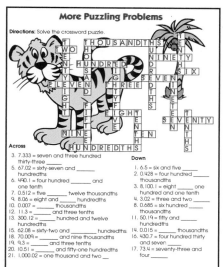

Across
3. 7.333 = seven and three hundred thirty-three _____
5. 67.02 = sixty-seven and _____ hundredths
6. 490.1 = four hundred _____ and one tenth
7. 0.512 = five _____ twelve thousandths
9. 8.06 = eight and _____ hundredths
10. 0.007 = _____ thousandths
12. 11.3 = _____ and three tenths
13. 300.12 = _____ hundred and twelve hundredths
15. 62.08 = sixty-two and _____ hundredths
18. 70.009 = _____ and nine thousandths
19. 9.3 = _____ and three tenths
20. 10.51 = _____ and fifty-one hundredths
21. 1,000.02 = one thousand and two _____

Down
1. 6.5 = six and five _____
2. 0.428 = four hundred _____ thousandths
3. 8,100.1 = eight _____ one hundred and one tenth
4. 3.02 = three and two _____
8. 0.685 = six hundred _____ thousandths
11. 50.19 = fifty and _____
14. 0.015 = _____ thousandths
16. 430.7 = four hundred thirty and seven _____
17. 73.4 = seventy-three and four _____

Page 124

Missing Train

Directions: Circle the . . .

1. smallest number	0.31 (A)	(0.05) (F)	0.20 (R)	
2. greatest number	0.001 (R)	(0.13) (T)	0.100 (A)	
3. greatest number	(9.910) (L)	9.010 (C)	9.909 (T)	
4. smallest number	0.110 (A)	(0.09) (L)	0.3 (R)	
5. greatest number	0.090 (S)	0.10 (P)	(0.12) (O)	
6. smallest number	0.131 (H)	0.2 (T)	(0.08) (W)	
7. greatest number	1.310 (E)	1.03 (H)	(1.33) (T)	
8. smallest number	(2.001) (H)	2.9 (A)	2.010 (U)	
9. greatest number	(0.3) (E)	0.03 (A)	0.003 (N)	
10. greatest number	1.01 (U)	1.001 (R)	(1.1) (T)	
11. greatest number	(3.04) (R)	3.009 (U)	3.039 (N)	
12. smallest number	(6.01) (A)	6.11 (H)	6.030 (O)	
13. greatest number	0.001 (T)	(0.100) (C)	0.090 (N)	
14. smallest number	(1.027) (K)	1.270 (R)	1.207 (P)	
15. smallest number	9.909 (N)	9.09 (G)	(9.009) (S)	

Directions: Fill in the circled letters to solve the riddle below.

How do you search for a missing train?

F O L L O W   T H E   T R A C K S
1 2 3 4 5 6   7 8 9   10 11 12 13 14 15

Page 125

The Missing Piece

Directions: Each puzzle piece on this page is missing its match. Cut out the pieces below. Match the word name with its decimal and tape the two pieces together along the broken lines. When complete, there should be a square, a triangle, a rectangle, a circle, a parallelogram, and a pentagon.

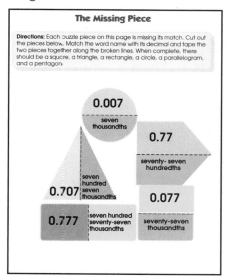

0.007 — seven thousandths

0.77 — seventy-seven hundredths

0.707 — seven hundred seven thousandths

0.077 —

0.777 — seven hundred seventy-seven thousandths

seventy-seven thousandths

Page 127

Decimals and Fractions

Directions: Write the letter of the fraction that is equal to the decimal.

0.25 = __G__
0.5 = __L__
0.7 = __O__
0.8 = __N__
0.37 = __J__
0.2 = __K__
0.65 = __C__
0.75 = __B__
0.6 = __D__
0.12 = __E__
0.33 = __A__
0.95 = __F__
0.24 = __M__
0.3 = __I__
0.4 = __H__

A. $\frac{33}{100}$ B. $\frac{3}{4}$ C. $\frac{13}{20}$

D. $\frac{3}{5}$ E. $\frac{3}{25}$ F. $\frac{19}{20}$

G. $\frac{1}{4}$ H. $\frac{2}{5}$ I. $\frac{3}{10}$

J. $\frac{37}{100}$ K. $\frac{1}{5}$ L. $\frac{1}{2}$

M. $\frac{6}{25}$ N. $\frac{4}{5}$ O. $\frac{7}{10}$

Page 128

Adding and Subtracting Decimals

Add and subtract with decimals the same way you do with whole numbers. Keep the decimal points lined up so that you work with hundreths, then tenths, then ones, and so on.

Directions: Add or subtract. Remember to keep the decimal point in the proper place.

0.5 + 0.8 = **1.3**
0.35 + 0.25 = **0.60**
47.5 − 32.7 = **14.8**
85.7 − 9.8 = **75.9**

13.90 + 4.23 = **18.13**
9.53 − 8.16 = **1.37**
72.8 − 63.9 = **8.9**
6.43 + 4.58 = **11.01**

638.07 − 19.34 = **618.73**
811.060 + 78.430 = **889.490**
521.09 − 148.75 = **372.34**

916.635 + 172.136 = **1,088.771**
287.768 − 63.951 = **223.817**
467.05 − 398.19 = **68.86**

Sean ran a 1-mile race in 5.58 minutes. Carlos ran it in 6.38 minutes. How much less time did Sean need?

0.8 minutes

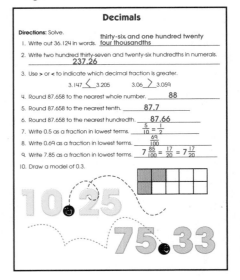

Page 129

Decimals

Directions: Solve.

1. Write out 36.124 in words. **thirty-six and one hundred twenty four thousandths**
2. Write two hundred thirty-seven and twenty-six hundredths in numerals. **237.26**
3. Use > or < to indicate which decimal fraction is greater.
   3.147 **<** 3.205   3.06 **>** 3.059
4. Round 87.658 to the nearest whole number. **88**
5. Round 87.658 to the nearest tenth. **87.7**
6. Round 87.658 to the nearest hundredth. **87.66**
7. Write 0.5 as a fraction in lowest terms. **$\frac{5}{10} = \frac{1}{2}$**
8. Write 0.69 as a fraction in lowest terms. **$\frac{69}{100}$**
9. Write 7.85 as a fraction in lowest terms. **$7\frac{85}{100} = \frac{17}{20} = 7\frac{17}{20}$**
10. Draw a model of 0.3.

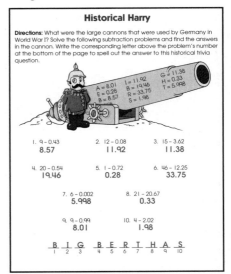

Page 130

Blast Off!

Directions: Solve the crossword puzzle.

Hint: Decimal points take up their own square. Do not use a zero before the decimal.

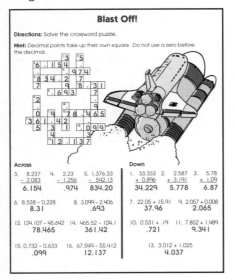

Across
3. 8.237 − 2.083 = **6.154**
4. 2.23 − 1.256 = **.974**
5. 1,376.33 − 542.13 = **834.20**
6. 8.538 − 0.228 = **8.31**
8. 3.099 − 2.406 = **.693**
12. 124.107 − 45.642 = **78.465**
14. 465.52 − 104.1 = **361.42**
15. 0.732 − 0.633 = **.099**
16. 567.549 − 55.412 = **12.137**

Down
1. 33.333 + 0.896 = **34.229**
2. 2.587 + 3.191 = **5.778**
3. 5.78 + 1.09 = **6.87**
7. 22.05 + 15.91 = **37.96**
9. 2.057 + 0.008 = **2.065**
10. 0.531 + .19 = **.721**
11. 7.852 + 1.489 = **9.341**
13. 3.012 + 1.025 = **4.037**

Page 131

Decimal Delight

Directions: Kooky Claude Clod, the cafeteria cook, has some strange ideas about cooking. He does not understand fractions—only decimals. Help Claude convert these measurements to decimals so he can get cooking!

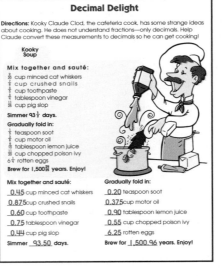

Kooky Soup

Mix together and sauté:
- $\frac{9}{20}$ cup minced cat whiskers
- $\frac{7}{8}$ cup crushed snails
- $\frac{3}{5}$ cup toothpaste
- $\frac{3}{4}$ tablespoon vinegar
- $\frac{11}{25}$ cup pig slop

Simmer $93\frac{1}{2}$ days.

Gradually fold in:
- $\frac{1}{5}$ teaspoon soot
- $\frac{3}{8}$ cup motor oil
- $\frac{9}{10}$ tablespoon lemon juice
- $\frac{11}{20}$ cup chopped poison ivy
- $6\frac{1}{4}$ rotten eggs

Brew for $1,500\frac{24}{25}$ years. Enjoy!

Mix together and sauté:
- **0.45** cup minced cat whiskers
- **0.875** cup crushed snails
- **0.60** cup toothpaste
- **0.75** tablespoon vinegar
- **0.44** cup pig slop

Simmer **93.50** days.

Gradually fold in:
- **0.20** teaspoon soot
- **0.375** cup motor oil
- **0.90** tablespoon lemon juice
- **0.55** cup chopped poison ivy
- **6.25** rotten eggs

Brew for **1,500.96** years. Enjoy!

Page 132

Historical Harry

Directions: What were the large cannons that were used by Germany in World War I? Solve the following subtraction problems and find the answers in the cannon. Write the corresponding letter above the problem's number at the bottom of the page to spell out the answer to this historical trivia question.

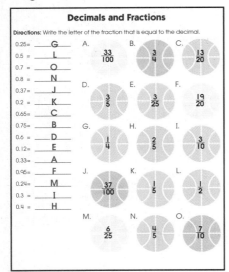

A = 8.01   I = 11.92   H = 0.33
E = 0.28   B = 19.46   G = 11.38
R = 33.75
B = 8.57   S = 1.98   T = 5.998

1. 9 − 0.43 = **8.57**
2. 12 − 0.08 = **11.92**
3. 15 − 3.62 = **11.38**
4. 20 − 0.54 = **19.46**
5. 1 − 0.72 = **0.28**
6. 46 − 12.25 = **33.75**
7. 6 − 0.002 = **5.998**
8. 21 − 20.67 = **0.33**
9. 9 − 0.99 = **8.01**
10. 4 − 2.02 = **1.98**

B I G   B E R T H A S
1 2 3   4 5 6 7 8 9 10

Page 133

Multiplying Decimals

Directions: Multiply with decimals the same way you do with whole numbers. The decimal point moves in multiplication. Count the number of decimal places in the problem and use the same number of decimal places in your answer.

Example:

```
    3.5
  x 1.5
   1 75
   3 5
   5.25
```

Directions: Multiply.

2.5 x .9 **2.25**	67.4 x 2.3 **155.02**	83.7 x 3.06 **820.26**	13.35 x 3.06 **40.851**
9.06 x 2.38 **21.5628**	28.97 x 5.16 **149.4852**	33.41 x .93 **31.0713**	28.7 x 11.9 **341.53**

The jet flies 1.5 times faster than the plane with a propeller. The propeller plane flies 165.7 miles per hour. How fast does the jet fly?

248.55 mph

Page 134

Multiple Design

Directions: Solve the problems on a separate sheet of paper. Find the answers in the design and color correctly.

green	blue	red
0.463 x 82 **37.966**	28.5 x 7.4 **210.9**	6.51 x 6.9 **44.919**

yellow	purple	purple
39.2 x 0.36 **14.112**	7.54 x 0.43 **3.2422**	0.670 x 0.94 **0.62980**

yellow	yellow	purple
64.9 x 3.26 **211.574**	0.592 x 40.6 **24.0352**	7.46 x 5.9 **44.014**

green	blue	blue	green	purple
92.4 x 0.62 **57.288**	32.8 x 0.26 **8.528**	85.1 x 0.95 **80.845**	7.32 x 1.6 **11.712**	6.05 x 8.3 **50.215**

green	blue	yellow	red	red
3.27 x 844 **2759.88**	5.56 x 3.94 **21.9064**	80.5 x 0.276 **22.218**	5.77 x 4.26 **24.5802**	95.8 x 7.41 **709.878**

red	yellow	yellow	yellow	yellow
0.784 x 6.92 **5.42528**	2.57 x 63.6 **163.452**	29.3 x 0.487 **14.2691**	6.80 x 0.42 **2.856**	0.245 x 3.6 **0.8820**

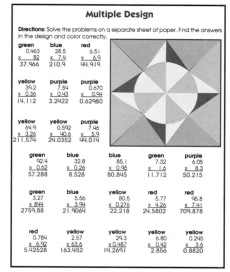

Page 135

Dividing With Decimals

Directions: When the dividend has a decimal, place the decimal point for the answer directly above the decimal point in the dividend. The first one has been done for you.

```
    12.5
3 ) 37.5
   -3
    07
   -6
    15
   -15
```

8.6	15.8	43.8
4) 34.4	2) 31.6	3) 131.4

37.5	25.9	56.8	32.7
5) 187.5	7) 181.3	6) 340.8	9) 294.3

45.2	52.9	67.3	94.3
3) 135.6	5) 264.5	2) 134.6	8) 754.4

7.05	11.35	3.19	5.54
5) 35.25	7) 79.45	9) 28.71	36) 199.44

Page 136

The Perfect Sweet-Treat Solution

Directions: Solve each division problem on a separate sheet of paper. Draw a line from the popcorn (problem) to the correct drink (answer).

Page 137

Dividing Decimals by Decimals

Directions: When the divisor has a decimal point you must eliminate it before dividing. You can do this by moving the decimal point to the right to create a whole number. You must also move the decimal point the same number of spaces to the right in the dividend.

Sometimes you need to add zeros to do this.

Example:

```
0.25 ) 85.50    changes to    25 ) 8550
                                  342
                                 -75
                                  105
                                 -100
                                   50
                                   50
                                    0
```

Directions: Divide.

93	71	91	119
0.3) 27.9	0.6) 42.6	0.9) 81.9	0.7) 83.3

58	81	9	63
0.4) 23.2	0.7) 56.7	1.2) 10.8	2.2) 138.6

450	120	98	543
12.6) 5,670	4.7) 564	8.6) 842.8	3.7) 2,009.1

325	320	318	2079
5.9) 1,917.5	4.3) 1,376	2.9) 922.2	2.7) 5613.3

Page 138

Working With Decimals

Directions: Solve.

1. Write 207.426 in words.
   two hundred seven and four hundred twenty six thousandths

2. Write forty-seven and thirteen thousandths in numerals. **47.013**

3. Use > or < to indicate which decimal fraction is greater.
   17.35 **>** 17.295

Directions: Fill in the blanks.

4. Round 12.836 to the nearest whole number. **13**

5. Round 12.836 to the nearest tenth. **12.8**

6. Round 12.836 to the nearest hundredth. **12.84**

7. Write 0.36 as a fraction in lowest terms. $\frac{36}{100} = \frac{9}{25}$

8. Write 0.25 as a fraction in lowest terms. $\frac{25}{100} = \frac{1}{4}$

9. Write $\frac{3}{4}$ as a decimal number. **0.75**

Directions: Solve.

10. 36.2 + 27.325 = **63.525**

11. 87.36 − 84.95 = **2.41**

12. 4.6 x 1.2 = **5.52**

13. 3.46 x 10 = **34.6**

14. 11.55 ÷ 7 = **1.65**

15. 39 ÷ 12 = **3.25**

16. 367.52 ÷ 10 = **36.752**

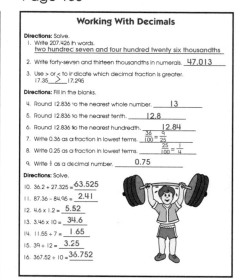

Page 139

Giving 100%

Example:
The word **percent** means "for each hundred." A test score of 95% means that 95 out of 100 answers are correct.

There are 100 squares in this grid. Each square represents one hundredth. Since 63 squares are shaded, 63% is shaded.

Directions: Write the percent of squares shaded.

Shade each grid to show the percent.

20%   55%   45%   10%

32%   4%   92%   100%

88%   0%   8%   67%

Page 140

Decimals, Fractions, and Percents

Decimals, fractions, and percents are different ways of representing the same number.

0.16 (sixteen hundredths) $\frac{16}{100}$ (or 4/25 in simplest form)   16%

Directions: Write the amount shaded as a decimal, a fraction in the simplest form, and a percent.

$0.33 \ \frac{33}{100} \ 33\%$ $0.06 \ \frac{3}{50} \ 6\%$ $0.65 \ \frac{13}{20} \ 65\%$ $0.20 \ \frac{1}{5} \ 20\%$

$0.78 \ \frac{39}{50} \ 78\%$ $1.00 \ 1 \ 100\%$ $0.22 \ \frac{11}{50} \ 22\%$ $0.50 \ \frac{1}{2} \ 50\%$

$0.49 \ \frac{49}{100} \ 49\%$ $0.75 \ \frac{3}{4} \ 75\%$ $0.91 \ \frac{91}{100} \ 91\%$ $0.80 \ \frac{4}{5} \ 80\%$

Page 141

Percents and Fractions

Directions: Write the fraction and percent represented in each situation.

Situation	Fraction	Percent
30 marbles out of 100 marbles are red.	$\frac{30}{100}$	30%
29 people out of 100 people voted.	$\frac{29}{100}$	29%
10 fish out of 100 fish are tropical.	$\frac{10}{100}$	10%
7 cats out of 100 cats live indoors.	$\frac{7}{100}$	7%
4 turtles out of 100 turtles laid eggs.	$\frac{4}{100}$	4%
7 out of 10 puppies had spots.	$\frac{7}{10} = \frac{70}{100}$	70%
5 out of 10 baskets were made.	$\frac{5}{10} = \frac{50}{100}$	50%
6 out of 25 rocks in my yard are igneous.	$\frac{6}{25} = \frac{24}{100}$	24%
17 out of 25 rulers are metric.	$\frac{17}{25} = \frac{68}{100}$	68%
18 out of 20 goldfish are orange.	$\frac{18}{20} = \frac{90}{100}$	90%
The dress was reduced $5 from $20.	$\frac{5}{20} = \frac{25}{100}$	25%

Page 142

Models

Directions: Draw the model and fill in the missing fraction, percent or decimal.

Draw	Fraction	Percent	Decimal
	$\frac{25}{100}$	25%	0.25
	$\frac{37}{100}$	37%	0.37
	$\frac{18}{100}$	18%	0.18
	$\frac{7}{10}$	70%	0.7
	$\frac{4}{100}$	4%	0.04

Page 143

Percents and Fractions

Example:

Steps to change a percent to a fraction, or a fraction to a percent:

Percent → Fraction
$67\% = 0.67 = \frac{67}{100}$
$8\% = 0.08 = \frac{8}{100} = \frac{2}{25}$
$125\% = 1.25 = \frac{125}{100} = \frac{5}{4} = 1\frac{1}{4}$

Fraction → Percent
$\frac{4}{5} = 4 \div 5 = 0.8 = 80\%$
$\frac{1}{3} = 1 \div 3 = 0.333 \ldots = 33.3\%$
$1\frac{1}{2} = \frac{3}{2} = 3 \div 2 = 1.5 = 150\%$

Directions: Match the percent with the fraction in simplest form. Write the letter on the line.

1. __H__ 5%   A. $\frac{3}{25}$ B. $\frac{11}{20}$ 2. __A__ 12%
3. __M__ 17%   C. $\frac{1}{3}$ D. $1\frac{1}{5}$ 4. __G__ 20%
5. __K__ 25%   E. $\frac{1}{2}$ F. $\frac{5}{6}$ 6. __C__ 33.3%
7. __O__ 48%   G. $\frac{1}{5}$ H. $\frac{1}{20}$ 8. __E__ 50%
9. __B__ 55%   I. $\frac{7}{10}$ J. $\frac{47}{50}$ 10. __I__ 70%
11. __N__ 75%   K. $\frac{1}{4}$ L. $1\frac{11}{25}$ 12. __F__ 83.3%
13. __J__ 94%   M. $\frac{17}{100}$ N. $\frac{3}{4}$ 14. __D__ 120%
15. __L__ 144%   O. $\frac{12}{25}$

Page 144

Percents and Decimals

Examples:
Steps to change a percent to a decimal, or a decimal to a percent:

Percent → Decimal
60% = 60 hundredths = 0.60
3% = 3 hundredths = 0.03
155% = 155 hundredths = 1.55

Decimal → Percent
0.35 = 35 hundredths = 35%
0.9 = 90 hundredths = 90%
1.24 = 124 hundredths = 124%

Directions: Write the equivalent decimal or percent.

0.54 = 54%   0.07 = 7%   0.8 = 80%
1.35 = 135%   35% = 0.35   125% = 1.25
50% = 0.50 or 0.5 2% = 0.02   2.44 = 244%
0.85 = 85%   23% = 0.23   0.5 = 50%
105% = 1.05   0.02 = 2%   8% = 0.08
10% = 0.10 or 0.1 3.00 = 300%   2.08 = 208%
0.05 = 5%   0.89 = 89%   120% = 1.20 or 1.2
43% = 0.43   3% = 0.03   90% = 0.90 or 0.9
1.85 = 185%   2.5 = 250%   0.4 = 40%

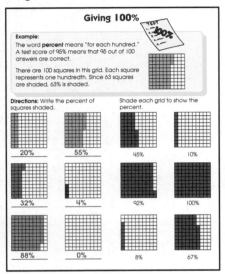
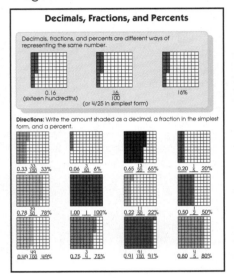
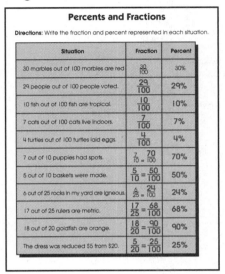
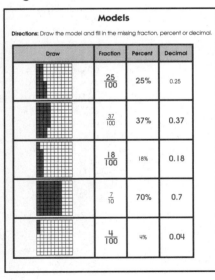
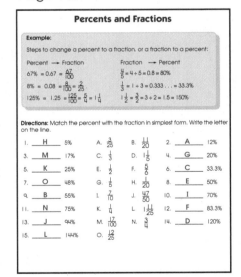

Page 145

Percent of a Number

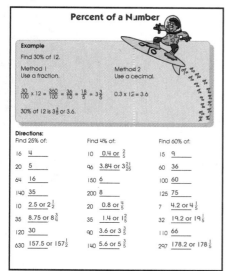

Example

Find 30% of 12.

Method 1
Use a fraction.

Method 2
Use a decimal.

$\frac{30}{100} \times 12 = \frac{360}{100} = \frac{36}{10} = \frac{18}{5} = 3\frac{3}{5}$ $0.3 \times 12 = 3.6$

30% of 12 is $3\frac{3}{5}$ or 3.6.

Directions:

Find 25% of:	Find 4% of:	Find 60% of:
16 _4_	10 _0.4 or $\frac{2}{5}$_	15 _9_
20 _5_	96 _3.84 or $3\frac{21}{25}$_	60 _36_
64 _16_	150 _6_	100 _60_
140 _35_	200 _8_	125 _75_
10 _2.5 or $2\frac{1}{2}$_	20 _0.8 or $\frac{4}{5}$_	7 _4.2 or $4\frac{1}{5}$_
35 _8.75 or $8\frac{3}{4}$_	35 _1.4 or $1\frac{2}{5}$_	32 _19.2 or $19\frac{1}{5}$_
120 _30_	90 _3.6 or $3\frac{3}{5}$_	110 _66_
630 _157.5 or $157\frac{1}{2}$_	140 _5.6 or $5\frac{3}{5}$_	297 _178.2 or $178\frac{1}{5}$_

Page 146

Sale!

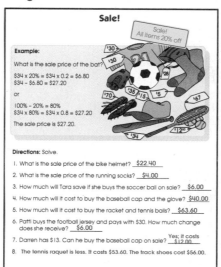

Sale! All items 20% off

Example:

What is the sale price of the bat?

$34 × 20% = $34 × 0.2 = $6.80
$34 − $6.80 = $27.20

or

100% − 20% = 80%
$34 × 80% = $34 × 0.8 = $27.20

The sale price is $27.20.

Directions: Solve.

1. What is the sale price of the bike helmet? _$22.40_
2. What is the sale price of the running socks? _$4.00_
3. How much will Tara save if she buys the soccer ball on sale? _$6.00_
4. How much will it cost to buy the baseball cap and the glove? _$40.00_
5. How much will it cost to buy the racket and tennis balls? _$63.60_
6. Patti buys the football jersey and pays with $30. How much change does she receive? _$6.00_
7. Darren has $13. Can he buy the baseball cap on sale? _Yes; it costs $12.00_
8. The tennis raquet is less. It costs $53.60. The track shoes cost $56.00.

Page 147

Percent

Directions: Percent is a ratio meaning "per hundred." It is written with a % sign. 20% means 20 percent or 20 per hundred.

Example:

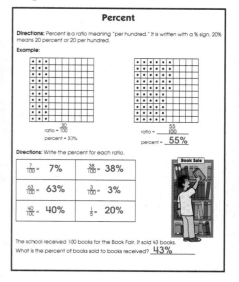

ratio = $\frac{30}{100}$
percent = 30%

ratio = $\frac{55}{100}$
percent = _55%_

Directions: Write the percent for each ratio.

$\frac{7}{100}$ = 7%	$\frac{38}{100}$ = 38%	Book Sale
$\frac{63}{100}$ = 63%	$\frac{3}{100}$ = 3%	
$\frac{40}{100}$ = 40%	$\frac{1}{5}$ = 20%	

The school received 100 books for the Book Fair. It sold 43 books.
What is the percent of books sold to books received? _43%_

Page 148

Using Calculators to Find Percent

A calculator is a machine that rapidly does addition, subtraction, multiplication, division, and other mathematical functions.

Example:

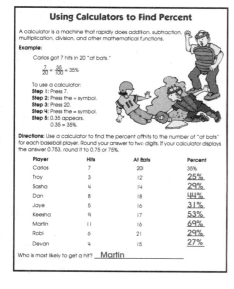

Carlos got 7 hits in 20 "at bats."

$\frac{7}{20} = \frac{35}{100} = 35\%$

To use a calculator:
Step 1: Press 7.
Step 2: Press the ÷ symbol.
Step 3: Press 20.
Step 4: Press the = symbol.
Step 5: 0.35 appears.
0.35 = 35%.

Directions: Use a calculator to find the percent of hits to the number of "at bats" for each baseball player. Round your answer to two digits. If your calculator displays the answer 0.753, round it to 0.75 or 75%.

Player	Hits	At Bats	Percent
Carlos	7	20	35%
Troy	3	12	_25%_
Sasha	4	14	_29%_
Dan	8	18	_44%_
Jaye	5	16	_31%_
Keesha	9	17	_53%_
Martin	11	16	_69%_
Robi	6	21	_29%_
Devan	4	15	_27%_

Who is most likely to get a hit? _Martin_

Page 149

Finding Percents

Find percent by dividing the number you have by the number possible.

Example:

15 out of 20 possible: $\frac{0.75}{20)15.00} = 75\%$
$\frac{-140}{100}$
$\frac{100}{}$

Annie has been keeping track of the scores she earned on each spelling test during the grading period.

Directions: Find out each percentage grade she earned. The first one has been done for you.

Week	Number Correct		Total Number of Words	Score in Percent
1	14	(out of)	20	70%
2	16		20	_80%_
3	18		20	_90%_
4	12		15	_80%_
5	16		16	_100%_
6	17		18	_94%_
Review Test	51		60	_85%_

If Susan scored 5% higher than Annie on the review test, how many words did she get right? _54_

Carrie scored 10% lower than Susan on the review test. How many words did she spell correctly? _48_

Of the 24 students in Annie's class, 25% had the same score as Annie. Only 10% had a higher score. What percent had a lower score? _65%_

Is that answer possible? _no   65% of 24 is 15.6_

Why? _cannot have a percent of a person_

Page 150

Ratio

A **ratio** is a comparison of two quantities.

Ratios can be written three ways: 2 to 3 or 2 : 3 or $\frac{2}{3}$.
Each ratio is read: two to three.

Example:

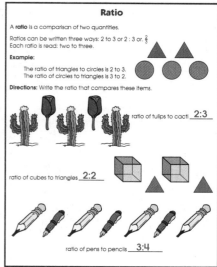

The ratio of triangles to circles is 2 to 3.
The ratio of circles to triangles is 3 to 2.

Directions: Write the ratio that compares these items.

ratio of tulips to cacti _2:3_

ratio of cubes to triangles _2:2_

ratio of pens to pencils _3:4_

Page 151

Ratios

A ratio compares two numbers.

Example:

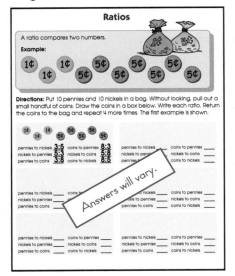

Directions: Put 10 pennies and 10 nickels in a bag. Without looking, pull out a small handful of coins. Draw the coins in a box below. Write each ratio. Return the coins to the bag and repeat 4 more times. The first example is shown.

pennies to nickels **3:5**	coins to pennies **8:3**
nickels to pennies **5:3**	nickels to coins **5:8**
pennies to coins **3:8**	coins to nickels **8:5**

Answers will vary.

pennies to nickels ____   coins to pennies ____
nickels to pennies ____   nickels to coins ____
pennies to coins ____   coins to nickels ____

pennies to nickels ____   coins to pennies ____
nickels to pennies ____   nickels to coins ____
pennies to coins ____   coins to nickels ____

Page 152

Proportions

Another way of writing a ratio is as a fraction. 3:7 is the same as $\frac{3}{7}$. Remember what you have learned about cross multiplication. $\frac{3}{7} \times \frac{6}{8}$

Because the products of cross multiplication are the same, the fractions are equivalent. When two ratios or fractions are equivalent, they form a proportion.

Example:

Steps to find an unknown term of a proportion:

Lisa uses 2 pots to plant 8 seeds. How many pots will she need to plant 24 seeds?

1. Write a proportion. $\frac{2 \text{ pots}}{8 \text{ seeds}} = \frac{n \text{ pots}}{24 \text{ seeds}}$

2. Cross multiply. $\frac{2}{8} \times \frac{n}{24}$

$8 \times n = 48$
$n = 6$ (Divide both sides of the proportion by 8.)
Lisa needs 6 pots to plant 24 seeds.

Directions: If the ratios form a proportion, write **yes** on the line. If not, write **no.**

$\frac{4}{5} = \frac{24}{30}$ __yes__ $\frac{1}{2} = \frac{36}{72}$ __yes__ $\frac{3}{7} = \frac{20}{35}$ __no__ $\frac{1}{23} = \frac{8}{184}$ __yes__

$\frac{6}{13} = \frac{75}{156}$ __no__ $\frac{9}{5} = \frac{171}{95}$ __yes__ $\frac{4}{21} = \frac{40}{210}$ __yes__ $\frac{11}{12} = \frac{154}{168}$ __yes__

Directions: Find the unknown term in each of these proportions.

$\frac{4}{5} = \frac{n}{15}$ __12__ $\frac{n}{104} = \frac{5}{13}$ __40__ $\frac{5}{6} = \frac{45}{n}$ __54__

Page 153

Probability

Probability is the ratio of favorable outcomes to possible outcomes of an experiment.

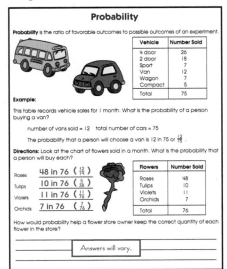

Vehicle	Number Sold
4 door	26
2 door	18
Sport	7
Van	12
Wagon	7
Compact	5
Total	75

Example:

This table records vehicle sales for 1 month. What is the probability of a person buying a van?

number of vans sold = 12   total number of cars = 75

The probability that a person will choose a van is 12 in 75 or $\frac{12}{75}$.

Directions: Look at the chart of flowers sold in a month. What is the probability that a person will buy each?

Roses   __48 in 76__ $\left(\frac{12}{19}\right)$
Tulips   __10 in 76__ $\left(\frac{5}{38}\right)$
Violets   __11 in 76__ $\left(\frac{11}{76}\right)$
Orchids   __7 in 76__ $\left(\frac{7}{76}\right)$

Flowers	Number Sold
Roses	48
Tulips	10
Violets	11
Orchids	7
Total	76

How would probability help a flower store owner keep the correct quantity of each flower in the store?

Answers will vary.

Page 154

What Are the Chances?

Probability is the chance that something will happen.

Example:

This spinner has 8 equal-sized spaces. What is the probability, or chance, that a person would spin:

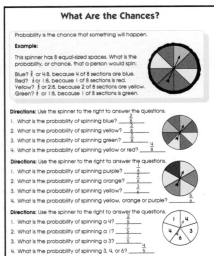

Blue? $\frac{4}{8}$ or 4:8, because 4 of 8 sections are blue.
Red? $\frac{1}{8}$ or 1:8, because 1 of 8 sections is red.
Yellow? $\frac{2}{8}$ or 2:8, because 2 of 8 sections are yellow.
Green? $\frac{1}{8}$ or 1:8, because 1 of 8 sections is green.

Directions: Use the spinner to the right to answer the questions.

1. What is the probability of spinning blue? $\frac{2}{8}$
2. What is the probability of spinning yellow? $\frac{2}{8}$
3. What is the probability of spinning green? $\frac{2}{8}$
4. What is the probability of spinning yellow or red? $\frac{4}{8}$

Directions: Use the spinner to the right to answer the questions.

1. What is the probability of spinning purple? $\frac{2}{6}$
2. What is the probability of spinning orange? $\frac{1}{6}$
3. What is the probability of spinning yellow? $\frac{3}{6}$
4. What is the probability of spinning yellow, orange or purple? $\frac{6}{6}$

Directions: Use the spinner to the right to answer the questions.

1. What is the probability of spinning a 4? $\frac{1}{5}$
2. What is the probability of spinning a 1? $\frac{1}{5}$
3. What is the probability of spinning a 3? $\frac{1}{5}$
4. What is the probability of spinning 3, 4, or 6? $\frac{4}{5}$

Page 155

Likely and Unlikely

The probability of an event happening can be written as a fraction between 0 and 1.

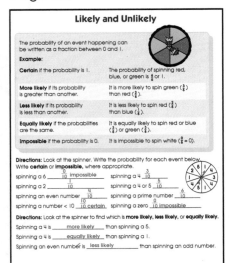

Example:

Certain if the probability is 1.   The probability of spinning red, blue, or green is $\frac{6}{6}$ or 1.

More likely if its probability is greater than another.   It is more likely to spin green ($\frac{3}{6}$) than red ($\frac{1}{6}$).

Less likely if its probability is less than another.   It is less likely to spin red ($\frac{1}{6}$) than blue ($\frac{2}{6}$).

Equally likely if the probabilities are the same.   It is equally likely to spin red or blue ($\frac{2}{6}$) or green ($\frac{2}{6}$).

Impossible if the probability is 0.   It is impossible to spin white ($\frac{0}{6}$ = 0).

Directions: Look at the spinner. Write the probability for each event below. Write **certain** or **impossible**, where appropriate.

spinning a 6 $\frac{0}{10}$ __impossible__   spinning a 4 $\frac{3}{10}$
spinning a 2 $\frac{1}{10}$ spinning a 4 or 5 $\frac{5}{10}$
spinning an even number $\frac{4}{10}$ spinning a prime number $\frac{6}{10}$
spinning a number < 10 $\frac{10}{10}$ __certain__   spinning a zero $\frac{0}{10}$ __impossible__

Directions: Look at the spinner to find which is **more likely**, **less likely**, or **equally likely**.

Spinning a 4 is __more likely__ than spinning a 5.
Spinning a 4 is __equally likely__ than spinning a 1.
Spinning an even number is __less likely__ than spinning an odd number.

Page 156

Flying Forks

Look at a plastic fork. What do you think will happen if you drop the fork—will it land faceup, facedown, or on its side? What is the probability of each position?

Directions: Write your answers below.

Predict:
Imagine dropping the fork 50 different times. Predict how many times the fork will land:

Faceup: _____
Facedown: _____
On its side: _____

Experiment:
Drop the fork 50 times. Record how many times it lands in each position.

Faceup: _____
Facedown: _____
On its side: _____

Organize the Data:
Graph the results.

[graph with y-axis 5 to 50 and x-axis: Up, Down, Side]

Answers will vary.

[...] the results mean. Why [...]ese results have occurred?

Page 157

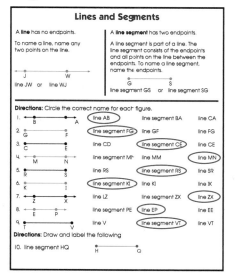

Lines and Segments

A **line** has no endpoints.

To name a line, name any two points on the line.

line JW or line WJ

A **line segment** has two endpoints.

A line segment is part of a line. The line segment consists of the endpoints and all points on the line between the endpoints. To name a line segment, name the endpoints.

line segment GS or line segment SG

Directions: Circle the correct name for each figure.

1. (line AB), line segment BA, line CA
2. (line segment FG), line GF, line FG
3. line CD, (line segment CE), line CE
4. line segment MN, line MM, (line MN)
5. line RS, (line segment RS), line SR
6. (line segment KI), line KI, line IK
7. line LZ, line segment ZX, (line ZX)
8. line segment PE, (line EP), line EE
9. line V, (line segment VT), line VT

Directions: Draw and label the following

10. line segment HQ

Page 158

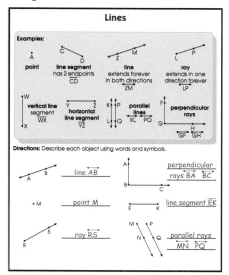

Lines

Examples:

point, line segment has 2 endpoints $\overline{CD}$, line extends forever in both directions $\overleftrightarrow{ZM}$, ray extends in one direction forever $\overrightarrow{LP}$

vertical line segment $\overline{WX}$, horizontal line segment $\overline{YZ}$, parallel lines $\overleftrightarrow{KL}$ $\overleftrightarrow{PQ}$, perpendicular rays $\overrightarrow{GF}$ $\overrightarrow{GH}$

Directions: Describe each object using words and symbols.

line $\overleftrightarrow{AB}$

perpendicular rays $\overrightarrow{BA}$ $\overrightarrow{BC}$

point M

line segment $\overline{EK}$

ray $\overrightarrow{RS}$

parallel rays $\overrightarrow{MN}$ $\overrightarrow{PQ}$

Page 159

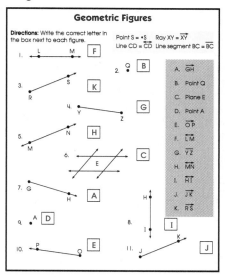

Geometric Figures

Directions: Write the correct letter in the box next to each figure.

Point S = •S Ray XY = $\overrightarrow{XY}$
Line CD = $\overleftrightarrow{CD}$ Line segment BC = $\overline{BC}$

1. F
2. B
3. K
4. G
5. H
6. C
7. A
8. I
9. D
10. E
11. J

A. $\overrightarrow{GH}$
B. Point Q
C. Plane E
D. Point A
E. $\overrightarrow{OP}$
F. $\overline{YZ}$
G. $\overleftrightarrow{LM}$
H. $\overrightarrow{MN}$
I. $\overline{HI}$
J. $\overrightarrow{JK}$
K. $\overleftrightarrow{RS}$

Page 160

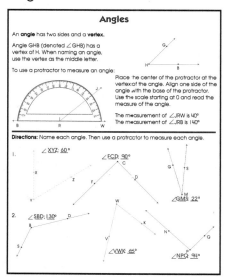

Angles

An **angle** has two sides and a **vertex**.

Angle GHB (denoted ∠GHB) has a vertex of H. When naming an angle, use the vertex as the middle letter.

To use a protractor to measure an angle:

Place the center of the protractor at the vertex of the angle. Align one side of the angle with the base of the protractor. Use the scale starting at 0 and read the measure of the angle.

The measurement of ∠JRW is 40°
The measurement of ∠JRB is 140°

Directions: Name each angle. Then use a protractor to measure each angle.

1. ∠XYZ; 60°
∠FCD; 90°
∠GMS; 22°

2. ∠SBD; 130°
∠VWK; 65°
∠NPQ; 94°

Page 161

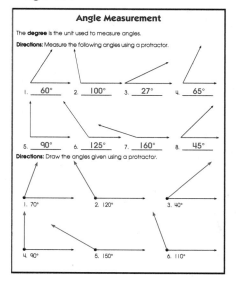

Angle Measurement

The **degree** is the unit used to measure angles.

Directions: Measure the following angles using a protractor.

1. 60°
2. 100°
3. 27°
4. 65°
5. 90°
6. 125°
7. 160°
8. 45°

Directions: Draw the angles given using a protractor.

1. 70°
2. 120°
3. 40°
4. 90°
5. 150°
6. 110°

Page 162

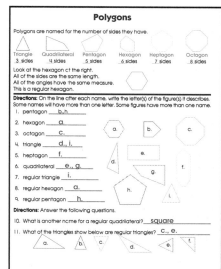

Polygons

Polygons are named for the number of sides they have.

Triangle 3 sides, Quadrilateral 4 sides, Pentagon 5 sides, Hexagon 6 sides, Heptagon 7 sides, Octagon 8 sides

Look at the hexagon at the right.
All of the sides are the same length.
All of the angles have the same measure.
This is a regular hexagon.

Directions: On the line after each name, write the letter(s) of the figure(s) it describes. Some names will have more than one letter. Some figures have more than one name.

1. pentagon b.,h.
2. hexagon a.
3. octagon c.
4. triangle d., i.
5. heptagon f.
6. quadrilateral e., g.
7. regular triangle i.
8. regular hexagon a.
9. regular pentagon h.

Directions: Answer the following questions.

10. What is another name for a regular quadrilateral? square
11. What of the triangles show below are regular triangles? c., e.

Page 163

Polygons

The word **polygon** means "many angles" and describes a shape that:

a) starts and stops at the same place (making it "closed").
b) can be traced without lifting the pencil or crossing or retracing any part.
c) is made of at least three line segments.

A **regular polygon** has sides that are all the same length.

shapes   polygons   regular polygons

Directions: Circle any shape that is a polygon. Color any shape that is a regular polygon. If the shape if not a polygon, explain why.

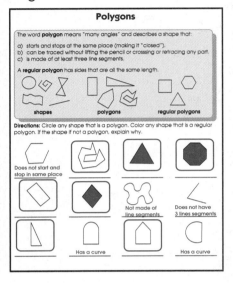

Does not start and stop in same place

Not made of line segments

Does not have 3 lines segments

Has a curve

Has a curve

Page 164

Polygons and Circles

To name a polygon, use the letters of the vertices (plural of vertex).

Figure ABCDE or Pentagon ABCDE

A line segment that connects two vertices, but is not a side is called a diagonal.

Diagonal SU   Diagonal VT

To name a circle, use the letters of the circle.

A line segment from the center of the circle to a point on the circle is a **radius**. A line segment that has endpoints on the circle and passes through the center of the circle is a **diameter.**

Radius LM
Diameter KN

Note that KL and LN are also radii (plural of radius).

Directions: Answer the following questions.

1. Draw and name all of the diagonals of figure FGHIJ
   JG, JH, IF, IG, FH
2. Are all of the diagonals of figure FGHIJ the same length? **NO**
3. Name a radius of circle P. **PQ, PR, PS, or PN**
4. Name a diameter of circle P. **SR**
5. In the circle P, draw a diameter that goes through point N.
6. Is figure RSTUVW a regular hexagon? **Yes**
7. Draw all the diagonals for figure RSTUVW.
8. How many diagonals does figure RSTUVW have? **9**
9. Are all of the diagonals of figure RSTUVW the same length? **No**

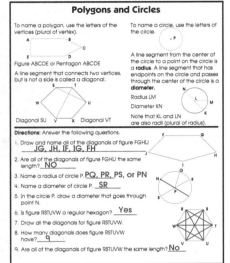

Page 165

Three-Dimensional Objects

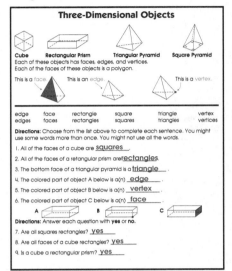

Cube   Rectangular Prism   Triangular Pyramid   Square Pyramid

Each of these objects has faces, edges, and vertices.
Each of the faces of these objects is a polygon.

This is a face.   This is an edge.   This is a vertex.

| edge | face | rectangle | square | triangle | vertex |
| edges | faces | rectangles | squares | triangles | vertices |

Directions: Choose from the list above to complete each sentence. You might use some words more than once. You might not use all the words.

1. All of the faces of a cube are **squares**.
2. All of the faces of a retangular prism are **rectangles**.
3. The bottom face of a triangular pyramid is a **triangle**.
4. The colored part of object A below is a(n) **edge**.
5. The colored part of object B below is a(n) **vertex**.
6. The colored part of object C below is a(n) **face**.

A   B   C

Directions: Answer each question with **yes** or **no**.

7. Are all squares rectangles? **yes**
8. Are all faces of a cube rectangles? **yes**
9. Is a cube a rectangular prism? **yes**

Page 166

Geometry

Geometry is the branch of mathematics that has to do with points, lines, and shapes.

Directions: Use the Glossary on pages 237-239 if you need help. Write the word from the box that is described below.

| triangle | square | cube | angle |
| line | ray | segment | rectangle |

a collection of points on a straight path that goes on and on in opposite directions **line**

a figure with three sides and three corners **triangle**

a figure with four equal sides and four corners **square**

part of a line that has one end point and goes on and on in one direction **ray**

part of a line having two end points **segment**

a space figure with six square faces **cube**

two rays with a common end point **angle**

a figure with four corners and four sides **rectangle**

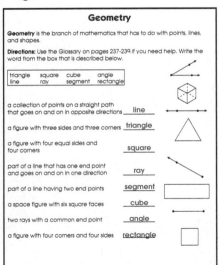

Page 167

Geometry

Review the definitions on the previous page before completing the problems below.

Directions: Identify the labeled section of each of the following diagrams.

AB = **segment**

ABC = **angle**

AB = **segment**

CD = **line**

AC = **ray**

AB = **segment**

EBC = **angle**

BC = **ray**

Page 168

Geometric Patterns

Directions: Draw the next three shapes in the pattern.

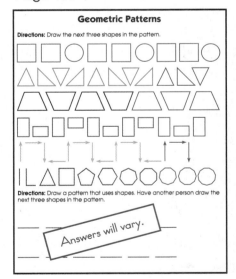

Directions: Draw a pattern that uses shapes. Have another person draw the next three shapes in the pattern.

Answers will vary.

Page 171

Shapes in Hiding

Directions: Shade triangles to make each shape.

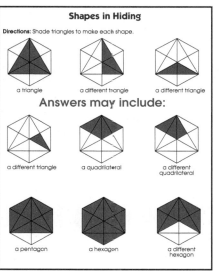

a triangle   a different triangle   a different triangle

Answers may include:

a different triangle   a quadrilateral   a different quadrilateral

a pentagon   a hexagon   a different hexagon

Page 172

The Rocketangular Puzzle

Directions: Take an $8\frac{1}{2}$" x 11" piece of paper. Fold it in half, half again, half again and half again. Open it up. It should look like this:

Directions: Draw in the two diagonals using a ruler and fold on them. Trace over all the fold lines on both sides. Cut on the dashed lines.

Fold Lines

Cut Lines - - - - - - -

Directions: Fold the piece of paper flat to make each shape below. Calculate the area of each shape and write it on the blank.

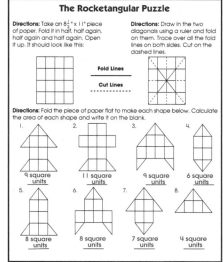

1. 9 square units
2. 11 square units
3. 9 square units
4. 6 square units
5. 8 square units
6. 8 square units
7. 7 square units
8. 4 square units

Page 173

Similar, Congruent, and Symmetrical Figures

Similar figures have the same shape but have varying sizes.

Figures that are **congruent** have identical shapes but different orientations. That means they face in different directions.

Symmetrical figures can be divided equally into two identical parts.

Directions: Cross out the shape that does not belong in each group. Label the two remaining shapes as similar, congruent, or symmetrical.

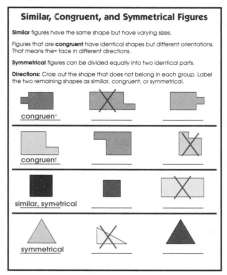

congruent

congruent

similar, symetrical

symmetrical

Page 174

Perimeter and Area

The **perimeter (P)** of a figure is the distance around it. To find the perimeter, add the lengths of the sides.

The **area (A)** of a figure is the number of units in a figure. Find the area by multiplying the length of a figure by its width.

Example:

P = 16 units
A = 16 units

Directions: Find the perimeter and area of each figure.

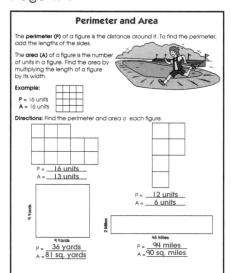

P = 16 units
A = 13 units

P = 12 units
A = 6 units

9 Yards
P = 36 yards
A = 81 sq. yards

2 Miles / 45 Miles
P = 94 miles
A = 90 sq. miles

Page 175

Perimeter and Area

Directions: Use the formulas for finding perimeter and area to solve these problems.

Julie's family moved to a new house. Her parents said she could have the largest bedroom. Julie knew she would need to find the area of each room to find which one was largest.

One rectangular bedroom is 7 feet wide and 12 feet long. Another is 11 feet long and 9 feet wide. The third bedroom is a square. It is 9 feet wide and 9 feet long. Which one should she select to have the largest room?

the 11 x 9 room

The new home also has a swimming pool in the backyard. It is 32 feet long and 18 feet wide. What is the perimeter of the pool?

100 ft.

Julie's mother wants to plant flowers on each side of the new house. She will need three plants for every foot of space. The house is 75 feet across the front and back and 37.5 feet along each side. Find the perimeter of the house.

225 ft.

How many plants should she buy? 675 plants

The family decided to buy new carpeting for several rooms. Complete the necessary information to determine how much carpeting to buy.

Den: 12 ft. x 14 ft. = 168 sq. ft.

Master Bedroom: 20 ft. x 18ft. = 360 sq. ft.

Family Room: 15ft. x 25 ft. = 375 sq. ft.

Total square feet of carpeting: 903 sq. ft.

Page 176

Volume

The formula for finding the **volume** (depth) of a box is length times width times height **(L x W x H)**. The answer is given in cubic units.

Directions: Solve the problems.

Example:

Height 8 ft.
Length 8 ft.
Width 8 ft.   **L x W x H** = volume
8' x 8' x 8' = 512 cubic ft. or 512 ft.³

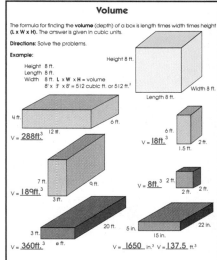

V = 288ft.³
V = 18ft.³
V = 189ft.³
V = 8ft.³
V = 360ft.³
V = 1650 in.³
V = 137.5 ft.³

Page 177

Cut and Paste

What is the area of a parallelogram?
Do this activity and find out.

1. Cut out the parallelogram at the bottom of the page.   1.

2. Cut out the triangle along the dotted line.   2.

3. Slide the triangle to make the parallelogram into a rectangle.   3.

4. Use the formula for the area of a rectangle to find the area of a parallelogram.

Area of a parallelogram = base x height = bh

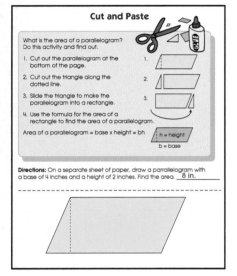

h = height
b = base

Directions: On a separate sheet of paper, draw a parallelogram with a base of 4 inches and a height of 2 inches. Find the area. __8 in.__

Page 179

Perimeter, Area, and Volume

Directions: Find the perimeter and area.

1. Length = 8 ft.
   Width = 11 ft.
   P = __38 ft.__   A = __88 sq. ft.__

2. Length = 12 ft.
   Width = 10 ft.
   P = __44 ft.__   A = __120 sq. ft.__

3. Length = 121 ft.
   Width = 16 ft.
   P = __274 ft.__   A = __1,936 sq. ft.__

4. Length = 72 in.
   Width = 5 ft.
   P = __22 ft.__   A = __30 sq. ft.__

Directions: Find the perimeter, area, and volume.

5. Length = 7 ft.
   Width = 12 ft.
   Height = 10 ft.
   P = __38 ft.__
   A = __84 sq. ft.__
   V = __840 cu. ft.__

6. Length = 48 in.
   Width = 7 ft.
   Height = 12 in.
   P = __22 ft.__
   A = __28 sq. ft.__
   V = __28 cu. ft.__

7. Length = 12 in.
   Width = 15 in.
   Height = 20 in.
   P = __54 in.__
   A = __180 sq. in.__
   V = __3,600 cu. in.__

8. Length = 22 ft.
   Width = 40 ft.
   Height = 10 ft.
   P = __124 ft.__
   A = __880 sq. ft.__
   V = __8,800 cu. ft.__

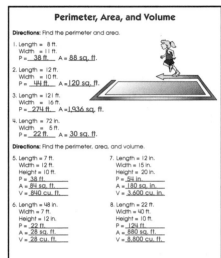

Page 180

Circumference

Circumference is the distance around a circle. The **diameter** is a line segment that passes through the center of a circle and has both end points on the circle.

To find the circumference of any circle, multiply 3.14 times the diameter. The number 3.14 represents **pi** (pronounced "pie") and is often written by this Greek symbol, π.

The formula for circumference is C = π x d

   C = circumference

   d = diameter

   π = 3.14

Example:

Circle A
d = 2 in.
C = 3.14 x 2 in.
C = 6.28 in.

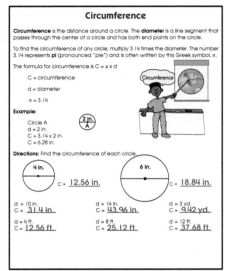

Directions: Find the circumference of each circle.

4 in.   C = __12.56 in.__

6 in.   C = __18.84 in.__

d = 10 in.
C = __31.4 in.__

d = 14 in.
C = __43.96 in.__

d = 3 yd.
C = __9.42 yd.__

d = 4 ft.
C = __12.56 ft.__

d = 8 ft.
C = __25.12 ft.__

d = 12 ft.
C = __37.68 ft.__

Page 181

Circumference

The **radius** of a circle is the distance from the center of the circle to its outside edge. The diameter equals two times the radius.

Find the circumference by multiplying π (3.14) times the diameter or by multiplying π (3.14) times 2r (2 times the radius).

C = π x d or C = π x 2r

Directions: Write the missing radius, diameter, or circumference.

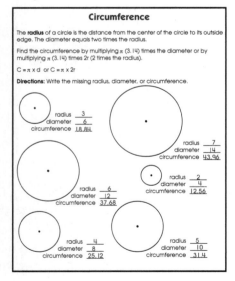

radius __3__
diameter __6__
circumference __18.84__

radius __7__
diameter __14__
circumference __43.96__

radius __6__
diameter __12__
circumference __37.68__

radius __2__
diameter __4__
circumference __12.56__

radius __4__
diameter __8__
circumference __25.12__

radius __5__
diameter __10__
circumference __31.4__

Page 182

The Circle Game

The perimeter of a circle is called the circumference. There is a formula for finding the circumference of a circle. The formula uses this special number, 3.14. We call this number pi (π). To find the circumference of a circle, use this formula:

Circumference = π x diameter
Circumference = π d

or

Circumference = π x 2 x radius
Circumference = 2πr

Examples:

C = π d   C = 2πr
C = 3.14 x 4   C = 2 x 3.14 x 2
C = 12.56   C = 12.56

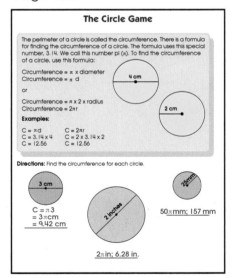

4 cm

2 cm

Directions: Find the circumference for each circle.

3 cm

C = π3
 = 3πcm
 = 9.42 cm

2 inches

2π in; 6.28 in.

25mm

50πmm; 157 mm

Page 183

Diameter, Radius, and Circumference

C = π x d or C = π x 2r

Directions: Write the missing radius, diameter or circumference.

Katie was asked to draw a circle on the playground for a game during recess. If the radius of the circle needed to be 14 inches, how long is the diameter?
__28 in.__

What is the circumference? __87.92 in.__

A friend told her that more kids could play the game if they enlarged the circle. She had a friend help her. They made the diameter of the circle 45 inches long.

What is the radius? __22.5 in.__

What is the circumference? __141.3 in.__

Jamie was creating an art project. He wanted part of it to be a sphere. He measured 24 inches for the diameter.

What would the radius of the sphere be? __12 in.__

Find the circumference. __75.36 in.__

Unfortunately, Jamie discovered that he didn't have enough material to create a sphere that large, so he cut the dimensions in half. What are the new dimensions for his sphere?

Radius __6__

Diameter __12__

Circumference __37.68 in.__

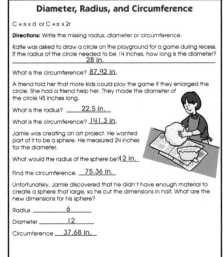

Page 184

Triangle Angles

A triangle is a figure with three corners and three sides. Every triangle contains three angles. The sum of the angles is always 180°, regardless of the size or shape of the triangle.

If you know two of the angles, you can add them together, then subtract the total from 180 to find the number of degrees in the third angle.

Directions: Find the number of degrees in the third angle of each triangle.

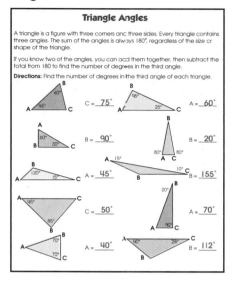

C = __75°__   A = __60°__

B = __90°__   B = __20°__

A = __45°__   B = __155°__

C = __50°__   A = __70°__

A = __40°__   B = __112°__

Page 185

Area of a Triangle

The area of a triangle is found by multiplying $\frac{1}{2}$ times the base times the height. A = $\frac{1}{2}$ x b x h

Example:

$\overline{CD}$ is the height.   4 in.
$\overline{AB}$ is the base.   8 in.
Area = $\frac{1}{2}$ x 4 x 8 = $\frac{32}{2}$ = 16 sq. in.

Directions: Find the area of each triangle.

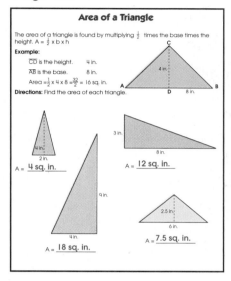

A = __4 sq. in.__

A = __12 sq. in.__

A = __18 sq. in.__

A = __7.5 sq. in.__

Page 186

I'm Hungry

Directions: Someone has already found the area for each triangle, but some are incorrect. Check each problem. Connect the problems with correct areas to make a path for the giraffe to the tree. Then, correct each wrong area.

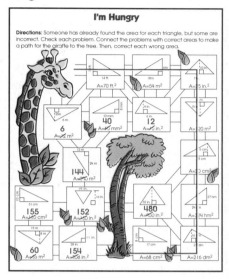

Page 187

Lines Across a Triangle

Directions: Draw the given number of straight lines to divide each triangle into the shapes listed. The first one has been done for you.

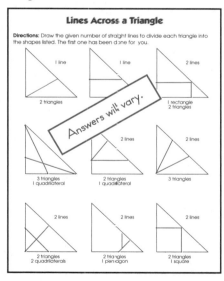

1 line
2 triangles

1 line

2 lines

Answers will vary.

1 rectangle
2 triangles

3 triangles
1 quadrilateral

2 lines
2 triangles
1 quadrilateral

2 lines
3 triangles

2 lines
2 triangles
2 quadrilaterals

2 lines
2 triangles
1 pentagon

2 lines
2 triangles
1 square

Page 188

Try a Triangle

Directions: A triangle is a three-sided polygon. It has three sides and three angles. Write the number of triangles there are in each drawing.

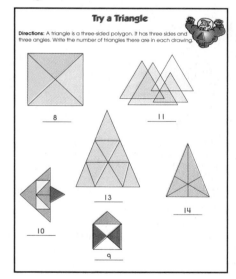

8   11

13   14

10

9

Page 189

Space Figures

Space figures are figures whose points are in more than one plane. Cubes and cylinders are space figures.

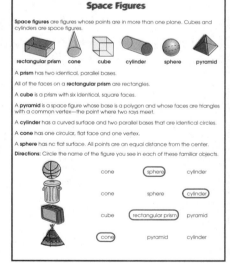

rectangular prism   cone   cube   cylinder   sphere   pyramid

A **prism** has two identical, parallel bases.

All of the faces on a **rectangular prism** are rectangles.

A **cube** is a prism with six identical, square faces.

A **pyramid** is a space figure whose base is a polygon and whose faces are triangles with a common vertex—the point where two rays meet.

A **cylinder** has a curved surface and two parallel bases that are identical circles.

A **cone** has one circular, flat face and one vertex.

A **sphere** has no flat surface. All points are an equal distance from the center.

Directions: Circle the name of the figure you see in each of these familiar objects.

cone   (sphere)   cylinder

cone   sphere   (cylinder)

cube   (rectangular prism)   pyramid

(cone)   pyramid   cylinder

Page 190

A Unit of My Own

Example:
Steps to make a nonstandard ruler:

1. Fold a sheet of paper in half along the longest side. Fold in that direction again, and once again.
2. Unfold the paper. Draw lines and labels like the ones shown here.
3. Name the units after yourself. For example, Julie's ruler measures 8 Julies long.
4. Use the ruler to measure objects in your units.

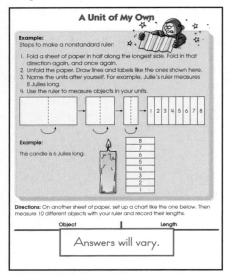

Example:
This candle is 6 Julies long.

Directions: On another sheet of paper, set up a chart like the one below. Then measure 10 different objects with your ruler and record their lengths.

Object	Length
Answers will vary.	

Page 191

Standard Length

Standardized units are units that are agreed upon all over the world, so that measurements made in India are the same as measurements made in Iceland, Israel, or Italy. The two main systems are **customary** and **metric**.

Examples:

The customary units for measuring length are **inch (in.)**, **foot (ft.)**, **yard (yd.)**, and **mile (mi.)**.

A paper clip is about 1 inch long.

A notebook is about 1 foot wide.

A baseball bat is about 1 yard long.

A mile is the distance 4 times around a running track.

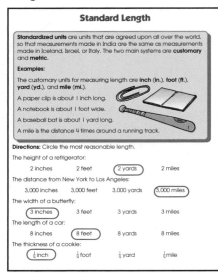

Directions: Circle the most reasonable length.

The height of a refrigerator:

2 inches   2 feet   (2 yards)   2 miles

The distance from New York to Los Angeles:

3,000 inches   3,000 feet   3,000 yards   (3,000 miles)

The width of a butterfly:

(3 inches)   3 feet   3 yards   3 miles

The length of a car:

8 inches   (8 feet)   8 yards   8 miles

The thickness of a cookie:

($\frac{1}{4}$ inch) $\frac{1}{4}$ foot $\frac{1}{4}$ yard $\frac{1}{4}$ mile

Page 192

Length

Inches, feet, yards, and miles are used to measure length in the United States.

12 inches = 1 foot (ft.)
3 feet = 1 yard (yd.)
36 inches = 1 yard
1,760 yards = 1 mile (mi.)

Directions: Circle the best unit to measure each object. The first one has been done for you.

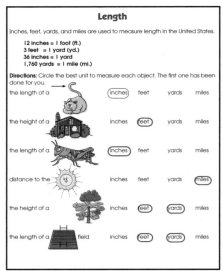

the length of a   (inches)   feet   yards   miles

the height of a   inches   (feet)   yards   miles

the length of a   (inches)   feet   yards   miles

distance to the   inches   feet   yards   (miles)

the height of a   inches   (feet)   (yards)   miles

the length of a   field   inches   (feet)   (yards)   miles

Page 193

Length

Directions: Use a ruler to find the shortest paths. Round your measurement to the nearest quarter inch. Then convert to yards using the scale.

Scale: 1 inch = 100 yards

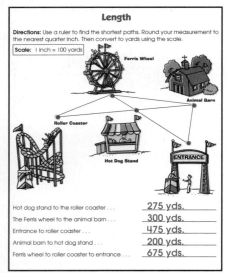

Hot dog stand to the roller coaster . . .	**275 yds.**
The Ferris wheel to the animal barn . . .	**300 yds.**
Entrance to roller coaster . . .	**475 yds.**
Animal barn to hot dog stand . . .	**200 yds.**
Ferris wheel to roller coaster to entrance . . .	**675 yds.**

Page 194

Measuring Perimeter

Directions: Use a ruler to measure and find the perimeter of each shape. Use inches.

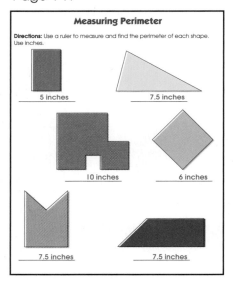

5 inches   7.5 inches

10 inches   6 inches

7.5 inches   7.5 inches

Page 195

Weight

Ounces, pounds, and **tons** are used to measure weight in the United States.

16 ounces = 1 pound (lb.)
2,000 pounds = 1 ton (tn.)

Directions: Circle the most reasonable estimate for the weight of each object. The first one has been done for you.

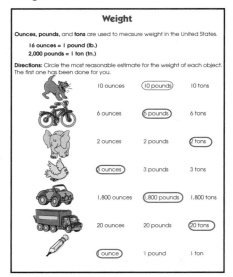

10 ounces   (10 pounds)   10 tons

6 ounces   (6 pounds)   6 tons

2 ounces   2 pounds   (2 tons)

(3 ounces)   3 pounds   3 tons

1,800 ounces   (1,800 pounds)   1,800 tons

20 ounces   20 pounds   (20 tons)

(1 ounce)   1 pound   1 ton

Page 196

Capacity

The **fluid ounce, cup, pint, quart,** and **gallon** are used to measure capacity in the United States.

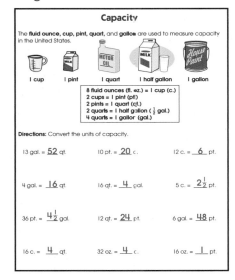

I cup   I pint   I quart   I half gallon   I gallon

8 fluid ounces (fl. oz.) = I cup (c.)
2 cups = I pint (pt.)
2 pints = I quart (qt.)
2 quarts = I half gallon ($\frac{1}{2}$ gal.)
4 quarts = I gallon (gal.)

Directions: Convert the units of capacity.

13 gal. = **52** qt.   10 pt. = **20** c.   12 c. = **6** pt.

4 gal. = **16** qt.   16 qt. = **4** gal.   5 c. = **2$\frac{1}{2}$** pt.

36 pt. = **4$\frac{1}{2}$** gal.   12 qt. = **24** pt.   6 gal. = **48** pt.

16 c. = **4** qt.   32 oz. = **4** c.   16 oz. = **1** pt.

Page 197

Length: Metric

Millimeters, centimeters, meters, and **kilometers** are used to measure length in the metric system.

I meter = 39.37 inches
I kilometer = about $\frac{5}{8}$ mile
10 millimeters = I centimeter (cm)
100 centimeters = I meter (m)
1,000 meters = I kilometer (km)

Directions: Circle the best unit to measure each object. The first one has been done for you.

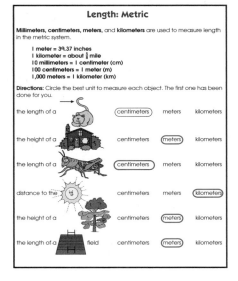

the length of a	(centimeters)	meters	kilometers
the height of a	centimeters	(meters)	kilometers
the length of a	(centimeters)	meters	kilometers
distance to the	centimeters	meters	(kilometers)
the height of a	centimeters	(meters)	kilometers
the length of a field	centimeters	(meters)	kilometers

Page 198

Weight: Metric

Grams and **kilograms** are units of weight in the metric system. A paper clip weighs about I gram. A kitten weighs about I kilogram.

I kilogram (kg) = about 2.2 pounds
1,000 grams (g) = I kilogram

Directions: Circle the best unit to weigh each object.

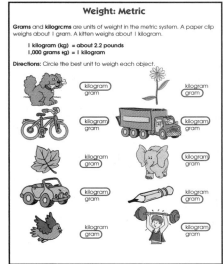

(kilogram) gram
kilogram (gram)

(kilogram) gram
(kilogram) gram

kilogram (gram)
(kilogram) gram

(kilogram) gram
kilogram (gram)

kilogram (gram)
(kilogram) gram

Page 199

Capacity: Metric

Milliliters and **liters** are units of capacity in the metric system. A can of soda contains about 350 milliliters of liquid. A large plastic bottle contains I liter of liquid. A liter is about a quart.

1,000 milliliters (mL) = I liter (L)

Directions: Circle the best unit to measure each liquid.

milliliters (liters)
milliliters (liters)

milliliters (liters)
milliliters (liters)

(milliliters) liters
milliliters (liters)

(milliliters) liters
(milliliters) liters

(milliliters) liters
milliliters (liters)

Page 200

Comparing Measurements

Directions: Use the symbols greater than (>), less than (<), or equal to (=) to complete each statement.

10 inches	>	10 centimeters
40 feet	<	120 yards
25 grams	<	25 kilograms
16 quarts	=	4 gallons
2 liters	>	2 milliliters
16 yards	>	6 meters
3 miles	>	3 kilometers
20 centimeters	<	20 meters
85 kilograms	>	8 grams
2 liters	<	I gallon

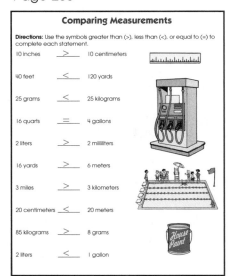

Page 201

Will It Fit?

I cup = 8 fluid ounces
I pint = 2 cups = 16 fluid ounces
I quart = 2 pints = 4 cups = 32 fluid ounces
I gallon = 4 quarts = 8 pints = 16 cups = 128 ounces

Directions: Complete the following table.

	fl. ounces	cups	pints	quarts	gallons
I fl. ounce =	1	$\frac{1}{8}$	$\frac{1}{16}$	$\frac{1}{32}$	$\frac{1}{128}$
I cup =	8	1	$\frac{1}{2}$	$\frac{1}{4}$	$\frac{1}{16}$
I pint =	16	2	1	$\frac{1}{2}$	$\frac{1}{8}$
I quart =	32	4	2	1	$\frac{1}{4}$
I gallon =	128	16	8	4	1

Directions: Write **yes** or **no**.

1. Will 6 cups fit in a I-quart container? **no**
2. Will 8 ounces fit in a I-cup container? **yes**
3. Will 16 pints fit in a 2-gallon container? **yes**
4. Will 3 quarts fit in a 5-pint container? **no**
5. Will 64 ounces fit in a $\frac{1}{2}$-gallon container? **yes**
6. Will 18 cups fit in an 8-pint container? **no**
7. Will 12 quarts fit in a 4-gallon container? **yes**
8. Will 8 gallons fit in a 16-quart container? **no**

Page 202

Weights and Measures

Example:

8 tons
16,000 pounds
256,000 ounces

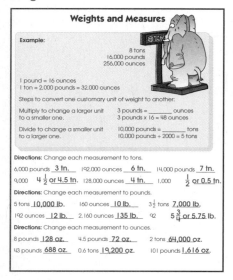

1 pound = 16 ounces
1 ton = 2,000 pounds = 32,000 ounces

Steps to convert one customary unit of weight to another:

Multiply to change a larger unit to a smaller one.
3 pounds = _____ ounces
3 pounds x 16 = 48 ounces

Divide to change a smaller unit to a larger one.
10,000 pounds = _____ tons
10,000 pounds ÷ 2000 = 5 tons

Directions: Change each measurement to tons.

6,000 pounds __3 tn.__   192,000 ounces __6 tn.__   14,000 pounds __7 tn.__
9,000 __4 $\frac{1}{2}$ or 4.5 tn.__   128,000 ounces __4 tn.__   1,000 __$\frac{1}{2}$ or 0.5 tn.__

Directions: Change each measurement to pounds.

5 tons __10,000 lb.__   160 ounces __10 lb.__   3$\frac{1}{2}$ tons __7,000 lb.__
192 ounces __12 lb.__   2,160 ounces __135 lb.__   92 __5$\frac{3}{4}$ or 5.75 lb.__

Directions: Change each measurement to ounces.

8 pounds __128 oz.__   4.5 pounds __72 oz.__   2 tons __64,000 oz.__
43 pounds __688 oz.__   0.6 tons __19,200 oz.__   101 pounds __1,616 oz.__

Page 203

Renaming Lengths

Example:

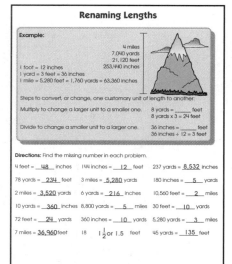

4 miles
7,040 yards
21,120 feet
253,440 inches

1 foot = 12 inches
1 yard = 3 feet = 36 inches
1 mile = 5,280 feet = 1,760 yards = 63,360 inches

Steps to convert, or change, one customary unit of length to another:

Multiply to change a larger unit to a smaller one.
8 yards = _____ feet
8 yards x 3 = 24 feet

Divide to change a smaller unit to a larger one.
36 inches = _____ feet
36 inches ÷ 12 = 3 feet

Directions: Find the missing number in each problem.

4 feet = __48__ inches   144 inches = __12__ feet   237 yards = __8,532__ inches
78 yards = __234__ feet   3 miles = __5,280__ yards   180 inches = __5__ yards
2 miles = __3,520__ yards   6 yards = __216__ inches   10,560 feet = __2__ miles
10 yards = __360__ inches   8,800 yards = __5__ miles   30 feet = __10__ yards
72 feet = __24__ yards   360 inches = __10__ yards   5,280 yards = __3__ miles
7 miles = __36,960__ feet   18   1$\frac{1}{2}$ or 1.5   feet   45 yards = __135__ feet

Page 204

Measurement Review

Directions: Write the best unit to measure each item: inch, foot, yard, mile, ounce, pound, ton, fluid ounce, cup, pint, quart, or gallon.

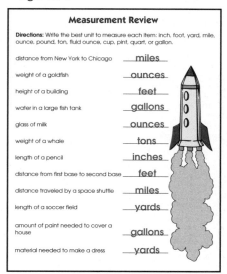

distance from New York to Chicago __miles__

weight of a goldfish __ounces__

height of a building __feet__

water in a large fish tank __gallons__

glass of milk __ounces__

weight of a whale __tons__

length of a pencil __inches__

distance from first base to second base __feet__

distance traveled by a space shuttle __miles__

length of a soccer field __yards__

amount of paint needed to cover a house __gallons__

material needed to make a dress __yards__

Page 205

Temperature: Fahrenheit

Degrees **Fahrenheit** (°F) is a unit for measuring temperature.

Directions: Write the temperature in degrees Fahrenheit (°F).

Example:

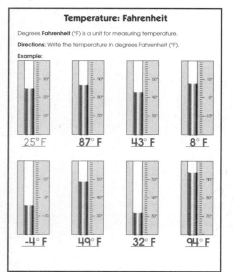

__25°__ F   __87°__ F   __43°__ F   __8°__ F

__-4°__ F   __49°__ F   __32°__ F   __94°__ F

Page 206

Temperature: Celsius

Degrees **Celsius** (°C) is a unit for measuring temperature in the metric system.

Directions: Write the temperature in degrees Celsius (°C).

Example:

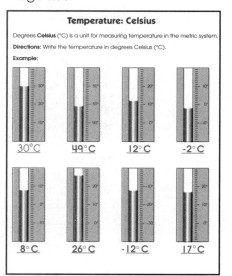

__30°C__   __49°C__   __12°C__   __-2°C__

__8°C__   __26°C__   __-12°C__   __17°C__

Page 207

Temperature

The customary unit of temperature is the degree Fahrenheit (°F). A thermometer is used to measure temperature.

Examples:

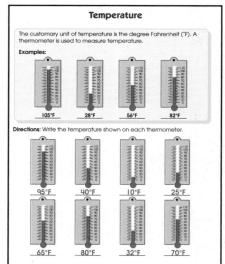

105°F   28°F   56°F   82°F

Directions: Write the temperature shown on each thermometer.

95°F   40°F   10°F   25°F

65°F   80°F   32°F   70°F

Page 208

Heat Wave

Example:

Water freezes at 32°F. It boils at 212°F.

30°F is cold   70°F is warm
50°F is cool   90°F is hot

Directions: Circle the most reasonable temperature for each item. The first one is done for you.

hot cocoa	30°F	70°F	**180°F**	300°F
snowy day	−60°F	**10°F**	65°F	80°F
iced tea	0°F	10°F	20°F	**40°F**
swimming pool	40°F	**75°F**	110°F	145°F
inside a refrigerator	**45°F**	60°F	75°F	90°F
room temperature	25°F	45°F	**70°F**	212°F
the air on a hot day	20°F	32°F	55°F	**90°F**
body temperature	60°F	80°F	**100°F**	120°F
top of a ski mountain	**0°F**	50°F	100°F	150°F
oven for baking cookies	75°F	200°F	**350°F**	500°F
spring day in Ohio	20°F	40°F	**60°F**	90°F
highest recorded shade temperature on Earth	95°F	100°F	**135°F**	180°F

Page 209

Metric Temperature

The metric unit of temperature is the degree Celsius (°C). A thermometer is used to measure temperature.

Example:

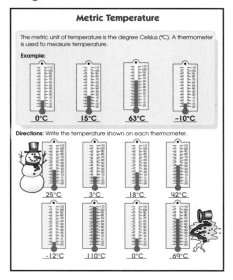

0°C   15°C   63°C   −10°C

Directions: Write the temperature shown on each thermometer.

25°C   3°C   18°C   42°C

−12°C   110°C   0°C   69°C

Page 210

Blowing Hot and Cold

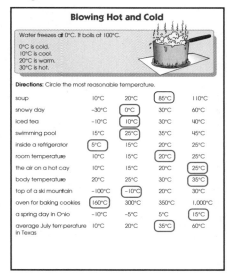

Water freezes at 0°C. It boils at 100°C.

0°C is cold.
10°C is cool.
20°C is warm.
30°C is hot.

Directions: Circle the most reasonable temperature.

soup	10°C	20°C	**85°C**	110°C
snowy day	−30°C	**0°C**	30°C	60°C
iced tea	−10°C	**10°C**	30°C	40°C
swimming pool	15°C	**25°C**	35°C	45°C
inside a refrigerator	**5°C**	15°C	20°C	25°C
room temperature	10°C	15°C	**20°C**	25°C
the air on a hot day	10°C	15°C	20°C	**25°C**
body temperature	20°C	25°C	30°C	**35°C**
top of a ski mountain	−100°C	**−10°C**	20°C	30°C
oven for baking cookies	**160°C**	300°C	350°C	1,000°C
a spring day in Ohio	−10°C	−5°C	5°C	**15°C**
average July temperature in Texas	10°C	20°C	**35°C**	60°C

Page 211

Temperature Change

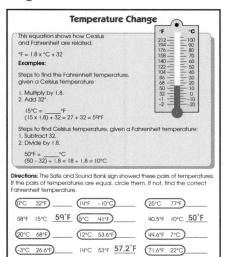

This equation shows how Celsius and Fahrenheit are related.

°F = 1.8 × °C + 32

Examples:

Steps to find the Fahrenheit temperature, given a Celsius temperature
1. Multiply by 1.8.
2. Add 32°.

15°C = _____ °F
(15 × 1.8) + 32 = 27 + 32 = 59°F

Steps to find Celsius temperature, given a Fahrenheit temperature:
1. Subtract 32.
2. Divide by 1.8.

50°F = _____ °C
(50 − 32) ÷ 1.8 = 18 ÷ 1.8 = 10°C

Directions: The Safe and Sound Bank sign showed these pairs of temperatures. If the pairs of temperatures are equal, circle them. If not, find the correct Fahrenheit temperature.

0°C   32°F   **14°F   −10°C**   **25°C   77°F**

58°F   15°C   **59°F**   **5°C   41°F**   40.5°F   10°C   **50°F**

20°C   68°F   **12°C   53.6°F**   **44.6°F   7°C**

−3°C   26.6°F   14°C   53°F   **57.2°F**   **71.6°F   22°C**

Page 212

Graphs

A **graph** is a drawing that shows information about changes in numbers.

Directions: Use the graph to answer the questions.

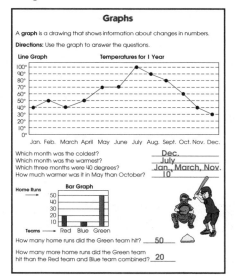

Line Graph   Temperatures for 1 Year

Jan. Feb. March April May June July Aug. Sept. Oct. Nov. Dec.

Which month was the coldest?   **Dec.**
Which month was the warmest?   **July**
Which three months were 40 degrees?   **Jan., March, Nov.**
How much warmer was it in May than October?   **10**

Home Runs   **Bar Graph**

Teams → Red   Blue   Green

How many home runs did the Green team hit?   **50**

How many more home runs did the Green team hit than the Red team and Blue team combined?   **20**

Page 213

Graphs

Directions: Read each graph and follow the directions.

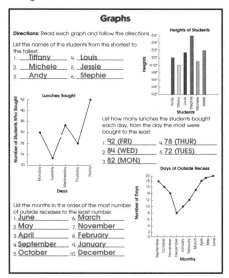

List the names of the students from the shortest to the tallest.
1. **Tiffany**   4. **Louis**
2. **Michele**   5. **Jessie**
3. **Andy**   6. **Stephie**

Heights of Students

Lunches Bought

List how many lunches the students bought each day, from the day the most were bought to the least.
1. **92 (FRI)**   4. **78 (THUR)**
2. **84 (WED)**   5. **72 (TUES)**
3. **82 (MON)**

Days of Outside Recess

List the months in the order of the most number of outside recesses to the least number.
1. **June**   6. **March**
2. **May**   7. **November**
3. **April**   8. **February**
4. **September**   9. **January**
5. **October**   10. **December**

Page 214

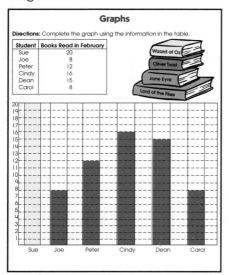

Graphs

Directions: Complete the graph using the information in the table.

Student	Books Read in February
Sue	20
Joe	8
Peter	12
Cindy	16
Dean	15
Carol	8

Page 215

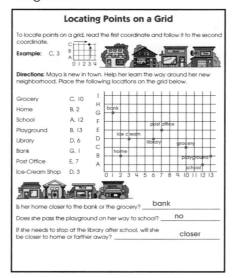

Locating Points on a Grid

To locate points on a grid, read the first coordinate and follow it to the second coordinate.

Example: C, 3

Directions: Maya is new in town. Help her learn the way around her new neighborhood. Place the following locations on the grid below.

Grocery — C, 10
Home — B, 2
School — A, 12
Playground — B, 13
Library — D, 6
Bank — G, 1
Post Office — E, 7
Ice-Cream Shop — D, 3

Is her home closer to the bank or the grocery? **bank**

Does she pass the playground on her way to school? **no**

If she needs to stop at the library after school, will she be closer to home or farther away? **closer**

Page 216

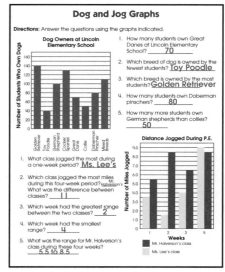

Dog and Jog Graphs

Directions: Answer the questions using the graphs indicated.

1. How many students own Great Danes at Lincoln Elementary School? **70**
2. Which breed of dog is owned by the fewest students? **Toy Poodle**
3. Which breed is owned by the most students? **Golden Retriever**
4. How many students own Doberman pinschers? **80**
5. How many more students own German shepherds than collies? **50**

1. What class jogged the most during a one-week period? **Ms. Lee's**
2. Which class jogged the most miles during this four-week period? **Mr. Halverson's** What was the difference between classes? **11**
3. Which week had the greatest range between the two classes? **2**
4. Which week had the smallest range? **4**
5. What was the range for Mr. Halverson's class during these four weeks? **5.5 to 8.5**

Page 217

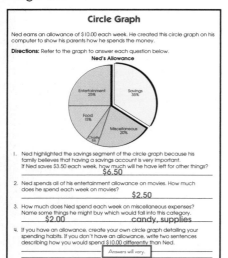

Circle Graph

Ned earns an allowance of $10.00 each week. He created this circle graph on his computer to show his parents how he spends the money.

Directions: Refer to the graph to answer each question below.

1. Ned highlighted the savings segment of the circle graph because his family believes that having a savings account is very important. If Ned saves $3.50 each week, how much will he have left for other things? **$6.50**
2. Ned spends all of his entertainment allowance on movies. How much does he spend each week on movies? **$2.50**
3. How much does Ned spend each week on miscellaneous expenses? Name some things he might buy which would fall into this category. **$2.00** **candy, supplies**
4. If you have an allowance, create your own circle graph detailing your spending habits. If you don't have an allowance, write two sentences describing how you would spend $10.00 differently than Ned. **Answers will vary.**

Page 218

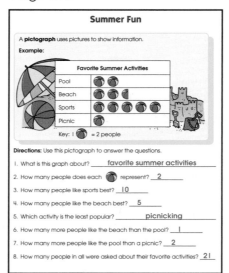

Summer Fun

A **pictograph** uses pictures to show information.

Example:

Favorite Summer Activities — Key: 1 = 2 people

Directions: Use this pictograph to answer the questions.

1. What is this graph about? **favorite summer activities**
2. How many people does each ball represent? **2**
3. How many people like sports best? **10**
4. How many people like the beach best? **5**
5. Which activity is the least popular? **picnicking**
6. How many more people like the beach than the pool? **1**
7. How many more people like the pool than a picnic? **2**
8. How many people in all were asked about their favorite activities? **21**

Page 219

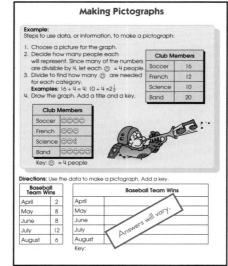

Making Pictographs

Example:
Steps to use data, or information, to make a pictograph:

1. Choose a picture for the graph.
2. Decide how many people each will represent. Since many of the numbers are divisible by 4, let each ☺ = 4 people.
3. Divide to find how many ☺ are needed for each category.
   Examples: 16 ÷ 4 = 4; 10 ÷ 4 = 2½
4. Draw the graph. Add a title and a key.

Club Members	
Soccer	16
French	12
Science	10
Band	20

Key: ☺ = 4 people

Directions: Use the data to make a pictograph. Add a key.

Baseball Team Wins	
April	2
May	8
June	4
July	12
August	6

Baseball Team Wins — Answers will vary.

Page 220

Bar Graphs

Bar graphs use bars to show information. They are good for showing information that can be easily counted.

Example:

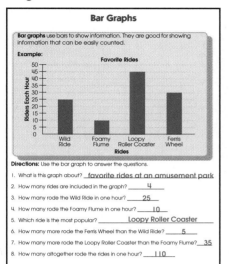

Directions: Use the bar graph to answer the questions.

1. What is this graph about? __favorite rides at an amusement park__
2. How many rides are included in the graph? __4__
3. How many rode the Wild Ride in one hour? __25__
4. How many rode the Foamy Flume in one hour? __10__
5. Which ride is the most popular? __Loopy Roller Coaster__
6. How many more rode the Ferris Wheel than the Wild Ride? __5__
7. How many more rode the Loopy Roller Coaster than the Foamy Flume? __35__
8. How many altogether rode the rides in one hour? __110__

Page 222

Double Bar Graphs

Double bar graphs use different colored bars to compare two sets of data. They are similar to bar graphs, and they include a key to show what the different bars mean.

Example:

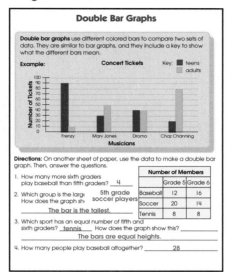

Directions: On another sheet of paper, use the data to make a double bar graph. Then, answer the questions.

	Grade 5	Grade 6
Baseball	12	16
Soccer	20	14
Tennis	8	8

1. How many more sixth graders play baseball than fifth graders? __4__
2. Which group is the large __5th grade__ How does the graph sh __soccer players__ __The bar is the tallest.__
3. Which sport has an equal number of fifth and sixth graders? __tennis__ How does the graph show this? __The bars are equal heights.__
4. How many people play baseball altogether? __28__

Page 223

Pie in the Sky

A **circle graph,** or pie chart, shows how parts relate to a whole. It makes it easy to see the data quickly.

Example:

This graph shows that pepperoni was the most popular topping.

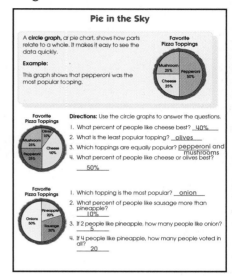

Directions: Use the circle graphs to answer the questions.

1. What percent of people like cheese best? __40%__
2. What is the least popular topping? __olives__
3. Which toppings are equally popular? __pepperoni and mushrooms__
4. What percent of people like cheese or olives best? __50%__

1. Which topping is the most popular? __onion__
2. What percent of people like sausage more than pineapple? __10%__
3. If 2 people like pineapple, how many people like onion? __5__
4. If 4 people like pineapple, how many people voted in all? __20__

Page 224

Color Wheels

Example:

Steps to use data to make a circle graph:

1. Find the total: 20.
2. Find what percent of the total each part is.

Favorite Colors	
Red	1
Green	4
Purple	10
Yellow	5

$1 \div 20 = 0.05 = 5\%$
$4 \div 20 = 0.20 = 20\%$
$10 \div 20 = 0.20 = 50\%$
$5 \div 20 = 0.25 = 25\%$

3. Divide the circle into the different parts.
4. Label the graph and give it a title.

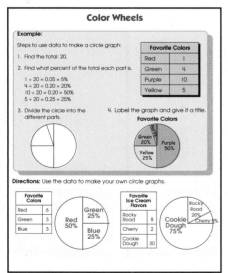

Directions: Use the data to make your own circle graphs.

Page 225

Braille Numbers

A **number line** is a simple kind of graph. It shows how numbers are ordered.

Example:

This number line shows the numbers 0 to 9.

Blind people can read letters and numbers by touching raised dots on paper. The dots are formed into patterns on a 2 x 3 grid. This system of raised dots is called Braille.

Braille symbols for the numbers and the comma:

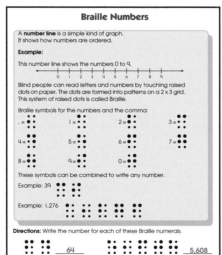

These symbols can be combined to write any number.

Example: 39

Example: 1,276

Directions: Write the number for each of these Braille numerals.

__64__ __5,608__

Page 226

Line Graphs

A **line graph** is a good way to show data that changes over time. This graph shows the company sales for Wacky Water Slides from 1994 to 2001.

Example:

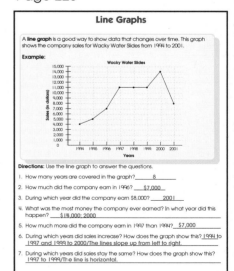

Directions: Use the line graph to answer the questions.

1. How many years are covered in the graph? __8__
2. How much did the company earn in 1996? __$7,000__
3. During which year did the company earn $8,000? __2001__
4. What was the most money the company ever earned? In what year did this happen? __$14,000; 2000__
5. How much more did the company earn in 1997 than 1994? __$7,000__
6. During which years did sales increase? How does the graph show this? __1994 to 1997 and 1999 to 2000/The lines slope up from left to right.__
7. During which years did sales stay the same? How does the graph show this? __1997 to 1999/The line is horizontal.__

Page 227

Hot and Cold

Directions: Use the data to make line graphs. Remember to include titles. Use abbreviations for the days and months.

Temperatures Week of March 7	
Day	**Temperature**
Sunday	11°C
Monday	12°C
Tuesday	8°C
Wednesday	9°C
Thursday	8°C
Friday	10°C
Saturday	12°C

High Temperatures	
Day	**Temperature**
January 1	6°C
February 1	4°C
March 1	10°C
April 1	16°C
May 1	16°C
June 1	23°C
July 1	27°C
August 1	27°C
September 1	23°C
October 1	20°C
November 1	14°C
December 1	9°C

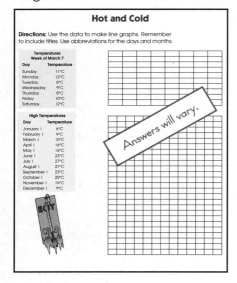

Answers will vary.

Page 228

Surveys

A **survey** is a way to collect data by asking people questions.

Directions: Follow these steps to conduct your own survey:

1. Decide what question to ask.
_____
_____

2. Decide who will be surveyed.
_____
_____

3. Do the survey and record the data. (In other words, ask lots of people your question, and write down what each person says.)

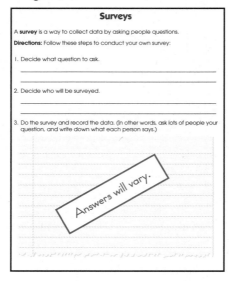

Answers will vary.

Page 229

Surveys

Directions: Show the results of your survey by summarizing your data.

4. Choose a kind of graph to show the data, then make the graph.

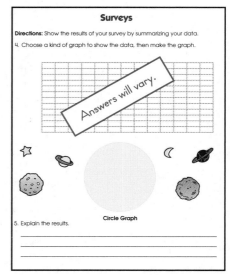

Answers will vary.

Circle Graph

5. Explain the results.
_____
_____
_____

Page 230

Tree Diagrams

A **tree diagram** shows the possible results of a group of events. It is very helpful in organizing probabilities and combinations.

Example:

A candy company offers white, milk, and dark chocolate candy shells with raspberry or caramel fillings. How many different candies do they make and what are they?

Shells	Fillings	Combinations

1. List all the possible outcomes of flipping a coin and rolling one die. (Hint: There are 12 possible outcomes.)

heads/1	heads/4	tails/1	tails/4
heads/2	heads/5	tails/2	tails/5
heads/3	heads/6	tails/3	tails/6

2. Tuna, turkey, and egg salad sandwiches can be made on white, wheat, or rye bread. List all the possible combinations.

tuna-white	turkey-white	egg salad-white
tuna-wheat	turkey-wheat	egg salad-wheat
tuna-rye	turkey-rye	egg salad-rye

3. Roma's makes pizzas in 3 sizes—small, medium, and large. They come in red (with sauce) or white (without). Each pizza can be made with regular or Sicilian crust. How many different ways can the pizzas be made? What are they?

12 ways

small/red/regular	medium/red/regular	large/red/regular
small/white/regular	medium/white/regular	large/red/Sicilian
small/red/Sicilian	medium/red/Sicilian	large/white/regular
small/white/Sicilian	medium/white/Sicilian	large/white/Sicilian

Page 231

Pennies From Heaven

Directions: On another sheet of paper, make a tree diagram to answer each question.

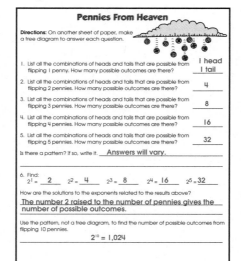

1. List all the combinations of heads and tails that are possible from flipping 1 penny. How many possible outcomes are there? **1 head 1 tail**

2. List all the combinations of heads and tails that are possible from flipping 2 pennies. How many possible outcomes are there? **4**

3. List all the combinations of heads and tails that are possible from flipping 3 pennies. How many possible outcomes are there? **8**

4. List all the combinations of heads and tails that are possible from flipping 4 pennies. How many possible outcomes are there? **16**

5. List all the combinations of heads and tails that are possible from flipping 5 pennies. How many possible outcomes are there? **32**

Is there a pattern? If so, write it. __Answers will vary.__
_____

6. Find:
$2^1 =$ **2** $2^2 =$ **4** $2^3 =$ **8** $2^4 =$ **16** $2^5 =$ **32**

How are the solutions to the exponents related to the results above?

__The number 2 raised to the number of pennies gives the number of possible outcomes.__

Use the pattern, not a tree diagram, to find the number of possible outcomes from flipping 10 pennies.

$2^{10} = 1,024$

Page 232

Coordinate Graphs

Coordinate graphs are line graphs that use ordered pairs to name the points. An **ordered pair** tells how many units to the right and up from the origin a point is located. It is written like this:

Example:
Move this many units to the right. $(2, 1)$ Move this many units up.

Example: Plot the point (4, 3).
What is the location of point H?
Point H is located at (2, 5).

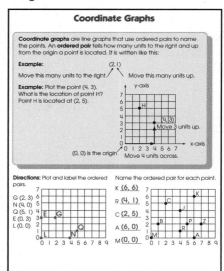

Move 3 units up.
Move 4 units across.
(0, 0) is the origin

Directions: Plot and label the ordered pairs.

G (2, 3)	K **(6, 6)**
N (4, 0)	R **(4, 1)**
Q (5, 1)	C **(2, 5)**
E (0, 3)	A **(6, 0)**
L (0, 0)	M **(0, 0)**

Name the ordered pair for each point.

Page 233

Graph Shapes

Example:

These four ordered pairs form a rectangle.

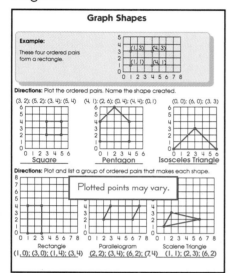

Directions: Plot the ordered pairs. Name the shape created.

(3, 2); (5, 2); (3, 4); (5, 4)   (4, 1); (2, 6); (0, 4); (4, 4); (0,1)   (0, 0); (6, 0); (3, 3)

Square   Pentagon   Isosceles Triangle

Directions: Plot and list a group of ordered pairs that makes each shape.

Plotted points may vary.

Rectangle   Parallelogram   Scalene Triangle
(1,0); (3, 0); (1, 4); (3,4)   (2, 2); (3, 4); (6, 2); (7,4)   (1, 1); (2, 3); (6, 2)

Page 234

Flying Experiment

Example:

Sally and Frank did an experiment with their flying disks. They threw disks of different sizes and measured how far they flew.

Disk Diameter (inches)	Distance (feet)
5	6
6	10
8	12
9	12
10	16

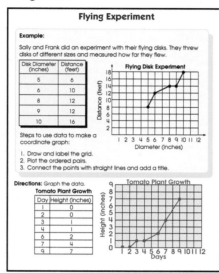

Steps to use data to make a coordinate graph:

1. Draw and label the grid.
2. Plot the ordered pairs.
3. Connect the points with straight lines and add a title.

Directions: Graph the data.

Tomato Plant Growth

Day	Height (inches)
1	0
2	0
3	1
4	1
6	2
7	4
9	7

Page 236

What's My Line?

Example:

A line on a graph can represent an equation. The table on the left lists some possible values for x and y in the equation y = 2x + 1. Each ordered pair is plotted and the points are joined to form a line.

Example: y = 2x – 1

x	y
–2	–3
–1	–1
0	1
1	3
2	5
3	7

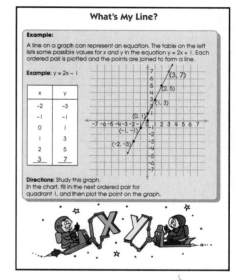

Directions: Study this graph.
In the chart, fill in the next ordered pair for quadrant 1, and then plot the point on the graph.

Test Practice

About the Tests

What Are Standardized Achievement Tests?

Achievement tests measure what children know in particular subject areas such as reading, language arts, and mathematics. They do not measure your child's intelligence or ability to learn.

When tests are standardized, or *normed,* children's test results are compared with those of a specific group who have taken the test, usually at the same age or grade.

Standardized achievement tests measure what children around the country are learning. The test makers survey popular textbook series, as well as state curriculum frameworks and other professional sources, to determine what content is covered widely.

Because of variations in state frameworks and textbook series, as well as grade ranges on some test levels, the tests may cover some material that children have not yet learned. This is especially true if the test is offered early in the school year. However, test scores are compared to those of other children who take the test at the same time of year, so your child will not be at a disadvantage if his or her class has not covered specific material yet.

Different School Districts, Different Tests

There are many flexible options for districts when offering standardized tests. Many school districts choose not to give the full test battery, but select certain content and scoring options. For example, many schools may test only in the areas of reading and mathematics. Similarly, a state or district may use one test for certain grades and another test for other grades. These decisions are often based on

the amount of time and money a district wishes to spend on test administration. Some states choose to develop their own statewide assessment tests.

On pages 280-282 you will find information about these five widely used standardized achievement tests:

- California Achievement Tests (CAT)
- Terra Nova/CTBS
- Iowa Test of Basic Skills (ITBS)
- Stanford Achievement Test (SAT9)
- Metropolitan Achievement Test (MAT).

However, this book contains strategies and practice questions for use with a variety of tests. Even if your state does not give one of the five tests listed above, your child will benefit from doing the practice questions in this book. If you're unsure about which test your child takes, contact your local school district to find out which tests are given.

Types of Test Questions

Traditionally, standardized achievements tests have used only multiple choice questions. Today, many tests may include constructed response (short answer) and extended response (essay) questions as well.

In addition, many tests include questions that tap students' higher-order thinking skills. Instead of simple recall questions, such as identifying a date in history, questions may require students to make comparisons and contrasts or analyze results, among other skills.

What the Tests Measure

These tests do not measure your child's level of intelligence, but they do show how well your child knows material that he or she has learned and that

is also covered on the tests. It's important to remember that some tests cover content that is not taught in your child's school or grade. In other instances, depending on when in the year the test is given, your child may not yet have covered the material.

If the test reports you receive show that your child needs improvement in one or more skill areas, you may want to seek help from your child's teacher and find out how you can work with your child to improve his or her skills.

California Achievement Tests (CAT/5)

What Is the California Achievement Test?

The *California Achievement Test* is a standardized achievement test battery that is widely used with elementary through high school students.

Parts of the Test

The CAT includes tests in the following content areas:

Reading
- Word Analysis
- Vocabulary
- Comprehension

Spelling

Language Arts
- Language Mechanics
- Language Usage

Mathematics

Science

Social Studies

Your child may take some or all of these subtests if your district uses the *California Achievement Test*.

Terra Nova/CTBS (Comprehensive Tests of Basic Skills)

What Is the Terra Nova/CTBS?

The *Terra Nova/Comprehensive Tests of Basic Skills* is a standardized achievement test battery used in elementary through high school grades.

While many of the test questions on the *Terra Nova* are in the traditional multiple choice form, your child may take parts of the *Terra Nova* that include some open-ended questions (constructed-response items).

Parts of the Test

Your child may take some or all of the following subtests if your district uses the *Terra Nova/CTBS:*

Reading/Language Arts
Mathematics
Science
Social Studies

Supplementary tests include:
- Word Analysis
- Vocabulary
- Language Mechanics
- Spelling
- Mathematics Computation

Critical thinking skills may also be tested.

Iowa Tests of Basic Skills (ITBS)

What Is the ITBS?

The *Iowa Test of Basic Skills* is a standardized achievement test battery used in elementary through high school grades.

Parts of the Test

Your child may take some or all of these subtests if your district uses the *ITBS*, also known as the *Iowa:*

Reading
- Vocabulary
- Reading Comprehension

Language Arts
- Spelling
- Capitalization
- Punctuation
- Usage and Expression

Math
- Concepts/Estimate
- Problems/Data Interpretation

Social Studies

Science

Sources of Information

Stanford Achievement Test (SAT9)

What Is the Stanford Achievement Test?

The *Stanford Achievement Test, Ninth Edition (SAT9)* is a standardized achievement test battery used in elementary through high school grades.

Note that the *Stanford Achievement Test (SAT9)* is a different test from the *SAT* used by high school students for college admissions.

While many of the test questions on the *SAT9* are in traditional multiple choice form, your child may take parts of the *SAT9* that include some open-ended questions (constructed-response items).

Parts of the Test

Your child may take some or all of these subtests if your district uses the *Stanford Achievement Test.*

Reading
- Vocabulary
- Reading Comprehension

Mathematics
- Problem Solving
- Procedures

Language Arts

Spelling

Study Skills

Listening

Critical thinking skills may also be tested.

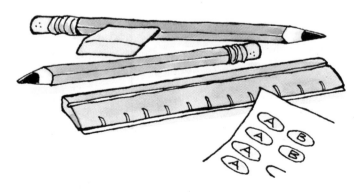

Metropolitan Achievement Test (MAT7 and MAT8)

What Is the Metropolitan Achievement Test?

The *Metropolitan Achievement Test* is a standardized achievement test battery used in elementary through high school grades.

Parts of the Test

Your child may take some or all of these subtests if your district uses the *Metropolitan Achievement Test*.

Reading
- Vocabulary
- Reading Comprehension

Math
- Concepts and Problem Solving
- Computation

Language Arts
- Pre-writing
- Composing
- Editing

Science

Social Studies

Research Skills

Thinking Skills

Spelling

Statewide Assessments

Today the majority of states give statewide assessments. In some cases these tests are known as *high-stakes assessments*. This means that students must score at a certain level in order to be promoted. Some states use minimum competency or proficiency tests. Often these tests measure more basic skills than other types of statewide assessments.

Statewide assessments are generally linked to state curriculum frameworks. Frameworks provide a blueprint, or outline, to ensure that teachers are covering the same curriculum topics as other teachers in the same grade level in the state. In some states, standardized achievement tests (such as the five described in this book) are used in connection with statewide assessments.

When Statewide Assessments Are Given

Statewide assessments may not be given at every grade level. Generally, they are offered at one or more grades in elementary school, middle school, and high school. Many states test at grades 4, 8, and 10.

State-by-State Information

You can find information about statewide assessments and curriculum frameworks at your state Department of Education Web site. To find the address for your individual state go to www.ed.gov, click on Topics A–Z, and then click on State Departments of Education. You will find a list of all the state departments of education, mailing addresses, and Web sites.

How to Help Your Child
Prepare for Standardized Testing

Preparing All Year Round

Perhaps the most valuable way you can help your child prepare for standardized achievement tests is by providing enriching experiences. Keep in mind also, that test results for younger children are not as reliable as for older students. If a child is hungry, tired, or upset, this may result in a poor test score. Here are some tips on how you can help your child do his or her best on standardized tests.

Read aloud with your child. Reading aloud helps develop vocabulary and fosters a positive attitude toward reading. Reading together is one of the most effective ways you can help your child succeed in school.

Share experiences. Baking cookies together, planting a garden, or making a map of your neighborhood are examples of activities that help build skills that are measured on the tests such as sequencing and following directions.

Become informed about your state's testing procedures. Ask about or watch for announcements of meetings that explain about standardized tests and statewide assessments in your school district.

Talk to your child's teacher about your child's individual performance on these state tests during a parent-teacher conference.

Help your child know what to expect. Read and discuss with your child the test-taking tips in this book. Your child can prepare by working through a couple of strategies a day so that no practice session takes too long.

Help your child with his or her regular school assignments. Set up a quiet study area for homework. Supply this area with pencils, paper, markers, a calculator, a ruler, a dictionary, scissors, glue, and so on. Check your child's homework and offer to help if he or she gets stuck. But remember, it's your child's homework, not yours. If you help too much, your child will not benefit from the activity.

Keep in regular contact with your child's teacher. Attend parent-teacher conferences, school functions, PTA or PTO meetings, and school board meetings. This will help you get to know the educators in your district and the families of your child's classmates.

Learn to use computers as an educational resource. If you do not have a computer and Internet access at home, try your local library.

Remember—simply getting your child comfortable with testing procedures and helping him or her know what to expect can improve test scores!

Getting Ready for the Big Day

There are lots of things you can do on or immediately before test day to improve your child's chances of testing success. What's more, these strategies will help your child prepare him or herself for school tests, too, and promote general study skills that can last a lifetime.

Provide a good breakfast on test day.
Instead of sugary cereal, which provides immediate but not long-term energy, have your child eat a breakfast with protein or complex carbohydrates such as an egg, whole grain cereal or toast, or a banana-yogurt shake.

Promote a good night's sleep. A good night's sleep before the test is essential. Try not to overstress the importance of the test. This may cause your child to lose sleep because of anxiety. Doing some exercise after school and having a quiet evening routine will help your child sleep well the night before the test.

Assure your child that he or she is not expected to know all of the answers on the test. Explain that other children in higher grades may take the same test, and that the test may measure things your child has not yet learned in school. Help your child understand that you expect him or her to put forth a good effort—and that this is enough. Your child should not try to cram for these tests. Also avoid threats or bribes; these put undue pressure on children and may interfere with their best performance.

Keep the mood light and offer encouragement. To provide a break on test days, do something fun and special after school—take a walk around the neighborhood, play a game, read a favorite book, or prepare a special snack together. These activities keep your child's mood light—even if the testing sessions have been difficult—and show how much you appreciate your child's effort.

Taking Standardized Tests

No matter what grade you're in, this is information you can use to prepare for standardized tests. Here is what you'll find:

- Test-taking tips and strategies to use on test day and year-round.
- Important terms to know for Math.
- A checklist of skills to complete to help you understand what you need to know in Math.
- General study/homework tips.

By opening this book, you've already taken your first step towards test success. The rest is easy—all you have to do is get started!

What You Need to Know

There are many things you can do to increase your test success. Here's a list of tips to keep in mind when you take standardized tests—and when you study for them, too.

Keep up with your school work.

One way you can succeed in school and on tests is by studying and doing your homework regularly. Studies show that you remember only about one-fifth of what you memorize the night before a test. That's one good reason not to try to learn it all at once! Keeping up with your work throughout the year will help you remember the material better. You also won't be as tired or nervous as if you try to learn everything at once.

Feel your best. One of the ways you can do your best on tests and in school is to make sure your body is ready. To do this, get a good night's sleep each night and eat a healthy breakfast (not sugary cereal that will leave you tired by the middle of the morning). An egg or a milkshake with yogurt and fresh fruit will give you lasting energy. Also, wear comfortable clothes, maybe your lucky shirt or your favorite color on test day. It can't hurt, and it may even help you relax.

Be prepared. Do practice questions and learn about how standardized tests are organized. Books like this one will help you know what to expect when you take a standardized test.

When you are taking the test, follow the directions. It is important to listen carefully to the directions your teacher gives and to read the written instructions carefully. Words like *not, none, rarely, never,* and *always* are very important in test directions and questions. You may want to circle words like these.

Look at each page carefully before you start answering. In school you usually read a passage and then answer questions about it. But when you take a test, it's helpful to follow a different order.

On math tests, look at the labels on graphs and charts. Think about what each graph or chart shows. Questions often will ask you to draw conclusions about the information.

Manage your time. *Time management* means using your time wisely on a test so that you can finish as much of it as possible and do your best. Look over the test or the parts that you are allowed to do at one time. Sometimes you may want to do the easier parts first. This way, if you run out of time before you finish, you will have completed a good chunk of the work.

For tests that have a time limit, notice what time it is when the test begins and figure out when you need to stop. Check a few times as you work through the test to be sure you are making good progress and not spending too much time on any particular section.

You don't have to keep up with everyone else. You may notice other students in the class finishing before you do. Don't worry about this. Everyone works at a different pace. Just keep going, trying not to spend too long on any one question.

Fill in answer circles properly. Even if you know every answer on a test, you won't do well unless you fill in the circle next to the correct answer.

Fill in the entire circle, but don't spend too much time making it perfect. Make your mark dark, but not so dark that it goes through the paper! And be sure you only choose one answer for each question, even if you are not sure. If you choose two answers, both will be marked as wrong.

It's usually not a good idea to change your answers. Usually your first choice is the right one. Unless you realize that you misread the question, the directions, or some facts in a passage, it's usually safer to stay with your first answer. If you are pretty sure it's wrong, of course, go ahead and change it. Make sure you completely erase the first choice and neatly fill in your new choice.

Use context clues to figure out tough questions. If you come across a word or idea you don't understand, use context clues—the words in the sentences nearby— to help you figure out its meaning.

Sometimes it's good to guess. Should you guess when you don't know an answer on a test? That depends. If your teacher has made the test, usually you will score better if you answer as many questions as possible, even if you don't really know the answers.

On standardized tests, here's what to do to score your best. For each question, most of these tests let you choose from four or five answer choices. If you decide that a couple of answers are clearly wrong but you're still not sure about the answer, go ahead and make your best guess. If you can't narrow down the choices at all, then you may be better off skipping the question. Tests like these take away extra points for wrong answers, so it's better to leave them blank. Be sure you skip over the answer space for these questions on the answer sheet, though, so you don't fill in the wrong spaces.

Sometimes you should skip a question and come back to it. On many tests, you will score better if you answer more questions. This means that you should not spend too much time on any single question. Sometimes it gets tricky, though, keeping track of questions you skipped on your answer sheet.

If you want to skip a question because you don't know the answer, put a very light pencil mark next to the question in the test booklet. Try to choose an answer, even if you're not sure of it. Fill in the answer lightly on the answer sheet.

Check your work. On a standardized test, you can't go ahead or skip back to another section of the test. But you may go back and review your answers on the section you just worked on if you have extra time.

First, scan your answer sheet. Make sure that you answered every question you could. Also, if you are using a bubble-type answer sheet, make sure that you filled in only one bubble for each question. Erase any extra marks on the page.

Finally—avoid test anxiety! If you get nervous about tests, don't worry. Test anxiety happens to lots of good students. Being a little nervous actually sharpens your mind. But if you get very nervous about tests, take a few minutes to relax the night before or the day of the test. One good way to relax is to get some exercise, even if you just have time to stretch, shake out your fingers, and wiggle your toes. If you can't move around, it helps just to take a few slow, deep breaths and picture yourself doing a great job!

Skills Checklists

Which math skills do you need more practice in? Use the following checklist to find out. Put a check mark next to each statement that is true for you. Then, use the unchecked statements to figure out which skills you need to review.

Keep in mind that if you are using these checklists in the middle of the school year, you may not have learned some skills yet. Talk to your teacher or a parent if you need help with a new skill.

Number Sense

❑ I can round numbers to the nearest ten, hundred, and thousand.

❑ I can identify the factors of a number.

❑ I can identify the multiples of a number.

❑ I can use roman numerals.

Addition and Subtraction

❑ I can add and subtract three- and four-digit numbers.

❑ I can add and subtract decimals to the thousandths places.

Multiplication and Division

❑ I can multiply by one-, two-, and three-digit numbers.

❑ I can divide two- and three-digit numbers and greater.

❑ I can divide one- and two-digit numbers.

Measurement

I can estimate and measure using the standard units for

- ☐ length (inch, foot, yard, mile).
- ☐ weight (ounce, pound, ton).
- ☐ capacity (cup, pint, quart, gallon).
- ☐ time (seconds, minutes, hours).

I can estimate and measure using the metric units for

- ☐ length (centimeter, decimeter, meter, kilometer).
- ☐ mass (gram, kilogram).
- ☐ capacity (milliliter, liter).
- ☐ I can solve simple problems with units of time, length, weight/mass, and capacity.

Fractions and Decimals

I can

- ☐ compare and order fractions.
- ☐ find the least common denominator.
- ☐ add and subtract fractions.
- ☐ add and subtract mixed numbers.
- ☐ multiply fractions.
- ☐ use ratios.
- ☐ find percents.
- ☐ find probabilities.

Geometry

I can identify

- ☐ polygons.
- ☐ lines, line segments, and rays.
- ☐ different types of angles, triangles, and quadrilaterals.
- ☐ I can find perimeter, area, volume, and circumference of plane shapes.

Problem Solving

I use different strategies to solve different kinds of problems:

- ☐ I estimate and use mental math.
- ☐ I make pictures, diagrams, and charts.
- ☐ I look for patterns.
- ☐ I work backwards.
- ☐ I collect data.
- ☐ I read and construct pictographs, line graphs, and bar graphs.

Preparing All Year Round

Believe it or not, knowing how to study and manage your time is a skill you will use for the rest of your life. There are helpful strategies that you can use to be more successful in school. The following is a list of tips to keep in mind as you study for tests and school assignments.

Get organized. To make it easy to get your homework done, set up a place in which to do it each day. Choose a location where you can give the work your full attention. Find a corner of your room, the kitchen, or another quiet place where you won't be interrupted. Put all the tools you'll need in that area. Set aside a drawer or basket for school supplies. That way you won't have to go hunting each time you need a sharp pencil! Here are some things you may want to keep in your study corner for homework and school projects:

- pencils and pens
- pencil sharpener
- notebook paper
- tape
- glue
- scissors
- stapler
- crayons, markers, colored pencils
- construction paper, printer paper
- dictionary

Schedule your assignments. The best way to keep track of homework and special projects is by planning and managing your time. Keep a schedule of homework assignments and other events to help you get organized. Make your own or make a copy of the Homework Log and Weekly Schedule provided on pages 294-295 of this book for each week you're in school.

Record your homework assignments on the log as completely as you can. Enter the book, page number, and exercise number of each assignment. Enter dates of tests as soon as you know them so that you can begin to study ahead of time. Study a section of the material each day. Then review all of it the day before the test.

Also make notes to help you remember special events and materials such as permission slips you need to return. List afterschool activities so you can plan your homework and study time around them. Remember to record fun activities on your log, too. You don't want to forget that party you've been invited to or even just time you'd like to spend hanging out or studying with friends.

Do your homework right away. Set aside a special time every day after school to do your homework. You may want to take a break when you first get home, but give yourself plenty of time to do your homework, too. That way you won't get interrupted by dinner or get too tired to finish.

If you are bored or confused by an assignment and you really don't want to do it, promise yourself a little reward, perhaps a snack or 15 minutes of playing ball after you've really worked hard for 45 minutes or so. Then go back to work for a while if you need to, and take another break later.

Get help if you need it. If you need help, just ask. Call a friend or ask a family member for help. If these people can't help you, be sure to ask your teacher the next day about any work you didn't understand.

Use a computer. If you have one available, a computer can be a great tool for doing homework. Typing your homework on the computer lets you hand in neat papers, check your spelling easily, and look up the definitions of words you aren't sure about. If you have an Internet connection, you can also do research without leaving home.

Before you go online, talk with your family about ways to stay safe. Be sure never to give out personal information (your name, age, address, or phone number) without permission.

Practice, practice, practice! The best way to improve your skills in specific subject areas is through lots of practice. If you have trouble in a school subject such as math, science, social studies, language arts, or reading, doing some extra activities or projects can give you just the boost you need.

Homework Log
and Weekly Schedule

	Monday	Tuesday	Wednesday
MATH			
SOCIAL STUDIES			
SCIENCE			
READING			
LANGUAGE ARTS			
OTHER			

Name _____

for the week of _____

	Thursday	Friday	Saturday / Sunday	
				MATH
				SOCIAL STUDIES
				SCIENCE
				READING
				LANGUAGE ARTS
				OTHER

What's Ahead in This Section?

As you know, you will have to take many tests while in school. But there is no reason to be nervous about taking standardized tests. You can prepare for them by doing your best in school all year. You can also learn about the types of questions you'll see on standardized tests and helpful strategies for answering the questions. That's what this section is all about. It has been developed especially to help you and other fifth graders know what to expect—and what to do—on test day.

Next, you'll find a section on math called subject help. You'll discover traps to watch for and tricks you can use to make answering the questions easier. And there are plenty of practice questions provided to sharpen your skills even more.

Finally, you'll find two sections of questions. One is called the Practice Test and the other is called the Final Test. The questions are designed to look just like the ones you'll be given in school on a real standardized math test. An answer key is at the back of the book so you can check your own answers. Once you check your answers, you can see in which areas you need more practice.

So good luck—test success is just around the corner!

Draw a Diagram

Math Story Problems

Many standardized tests will ask you to solve math story problems, or word problems. You have probably already done problems like this in school, so this format will not be new to you. When you see story problems on a test, though, you will have limited time to find your answer.

Use the following strategies to help solve story problems quickly. Remember, though, not every strategy can be used with every story problem. You will have to choose the best strategy to use for each one.

Draw a Diagram

Sometimes you can draw a diagram to help solve a math problem. Venn diagrams organize data into circles. Overlapping sections show data that applies to more than one category.

Of 16 people on the Bulldogs soccer team, 8 play only defense. Two of the players play both offense and defense. How many players are on offense, but not defense?

- Ⓐ 6 people
- Ⓑ 8 people
- Ⓒ 2 people
- Ⓓ 10 people

- Draw a Venn diagram with two overlapping circles, one to represent offense and one to represent defense. The overlapping section is for students who play both offense and defense.

- You can find the number of students playing only offense by adding the number who play only defense and both positions and then subtracting that number from the total number of players.

Offense | Offense and Defense | Defense

- The Venn diagram shows that 6 students only play offense on the soccer team. So **A** is the correct answer.

When you draw a Venn diagram:

- ☐ Read the problem carefully.
- ☐ Determine what data is helpful for solving the problem.
- ☐ Determine how to organize your Venn diagram.
- ☐ Draw your diagram based on the data from the problem.
- ☐ Solve the problem.

Diagram Practice

Directions: Make a Venn diagram to help solve each problem.

1 There are 26 students in a fifth grade gym class. Sixteen students decide to play basketball and 14 students decide to play soccer. Four students will play both. How many students will play only basketball?

Ⓐ 16 students

Ⓑ 12 students

Ⓒ 10 students

Ⓓ 8 students

2 Carol took a survey of her class to find out who likes to do puzzles on rainy days and who likes to play checkers on rainy days. She found out that 15 students like to do puzzles and 17 students like to play checkers; she also found 6 additional students that like to do both. How many students did Carol survey?

Ⓕ 38 students

Ⓖ 32 students

Ⓗ 9 students

Ⓙ 2 students

Trick Questions

Some test questions contain the word *not*. You must be careful to notice when the word *not* is used. These are a type of trick question; you are being tested to see if you have read and understood the material completely.

EXAMPLE | **Which of the following is not a fraction?**

    Ⓐ $1\frac{2}{3}$

    Ⓑ $4\frac{5}{9}$

    Ⓒ $\frac{7}{16}$

    Ⓓ   9.04

- When solving this type of problem, first figure out how the word *not* applies to the problem. In this case, you must find the number that is not a fraction.

- Next, you need to know what a fraction is and compare what you know to your answer choices.

You read the answer choices and decide that

    $1\frac{2}{3}$ is a fraction.

    $\frac{7}{16}$ is a fraction.

    $4\frac{5}{9}$ is a fraction.

    9.04 is a decimal.

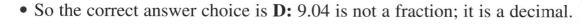

- So the correct answer choice is **D**: 9.04 is not a fraction; it is a decimal.

When you are asked questions containing the word *not*:

- ☐ Read the problem carefully.
- ☐ Determine how the word is used in the problem.
- ☐ Solve the problem.
- ☐ Check your work.

Trick Questions Practice

Directions: Solve each problem. Look carefully for the word *not*.

1 Cora went to the park on Tuesday, Wednesday, and Saturday. She went to the library on Monday and Sunday. On Friday, she went to the museum. On what days did Cora not go to the park or library?

Ⓐ Thursday and Sunday

Ⓑ Thursday

Ⓒ Tuesday and Friday

Ⓓ Thursday and Friday

2 Jessica must find the area of a square with one side that is 12 inches long. How can Jessica figure it out?

Ⓕ She can add all the sides together.

Ⓖ She can multiply 2 sides together.

Ⓗ She can divide 2 sides by each other.

Ⓙ She cannot figure out the area with the information she has.

3 Lance and Heath collected cans for a school fundraiser. Lance collected 128 cans and Heath collected 95 cans. If each can is worth five cents, how much money did they raise for the school fundraiser altogether?

Ⓐ $11.15

Ⓑ $6.40

Ⓒ $4.75

Ⓓ $2.23

4 Toby hiked 36 miles every day for 8 days. What mathematical operations could not be used to find how far he hiked altogether?

Ⓕ addition

Ⓖ multiplication

Ⓗ division

Ⓙ All of the above

Paper and Pencil

On tests, it often helps to work a problem out using paper and pencil. This helps you to visualize the problem and double-check your answer. It is especially useful when you must solve an equation.

EXAMPLE

Mr. Thomas is planning the seating for a party he is having. There will be 167 guests altogether and 8 people can sit at one table. How many tables will Mr. Thomas need so everyone can have a seat?

Ⓐ 23 tables

Ⓑ 20 tables

Ⓒ 21 tables

Ⓓ 18 tables

- Since it would be difficult to solve the problem mentally, you need to do the work for the problem using paper and pencil.
- Use paper and pencil to divide 167 by 8.

$$
\begin{array}{r}
20 \ \text{R7} \\
8\overline{\smash{)}167} \\
\underline{16} \\
7 \\
\underline{0} \\
7
\end{array}
$$

- There is a remainder of 7. Since Mr. Thomas needs enough tables to seat everyone, he must have 21 tables altogether. The correct answer is **D.**

When you use pencil and paper:

☐ Read the problem carefully.

☐ Write neatly so that you do not make errors.

☐ Solve the problem.

☐ Check your work.

Paper and Pencil Practice

Directions: Solve the problems. Use the work area to show your work.

1 Nadia sailed 3.5 hours a day for 5 days. How many hours did Nadia sail altogether?

   Ⓐ 25.5 hours

   Ⓑ 17.5 hours

   Ⓒ 15 hours

   Ⓓ 3.5 hours

2 It costs $15.75 per student to take a field trip to the aquarium. If 17 students go on the trip, what is the total cost?

   Ⓕ $255.00

   Ⓖ $267.75

   Ⓗ $268.75

   Ⓙ $298.50

3 A Tasmanian devil weighs 12,000 grams. A mole weighs about $\frac{1}{200}$ of what a Tasmanian devil weighs. How much does a mole weigh?

   Ⓐ 60 grams

   Ⓑ 600 grams

   Ⓒ 240,000 grams

   Ⓓ 2,400,000 grams

Guess and Check

One way to solve a word problem is to make your best guess and then work backwards to check your answer.

EXAMPLE **Manuel sends letters and postcards to his family and friends about his time at summer camp. A letter costs $0.33 to mail and a postcard costs $0.20 to mail. Manuel writes to 6 people and spends $1.46 altogether. How many letters and postcards did he send?**

Ⓐ 3 letters, 3 postcards   Ⓒ 4 letters, 2 postcards

Ⓑ 2 letters, 4 postcards   Ⓓ 1 letter, 5 postcards

• To guess and check here, pick the set of numbers that looks the most logical. Then fit it into an equation to see if the answer is $1.46.

Guess: 3 letters and 3 postcards

$3 \times \$0.33 = \$0.99$
$3 \times \$0.20 = \$0.60$
$\$0.99 + \$0.60 = \$1.56$
$\$1.56 > \$1.46$

• Since your answer is too large, you should try a smaller number of letters and a larger number of postcards.

Guess: 2 letters and 4 postcards

$2 \times \$0.33 = \$0.66$
$4 \times \$0.20 = \$0.80$
$\$0.66 + \$0.80 = \$1.46$
$\$1.46 = \$1.46$

• Your guess is correct. By sending 2 letters and 4 postcards, Manuel spent $1.46. The correct answer is **B**.

When you use guess and check:

☐ Read the problem carefully.

☐ Make a reasonable first guess.

☐ Revise your guess based on whether your answer was too high or low.

☐ Check that your answer is reasonable based on the question.

Guess and Check Practice

Directions: Use the guess and check method to solve these problems.

1 Jesse buys a T-shirt and a stuffed animal at a souvenir shop for $17.50. If the T-shirt costs $3.50 more than the stuffed animal, how much does the T-shirt cost?

Ⓐ $7.00

Ⓑ $10.50

Ⓒ $14.50

Ⓓ $21.00

2 There are two numbers whose product is 108 and whose quotient is 12. What are the two numbers?

Ⓕ 9, 12   Ⓗ 36, 3

Ⓖ 7, 16   Ⓙ 54, 6

3 There are several uninvited ants at a picnic in the park. Among the 9 guests that are ants or people, there are 30 legs altogether. How many ants are at the picnic?

Ⓐ 9 ants

Ⓑ 6 ants

Ⓒ 4 ants

Ⓓ 3 ants

4 Mr. Grace purchased two programs for the classroom computer. He spent a total of $35.45. What programs did he buy?

Ⓕ Math Busters and Spelling Practice

Ⓖ Math Busters and Reading Classics

Ⓗ Spelling Practice and Reading Classics

Ⓙ None of the above

Estimation

Directions: Use estimation to help you narrow down answer choices on a multiple choice test.

A band gave 204 concerts in one year. One-fourth of these concerts were performed in the United States. How many concerts did the band perform in the United States?

Ⓐ 97 concerts   Ⓒ 59 concerts

Ⓑ 82 concerts   Ⓓ 51 concerts

- First, estimate the answer by rounding up or down. When rounding, you should round to the most precise place needed for the problem. In this case, you should round to the nearest ten, which happens to become the nearest hundred: 204 rounds to 200.
- You do not need to round $\frac{1}{4}$ because it multiplies and divides easily with 200. Now you can estimate the answer to the problem using these two numbers.
- You can cross off choices **A** and **B** since they do not have a five in the tens place.
- Find the exact answer by dividing: $\frac{51}{4\overline{)204}}$

$$\frac{50}{4\overline{)200}}$$

- Now you can be sure that **D** is the correct answer.

When you estimate and answer:

☐ Read the problem carefully.

☐ Round the numbers you need to estimate the answer.

☐ Estimate the answer.

☐ Eliminate any answers not close to your estimate.

☐ Find the exact answer.

Estimation Practice

Directions: Use estimation to solve these problems.

1 Stacey spent $14.83 at the store. Harry spent $35.32 at the store. How much more did Harry spend than Stacey?

Ⓐ $21.60

Ⓑ $20.49

Ⓒ $49.95

Ⓓ $50.31

2 Golden lion tamarins are an endangered species. Only about 416 still live in the wild. They live in groups of 8. How many groups still live in the wild if there are 416 golden lion tamarins?

Ⓕ 52

Ⓖ 51

Ⓗ 42

Ⓙ 41

3 Colby surveyed 1,972 people and found that 1/4 of them enjoyed spending a sunny day at the beach. How many people enjoyed spending a sunny day at the beach?

Ⓐ 468 people

Ⓑ 479 people

Ⓒ 493 people

Ⓓ 498 people

4 The length of one side of a rectangle is 82 inches. The area of the rectangle is 6,068 inches. What is the length of the other side of the rectangle?

Ⓕ 74 inches

Ⓖ 76 inches

Ⓗ 82 inches

Ⓙ 89 inches

Incomplete Information

Some test problems may include "Not enough information" as one of the answer choices. When you see a problem with this as an answer choice, watch out! The problem may not contain enough information for you to solve it.

EXAMPLE

Jonas polled his school of 1,390 students. He found that 25% of the students enjoy going to the movies. Students' other favorite pastimes are reading, playing sports, and playing video games. How many students enjoyed reading?

Ⓐ 569 students   Ⓒ 86 students

Ⓑ 347 students   Ⓓ Not enough information

- Read the problem to find out the question you need to answer.

  How many students enjoy reading?

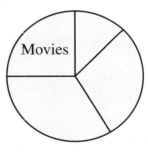

- Determine what information you have.
  —how many students there are in the school
  —how many students like going to the movies
  —the other pastimes of the students
- Since you do not know what percentage of students enjoy reading, you do not have enough information to answer the question.
- Reread the problem to verify that you do not have enough information.
- Since you do not have enough information, **D** is your answer.

When you think you have incomplete information:

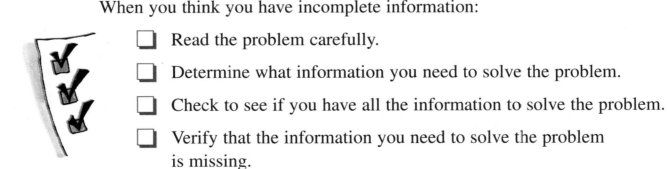

☐ Read the problem carefully.

☐ Determine what information you need to solve the problem.

☐ Check to see if you have all the information to solve the problem.

☐ Verify that the information you need to solve the problem is missing.

Incomplete Information Practice

Directions: Solve the problems below.

1 Brenda finished the 100-meter dash in 22.4 seconds. Tony finished the dash 1.3 seconds slower than Brenda. How long did it take Tony to complete the 100-meter dash?

Ⓐ 24.5 seconds

Ⓑ 23.7 seconds

Ⓒ 21.1 seconds

Ⓓ Not enough information

2 Monica ate $\frac{1}{8}$ of her sandwich for lunch, Sam ate $\frac{2}{3}$ of his apple, and Rick drank all of his milk. How much of her milk did Monica drink?

Ⓕ $\frac{1}{8}$ of the milk

Ⓖ $\frac{2}{3}$ of the milk

Ⓗ all of the milk

Ⓙ Not enough information

3 There were 258 cans of soup on the grocery store shelf in the morning. At 1:00 p.m., there were 156 cans of soup on the shelf. By the time the store closed at 7:00 p.m., several more cans of soup were on the shelf. How many cans of soup did the store sell in the entire day?

Ⓐ 102 cans

Ⓑ 288 cans

Ⓒ 414 cans

Ⓓ Not enough information

4 Sasha went to the park at 9:30 a.m. She played for 45 minutes and then started soccer practice. She had soccer practice for 90 minutes. At what time did soccer practice end?

Ⓕ 10:45 a.m.

Ⓖ 11.15 a.m.

Ⓗ 11:45 a.m.

Ⓙ Not enough information

Use a Calculator

You may be allowed to use a calculator with some standardized tests. Using a calculator can save you time, especially when you need to compute multi-digit numbers. A calculator can also allow you to double-check your work quickly.

EXAMPLE

Yo-yos cost $1.79 at the store. Marcia bought 17 yo-yos as presents. How much did Marcia spend on yo-yos?

Ⓐ $30.43

Ⓑ $21.34

Ⓒ $18.79

Ⓓ $9.58

- To solve the problem, you need to multiply a three-digit number by a two-digit number. It is quicker and easier, especially on a timed test, to use your calculator.

$ 1.79
× 17
$30.43

The correct answer is **D**.

- When you use a calculator, you can easily find a correct answer and the proper location of a decimal point. However, you must be sure to key in the correct numbers.

When you use a calculator:

☐ Read the problem carefully.

☐ Be sure you key in the correct numbers.

☐ Solve the problem.

☐ Check to see that your answer is reasonable.

Calculator Practice

Directions: Solve the problems below.

1 A case of crayons costs $55.20. Twelve boxes come in one case. How much does each box of crayons cost?

- Ⓐ $4.65
- Ⓑ $3.95
- Ⓒ $4.60
- Ⓓ $7.45

2 What is the sum of 41.78 and 67.893?

- Ⓕ 26.113
- Ⓖ 109.67
- Ⓗ 109.673
- Ⓙ 109.683

3 It costs $19.50 for an adult ticket to the amusement park. Children's tickets cost $11.50. If 2 adults and 3 children go to the amusement park, how much does it cost to get inside?

- Ⓐ $34.50
- Ⓑ $39.00
- Ⓒ $73.50
- Ⓓ $74.50

4 If you divide 47.34 into 9 equal parts, what is the result?

- Ⓕ 5.26
- Ⓖ 5.37
- Ⓗ 3.89
- Ⓙ 38.34

5 Chad swam 100 meters in 36.8 seconds. Zoe was 2.3 seconds faster than Chad. What was Zoe's time?

- Ⓐ 84.64 seconds
- Ⓑ 34.5 seconds
- Ⓒ 39.1 seconds
- Ⓓ 16 seconds

6 What is the product of 21.2 and 53.8?

- Ⓕ 1140.66
- Ⓖ 1140.46
- Ⓗ 1140.56
- Ⓙ 1040.56

Computation

Most standardized tests contain math sections where you must solve a variety of number equations. These questions test your ability to find exact answers to math problems. You will often be allowed to use scrap paper to work out these problems, but the work you show on scrap paper will not count.

The following is a list of skills that are often tested in the Computation segments of standardized tests. The list also contains tips for how to solve tough problems.

Using Operations

Your ability to perform basic mathematical operations (such as addition, subtraction, multiplication, and division) will be tested. Whenever you are solving a math equation, be sure of which operation you must use to solve the problem. Here are some tips:

- Even though you will be given answer choices, it's best to work the problem out first using scrap paper. Then you can compare the answer you found to the choices that are given.

- If you have time, double-check your answer to each problem by using the inverse operation.

- Keep in mind that the same equation may be written differently. Even though these problems look different, they ask you to do the exact same thing. Here are two equations for the same problem:

$$56 \div 12 = ? \qquad 12\overline{)56}^{\,?}$$

Other Things to Keep in Mind

- When using decimals, make sure your answer choice shows the decimal point in the correct place.

- Double-check the numerators and denominators of answers with fractions.

- If your problem contains units (such as 2 centimeters + 50 millimeters = X millimeters), be sure the answer choice has the correct units labeled. Many tests will try to confuse you by substituting one unit for another in an answer choice.

- Finally, if you get to a tough problem, use logic to decide which answer choice makes the most sense. Then plug this choice into the equation and see if it works.

Computation Practice

Directions: Find the answer to each problem below.

1 $95 \times 31 =$

Ⓐ 3,045

Ⓑ 2,954

Ⓒ 2,945

Ⓓ None of the above

2 $56,981 - 31,220 =$

Ⓕ 88,597

Ⓖ 26,761

Ⓗ 25,761

Ⓙ 21,961

3 $\frac{15}{16} + \frac{13}{16} =$

Ⓐ $\frac{2}{16}$

Ⓑ $\frac{28}{16}$

Ⓒ $\frac{16}{28}$

Ⓓ None of the above

4 $3689 \div 527 =$

Ⓕ 7

Ⓖ 9

Ⓗ 17

Ⓙ None of the above

5 $\$16.27 + \$8.40 + \$3.22 =$

Ⓐ $27.69

Ⓑ $27.89

Ⓒ $37.89

Ⓓ $37.90

6 $321.56 - 52.705 =$

Ⓕ 268.85

Ⓖ 268.855

Ⓗ 2688.55

Ⓙ 2680.855

Concepts

Standardized tests also test your understanding of important math concepts you will have learned in school. The following is a list of concepts that you may be tested on.

Number Concepts

- recognizing the standard and metric units of measure used for weighing and finding length and distance.

- recognizing place value (through the millions place and the thousandths place).

- telling time to the nearest minute.

- using a calendar.

- reading a thermometer.

- rounding up and down to the nearest whole number or five, ten, or hundred.

- prime numbers.

- mixed numbers and improper fractions.

- equivalent fractions.

- fraction/decimal equivalents.

Geometry

- identifying solid shapes such as prisms, spheres, cubes, cylinders, and cones.

- finding the area and perimeter of flat shapes.

- finding the line of symmetry in a flat shape.

- telling about the number of angles and sides of flat shapes.

- telling about the number of vertices, faces, and edges of a solid shape.

- recognizing parallel, perpendicular, and intersecting lines.

- recognizing congruent shapes.

- knowing the difference among acute, obtuse, and right angles.

Other Things to Keep in Mind

- If you come to a difficult problem, think of what you do know about the topic and eliminate answer choices that don't make sense.

- You may be given a problem that can't be solved because not enough information is provided. In that case, "not enough information" or "none of the above" will be an answer choice. Carefully consider each of the other answer choices before you decide that a problem is not solvable.

Concepts Practice

Directions: Find the answer to each problem below.

1 Which unit would be the best to find the distance between one town and another town?

- Ⓐ centimeters
- Ⓑ inches
- Ⓒ millimeters
- Ⓓ kilometers

2 How many edges does this shape have?

- Ⓕ 4
- Ⓖ 6
- Ⓗ 8
- Ⓙ None of these

3 Which of the following angles is obtuse?

- Ⓐ
- Ⓑ
- Ⓒ
- Ⓓ

4 Which one of the following letters contains a line of symmetry?

- Ⓕ J
- Ⓖ G
- Ⓗ L
- Ⓙ E

5 $\frac{35}{8}$ is equal to

- Ⓐ $4\frac{3}{8}$
- Ⓑ $4\frac{8}{3}$
- Ⓒ 8
- Ⓓ $8\frac{1}{8}$

6 .6 is equal to which of the following fractions?

- Ⓕ $\frac{1}{8}$
- Ⓖ $\frac{6}{12}$
- Ⓗ $\frac{1}{5}$
- Ⓙ $\frac{3}{5}$

Applications

You will often be asked to apply what you know about math to a new type of problem or set of information. Even if you aren't exactly sure how to solve a problem of this type, you can usually draw on what you already know to make the most logical choice.

When preparing for standardized tests, you may want to practice some of the following:

- how to use a number line with whole numbers and decimals.

- putting numbers in order from least to greatest and using greater than/less than symbols.

- recognizing complex number patterns and object patterns and extending them.

- writing an equation to solve a problem.

- solving time duration problems.

- reading bar graphs, tally charts, or pictographs.

- reading pie charts.

- reading simple line graphs.

- reading and making Venn diagrams.

- reading and plotting x-y coordinates.

Other Things to Keep in Mind

- When answering application questions, you may want to use scrap paper to work out some problems.

- If you come to a problem you aren't sure how to solve or a word or idea you don't recognize, try to eliminate answer choices by using what you do know. Then go back and check your answer choice in the context of the problem.

Applications Practice

Directions: Find the answer to each problem below.

1 What is the next number in this pattern? 2, 4, 12, 48, 240, _____

Ⓐ 1440

Ⓑ 480

Ⓒ 320

Ⓓ 240

2 If you wanted to use a pie graph to show that 4 out of 16 students wore jeans to school one day, about what fraction of the pie chart would you shade in to represent them?

Ⓕ $\frac{1}{5}$

Ⓖ $\frac{1}{4}$

Ⓗ $\frac{1}{2}$

Ⓙ Not enough information

3 What are the coordinates of point F?

Ⓐ (5, 6)

Ⓑ (4, 5)

Ⓒ (6, 4)

Ⓓ (4, 6)

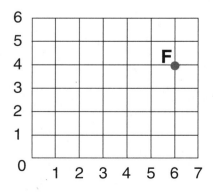

4 What equation would you use to figure out the number of inches in 3.7 miles?

Ⓕ $3.7 \times 5280 + 12$

Ⓖ $3.7 \times 5280 - 12$

Ⓗ $(3.7 + 5280) \times 12$

Ⓙ $(3.7 \times 5280) \times 12$

5 If it takes an airplane 422 minutes to make a flight and it leaves at 2:30 P.M., at what time will the plane arrive at its destination?

Ⓐ 8:30 P.M.

Ⓑ 8:32 P.M.

Ⓒ 9:32 P.M.

Ⓓ None of the above

6 What type of graph would be best to show the amount of rainfall per year in a small town over a period of 10 years?

Ⓕ a pie chart

Ⓖ a bar graph

Ⓗ a pictograph

Ⓙ a line graph

Introduction

The remainder of this book is made up of two tests. On page 321, you will find a Practice Test. On page 332, you will find a Final Test. These tests will give you a chance to put the tips you have learned to work. There is also a name and answer sheet preceding each test and an answer key at the end of the book.

Here are some things to remember as you take these tests:

- Be sure you understand all the directions before you begin each test.

- Ask an adult questions about the directions if you do not understand them.

- Work as quickly as you can during each test. There are no time limits on the Practice Test, but you should try to make good use of your time. There are suggested time limits on the Final Test to give you practice managing your time.

- You will notice little **GO** and **STOP** signs at the bottom of the test pages. When you see a **GO** sign, continue on to the next page if you feel ready. The **STOP** sign means you are at the end of a section. When you see a **STOP** sign, take a break.

- You can guess at an answer or skip difficult items and go back to them later.

- Use the tips you have learned whenever you can.

- It is OK to be a little nervous. You may even do better.

- When you complete all the lessons in this book, you will be on your way to test success!

- After you have completed your tests, check your answers with the answer key. You can record the number of questions you got correct for each unit on the recording sheet on page 319.

Name Sheet

Fill in **only one** letter for each item. If you change an answer, make sure to erase your first mark completely. This is a practice name sheet like the ones you will use in school. Follow these directions:

1. Use a No. 2 pencil.

2. Write your name in the boxes. Put only one letter in each box. Then fill in one little circle below each letter that matches that letter of your name.

3. Fill in all the other information.

STUDENT'S NAME			SCHOOL		
LAST	FIRST	MI	TEACHER		
			FEMALE ○ MALE ○		

BIRTHDATE

MONTH	DAY		YEAR
JAN ○	⓪	⓪	⓪
FEB ○	①	①	①
MAR ○	②	②	②
APR ○	③	③	③
MAY ○		④	④
JUN ○		⑤	⑤ ⑤
JUL ○		⑥	⑥ ⑥
AUG ○		⑦	⑦ ⑦
SEP ○		⑧	⑧ ⑧
OCT ○		⑨	⑨ ⑨
NOV ○			
DEC ○			

GRADE

④   ⑤   ⑥   ⑦   ⑧

The name grid contains columns of bubbles A through Z for each letter box (LAST, FIRST, MI).

Record Your Scores

After you have completed and checked each test, record your scores below. Do not count your answers for the sample questions.

Practice Test

Mathematics

Number of Questions: 31   Number Correct _____

Final Test

Mathematics

Number of Questions: 43   Number Correct _____

Practice Test Answer Sheet

Fill in **only one** letter for each item. If you change an answer, make sure to erase your first mark completely.

Mathematics, pages 321-330

A Ⓐ Ⓑ Ⓒ Ⓓ Ⓔ   7 Ⓐ Ⓑ Ⓒ Ⓓ   16 Ⓕ Ⓖ Ⓗ Ⓙ Ⓚ   24 Ⓐ Ⓑ Ⓒ Ⓓ

B Ⓕ Ⓖ Ⓗ Ⓙ Ⓚ   8 Ⓕ Ⓖ Ⓗ Ⓙ   17 Ⓐ Ⓑ Ⓒ Ⓓ Ⓔ   25 Ⓕ Ⓖ Ⓗ Ⓙ

1 Ⓐ Ⓑ Ⓒ Ⓓ Ⓔ   9 Ⓐ Ⓑ Ⓒ Ⓓ   18 Ⓕ Ⓖ Ⓗ Ⓙ Ⓚ   26 Ⓐ Ⓑ Ⓒ Ⓓ

2 Ⓕ Ⓖ Ⓗ Ⓙ Ⓚ   10 Ⓕ Ⓖ Ⓗ Ⓙ   19 Ⓐ Ⓑ Ⓒ Ⓓ Ⓔ   27 Ⓕ Ⓖ Ⓗ Ⓙ

3 Ⓐ Ⓑ Ⓒ Ⓓ Ⓔ   11 Ⓐ Ⓑ Ⓒ Ⓓ   20 Ⓕ Ⓖ Ⓗ Ⓙ Ⓚ   28 Ⓐ Ⓑ Ⓒ Ⓓ

4 Ⓕ Ⓖ Ⓗ Ⓙ Ⓚ   12 Ⓕ Ⓖ Ⓗ Ⓙ   21 Ⓐ Ⓑ Ⓒ Ⓓ Ⓔ   29 Ⓕ Ⓖ Ⓗ Ⓙ

C Ⓐ Ⓑ Ⓒ Ⓓ   13 Ⓐ Ⓑ Ⓒ Ⓓ   D Ⓐ Ⓑ Ⓒ Ⓓ   30 Ⓐ Ⓑ Ⓒ Ⓓ

5 Ⓐ Ⓑ Ⓒ Ⓓ   14 Ⓕ Ⓖ Ⓗ Ⓙ   22 Ⓐ Ⓑ Ⓒ Ⓓ   31 Ⓕ Ⓖ Ⓗ Ⓙ

6 Ⓕ Ⓖ Ⓗ Ⓙ   15 Ⓐ Ⓑ Ⓒ Ⓓ   23 Ⓕ Ⓖ Ⓗ Ⓙ

Mathematics

Lesson 1 Computation

SAMPLE A

413
+ 133

A 320
B 446
C 546
D 556
E None of these

SAMPLE B

55 − 19 =

F 34
G 44
H 46
J 74
K None of these

Skim the problems and do the easiest ones first. Check your answer by the opposite operation.

1

7291
+ 296

A 7005
B 6587
C 7585
D 7587
E None of these

3

3106
× 3

A 3109
B 9418
C 9318
D 9609
E None of these

2

4008
− 2021

F 2027
G 1987
H 2987
J 6029
K None of these

4

$\frac{1}{3} + \frac{1}{3} =$

F 0
G $\frac{1}{6}$
H $\frac{11}{13}$
J $\frac{1}{8}$
K None of these

STOP

Lesson 2 Mathematics Skills

SAMPLE C

What is the area of the shaded figure?

    A 5 square units

    B $5\frac{1}{2}$ square units

    C 6 square units

    D $6\frac{1}{2}$ square units

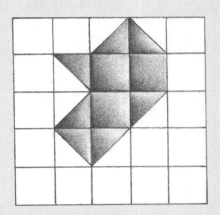

☐ = 1 square unit

Think about what you are supposed to do before you start working.

Eliminate answers you know are wrong.

Before you mark your answer, compare it with the question. Does your answer make sense?

GO

Our Hockey Team

5 Carla has 6 hockey cards. Ed and Carla together have 16 hockey cards. Judith and Ed together have 25 hockey cards. How many hockey cards does Judith have?

A 6

B 9

C 15

D 20

6 The table shows the number of goals Luke, Jacques, Pierre, and Roland have scored during the hockey season. If the trend continues, which player is most likely to score a goal in the next game?

Players	Luke	Jacques	Pierre	Roland
Number of Goals	✓✓✓✓✓ ✓	✓✓✓✓✓ ✓✓✓✓✓ ✓✓✓✓	✓✓✓✓✓ ✓✓✓	✓✓✓

F Luke

G Jacques

H Pierre

J Roland

7 The number of people watching a hockey game is 900 when rounded to the nearest hundred and 850 when rounded to the nearest ten. Which of these could be the number of people watching the game?

A 847

B 849

C 856

D 852

GO

Name _____

8 After the hockey game, each of these players bought a can of soda from a machine that takes both coins and bills.

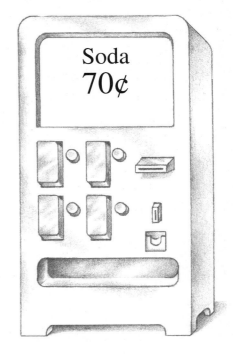

Soda
70¢

– Luke used only dimes.

– Jacques used only quarters.

– Pierre used only half-dollars.

– Roland used a dollar bill.

Which two players got the same amount of change?

F Luke and Jacques

G Jacques and Pierre

H Pierre and Roland

J Roland and Luke

9 The Card Shop receives a shipment of trading cards each month. There are 8 hockey cards in a pack, 12 packs in a box, and 16 boxes in a shipping crate. Which is the total number of hockey cards in the shipping crate?

A 1536

B 672

C 1436

D 662

8 cards
in a pack

12 packs
in a box

16 boxes
in a crate

GO

Name _____

Hair Color

Directions: The tally chart shows the hair color of some 5th-grade students. Study the chart. Then do numbers 10–12.

10 **Which of these questions could you answer using the information on the tally chart?**

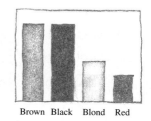

   F How often do the students get their hair cut?

   G How many students dye their hair?

   H Which students have long hair?

   J How many more brown-haired students are there than blond-haired students?

11 **Which graph below shows the data on the tally chart?**

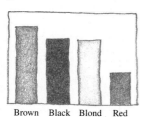 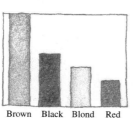 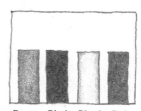 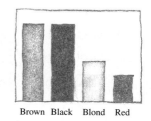

    A   **B**   **C**   **D**

12 **Which circle shows the fraction of the students on the tally chart that have black hair?**

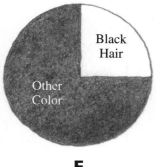  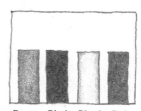 

    F   **G**   **H**   **J**

GO

13 Lori's class used hobby sticks to make skeletons of solid figures. Study the picture of the prism and its skeleton.

How many hobby sticks would be needed to make a skeleton of a rectangular pyramid?

A 9

B 8

C 7

D 4

14 How many pairs of congruent figures are on the grid?

F 4

G 5

H 6

J 7

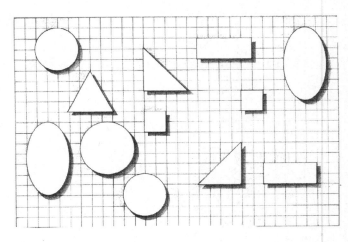

15 If = 1, then which of these pictures represents $1\frac{3}{8}$?

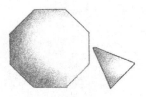

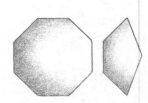

A   **B**   **C**   **D**

GO

Name _____

16   1.14
     + 4.53

F   5.57

G   5.66

H   5.76

J   5.77

K   None of these

17 $20\frac{7}{8}$
     $- \ 5\frac{3}{8}$

A $25\frac{1}{2}$

B $15\frac{1}{2}$

C $14\frac{1}{2}$

D $15\frac{2}{7}$

E   None of these

18   3000
     $\times$ 42

F   126,000

G   120,420

H   300,420

J   300,042

K   None of these

19 $31\overline{)1085}$

A   34

B   34 R1

C   35

D   35 R1

E   None of these

20 $\frac{5}{6} - \frac{2}{3} =$

F $\frac{1}{3}$

G $1\frac{1}{9}$

H $\frac{1}{6}$

J   1

K   None of these

21 $490 \div 7 =$

A   70

B   90

C   420

D   560

E   None of these

STOP

Lesson 3 Review

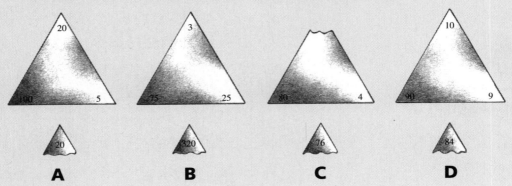

SAMPLE D The numbers in each triangle are related according to a certain rule. Which of these is the missing top of the triangle?

A 20 **B** 320 **C** 76 **D** 84

Directions: For numbers 22–25, you do not need to find exact answers. Use estimation to choose the best answer.

22 Jay took a test that had a true/false section, a matching section, and a multiple choice section. Look at the score card below. Which of these is the best estimate of his point total on the multiple choice section?

A 20 points

B 30 points

C 40 points

D 50 points

True/False	1-10
1 Wrong	
Matching	1-15
2 Wrong	
Multiple Choice	1-25
5 Wrong	
2 pts. per question.	

23 5700 ÷ 7
The answer to this problem is about

F 8000   **H** 80

G 800   **J** 8

24 Which of these is the best estimate of 57.4 + 79.7?

A less than 100

B between 100 and 150

C between 150 and 200

D greater than 200

25 Sharon earned $125.50 baby-sitting on weekend nights. She had $46.89 left after she bought some new clothes. Which of these is the best estimate of the cost of her clothes?

F $20.00   **H** $60.00

G $40.00   **J** $80.00

GO

Our Favorite Subjects

Directions: The 5th graders at Memorial School voted for their favorite subject in school. They made a graph to show how they voted.

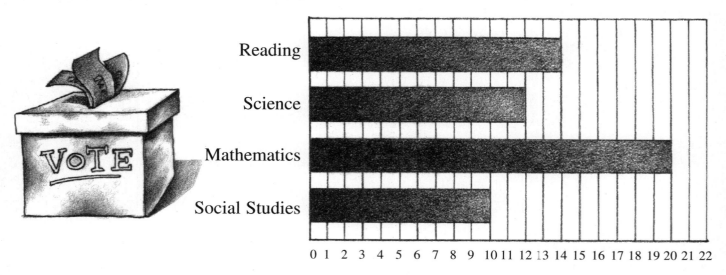

Reading

Science

Mathematics

Social Studies

0 1 2 3 4 5 6 7 8 9 10 11 12 13 14 15 16 17 18 19 20 21 22

26 **How many more students voted for mathematics than voted for science?**

A 2   **C** 6

B 4   **D** 8

27 **Which of these could not happen if 8 more 5th graders added their votes to the graph?**

F Social studies could have the most votes.

G Science and math could have the same number of votes.

H Science could have more votes than reading.

J Social studies could have more votes than science.

28 **Which of these statements about the vote is true?**

A More than three-quarters of the 5th graders voted for mathematics.

B Exactly one-quarter of the 5th graders voted for reading.

C More than one-quarter of the 5th graders voted for social studies.

D Exactly one-quarter of the 5th graders voted for science.

GO

29 Which shape is exactly two-thirds shaded?

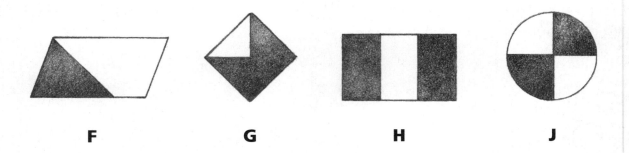

F   **G**   **H**   **J**

30 Xavier cut an eight-sided piece of paper along a line of symmetry. Which of these could not be the result?

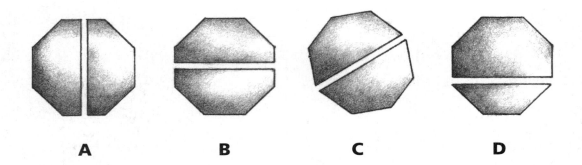

A   **B**   **C**   **D**

31 Which of these points shows about where 3 × 87 would be put on the number line?

F Point A

G Point B

H Point C

J Point D

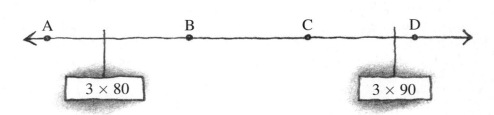

STOP

Final Test Answer Sheet

Fill in **only one** letter for each item. If you change an answer, make sure to erase your first mark completely.

Mathematics, pages 332–340

A Ⓐ Ⓑ Ⓒ Ⓓ   10 Ⓕ Ⓖ Ⓗ Ⓙ   22 Ⓕ Ⓖ Ⓗ Ⓙ   34 Ⓕ Ⓖ Ⓗ Ⓙ

B Ⓕ Ⓖ Ⓗ Ⓙ Ⓚ   11 Ⓐ Ⓑ Ⓒ Ⓓ   23 Ⓐ Ⓑ Ⓒ Ⓓ   35 Ⓐ Ⓑ Ⓒ Ⓓ

1 Ⓐ Ⓑ Ⓒ Ⓓ Ⓔ   12 Ⓕ Ⓖ Ⓗ Ⓙ   24 Ⓕ Ⓖ Ⓗ Ⓙ   36 Ⓕ Ⓖ Ⓗ Ⓙ

2 Ⓕ Ⓖ Ⓗ Ⓙ Ⓚ   13 Ⓐ Ⓑ Ⓒ Ⓓ   25 Ⓐ Ⓑ Ⓒ Ⓓ   37 Ⓐ Ⓑ Ⓒ Ⓓ

3 Ⓐ Ⓑ Ⓒ Ⓓ Ⓔ   14 Ⓕ Ⓖ Ⓗ Ⓙ   26 Ⓕ Ⓖ Ⓗ Ⓙ   38 Ⓕ Ⓖ Ⓗ Ⓙ

4 Ⓕ Ⓖ Ⓗ Ⓙ Ⓚ   15 Ⓐ Ⓑ Ⓒ Ⓓ   27 Ⓐ Ⓑ Ⓒ Ⓓ   39 Ⓐ Ⓑ Ⓒ Ⓓ

5 Ⓐ Ⓑ Ⓒ Ⓓ Ⓔ   16 Ⓕ Ⓖ Ⓗ Ⓙ   28 Ⓕ Ⓖ Ⓗ Ⓙ   40 Ⓕ Ⓖ Ⓗ Ⓙ

6 Ⓕ Ⓖ Ⓗ Ⓙ Ⓚ   17 Ⓐ Ⓑ Ⓒ Ⓓ   29 Ⓐ Ⓑ Ⓒ Ⓓ   41 Ⓐ Ⓑ Ⓒ Ⓓ

C Ⓐ Ⓑ Ⓒ Ⓓ   18 Ⓕ Ⓖ Ⓗ Ⓙ   30 Ⓕ Ⓖ Ⓗ Ⓙ   42 Ⓕ Ⓖ Ⓗ Ⓙ

7 Ⓐ Ⓑ Ⓒ Ⓓ   19 Ⓐ Ⓑ Ⓒ Ⓓ   31 Ⓐ Ⓑ Ⓒ Ⓓ   43 Ⓐ Ⓑ Ⓒ Ⓓ

8 Ⓕ Ⓖ Ⓗ Ⓙ   20 Ⓕ Ⓖ Ⓗ Ⓙ   32 Ⓕ Ⓖ Ⓗ Ⓙ

9 Ⓐ Ⓑ Ⓒ Ⓓ   21 Ⓐ Ⓑ Ⓒ Ⓓ   33 Ⓐ Ⓑ Ⓒ Ⓓ

Mathematics

	SAMPLE A		
	469	**A**	244
	+ 225	**B**	684
		C	694
		D	695
		E	None of these

	SAMPLE B		
	87.8	**F**	5.4
	− 72.4	**G**	14.5
		H	16.2
		J	15.4
		K	None of these

1 23
$\times$ 32

A 736
B 636
C 55
D 115
E None of these

2 $6.00 − $0.35

F $6.35
G $5.65
H $5.75
J $5.35
K None of these

3 $18\overline{)90}$

A 5
B 4
C 4 R2
D 5 R4
E None of these

4 $5\frac{7}{8} - 2\frac{3}{8} =$

F $2\frac{1}{2}$
G $3\frac{3}{4}$
H $3\frac{3}{8}$
J $3\frac{1}{2}$
K None of these

5 $510 \times 38 =$

A 19,380
B 548
C 51,038
D 18,390
E None of these

6 89.7
+ 25.6

F 114.3
G 64.3
H 105.3
J 104.3
K None of these

GO

SAMPLE C

Points M and N represent certain numbers on the number line. Which of these problems would give an answer of about 10?

A N + M

B N − M

C N × M

D N ÷ M

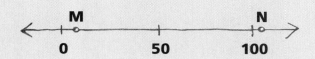

---

7 Parallelogram QRST slid to a new position on the grid as shown. Which moves describe the slide?

A 1 right, 4 down

B 1 right, 5 down

C 2 right, 4 down

D 1 right, 3 down

---

8 Study this pattern. If the pattern continues, how many stars will be in the fourth position?

F 14

G 16

H 18

J 20

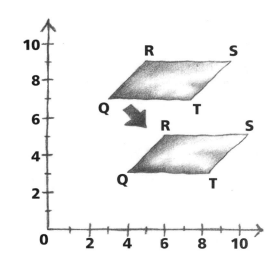

Position		Number of Stars
1	★ ★ ★ ★	4
2	★ ★ ★ ★ ★ ★ ★ ★	8
3	★ ★ ★ ★ ★ ★ ★ ★ ★ ★ ★ ★	12
4		?

GO

Name _____

The Hundreds Hunt

Directions: Mr. Pontario's students are making number charts and labeling the squares from 1 to 100. Use Harry's number chart to do numbers 9 and 10.

9 **Liza is making a number chart. If she shades only the multiples of 4, her chart will have**

    A about three-fourths as many shaded numbers as Harry's.

    B about two-thirds as many shaded numbers as Harry's.

    C about one-half as many shaded numbers as Harry's.

    D about twice as many shaded numbers as Harry's.

HARRY'S CHART

1	2	3	4	5	6	7	8	9	10
11	12	13	14	15	16	17	18	19	20
21	22	23	24	25	26	27	28	29	30
31	32	33	34	35	36	37	38	39	40
41	42	43	44	45	46	47	48	49	50
51	52	53	54	55	56	57	58	59	60
61	62	63	64	65	66	67	68	69	70
71	72	73	74	75	76	77	78	79	80
81	82	83	84	85	86	87	88	89	90
91	92	93	94	95	96	97	98	99	100

10 **Tenisha just made a number chart on which she shaded all the multiples of 5. Which pattern shows the shading on her number chart?**

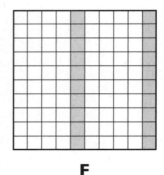

F

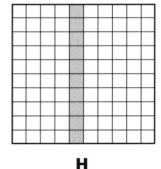

G

H

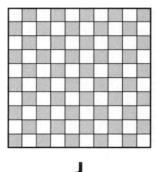

J

GO

Name _____

11 Which of these number sentences could be used to find the cost of 6 dozen pens?

  A $\$4.59 + 6 =$

  B $\$4.59 - 6 =$

  C $\$4.59 \times 6 =$

  D $\$4.59 \div 6 =$

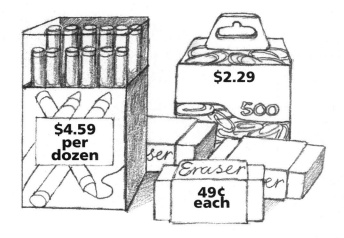

12 Mrs. Lynch showed a container of jelly beans to her class. She said she would give it to the student who guessed the correct number of jelly beans inside it. The first four students guessed 352, 267, 195, and 454, respectively. What was the average of these four guesses?

  F 300

  G 317

  H 320

  J 323

13 If all these chips were put into a bag, what is the probability that you would pick a chip with a letter that comes before M in the alphabet?

  A $\frac{3}{5}$

  B $\frac{3}{8}$

  C $\frac{5}{3}$

  D $\frac{5}{8}$

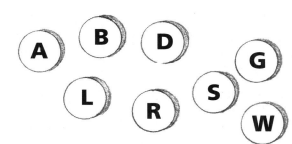

GO

Bake Sale

Directions: The 5th grade is having a bake sale for the rest of the school and the outside community. Numbers 14–17 are about the bake sale.

14 There are 120 students in the fifth grade. Only 87 of these students contributed baked goods. How many students did not contribute baked goods?

- **F** 87
- **G** 207
- **H** 43
- **J** 33

15 The oatmeal cookies are small, so there are 3 cookies in each plastic bag. There are 45 bags of these cookies. How many oatmeal cookies are there in all?

- **A** 48
- **B** 120
- **C** 135
- **D** 15

16 The local bakery donated 112 blueberry muffins. There are 16 blueberries in each muffin. How many blueberries did the bakery use in all?

- **F** 784
- **G** 128
- **H** 1782
- **J** 1792

17 Thelma and Arnold collected the money. Thelma sat 71.52 inches from the exit door, and Arnold sat 63.31 inches farther from the exit door than Thelma sat. How far from the door did Arnold sit?

- **A** 134.83 in.
- **B** 135.83 in.
- **C** 8.21 in.
- **D** 9.21 in.

GO

Name _____

Directions: Find the correct answer to solve each problem.

18 **What number does CXVII represent?**

F   62   H   117

G   67   J   542

19 **What is the name of this figure?**

A   sphere

B   rectangular prism

C   triangular prism

D   cylinder

20 **What is 456,517 rounded to the nearest thousand?**

F   460,000

G   457,000

H   454,000

J   456,000

21 **Which of the following is a right triangle?**

A

B

C

D

22 **What letter represents point 4, 2?**

F   A

G   C

H   B

J   D

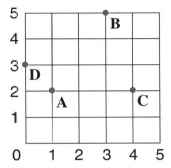

23 **What is the square root of 16?**

A   256   C   4

B   8   D   1

24 **Which figure shows intersecting lines, but not perpendicular lines?**

F   **S**

G   _____

H   **X**

J

25 **What number has an 8 in the millions place and a 2 in the ten-thousands place?**

A   8,912,703

B   8,721,034

C   8,241,037

D   2,781,654

GO

26 **What figure has vertical and horizontal symmetry?**

F

H

G

J

27 **Which animal is longer than 156 inches and shorter than 216 inches?**

A African elephant

B Hippopotamus

C White rhinoceros

D Giraffe

Animal	Length (in feet)	Weight (in pounds)
African Elephant	24	14,432
White Rhinoceros	14	7,937
Hippopotamus	13	5,512
Giraffe	19	2,257

28 **What is the perimeter of this figure?**

F 101 inches

G 98 inches

H 76 inches

J 38 inches

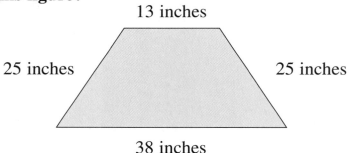

13 inches

25 inches

25 inches

38 inches

29 **Which is the best estimate for the height of a room?**

A 3 inches

B 3 feet

C 3 yards

D 3 miles

GO

Directions: Find the correct answer to solve each problem.

30 23,300 – 17,984 =

    F 5,316

    G 5,326

    H 6,626

    J 41,284

31 0.36 $\square$ $\frac{3}{5}$

    A >

    B =

    C <

    D Not enough information

32 78.576 + 412.82 =

    F 1,198.58

    G 491.396

    H 490.396

    J 119.848

33 1984 – 894.5 =

    A 986.5

    B 1,089.5

    C 1,189

    D 2,879

34 24,000 ÷ 60 =

    F 4,000

    G 400

    H 40

    J None of these

35 765 + 456 + 835 + 490 =

    A 2,056

    B 2,456

    C 2,546

    D None of these

36 Find the average for this set of numbers: 47, 83, 15, 22, 67.

    F 58.5   **H** 43.5

    G 47   **J** None of these

37 $\frac{1}{3} + 2\frac{1}{3} + \frac{4}{9}$ =

    A $3\frac{1}{9}$

    B 3

    C $2\frac{2}{3}$

    D None of these

GO

Directions: Find the correct answer to solve each problem.

38 Five friends each had 36 prize tokens from the arcade. Two other friends each had 25 prize tokens. The 7 friends decided to combine their tokens and then divide them equally. How many tokens will each friend get?

   F 8 tokens   **H** 32 tokens

   G 25 tokens   **J** 33 tokens

39 James earned $15.85 each week for his chores. If James saves all of his money for 8 weeks, how much money will he have?

   A $12.68

   B $120.00

   C $125.40

   D $126.80

40 Luca finished his homework at 8:37 p.m. If he started his homework 92 minutes earlier, at what time did Luca begin his homework?

   F 7:05 p.m.

   G 7:09 p.m.

   H 7:35 p.m.

   J 11:09 p.m.

41 Martin made a bowl of punch using 14 gallons of juice. How many quarts of punch did Martin make?

   A 112 quarts   **C** 28 quarts

   B 56 quarts   **D** None of the above

42 Jaime read for 30 minutes on Monday, 47 minutes on Tuesday, 64 minutes on Wednesday, and 81 minutes on Thursday. Which statement describes Jaime's pattern for reading?

   F Add 15 minutes each day

   G Subtract 17 minutes each day

   H Add 12 minutes each day

   J Add 17 minutes each day

43 An aquarium has a collection of 148 fish. It is going to expand its collection to 500 fish. If 8 new fish are added each week, how long will it take to get to 500 fish?

   A 15 weeks

   B 19 weeks

   C 43 weeks

   D 44 weeks

STOP

Test Practice Answer Key

Page 298
1. B
2. F

Page 300
1. D
2. G
3. A
4. H

Page 302
1. B
2. G
3. A

Page 304
1. B
2. H
3. B
4. G

Page 306
1. B
2. F
3. C
4. F

Page 308
1. B
2. J
3. D
4. H

Page 310
1. C
2. H
3. C
4. F
5. B
6. H

Page 312
1. C
2. H
3. B
4. F
5. B
6. G

Page 314
1. D
2. J
3. C
4. J
5. A
6. J

Page 316
1. A
2. G
3. C
4. J
5. C
6. J

Page 321
A. C
B. K
1. D
2. G
3. C
4. K

Page 322
C. D

Page 323
5. C
6. G
7. D

Page 324
8. H
9. A

Page 325
10. J
11. B
12. F

Page 326
13. B
14. F
15. D

Page 327
16. K
17. B
18. F
19. C
20. H
21. A

Page 328
D. A
22. C
23. G
24. B
25. J

Page 329
26. D
27. F
28. B

Page 330
29. H
30. D
31. H

Page 332
A. C
B. J
1. A
2. G
3. A
4. J
5. A
6. K

Page 333
C. B
7. A
8. G

Page 334
9. D
10. F

Page 335
11. C
12. G
13. D

Page 336
14. J
15. C
16. J
17. A

Page 337
18. H
19. C
20. G
21. D
22. G
23. C
24. H
25. B

Page 338
26. G
27. C
28. F
29. C

Page 339
30. F
31. C
32. G
33. B
34. G
35. C
36. J
37. A

Page 340
38. H
39. D
40. F
41. B
42. J
43. D

Pentomino Activities

Directions: Cut out the pentomino pattern pieces on the two pages in the back of this workbook. Then, use these pieces to solve the puzzles on pages 342–351.

Cover this shape with pieces.

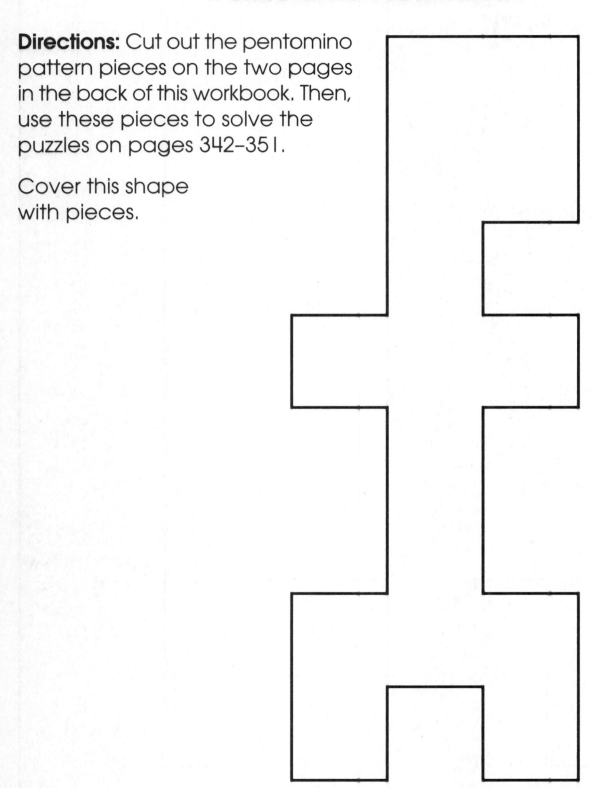

Cover this shape with pieces.

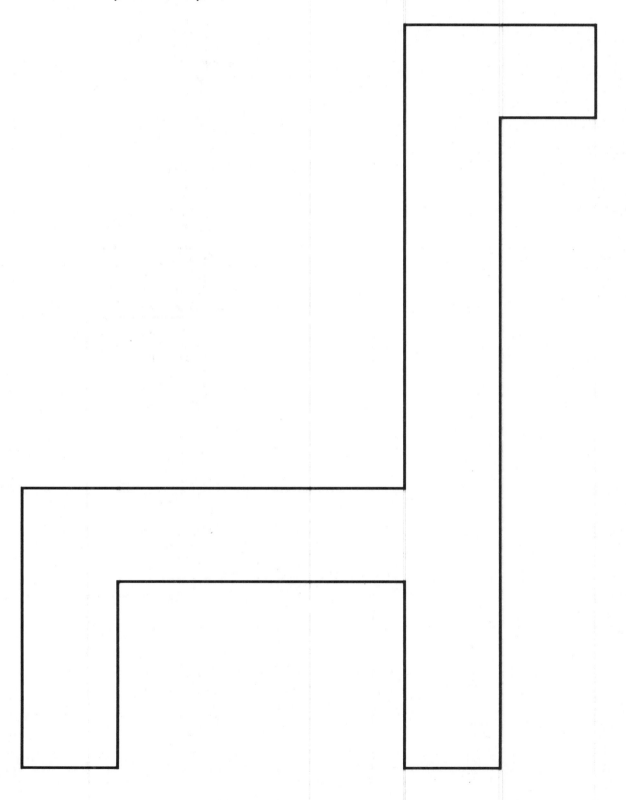

Cover this shape with pieces.

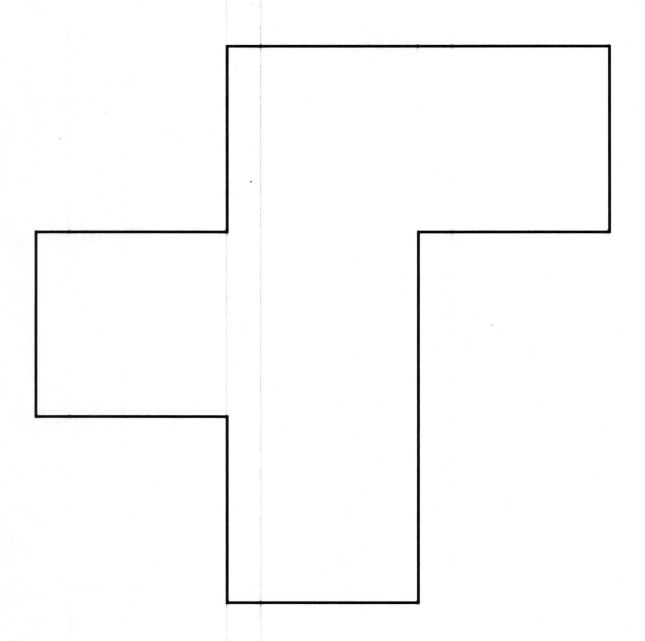

Cover this shape with pieces.

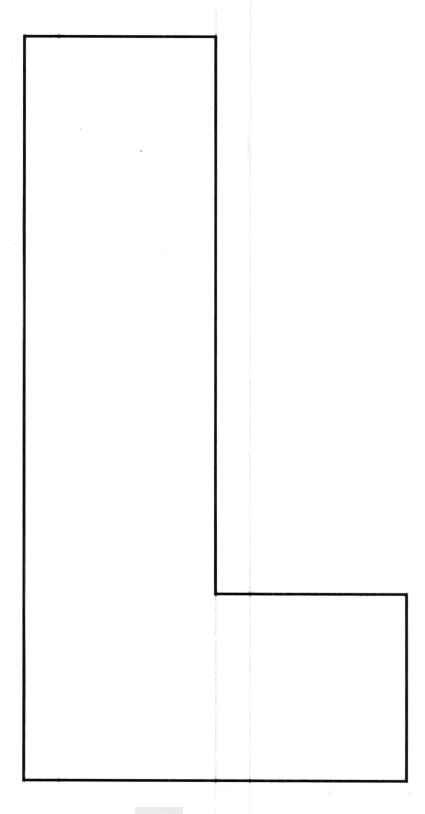

Cover this shape with pieces.

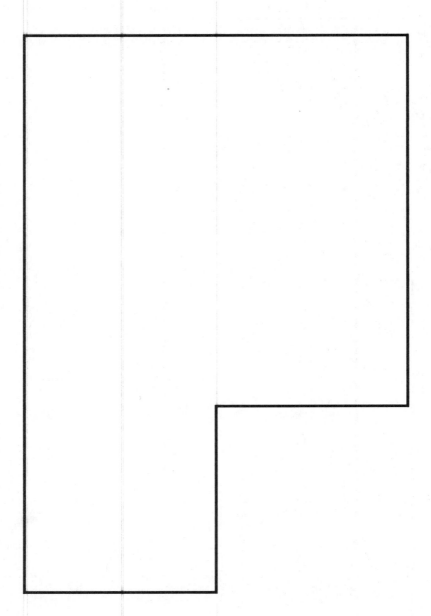

Cover this shape with pieces.

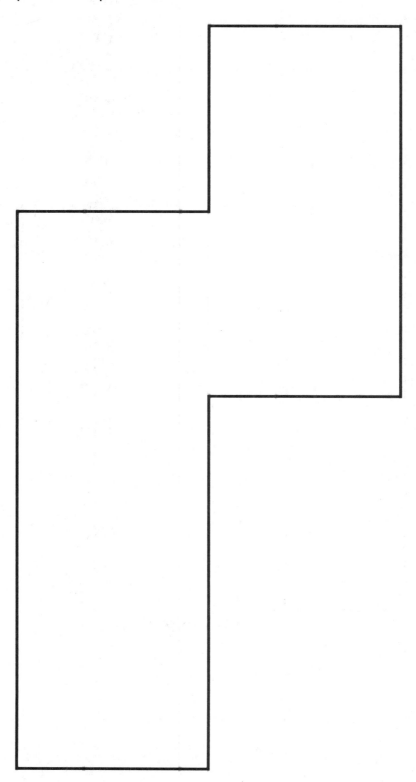

Cover this shape with pieces.

Cover this shape with pieces.

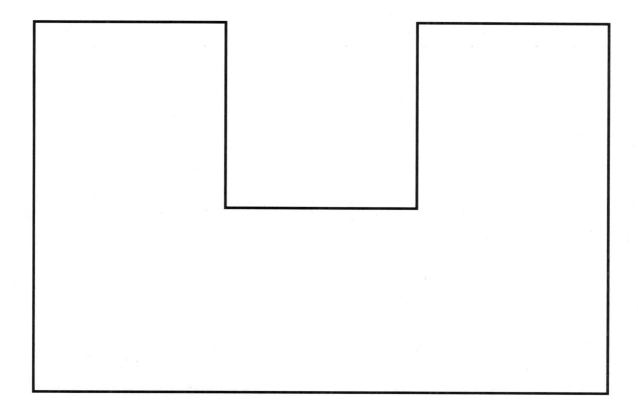

Cover this shape with pieces.

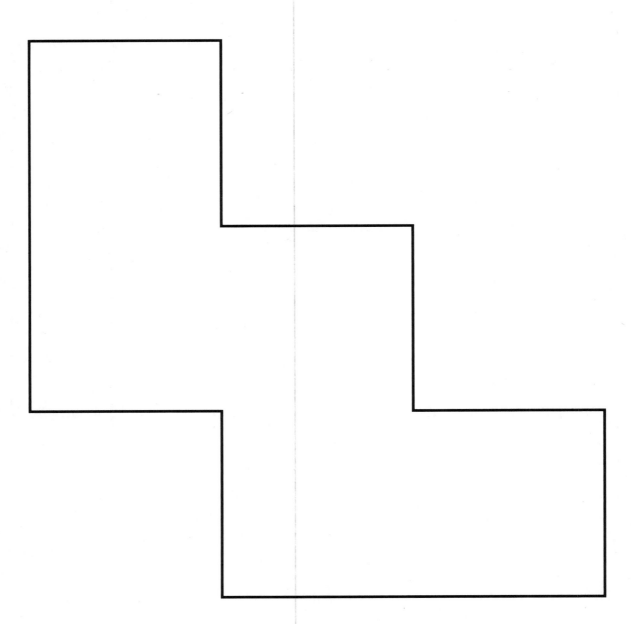

Cover this shape with pieces.

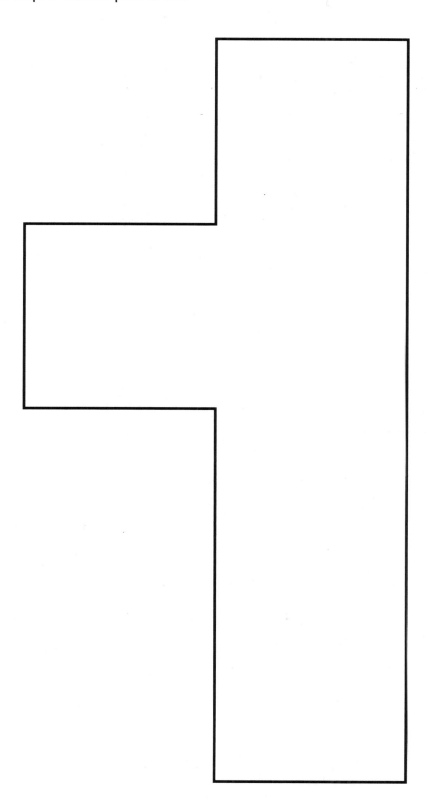

Pentomino Activities Answer Key

The following are possible solutions for the Pentomino Activities on pages 342–351.

Page 342

Page 343

Page 344

Page 345

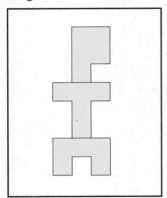
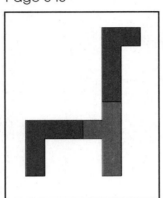
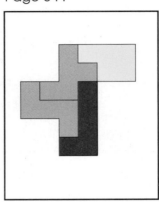
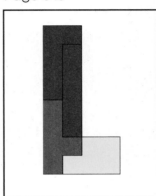

Page 346

Page 347

Page 348

Page 349

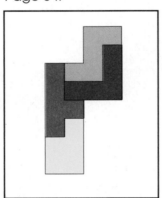
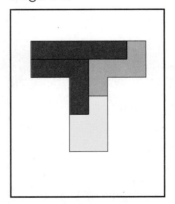
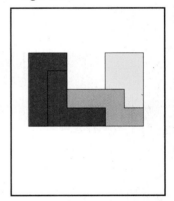

Page 350

Page 351

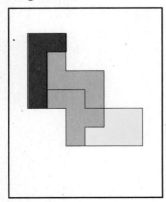

Pentomino Pieces

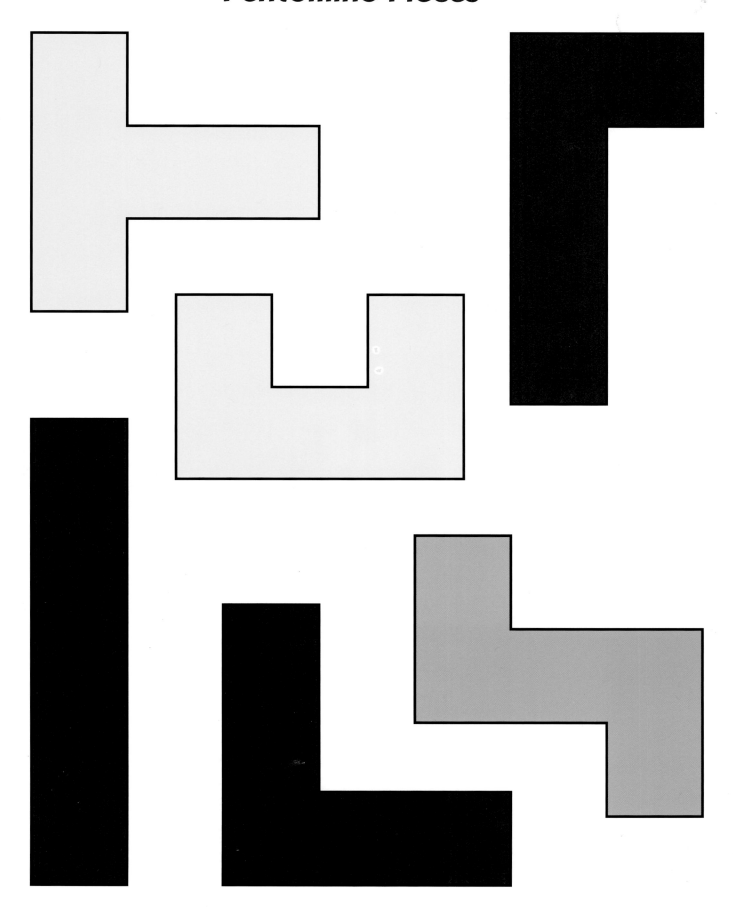

 **MATH**

Graphs

Bar Graph

Favorite Foods

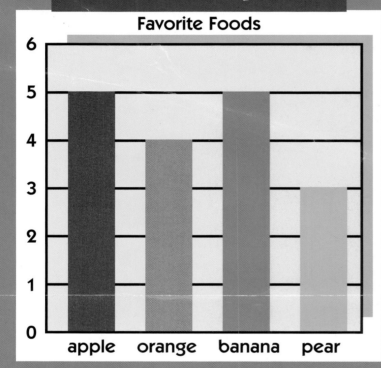

In a bar graph, the length of a bar tells how much or how many.

Line Graph

Number of Students at Kent School

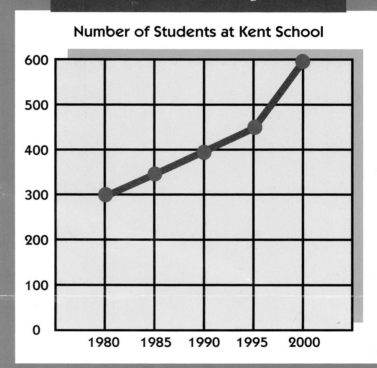

In a line graph, a line shows how something changes over a period of time.

Picture Graph

Number of Books Read at Greenvale School

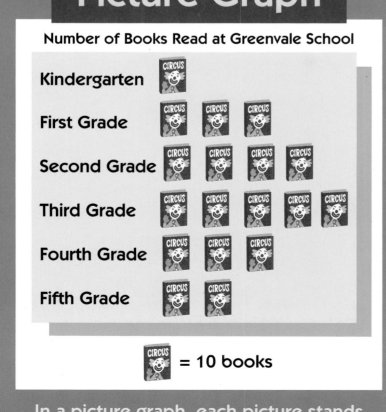

In a picture graph, each picture stands for a certain amount.

Circle Graph

Kelly's Sticker Collection

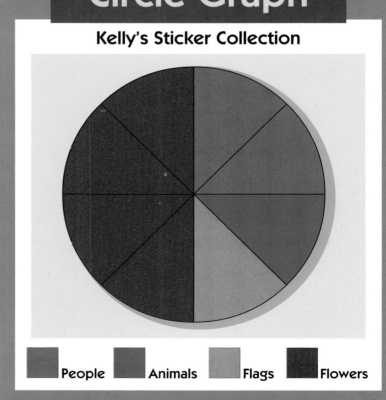

In a circle graph, the parts of a circle tell how much or how many.